International
Organizations
and
Ethnic Conflict

International Organizations and Ethnic Conflict

EDITED BY

Milton J. Esman and Shibley Telhami

Cornell University Press · *Ithaca and London*

First published 1995 by Cornell University Press.

Library of Congress Cataloging-in-Publication Data

International organizations and ethnic conflict / edited by Milton J.
    Esman, Shibley Telhami.
      p. cm.
    Includes bibliographical references and index.
    ISBN 0-8014-3107-7 (cloth).—ISBN 0-8014-8259-3 (pbk.)
     1. Intervention (International law) 2. International politics.
  3. Ethnic relations. 4. International agencies. I. Esman, Milton
J. (Milton Jacob), 1918– . II. Telhami, Shibley.
JX4481.I5545 1995
341.5'84—dc20   95-2529

Printed in the United States of America

∞ The paper in this book meets the minimum requirements
of the American National Standard for Information Sciences—
Permanence of Paper for Printed Library Materials, ANSI Z39.48-1984.

To Janice and Kathryn

Contents

Acknowledgements

The idea for this project began with the observation that the end of the cold war resulted in the spread and intensification of ethnic conflict in several regions around the world. At the same time expectations were rising that international organizations would become more effective in dealing with ethnic conflict and civil strife in the new era. We thus proposed a project to study the changing role of international organizations in ethnic conflict. It was ultimately funded by the United States Institute of Peace and resulted in a conference held at Cornell University, April 16–17, 1993. Most of the chapters in this volume resulted from that conference; Michael Hudson agreed immediately after it to write a new article, and the essay by V. P. Gagnon was solicited later, in response to ideas expressed at the conference and to helpful suggestions of anonymous reviewers for Cornell University Press.

Within Cornell, two programs were especially helpful in sponsoring the project: Peace Studies and European Studies, both of which provided logistical and financial support. Their respective directors, Judith Reppy and Valerie Bunce, provided valuable contributions to the original proposal and to subsequent discussions. John Oakley, as project coordinator, should be singled out for invaluable efforts in getting the project under way and seeing it to completion. Bablu Naidu compiled helpful research material in the early stages of the project, and Debbie Stroeber made management of difficult details much easier in her capacity as a research assistant.

Several conference participants made useful contributions to the discussions and to the draft chapters: Peter Katzenstein, Misha Glenny, Carl Kaysen, David Wippman, Richard Herrmann, Jonathan Kirshner, Larry Scheinman, Gale Stokes, Norman Uphoff, and David Smock. Their input was helpful to the authors in this volume, especially to the editors in writing the introductory and concluding chapters. We are also thankful to the staff of Cornell University Press for excellent editorial suggestions and timely production. As always, however, shortcomings in this volume are our responsibility alone.

M. E.
S. T.

A Note to the Reader

On January 1, 1995, the name of the Conference on Security and Cooperation in Europe (CSCE) was changed to the Organization for Security and Cooperation in Europe (OSCE). As this book was already in press, references to the CSCE throughout have not been changed.

International
Organizations
and
Ethnic Conflict

Introduction

Milton J. Esman and Shibley Telhami

One noticeable outcome of the end of the cold war has been the great disparity between the rising demand and expectations for intervention by the United Nations and other international organizations and the limited capabilities of these IOs to meet these demands and expectations. The demise of the Soviet-U.S. rivalry has exacerbated and highlighted ethnic conflicts, not only increasing the need for IOs but also testing the limits of existing norms. Most ethnic conflicts are "internal" matters within the "domestic jurisdiction" of states. Thus, where there are no obvious "threats to international peace and security," the legal basis for intervention is difficult to establish, especially when there is no clear "consent" by the local parties. International law and the Charter of the UN have always contained two value clusters, state system values and human rights values, but the former have usually won out over the latter (Damrosch 1993). Thus, the debate about the changing role of IOs pertains to three issues: their norms, their capabilities, and the degree of their autonomy from member states.

Two recent cases of UN intervention raised expectations about changing norms and capabilities. The first, the Iraq-Kuwait conflict, is remarkable in its use of substantial capabilities of member states under the authorization of the UN Security Council to implement UNSC resolutions, and in the degree of international intrusion into the sover-

This project has been funded by a grant from the United States Institute of Peace and by additional support from the Peace Studies and European Studies programs at Cornell University.

eignty of Iraq, even after it was forced to withdraw from Kuwait. The second, the civil war in Somalia, stands out because intervention was motivated much more by humanitarian concerns than by the need to address "threats to international peace," even though both justifications were employed in the UNSC resolution authorizing the intervention.

Are the norms that limit and legitimate IO intervention in ethnic conflicts adequate to present conditions and changing expectations? Are international expectations about the new role of IOs justified? Are IOs capable of meeting the increasing demand? If not, what are the consequences of the disparities between established norms, actual capabilities, and international expectations? How might these disparities be narrowed? These are some of the general questions that motivate this book. A second set of derivative and practical questions pertains to the desirability and potential effectiveness of IO interventions. Under what circumstances can IOs be helpful in reducing bloodshed, preventing civil war, and managing ethnic rivalries? When do they succeed and when do they fail in these areas? What steps can bolster the role of IOs to reduce ethnic conflicts? We hope to gain insight into these questions by focusing on two specific cases of severe and violent ethnic conflict, Lebanon and Yugoslavia. These cases were selected because they are consequential, complex, well documented, and representative. The IO intervention in Lebanon was conducted under the auspices of a regional body (the Arab League) and took place during the cold war; the crisis in Yugoslavia occurred after the cold war and involved several IOs, regional (European Community, Conference on Security and Cooperation in Europe) and universal (UN).

Several definitional and conceptual questions emerge at the outset. What constitutes an international organization? What differentiates ethnic conflicts from civil wars or other types of conflict? What activities by an IO amount to intervention? One goal of this chapter is to develop some helpful distinctions.

The Changing Role of International Organizations

Although the term "international organizations" might in some contexts embrace nongovernmental associations, this book restricts the term to those organizations whose members are states. Moreover, although the acts of "international" organizations are multilateral, not all multilateral acts are organizational. For example, the British-French-Israeli intervention in Egypt in 1956 and the U.S.-led international intervention in Lebanon in 1982 were multinational but not carried out by an IO. Finally, international organizations need not have global membership; regional or issue-specific organizations are included in this definition.

By our definition, such entities as the United Nations, the Organization of African Unity, and the Arab League are international organizations, but alliances such as the North Atlantic Treaty Organization and cartels such as the Organization of Petroleum Exporting Countries are not. The basic criterion for inclusion is the central function of the organization: Is it primarily intended to regulate relations among member states or between member and nonmember states? Whereas all organizations monitor both external and internal interaction, they differ in how they place their priorities. The primary purpose of alliances such as NATO is to defend the interests of members against nonmembers, even if they also have some regulatory function among members. The European Union (formerly the European Community) performs both functions. The United Nations is the ideal type of our definition. Virtually its only function is to regulate relations among members; there are very few nonmembers to be targeted.

Common usage provides a guide, but we also differentiate IOs from alliances and other multilateral groups by the degree of their international legitimacy and acceptability. How inclusive or exclusive is the organization? What is its relation to the UN (the most inclusive organization)? Does it have a "competitive" relationship with another IO?

That the role of IOs in the Gulf War, Somalia, and Cambodia constitutes an important departure from their role during the cold war cannot be denied. The legal justification for intervention aside, the *extent* of UN interventions and the practical basis for intervention are unprecedented; the annual cost of UN peace-keeping operations has escalated from $400 million in 1990 to over $3 billion in 1993 and threatens to continue increasing. The question is how to interpret this change. There are three possibilities: that this change is *transitional* and quite reversible; that it is *incremental* but progressive and irreversible; or that it constitutes a *fundamental transformation* in international politics.

On one extreme end of the literature is the "realist" view, the transitional explanation represented in this volume most closely by Jack Donnelly, that international organizations are primarily instruments of policy for their powerful members. To find out what the given organization does or does not do, one has to investigate the basic interests of dominant members. In this view, the UN action in Kuwait was largely an American intervention to serve U.S. interests. Even the UN intervention in Somalia, which would have been unlikely without U.S. support, would be interpreted by this school as emanating from the preferences of the United States, perhaps in response to domestic pressure.

To explain the recent change in the role of the UN, this school of thought would emphasize the transition in global politics following the demise of the Soviet Union and the ending of the cold war, which, it is said, has given rise, perhaps temporarily, to the political hegemony of the United States. As soon as a new configuration of power emerges, the role of the UN will also change to reflect the new distribution of power.

The incremental explanation accepts the argument of the realists that the post-cold-war era does not constitute a fundamental transformation in global politics. Nonetheless, it sees some incremental, progressive, and irreversible trends. Just as the shift from the League of Nations to the UN constituted a progressive shift that accompanied changes in the global distribution of power following World War II, so will the end of the cold war be accompanied by a transformation from United Nations I to United Nations II.

This interpretation of IOs is consistent with much of the "regime" literature in international relations, which argues that regimes, regardless of how they are created, ultimately acquire a life of their own (*International Organization* 36(2) 1982:185–510). In this literature, international regimes are defined as norms, rules, and procedures that regulate an issue area of international relations. Although the most powerful states exert substantial influence in shaping the behavior of IOs, the norms, rules, and procedures of these organizations, once they are established, have some influence of their own, which even their more powerful members cannot disregard. Indeed, even if one takes the view that IOs are used as instruments of policy by their powerful members, those members would stand to lose much by blatantly violating the norms of these organizations in any given instance.

The incrementalists, thus, might agree with the realists that the United States used the UN as an instrument of policy during the Gulf War. Nonetheless, they would say, the intervention established a precedent and created new international expectations. The United States then could not simply ignore these expectations in other cases. Indeed, the UN intervention in Somalia, where no major U.S. interests were at stake, might never have taken place without the Gulf precedent. Still, the incrementalists share the realists' belief that no matter what the norms of IOs are, if the central interests of one or more of the major powers are violated by their application in a particular case, the IO will not prevail. For example, the United States in 1993 managed a political deal that averted implementation of the UNSC resolution demanding the immediate return of Palestinians deported by Israel.

According to the "transformation" school of thought, the role of IOs cannot be evaluated without understanding the fundamental transformation that has recently occurred in international politics and economics and without taking note of the gap that exists between international norms and international behavior. There are at least two variants to this interpretation.

In the first variant, the end of the cold war has revealed the extent of transnational activity in world politics, which has substantially reduced the significance of states as actors (Keohane and Nye 1974 and 1977; Mansbach et al. 1976; Huntington 1973; Keohane 1989; Young 1989; Kratochwil 1989). IOs, according to this interpretation, are acquiring an independent power of their own at the expense of member states. Transformationists find the study of the role of IOs in ethnic conflict especially interesting because ethnic identities challenge existing state identities and draw boundaries that are not necessarily territorial. In this approach, a disjuncture exists between norms and practices in international relations (Meyer 1980).

The second variant emphasizes not so much the declining importance of the state as *the changing interests of states*, which are said to be substantially affected by international norms. For example, during the cold war, U.S. interests were defined through competition with the Soviet Union, and therefore, the end of the cold war has led to the rearrangement of U.S. priorities. Moreover, governments are no longer the primary *agents* for formulating concepts of security and national interest. Americans watching the horrors of famine on television may have forced the intervention in Somalia, despite the reluctance of the U.S. government. IOs could thus be acquiring more power because their norms now correspond to redefined interests that bypass governments representing states (Wendt 1992; Keohane 1988; Haggard 1991; Kratochwil 1982).

Each theoretical interpretation leads to several important questions about the changing role of IOs. One set of questions, addressed in Part I of this book, derives from the "transitional" and the "incremental" interpretations, in their assumption that sovereignty norms will continue to dominate international relations, even though sovereignty may be eroding at the margins, and in not foreseeing a major change in the mission of IOs. Will the scope and volume of activities by IOs increase in the post-cold-war period? On the one hand, the end of the Soviet-U.S. rivalry has removed important barriers to intervention in regional and ethnic conflicts; on the other hand, the decline in superpower competition has diminished the incentives for powerful states to expend resources in regions remote from their borders, such as Angola, Afghanistan, and Bosnia. How will this disjuncture between possibilities and incentives reflect itself in the changing role of IOs? Will the diminishing incentives for direct intervention by powerful states lead to their support for multilateral actions, thus enhancing the power and role of IOs? If so, who will pay the costs of this increased role? Will local problems increasingly become "regionalized," thus enhancing the power of regional organizations at the expense of the UN (Weiss and MacFarlane 1992)? Or will there be a division of labor?

Both the transitionalists and the incrementalists envision continued domination by the more powerful states in shaping the behavior of IOs. Given that the United States has emerged as the dominant state in world politics, how will the new U.S. priorities in the post-cold-war era affect IOs?

If we agree that there is a disjuncture between international expectations of IOs and their capabilities, what are its consequences? What realistic intermediate steps could be taken by the international community to diminish this disjuncture and to raise capabilities to the level of expectations?

Has there been an incremental shift in the intervention norms of IOs from "state system values" to "human rights values" (Damrosch 1993)? Has there been a detectable differentiation between *individual* human rights and *collective* human rights which would apply to ethnic and other minority groups? If no shift in the legal norms of IOs can be detected, has there been a *practical* shift in the behavior of IOs toward human rights values or is there a *perception* of such a shift? Is there reason to expect that shifts in perception and practice constitute important precedents that will ultimately affect the legal norms of intervention?

Another set of questions derives from the theoretical proposition of fundamental transformation. Proponents of this proposition generally assume that international norms of sovereignty have substantially weakened, largely as a consequence of a major increase in transnational activity—economic and environmental, for example—and that the weakness of states has been exposed by the end of the cold war. How empirically valid is this claim?

How will the weakening of the state as an actor affect IOs? The transformation position implies that the very norms that IOs are designed to defend are themselves a cause of disjuncture: the more IOs are strengthened, the more governments with declining popular legitimacy are propped up, thus increasing stress on the resources of IOs and decreasing their chances of success. This view presents a fundamental challenge to the very notion that IOs representing sovereign states can play a constructive role in a world where state sovereignty has irreversibly diminished (McNeely 1993).

Can sovereign states in pursuit of their own self-interest accept increasing intrusions into their sovereignty? Theoretically, one can envision a situation in which states have interests in seeing intrusions into *other* states and where the absence of limited coordinated intrusions by IOs, for example, for environmental protection or to stop the flow of narcotics, may pose a *bigger challenge* to their sovereignty. If this is the claim, how empirically valid is it?

What are the consequences of the proposition that priorities and concepts of national interest are being transformed by the demise of the Soviet-U.S. rivalry and the increase in transnational activity? Are governments no longer the primary agents for defining national interest and for setting priorities? What are the implications of this proposition for the changing role of IOs in ethnic conflict?

Answers to the general questions we have posed cannot be given outside the empirical context. In each case we must ask what issues face concrete IOs in specific situations? What forms of intervention is contemplated? How costly is the intervention? What are the prospects that it is likely to be effective? What kind of precedents might it set? What are the interests of the powerful members?

It is important, too, to identify the different methods of intervention before one can decide what leads a given IO to intervene in an ethnic conflict. For example, since humanitarian relief is substantially easier to accomplish than military intervention, it is likely to be determined more by the norms of the organization than by the immediate interests of individual members.

One would expect different criteria to apply in cases of peace enforcement (as opposed to peace keeping) which require military intervention, since it is the most difficult to approve and usually the costliest. In the few cases where such interventions have taken place under IO auspices, three conditions obtained; at least one member state believed its vital interests were at stake and was willing to employ its own military resources to make intervention possible; the vital interests of the more powerful members of the organization were not violated by the intervention; and the vital interests of a superpower were not violated (whether or not the superpower was a member of the organization).

The Arab League, for instance, supported Syria's military intervention in the Lebanese civil war in the mid-1970s, sending additional troops and underwriting the economic costs. Syria believed that the Lebanese civil war could have far-reaching implications for its foreign policy. Perhaps more important, had Syria not intervened on behalf of the losing party (a primarily Christian alliance), there was a good chance that Israel or the United States would do so—a prospect that the Syrians found especially threatening. In short, the Syrians took the risks of military intervention because the outcome of the civil war would have affected vital Syrian interests. Other key members of the Arab League, most notably Egypt and Saudi Arabia, found it in their interest (though perhaps not "vital" interest) to support the intervention. Meanwhile, neither superpower viewed the Syrian-led intervention as threatening to its vital interests: the Soviet Union was Syria's ally, and the United States, fearful of the consequences of the Lebanese civil war and of possible Israeli intervention, gave Syria the "green light." Similar conditions appear to have obtained in the international intervention in Kuwait in 1990-91 and, to some extent, in the U.S.-led intervention in Korea in 1950. In Kuwait it is doubtful that the UN would have acted militarily had the United States not been willing to undertake the risks of military intervention. Other powerful UN members, most notably veto-wielding permanent members of the Security Council, did not see the intervention as a threat to their vital interests even if they disapproved of it. China and the former Soviet Union feared that military intervention would set a bad precedent; yet, neither had interests in Kuwait which were so vital as to warrant jeopardizing their relations with the powerful member that cared most: the United States. In the case of Korea, the Soviet Union, would certainly have vetoed the UNSC resolution authorizing military intervention, if its delegate had not made the mistake of missing the meeting. Korea thus stands as an exception.

In contrast to these examples, consider the case of ethnic conflict in Yugoslavia in 1991-1994. The absence of threat to the vital interests of any state or coalition of states capable of taking on the burden of military intervention makes such intervention unlikely, for under present rules, no IO, including the UN, has its own military forces or the independent ability to mobilize them.

Comparison of the cases of Yugoslavia and Lebanon reveal that intervention is more likely when the targets are members of the intervening organization. Recall our central distinction between IOs and alliances based on whether the basic norms of the entity are intended to regulate relations among member states or between members and nonmembers. In the former case, intervention, especially where norms are violated by members, has more "legitimacy." When an organization intervenes militarily against nonmembers, it behaves like an alliance. In the case of Kuwait, Iraq, a member state, violated the most fundamental norm of the UN by invading and annexing another sovereign member, Kuwait. In the case of Lebanon, the Arab League acted on the grounds that Lebanon, a member state, required protection from internal forces. By contrast, the European Union finds it difficult to become involved in Yugoslavia, which, although in Europe, is not a member of the EU.

Currently, IOs may not legally intervene in the domestic affairs of member states unless invited, but who decides what party speaks for the state when it is engulfed in ethnic war? The Arab League and Syria were "invited" by the president of Lebanon, who was also a leader of one of the parties to the internal conflict. It is more often the case, however, that the party in need of outside intervention—for example, the Kurds in Iraq—is not the government. Is intervention less likely in such cases? Has this criterion been relevant in Yugoslavia?

What our examples of one extreme form of intervention (military intervention/peace enforcement) by IOs indicate is that an assessment of the role of IOs in ethnic conflicts requires differentiating types and costs of intervention, articulating the basic norms of the given IO, and specifying the vital interests of the powerful members of the IOs as well as the superpowers.

The empirical comparison of the role of IOs in the conflict in Yugoslavia following the end of the cold war with the international intervention in Lebanon during the cold war promises to shed some light on these issues. Comparison also illustrates the consequences of IO interventions and the degree of their success or failure both in mitigating immediate conflict and in reducing the prospects of future conflict. Some scholars warn, for example, that well-meaning interventions could actually retard constructive change and prolong conflict (Haas, 1993).

It is useful to study the consequences of international intervention and compare them to their intended goals if member states and IOs are to learn from previous cases. If the international intervention in Kuwait was partly meant to signal a new UN willingness to use force, for instance, why have the Serbs not learned this lesson? Comparative assessments of the consequences of international interventions are a concern of all the authors in the chapters that follow.

Ethnic Conflict and International Organizations

Inasmuch as we have limited the scope of this book to intervention in *ethnic* conflicts, it is important to differentiate such conflicts from other cases of domestic strife and civil war (Schecterman and Slann 1993; Ryan 1990a; Midlarsky 1992; Moynihan 1993). Ethnic conflict is a consequence of ethnic pluralism, the presence of two or more ethnic communities under the same political authority. More than 90 percent of the 180 or so states that are members of the UN include two or more ethnic communities of significant size. Most of these communities want to maintain their distinctive collective identity, or they find that a collective identity is imposed on them by outsiders. Such identity may be based on a distinctive culture marked by its own language or dialect and by sentiments of common origin, historical experience, or nationality; a common religion, belief system, and practices; racial differences; or a combination of these factors. Collective ethnic identity, ascriptive in origin, may be shaped by experience in a common territory regarded as the exclusive homeland of a people or by immigration through which a community is formed apart from the dominant indigenous society.

Ethnic distinctiveness does not necessarily generate conflict. Ethnic communities may coexist peacefully for extended periods of time. In most societies, however, ethnicity is close to the core of individual identity. Perceived slights or threats from outsiders can generate powerful collective reactions, which can be mobilized and politicized by ethnic entrepreneurs who are motivated partly by genuine concern for their people and partly by a desire to build a constituency in pursuit of personal political ambitions. Ethnic entrepreneurs precipitate conflict by politicizing collective identity, that is, by dramatizing grievances or threats to common interests or by pointing out opportunities to promote and further such interests by organized action.

These competitive interests may run the gamut from control of territory to eligibility for citizenship and the exercise of political rights, from official recognition of language to the status of religion, from access to education to opportunities for employment, landownership, business enterprise, and the distribution of government investments and public services. Even in the face of such competition, ethnic communities are normally beset by internal cleavages and factions, disagreement about goals and tactics, and competition for support among constituents and relevant outsiders.

Political action by organized ethnic communities may take a variety of forms, ranging from conformity with the rules and practices of the polity to various expressions of civil disobedience and collective violence. Two or more organized ethnic communities may be involved, particularly when a government is too weak to enforce its authority over society. Normally the state, the principal allocator of values in contemporary societies, is a party to such disputes, often as the agent or instrument of the dominant ethnic community. Under these circumstances the state may actively promote the ambitions of that community, thereby aggravating the grievances and insecurities of their ethnic competitors. Even when the state attempts to be neutral, its elites may be forced to cope with challenges to a status quo that is regarded as unjust or unacceptable by spokespersons for an organized and aggrieved ethnic community.

In the contemporary world, there are few closed political systems. Persons, goods, weapons, money, information, and ideas move rather freely across international borders. As a consequence, external intrusions in ethnic disputes within recognized international borders are quite common. Such intrusions may be solicited from the inside by a party to the dispute seeking to buttress its position by diplomatic support, favorable propaganda, funds, weapons, and even personnel provided by sympathetic outsiders. Often those who have joined the diaspora support ethnic kinspeople in their country of origin. The Palestinian diaspora has provided steadfast assistance to the Palestinians under Israeli occupation, just as the Jewish diaspora extended itself on behalf of the Zionist movement and the state of Israel. External intervention may sometimes be initiated by foreign governments seeking strategic benefits by championing and even provoking one contestant in an ethnic dispute in another country, as Hitler supported the Sudeten Germans in pre-World War II Czechoslovakia. Political elites may attempt to solidify their domestic political backing, an example being President Boris Yeltsin's expressions of concern for Russian minorities in the successor states of the USSR. By their allocations of economic assistance, international development agencies may, usually inadvertently, provide resources that favor a party to an ethnic dispute, usually the government. Thus, in this era of rapid communication and growing economic interdependence, international borders have become increasingly porous; ethnic disputes cannot be totally insulated from external "interference" from non governmental sources or even from other states (Schecterman and Slann 1993; Ryan 1990a; Midlarsky 1992; Moynihan 1993).

All parties to an ethnic dispute may welcome and even solicit external intervention on their behalf. The stronger party is most likely to resist or condemn such intervention if it calculates that its weaker adversary will benefit. Governments endowed with the legitimate monopoly of force and with more ready access to weaponry are more likely than their ethnic challengers to stand for the principle of nonintervention. For four decades the government of South Africa resisted international intervention, while the African National Congress and its allies solicited and welcomed intervention by IOs, including the UN and the Organization of African Unity.

State sovereignty is a long-established norm or principle of international law and international relations. Within recognized borders the state is formally endowed with absolute sovereignty over its territory and population; any interference by outsiders without the state's consent is regarded as ipso facto illegitimate. The recognized principle of noninterference in matters of domestic jurisdiction is intended to limit all outside parties, including nongovernmental organizations, but it applies especially to the behavior of states and IOs. Therefore in analyzing and evaluating an emergent role for IOs in domestic ethnic conflicts, the relevant point of departure must be the established norms of state sovereignty and noninterference. The presumption of state sovereignty holds unless a compelling case can be made to override it.

Beginning with the Minorities Treaties under the League of Nations and culminating in the 1992 Declaration by the Conference on Security and Cooperation in Europe (CSCE)—an evolution that will be treated in detail in Chapter 2—a set of norms has emerged which justifies and may even require action by IOs, compromising the established doctrines of state sovereignty and noninterference in domestic affairs. An international consensus has developed in support of intervention under the following conditions:

1. When there are threats to international peace and order, that is, when it appears that domestic ethnic violence may spread beyond national borders, involving parties not previously engaged, thus expanding the scope and scale of conflict. This condition comports with one of the basic purposes of IOs, to maintain peace by preventing and containing international conflicts.
2. When there is large-scale suffering among civilian populations, including refugees victimized by violence resulting from ethnic conflict. IOs, expressing emergent universal humanitarian values, mobilize and deliver resources to sustain the lives of innocent victims, often in cooperation with states and nongovernmental organizations.
3. When there are flagrant violations of human rights. When domestic ethnic conflicts are associated with abuses of human rights by governments, ranging from repression of free expression to genocide, IOs are increasingly urged to intervene. A consensus has been developing in favor of the universalization of human rights to the point that state sovereignty can be abridged by the international community in the face of gross and flagrant violations. In international declarations, the main tendency has been to define human rights as inhering only in individuals, in individual freedom of expression, nondiscriminatory political participation, economic opportunities, and criminal justice.

More recently the definition of human rights has been expanding to incorporate group rights, especially the rights of ethnic minorities (Van Dyke 1977). Once it is recognized that collectivities are also endowed with rights that qualify for international protection, how are such rights to be identified and defined? Should all ethnic groups enjoy the right to self-determination? If so, what are the limits to this right? Spokespersons for IOs adhere to the principle that minority rights cannot be permitted to extend to the revision of international borders. In effect, they reject any claim to territorial separation as a valid human right. Are the human rights of ethnic minorities limited to immunity from oppression and to nondiscrimination? Or do they include such collective rights as regional autonomy/self-determination, separate representation in parliaments, separate schools in the ethnic language, or "affirmative action" for members of historically disadvantaged ethnic communities? Which collective rights of ethnic communities should IOs recognize and attempt to vindicate?

The kind of intervention IOs may pursue varies widely. They may apply diplomatic pressure, through resolutions calling attention to evident violations and condemning them, urging the offending party, a government or an ethnic community, to cease and desist. The purpose is to make the offender aware of negative international opinion in the hope of inducing compliance with international norms.

A second possibility is the provision of humanitarian relief, shipments of food, medicine, and emergency shelter for the victims of ethnic conflict, including refugees and other displaced persons. Distribution is supervised where possible by representatives of IOs with the help of nongovernmental organizations to ensure that relief supplies reach their intended beneficiaries.

Third, IOs may assemble a team to observe, monitor, and report on the situation, hoping that their presence and the publicity it generates will serve to limit and contain the conflict and perhaps induce the parties to mediate their differences.

Fourth, IOs may use their good offices, may encourage the parties to an ethnic dispute to allow the IO to mediate with the objective of suspending or ending violence, relieving human suffering, and achieving the basis for negotiations leading to a longer-term settlement.

Fifth, the IO may employ economic sanctions—embargoes on imports, exports, and capital flow—against states considered to be in flagrant violation of international norms. Punitive economic measures may be complemented by arms embargoes intended to deprive the offending state of additional weaponry, military supplies and equipment.

Sixth, with the agreement of the parties to an ethnic dispute, an IO may dispatch teams of military and civilian personnel to supervise armistice or cease-fire arrangements, to mediate minor disputes, in effect to separate the combatants, keep them separated, and thus pre-empt violent hostilities. Peace keeping may build confidence as a prelude to the negotiation of more permanent settlements.

Seventh, IOs may attempt to make peace themselves, to design terms for interim or even long-term settlements of ethnic disputes. Where it is possible, the disputing parties may participate in the negotiation and formulation of such terms. The IO may assist in their implementation, for example, by supervising elections.

Eighth, where treaties provide for the management of ethnic conflicts, IOs may be designated as agencies for exercising surveillance over their implementation. They may hear and adjudicate complaints by aggrieved parties and participate in enforcement by the methods stipulated in the treaties.

Finally, when a party to an ethnic conflict refuses to comply with the decisions of an IO and continues to pursue its goals by violent means, the IO may feel compelled to intervene militarily to enforce its will. This is the most risky and most costly form of intervention, entailing the possibility that forces sponsored by an IO may, in effect, become a party to a violent conflict and suffer heavy casualties.

None of these methods is automatic or self administering. None can operate independently of the internal politics of IO; decisions, of necessity, reflect the diverse perspectives, interests, and relative influence of their various members. Nor can success be guaranteed in the face of limited resources, uncertain commitment of members, and the obduracy of parties to the conflict.

One of the aims of this book is to assess the causes and objectives of international intervention. We want to examine how the specific interests of powerful member states affect intervention patterns, compared with the role played by the norms of IOs. But when IOs decide to act—and such decisions are usually selective, often hesitant, less than unanimous, and constrained by concerns about costs and uncertain effectiveness—they ostensibly aim to achieve one or more of the following goals: to terminate violence between the parties, prevent the renewal of hostilities, and restore order; to relieve suffering, especially among civilians, and restore some of the normal routines of living by, for example, repairing damaged infrastructure and renewing essential public services; to initiate negotiations between the conflicting parties leading to cessation of hostilities, interim arrangements, and eventually permanent settlements; to apply emergent international norms to protect and promote the human rights of individuals and especially the collective rights of ethnic communities; to punish and delegitimate regimes or parties judged to be in flagrant, persistent, and large-scale violation of international norms; and to establish precedents for intervention which will deter future violations of international norms.

Assessing the Role of IOs in Ethnic Conflict: Some Questions

Whatever the stated objectives of IOs when they intervene in ethnic conflict, several questions arise about the consistency of their behavior, criteria for intervention, changes in their norms over time, and the actual consequences of interventions as compared to stated objectives. More specifically, certain questions can be asked.

What factors determine why IOs intervene in some domestic ethnic disputes and not in others that appear equivalent in terms of violence, suffering, and abuses of rights? Why Cyprus but not Sudan? why Lebanon but not Sri Lanka? Why on behalf of Kurds but not of Tibetans? Is this apparent inconsistency related to the internal politics of IOs, including the goals and interests of their more influential members, to the vagueness of international norms, to concerns about financial capacities and who will pay, to fears that interventions may be both costly and ineffectual? Are selectivity and hesitancy about intervention in domestic ethnic disputes inherent in the current structures and procedures of IOs?

What can be said of the stages of domestic ethnic conflict which prompt intervention? Does the timing of intervention influence its effectiveness? Do IOs tend to consider intervention only when action may be too late to be effective? Are there opportunities or possibilities to facilitate early and *preventive* intervention? What forms might it take? What changes in IO policies and practices would be required to implement this type of institutional reform? Would such changes necessarily enhance the autonomy of IO senior officials, especially the UN secretary-general (Boutros-Ghali 1992a)? Could the more influential member states be reconciled to this enhanced role? Where would the necessary additional resources come from?

How do the attitudes of local actors in the ethnic conflict affect the decisions of IOs? Does it matter whether the initiative for intervention comes from local or external actors? Is the extent of local support for or opposition to international intervention an important criterion in the decisions of IOs?

What norms and criteria guide IOs in decisions concerning intervention, and how should these criteria change: The prospect that violent conflict will spread and threaten international peace? The *severity* of violence, of human suffering, of abuses of rights? The *feasibility* of intervention expressed in financial costs, risks to lives and safety of agents of the IOs, or the possibility of effectiveness on the ground? Is it true that the more severe and large scale the violence, suffering and abuses, the less IOs will be inclined or able to act and that the more powerful the offending state, the more immune it is from IO limitations on its freedom of action?

Is there evidence that the principle of state sovereignty and noninterference is yielding to the vindication of human rights as a criterion for organized international action? Which collective rights of ethnic communities are accepted, and which should be accepted as actionable by IOs? How can IOs reduce the growing gap between ever more expansive declarations of human rights and their capacities and willingness to act?

Would it be feasible to develop complementary divisions of labor between universal and regional IOs and between IOs and nongovernmental organizations such as the International Red Cross and the World Council of Churches on how and when to intervene in domestic ethnic conflicts? Are there some situations and some tasks for which certain kinds of actors are better suited? How might their different capabilities be used to enhance their combined effectiveness?

What criteria should be used to assess the consequences of international intervention: success or failure in the specific case, overall tendency to preserve international norms, short-term mitigation of immediate suffering, or long-term reduction of the chances of future conflict?

Organization of the Book

With these analytical questions in mind, we have divided the book into three parts. Milton Esman begins Part I with a survey of the historical record of IO interventions in ethnic conflicts. Next, in theoretical chapters, Jack Donnelly and Raymond Hopkins address general questions about the evolving role of international organizations in ethnic conflict, the relative weight that these organizations have acquired in comparison to the individual power of member states, the changing norms of IOs, and how local actors in ethnic conflict view IOs. Part I functions as a prelude to the empirical examination of our two primary cases, Lebanon and Yugoslavia.

In Part II of the book, the role of IOs in Lebanon is thoroughly examined. In Chapter 4 Samir Khalaf provides the historical background of the civil strife and the outside action it has provoked. Although it is not specifically about IOs, the chapter draws general conclusions about intervention, setting the stage for Michael Hudson's assessment of the role of IOs from the point of view of local actors. In what sense is the conflict in Lebanon ethnic? Who are the key actors and how did they view the role of IOs? Who supported and who opposed international interventions? Have the interests of the local actors (and thus their attitude toward IOs) changed over time?

In Chapter 6, Naomi Weinberger focuses primarily on how IOs, especially the Arab League and the UN, viewed the conflict in Lebanon. She compares the role of the UN with that of the U.S.-led multinational force in 1982-1983. What were the interests of these organizations, and why did they intervene? Can these interests be differentiated from the interests of individual member states? What were the consequences of intervention?

Part III describes the case of Yugoslavia and its successor states, especially Bosnia. V. P. Gagnon evaluates the historical forces that led to the crisis of the multiethnic Yugoslav state in the 1980s and precipitated its dissolution. In Chapter 8 Susan Woodward describes and evaluates the role of IOs in this conflict from the perspective of local actors. Steven Burg completes Part III by examining this case from the point of view of relevant IOs—the UN, the EC, and the CSCE.

Two concluding chapters, by Barry Preisler and Shibley Telhami draw lessons from the preceding essays, both about the historical evolution of international intervention in ethnic conflict and about the degree of success and failure of these interventions. An effort is made to distinguish conditions under which IOs can intervene more effectively and to assess the likelihood of change in the norms of intervention following the end of the cold war. Finally, criteria are proposed for the empirical study of additional cases of intervention by international organizations.

PART I

The Role of International Organizations in the Post-Cold-War Era

1

A Survey of Interventions

Milton J. Esman

This chapter surveys interventions by international organizations in domestic ethnic conflicts. Though not exhaustive, it reviews the activities and responses of enough IOs to permit judgments about their effectiveness, potential, and limitations in the kinds of disputes that have become the principal threat to international peace. I have chosen examples from the main categories of intervention: good offices and mediation, peace making and peace keeping, protection of human rights, humanitarian assistance, and stigmatization of regimes deemed guilty of flagrant violation of international norms. I have excluded the cases of Lebanon and Yugoslavia, which are analyzed in other chapters, and IO-sponsored interventions that do not involve ethnic conflicts, such as the Korean conflict of the 1950s and more recent UN operations in Cambodia and El Salvador.

The modern international "system" of territorial states has evolved a set of norms, practices, and structures that have become highly institutionalized and change very slowly. The main actors have been and remain territorially delimited states. The controlling doctrine is that of state sovereignty; outsiders, including other states and IOs, may not interfere in matters of "domestic jurisdiction" without the explicit consent of that state's government. Though this doctrine has been eroded at the margins by growing economic interdependency, environmental concerns, and human rights violations, it is jealously guarded by state

The author acknowledges, with gratitude, research assistance provided by Boblu Naidu.

elites everywhere. The presumption against external interference continues to govern the behavior of IOs; members are hesitant to establish precedents that might justify subsequent interference in what they regard as their internal affairs. Equally rigid has been the related principle concerning the inviolability of established international borders. There has been a strong presumption that any settlement of an ethnic dispute should respect this principle. The international system may yield to faits accomplis, such as the partition of Pakistan, the secession of Eritrea from Ethiopia, and the dissolution of the Soviet and Yugoslav states, but such outcomes are not likely to be promoted by IOs (Hannum 1990).

The IOs that have emerged during the twentieth century, especially those that deal with political and security matters, are voluntary associations of member states. Neither global nor regional IOs have any independent access to resources. Their funds are provided by member states, but IOs have no effective capacity to enforce payment. Nor do their administrators have any autonomous capacity to act. The charters of IOs proscribe interference in the domestic affairs of member states and their activities require explicit approval of the membership, often by extraordinary majorities that must include the more powerful and influential member states. In the case of the UN, proposed actions can be vetoed by any one of the five permanent members of the Security Council. Decisions to intervene in ethnic conflicts are conditioned not only by international norms and perceptions of justice but also by the interests of member states, including security concerns, competitive economic and political considerations, and willingness to bear the costs of interventions in money and in manpower. IOs are political bodies with limited resources and they behave as such. Decisions about intervening in ethnic conflicts are necessarily hesitant and selective (Haas 1987).

During the past two centuries the dominant bias among ruling elites in the face of domestic ethnic pluralism has been assimilationist. Enlightened governments do not oppress ethnic minorities or discriminate against them. Instead, they encourage members of ethnic minorities to join the mainstream, hoping thereby to build a unified, "indivisible" nation. Individual members of ethnic minorities, it is thought, should be pleased to accept the privilege of full incorporation into the nation. Policies and measures that recognize permanent collective rights or special status for minorities have been considered impediments to the normal and desirable processes of "nation building." Consequently, as IOs have struggled with the implementation of the human rights to which their charters pay homage, they have emphasized the rights of individuals to nondiscriminatory treatment, not the collective rights of ethnic minorities to official status for their language, separate schools, or equitable representation in political and administrative bodies (Donnelly 1989). Though the question of collective minority rights never disappeared from the agendas of IOs and has won new attention since the dissolution of the multiethnic USSR and Yugoslavia, state elites have felt much more comfortable pursuing individual human rights in an assimilationist framework.

Nor have IOs been certain about their mandate to intervene when the primary issue is perceived as protection of human rights or even the need for humanitarian assistance. Member states have been more likely to act out of concerns that an ethnic conflict might constitute a threat to international stability and peace, whose preservation forms the bedrock purpose for the establishment of IOs. Thus, not only because of uncertain mandates and limited resources but also because intervention normally requires the consent of the member states, IOs tend to exercise extreme caution in the absence of a persuasive case that international peace and stability are at risk. It has been from within this well-established structural and normative framework that IOs have addressed the challenge of intervention in domestic ethnic conflicts during this century.

The League of Nations Minorities Treaties

The minorities treaties executed as part of the post-World War I peace settlement were a precedent-setting effort to involve the League of Nations in domestic ethnic conflicts. As part of his crusade to "make the world safe for democracy" President Woodrow Wilson popularized the idea of "self-determination of nations." Where possible, every nation should be entitled to its own self-governing state; where establishment of such a state is impracticable, national minorities should be entitled to fair treatment, including reasonable autonomy and the opportunity to maintain their distinctive culture.

Application of the principle of national self-determination in the postwar peace settlement was limited. It was to apply not to the victorious powers, to the Irish in the United Kingdom, Bretons in France, or African-Americans in the United States, and certainly not to their colonial possessions, but mainly to Eastern European states that were created or enlarged by the terms of the Versailles peace settlement, specifically Poland, Czechoslovakia, Romania, Yugoslavia, and Greece. (As other Eastern European states, including Latvia, Estonia, Lithuania, and Finland, were later admitted to the League of Nations, they agreed to be bound by the same principles, as did the defeated powers in their peace treaties, Austria, Bulgaria, Turkey, and Hungary, but not Germany.) Despite the rhetoric of self-determination, the main political purpose of these treaties was not so much to vindicate minority rights as to prevent destabilization of the peace settlement. The principal minorities in these new states were Germans and Hungarians, formerly members of dominant majorities, now reduced to the status of vulnerable minorities. By internationalizing the rights of minorities, by providing a forum for their grievances, the victorious powers hoped to prevent Germany and Hungary from seizing upon the status of their kinspeople as bilateral issues with which to destabilize the new order in Eastern Europe.

By treaties with the allied powers, the new states committed themselves first, to protect the rights of individual members of national minorities to nondiscriminatory treatment and to the enjoyment of full and equal rights of citizenship and, second, to allow minorities as distinct communities to preserve and develop their cultures—to use their language freely, to operate their own cultural and social institutions, and to receive government financing for education in their minority language. Both individual and collective human rights were thus recognized and incorporated in these treaties.

The Allied powers committed the administration of the Minorities Treaties to the League of Nations—which they effectively controlled. The treaty rights became international obligations of the signatory states, guaranteed by the Council of the League. A minorities section was established in the League's secretariat. Aggrieved minorities could petition the council for redress. The petition would be remanded to the accused state for comments, and then petition and comments would be referred to a three-nation committee of the council, which could dismiss the petition, attempt to negotiate a settlement, or refer it to the full council. The accused state was invited to participate in council discussions, but the petitioning minority could not be present. Legal issues involving interpretation of the language of the treaties could be referred to the Permanent Court of International Justice. The assumption underlying these cumbersome procedures was that the ventilation of these issues would normally lead to the mutually satisfactory adjustment of grievances. The treaty rights of the minorities would thus be protected, while the sovereignty of member states was fully respected (Claude 1955, Hannum 1990, Kohn 1965).

In fact, the minorities complained that their treaty rights were hopelessly compromised by these procedures. Once their petitions were submitted, they were excluded from any further participation in deliberations, whereas the violating state was present at all stages of the proceedings. Germany and Hungary considered themselves deprived of their inherent power under international law to defend by diplomatic action the rights of oppressed ethnic kinspeople in neighboring countries. The new states that were subject to these treaty provisions resented the imposition of special obligations to minorities, especially after the League rejected efforts to universalize such obligations. They argued that the system undermined domestic tranquillity and stability, because it compromised the process of assimilation by encouraging minorities to perpetuate their sense of separateness; it diminished respect for government by allowing minorities to appeal over their heads to a foreign body; it generated popular animosity toward minorities by emphasizing their distinctiveness, marking them as a privileged "foreign" group and in some cases identifying them with a potentially irredentist neighboring state; it impeded economic reforms, since in many instances the immunities accorded to minorities had the effect of protecting an economically privileged class; and it exempted minorities from the obligation of loyalty to the new states. The political elites of most of the treaty states, notably Poland and Romania, were ethnic nationalists opposed in principle to institutionalizing ethnic pluralism and minority rights.

As the 1919 peace settlement began to unravel, Poland in September 1934 informed the League that it would no longer cooperate on minorities issues, in effect denouncing the minorities treaty. Since the dominant powers, Britain and France, were not prepared to confront Poland on this issue, the other signatories tacitly followed Poland's example and the structure supporting the treaties was allowed to collapse. As the Council of the League defaulted on its "guarantees," minorities learned that they had nothing to gain by petitioning. In 1939 the minorities section of the secretariat was disbanded.

Thus the League of Nations machinery for the protection of minority rights, limited as it was to Eastern European states, could not be sustained. It was, however, the first significant effort by an IO to intervene in domestic ethnic conflicts. It pioneered in promoting the principle that state sovereignty may be constrained by the international community in defense of human rights. And it defined human rights as pertaining not only to individuals, but also to ethnic communities (national minorities) as collectivities.

While these treaty provisions and their enforcement machinery were in effect, they did offer minorities some protection. They restrained the behavior of governments and they resolved some minority grievances. The procedures, however, were ponderous, and they favored accused states over petitioning minorities, reflecting the reluctance of the League and its members to compromise the principle and practice of state sovereignty. Then, as now, IOs had little autonomous capacity to act. When the members, especially the more powerful states, Britain and France, failed to respond to Poland's defiance, the League was powerless to act. The international norms that the minorities treaties represented were fragile, but even had they been more robust and commanded a larger following, they could not have been implemented against a determined violator without the active support of the more influential members.

Palestinians and Israelis

The dispute between Palestinians and Israelis, in which the United Nations has been involved for forty-five years, exhibits every dimension of IO intervention. Here, it is possible only to summarize the highlights of this lengthy and complex historical record, evaluate their consequences, and attempt to draw some general inferences about what IOs can achieve in disputes of this kind.

What makes the Israeli-Palestinian confrontation so intractable is that two highly mobilized nationalist movements, Zionist and Palestinian, claimed exclusive rights to this small territory between the Jordan River and the Mediterranean. Until the Israel-Palestine Liberation Organization (PLO) accord in September 1993, a consensual settlement based on power sharing, federalism, or territorial compromise had been unacceptable to the parties or to factions within the two camps which were able to exercise veto power over terms of settlement (Geddes 1991, Hadawi 1989, Kimchi 1991).

Britain acquired control of Palestine in 1918, displacing the Ottoman Turks. In 1917 the British government had committed itself in the Balfour Declaration to "the establishment in Palestine of a national home for the Jewish people" but had declared that "nothing shall be done which may prejudice the civil or religious rights of existing non-Jewish communities." The League of Nations assigned Palestine to Britain as a mandate, incorporating in its resolution the language of the Balfour Declaration. For more than a quarter of a century the British attempted to manage the increasingly violent confrontation between Palestinians, supported by all the Arab states, and the growing Zionist community, satisfying neither party. After World War II, Britain decided to abandon the mandate and remand it to the new United Nations Organization, successor to the defunct League. In May 1947 a UN Special Committee on Palestine was formed; in September its majority report recommended the partitioning of Palestine into a predominantly Jewish and a predominantly Palestinian state. Jerusalem would remain an enclave under international administration. The Zionists accepted this proposal, but all the Arab states as well as spokesmen for the Palestinians categorically rejected partition. The first UN effort at peace making had failed.

With the departure of the British, war broke out. The UN attempted mediation and after many months of hostilities achieved a series of armistices along existing battle lines. These armistices were to be monitored by a UN Truce Supervision Organization, which exists to this day. In 1949 the UN Relief and Works Agency (UNRWA) was established to provide relief and subsistence to Palestinian refugees displaced to neighboring countries. This agency continues to operate four and a half decades later. In 1956 in the wake of the aborted Israeli-British-French invasion of Egypt, a UN Emergency Force (UNEF) was organized to keep the peace and separate the parties on the Israel-Egypt border. The sudden withdrawal of this force without protest by the secretary-general, as demanded by President Gamal Abdel Nasser of Egypt, helped to precipitate the Six-Day or June War in 1967. After the defeat of the Arab armies, the UN Security Council brokered a cease-fire and peace-keeping units were stationed on the Egyptian and Syrian borders. A few months later the Security Council issued resolution 242, a second UN effort at peace making, which called for Israeli withdrawal from territories occupied during the war and recognition by the Arab states of Israel's right to exist behind secure and recognized borders. From 1968 to 1971, Gunnar Jarring, representing the secretary-general, unsuccessfully attempted to broker settlements among the parties. After the Yom Kippur War of October 1973, a UNEF II was activated to police the cease-fire on the Egyptian and Syrian borders. In 1978 the UN Interim Force in Lebanon (UNIFIL) was set up to separate the parties, including Israeli regulars and their Lebanese Christian allies, and enforce a cease-fire in southern Lebanon. Thus, since 1948, there have been several UN-sponsored unarmed observer groups in this area, as well as five major peace-keeping forces, of which three remain in operation (al-Rfouh 1984, Beker 1988, Tessitore and Wolfson 1990).

Following the 1967 war, a coalition emerged which was to set the tone in the UN for over two decades. The African states agreed to support the Arabs and their Muslim allies on Middle East matters in return for support on questions affecting South Africa. The Soviet bloc participated in this coalition in order to undermine the United States and its allies, and the nonaligned states joined as an expression of Third World solidarity. The coalition achieved a guaranteed two-thirds majority in the UN General Assembly and the specialized agencies for annual resolutions endorsing the Palestinian cause, recognizing the PLO as sole representative of the Palestinian people, harshly condemning Israel, and activating a series of special committees and agencies that for the most part promoted the Palestinian version of the conflict. The culmination of these efforts was the 1975 General Assembly resolution equating Zionism with racism and the 1983 special General Assembly session in Geneva devoted entirely to Palestine. Inasmuch as these measures were routinely vetoed by the United States and its allies in the Security Council, their effects were primarily declaratory and propagandistic, but they crippled the ability of the UN to act as interlocutor or honest broker between the parties. The Camp David accord between Egypt and Israel was sponsored and managed by the United States; the current round of Middle East peace negotiations are sponsored by the United States and Russia. With the end of the cold war and the outcome of the Gulf War, the anti-Israel coalition in the General Assembly collapsed, and the Zionism-racism resolution was formally rescinded in 1991. Israel, however, continues to distrust and resist any role for the UN as peacemaker.

In this complex and extended history of interventions, the UN has played a variety of roles. In peace making its 1947 partition proposal failed, as did the Jarring missions from 1968 to 1971. Though it has yet to be implemented, Security Council resolution 242 has been formally accepted by Israel, by most Arab governments, and since 1988, by the PLO. The principle that Israel should yield territories and that Arab states should recognize the statehood of Israel continues to provide the basis for negotiation, though the parties and factions involved differ widely on their meaning and how they should be implemented.

The UN has also been involved in a variety of costly and lengthy peace-keeping operations. Except for the 1967 withdrawal of the UNEF at Nasser's insistence and the inability of UNIFIL to deter Israel's invasion of Lebanon in 1982, the peace-keeping forces have served their intended purposes—enforcing cease-fires, separating the parties and keeping them disengaged, maintaining armistice agreements, and preventing minor incidents from flaring up into serious hostilities. The stationing of peace-keeping forces requires the consent of the contending parties and their ability to control and discipline groups associated with their ethnic community. That Israelis and Arabs have generally tolerated the status quo has facilitated the task of the peace-keepers. Nevertheless, these operations have strained the fragile UN budgets for many years. The cumulative costs through 1990 totaled $3.184 billion, averaging $80 million annually since the peace-keeping operations began. Many members have failed to pay their assessments for these operations; in 1990 unpaid assessments for UNIFIL totaled $318 million, the equivalent of two years of current operating costs.

The UN's main humanitarian role for more than four decades has been to finance and operate UNRWA, devoted entirely to maintaining Palestinian refugees in their diaspora, including camps in Lebanon, Syria, Jordan, and the occupied territories. UNRWA has relieved both Israel and the Arab states of the responsibility of caring for and integrating the refugees, now in their third generation. The camps, where isolation and hopelessness breed frustration and extremism, have become centers for the recruitment of fighters for the various Palestinian resistance organizations and staging grounds for terrorist operations against Israel. UNRWA has provided for survival needs and for education, health, and other public services at international expense, but it has also provided the material base for maintaining the Arab and Palestinian political demand for the refugees' right to return to their former homeland. UNRWA in 1949 served 750,000 refugees and displaced persons; forty years later the number had increased to 2.6 million, including about 900,000 in sixty-one camps. Annual costs in 1992 totaled $286 million, financed by voluntary contributions of member states.

Two roles, protection of human rights and partisan promotion, have been interlinked in the Israeli-Palestinian confrontation. The decades of the 1970s and 1980s witnessed an annual barrage of General Assembly resolutions reinforced by the activities of a network of special committees and agencies designed to promote the Palestinian cause and to isolate and delegitimate Israel. Prominent in these debates were attacks on Israel for flagrant violations of human rights, ranging from arbitrary arrests, detentions, torture, and expulsions to discrimination in education, exploitation of labor, expropriation of land, and denial of the right of self-determination. Though these attacks were condemned by Israel and its allies as cynical, exaggerated, and highly selective, they increased international sympathy for the plight of Palestinians in the occupied territories and may have reinforced liberal opinion in Israel. They also had the effect of disabling the UN as a neutral interlocutor between the parties.

The UN's involvement in the dispute between these two hostile and highly mobilized national movements constitutes the most intense, long-lasting, and costly participation by any IO in an ethnically based conflict. The Palestinian-Israeli dispute has been and remains a major claimant on UN resources. The combined financial costs of the peacekeeping and humanitarian activities, now in their fifth decade, exceed $360 million annually. The leading members of the UN have been willing to support these extended operations because they serve their mutual interests in stabilizing a potentially dangerous situation in a strategically important region.

Cyprus

On Cyprus, an island about sixty miles south of the Turkish mainland, more than 80 percent of the 700,000 inhabitants are Greek-speaking, while Turks comprise fewer than 20 percent. In 1878 Britain took effective control of the island from the Ottoman Empire. It subsequently installed two large military bases and was able to maintain peace between the Greek and Turkish communities until after World War II. At that time agitation for union with Greece, *enosis*, became a major issue, supported by nationalist elements in Greece, and it led to major acts of violence against British forces. After lengthy negotiations involving Britain, Greece, and Turkey, Cyprus in 1960 became an independent unitary state with a Greek Cypriot president and a Turkish Cypriot vice-president, each of whom could exercise a veto over matters deemed to be prejudicial to the interests of their respective communities. Thirty percent of the seats in the parliament and an equal proportion of positions in the civil service were reserved for members of the Turkish minority, substantially above their percentage of the population. Britain retained its military bases.

In 1963 the Greek-speaking president, Archbishop Makarios III, proposed constitutional changes that the Turkish leadership believed would be damaging to the interests of the Turkish minority. Communal violence soon erupted. To prevent the extension of hostilities to the two "protecting" powers, Greece and Turkey, both members of NATO, the United States and Britain, with the approval of the Soviet Union, decided to request UN intervention. The secretary-general in 1964 selected a mediator to seek a peaceful modus vivendi between the parties. The Security Council also authorized, originally for a limited period of three months, the UN Peace-keeping Force in Cyprus (UNFICYP) to serve as buffer between the communities, prevent external interference, patrol sensitive areas, and restore normal activities, including free movement of goods and people, as well as water, electricity, judicial, educational, health, and welfare services. The UN contingents were unable to eliminate all violence, but they reduced it very considerably and were successful in protecting life and property and in restoring the normal rhythms of life. The fundamental issues could not be resolved, many in Greece and among the Greek Cypriot majority favoring *enosis*, Turkey and the Cypriot Turks favoring some form of partition. Though sporadic violence continued during this period, it was possible to reduce the UN force from 6,400 in 1964 to 3,500 in 1970.

In 1974 the military junta in control of Greece initiated an insurrection in favor of *enosis* and succeeded in deposing President Makarios. Turkey reacted with a military invasion, seizing control of 40 percent of the territory in the north and east, in effect partitioning the island. Greeks were expelled en masse from the Turkish-occupied zone and many Turks moved in from the Greek zone to take over abandoned homes, shops, and agricultural land. Later Turkish colonists were brought in from the mainland to strengthen the Turkish presence.

Since the invasion of 1974, several UN-sponsored efforts to restore the political and economic unity of the island have uniformly failed. Turkey and its Cypriot clients are disinclined to yield the territory they now occupy, which they have designated as the Turkish Republic of North Cyprus, unrecognized by the international community. After the invasion, the UN shifted operational priorities to humanitarian work, which was placed under the control of the UN High Commissioner for Refugees, whose mission was to care for the 240,000 or so refugees and displaced persons, more than a third of the population, providing relief convoys, temporary housing, health services, assistance in resettlement, and opportunities to earn livelihoods in their new locations.

The UN has been unable to achieve withdrawal of foreign (Turkish) forces, to eliminate checkpoints and fortifications, or to prevent separate economic development in the two sectors. UN peace-keeping forces have, however, helped to prevent further outbreaks of hostilities and of communal violence and have stabilized the cease-fire along the present buffer zone, the de facto border. In the absence of a formal settlement, the parties concerned—Greece, Turkey, Greek Cypriots, and Turkish Cypriots—accept the UN presence because it has helped to maintain a precarious peace. This peace has enabled Greek Cypriots, despite loss of territory, to achieve an unprecedented level of economic development and material prosperity, far above the income levels attained in the Turkish zone.

The Security Council routinely extends UNFICYP for six-month periods. Through 1990, $635 million has been spent to maintain the UN presence in Cyprus, about $25 million annually, exclusive of the estimated cost of $65 million annually which is borne by the countries that provide the military detachments. Voluntary contributions from member countries have fallen short of requirements, leaving the UN with a cumulative deficit (as of 1990) of $191 million for these operations. The secretary-general has so far failed to persuade the Security Council to cover these costs by assessments rather than voluntary contributions. The resources used in Cyprus could be used to good effect in many other ethnic flashpoints, but the UN has not found a way to withdraw, despite the urgings of the secretary-general and the manifest impatience of the states that provide the peace-keeping forces, without serious risk of renewed communal violence that might involve Greece and Turkey. The operation has continued for thirty years largely because the most powerful member states have remained interested in preventing such violence. The failure in November 1992 to find an acceptable formula for a negotiated settlement would seem to condemn the UN to an indefinite extension of its costly peace-keeping presence in Cyprus. So effective has been the UN presence in stabilizing the status quo that its presence may have become permanent and indispensable (James 1989, Kaloudis 1991, Mackinlay 1989, UN Department of Public Information 1990).

Sudan

The northern two-thirds of the large territory of Sudan was gradually Islamicized and Arabized over several centuries following Arab-Muslim invasions in the seventh century. The southern third, however, remained divided among several indigenous ethnic communities that remain Christian or animist in their cultures. The north, technologically and economically more advanced, was able to control the major trade routes, including the Nile, on which the south depended and to raid the area for slaves. Northern domination continued under Ottoman and Egyptian rule beginning in the sixteenth century and under the brief period of Mahdist control until 1898 when the British consolidated their rule under the Anglo-Egyptian condominium. British policy was to protect the weaker southern peoples from northern domination, setting up "closed districts" in the south for separate economic and cultural development. British investment and trade policies, however, benefited northern traders and farmers, further marginalizing the south. Though insulated and protected from northern Arab-Muslim influences, the southerners lost more and more economic ground and their dependence on the north increased. North-south cleavages over religion, language, and region were reinforced by severe economic grievances.

When Britain terminated its rule in 1956 the south was guaranteed a share of power in the newly independent state and promised substantial resources for economic development. These promises were disregarded, however, and an armed insurrection broke out, led by multiethnic southern armies, which fought in guerrilla style. They received some assistance from Israel and from the neighboring non-Muslim states of Ethiopia, Kenya, and Uganda. After fifteen years of destructive but indecisive conflict, both parties were exhausted and ready to negotiate. An influential nongovernmental organization, the World Council of Churches, seized the opportunity and used its networks of contacts with rebel Christian leaders inside and outside Sudan to obtain an agreement with the president, General Jaafar al-Nimairi and his military regime with the goal of terminating the conflict. The council made arrangements to hold negotiations outside Sudan on neutral ground in Addis Ababa, Ethiopia, headquarters city for the Organization of African Unity (OAU), which made its facilities available for these meetings. The Ethiopian emperor, Haile Selasie, Africa's senior statesman at that time, took charge of the negotiations and helped to secure the Addis Ababa Agreement of 1972.

Under the terms of this agreement Sudan remained a single polity, but the three southern provinces were combined into a regional entity under a form of federalism in which an elected regional government would enjoy considerable domestic autonomy. Southern military formations would be disbanded and their members absorbed into the national army. Islam would be the state religion and Arabic the official language, but Christianity and other religions could be freely practiced and English would be used in education and in government in the southern region. It was understood that the south would be awarded a generous share of governmental resources for economic development and would be represented equitably in the cabinet and in other decision-making positions in the central government.

The 1972 agreement was hailed as a signal triumph for African statesmanship and the good offices of the OAU, and it succeeded in keeping peace for about ten years. Unfortunately, it led to intense political competition for patronage among the southern tribes, diverting them from the pursuit of economic development and from applying sufficient pressure to win favorable policies and financial allocations from the central government. Through patronage and arms shipments, the central government capitalized on these local cleavages to limit the flow of resources to the south and to attempt to gain control of the recently discovered oil resources in the region.

In 1982 the communists who had supported Nimairi's military regime defected. Their rebellion was quelled with timely assistance from Libya. In an effort to shore up his weakened regime Nimairi, previously a secularist, turned to Islamic fundamentalists, always a factor in Sudanese politics. In return for continuing financial and military support from Libya, Nimairi agreed to enforce Islamic law throughout the country, including the South. This effort, along with Nimairi's orders to southern military formations to serve in the north, precipitated renewal of the insurrection and the formation of the Southern Peoples' Liberation Army (SPLA), committed to defending southern autonomy and restoring democratic, secular rule in Khartoum. The stated goals of the insurrection were not secessionist but called for power sharing, respect for minority rights, and the equitable distribution of economic resources.

After Nimairi's overthrow and a brief democratic interlude, the military seized power in 1989 and installed an explicitly Islamic regime committed to achieving Muslim and Arabic hegemony throughout the country. With military assistance from Libya and Iran, the war in the south was intensified. Large areas were devastated. The UN and voluntary agencies tried to bring food to beleaguered southern areas but the government blocked these efforts as indirectly assisting the rebels. Meanwhile, certain rebel factions similarly hijacked for profit and blocked the provision of food to hungry victims of the fighting. The result has been the total disruption of southern society and its economy and the flight of an estimated three million destitute refugees to neighboring countries and north to Khartoum. The military regime will not consider a pluralist society or polity for Sudan. In its determination to impose Arabic Islamic culture on the entire country, it has practiced or at least acquiesced in massive atrocities and denied international and nongovernmental organizations the ability to distribute desperately needed food and medicine to millions of sick, starving people. Southern Sudan is now the scene of a human tragedy on the scale of Bosnia or Somalia. (Deng 1990, Kasfir 1990, Voll 1990)

IOs have been completely ineffective in mitigating the fury of this ethnic dispute or in preventing the resulting deaths, displacements, and suffering. The OAU's rigid policy of respecting the absolute sovereignty of member states and its members' wariness of any precedent that might justify external intervention in their affairs have prevented it from playing any role in this conflict. UN intervention has not been requested by and would not be acceptable to Sudan's government, which believes it is winning the campaign to impose its rule on the entire country. Even humanitarian efforts have been hampered by the government and at times by the SPLA as well; relief workers have been harassed, and access to some of the most needy populations has been denied. Despite clear evidence of flagrant abuses that resemble "ethnic cleansing," UN members have not been willing to challenge the Khartoum regime by any measures that might stop the killing and protect the human rights of Sudan's minorities. The situation exemplifies the reluctance of IOs to intervene in an ethnic conflict when their more powerful members do not believe their interests warrant the risks and costs of intervention; a bloc of member states, Muslim and Arab in this case, oppose intervention; and the government on whose territory the conflict is being waged will not consent.

South Africa

The racist policies and practices of the government of South Africa have been a major concern of the UN since its inception. (Riley 1991). The objective has been to isolate, delegitimate, and punish the racist regime, encourage its domestic opponents, and persuade member states to adopt diplomatic and economic measures that would compel abandonment of the structures of apartheid. The resolutions adopted by the General Assembly and the Security Council, though they differed considerably in substance and tone, were directed to the same objectives. The methods employed to intervene in this ethnic and racial conflict were entirely declaratory, since there was at no time a UN presence on the ground in South Africa. Many factors contributed to the eventual elimination of apartheid beginning in 1990, but the persistent and unrelenting campaign in the UN certainly played an important part. The UN brought this issue to the forefront of world attention, kept it at the head of the global agenda despite disappointments and setbacks year after year, encouraged domestic and foreign opponents of apartheid, and maintained moral and political pressure on member states to adopt measures intended to isolate and punish the South African government and compel it to abandon its racist policies and practices (Grundy 1991, Ozgur 1982, Beddy 1986).

The UN involvement with South African racism can be divided into three phases.

From 1946 to 1962, the focus was on South Africa's Asian minority. India, the first of the ex-colonial members of the UN, placed on its agenda the issue of racial discrimination against persons of Indian origin. During this period the General Assembly adopted twenty-four resolutions deploring racial discrimination, offering the UN's good offices, and urging India, Pakistan, and South Africa to negotiate a resolution of this dispute. Pretoria refused to cooperate with these initiatives, contending that the UN had no authority to entertain this question, since the issue fell entirely within South Africa's "domestic jurisdiction," which, under article 2, chapter 7, of the charter, is explicitly excluded from the UN's purview.

From 1962 to 1980 attention abruptly shifted to the black majority. The Sharpeville massacre of June 21, 1960, dramatized to a global audience the brutality of South African racism at the very time that decolonization was producing a substantial bloc of African states dedicated to removing the vestiges of white domination from the continent. Beginning in 1962 South African racism became one of the preoccupations of the General Assembly. Annual resolutions urged member states to sever diplomatic, cultural, and sports relations with the apartheid regime, to embargo arms shipments, and to apply economic sanctions, so as to assist the South African majority to displace the apartheid regime. After 1977 the resolutions also endorsed "armed struggle." The South African delegation was not allowed to take its seat in the General Assembly or in the various specialized agencies of the UN. By the late 1970s the General Assembly was enacting an average of eighteen resolutions annually. A network of special committees and working groups, including the Special UN Committee on Apartheid, was activated to collect information, convene meetings, and publicize data condemning apartheid. The General Assembly had no difficulty overriding state sovereignty in the face of flagrant violations of human rights and the right of self-determination, at least when the offending state could be identified as a racist residue of European colonialism.

During this period the Security Council was more cautious, reflecting the dominant position of the Western powers. Security Council resolutions condemned racism and the policies and practices of apartheid, and urged the South African government to abandon them and release political prisoners. It recommended that member states institute an arms embargo. After the Soweto violence in 1976 the Security Council, under the influence of the Carter administration, for the first time demanded the right of self-determination for the people of South Africa regardless of race or color and urged a mandatory arms embargo but declined to recommend economic sanctions or the expulsion of South Africa from the UN.

During the decade of the 1980s the General Assembly maintained pressure with its annual resolutions, intensified its campaign for mandatory economic sanctions and disinvestment by multinational corporations, and condemned alleged Israeli-South African cooperation on nuclear weapons. The Security Council became more militant, demanding the elimination of all aspects of apartheid; rejecting the 1982 constitution, which established a tricameral parliament that excluded blacks; condemned South Africa's attacks on "frontline states" that harbored enemies of the regime; and criticized the regime's draconian "emergency" measures to counteract the urban insurrection that broke out in 1984. The Thatcher and Reagan governments, however, vetoed mandatory economic sanctions, even though the European Community and the United States (Congress having overridden Reagan's veto) had adopted and begun to enforce comprehensive economic sanctions.

With the release of Nelson Mandela and other prominent political prisoners in February 1990, the rapid dismantling of the structures of apartheid in 1990-1991, and the beginning of negotiations in December 1992 for a new nonracial constitution, pressures from the Security Council ceased. The General Assembly, in turn, voted in October 1993 to lift economic sanctions. With the approval of the South African government, the UN dispatched a contingent of fifty observers to monitor preparations and then to supervise the April 1994 elections to the postapartheid constituent assembly.

The UN was the main arena in the global struggle against apartheid, but the OAU also contributed. It helped to anathematize the apartheid regime, legitimate the antiapartheid struggle, and serve as a vigorous pressure group within the UN and its specialized agencies. Although its members lacked the economic and military resources to punish South Africa, the OAU was effective in assisting political exiles and in helping frontline states, which provided sanctuary for political exiles and training facilities for antiregime fighters, exposing themselves to punitive reprisal by the South African military. Despite the uncompromising posture of the OAU, however, several members and their allies in the nonaligned movement conducted profitable covert economic relations with South Africa.

Because there were no UN forces on the ground during the long campaign against apartheid, the financial burden was not significant. The aim was to create and sustain a global moral climate that would delegitimate, isolate, and punish the apartheid regime. UN pressure was an important factor in keeping this issue at the forefront of the global agenda, sustaining morale during this lengthy and often disappointing struggle, gradually eroding the confidence of the racist government and its domestic constituents, and persuading member states, including the initially reluctant members of the European Community and the United States, to enact and enforce punitive measures.

The UN majority and eventually the Security Council were willing to override the charter provision regarding "domestic jurisdiction" in defense of human rights and the right of self-determination for an oppressed racial majority. Does this successful campaign constitute a precedent justifying or mandating UN intervention in other cases where governments are flagrantly denying basic human rights, including the right of self-determination to oppressed ethnic or racial communities (Tibetans, southern Sudanese, Bosnian Muslims, Guatemalan Indians)? Or was South Africa a unique case involving the oppression of an indigenous racial majority by a minority post-colonial European settler regime and consequently of little precedent value?

Namibia

Namibia proved to be the most successful intervention ever undertaken by the UN. Its success was due not only to competent management of a complex set of military, police, and civilian activities, but also to an agreement among all the concerned parties, the two superpowers in the Security Council, and regional forces on the ground about what needed to be done. After four decades of controversy over the status of this territory, in the late 1980s the time seemed ripe for a settlement and UN diplomacy was able to seize the moment. The costs were relatively high: 8,000 men and women from 120 countries and $383 million for an operation that lasted less than eighteen months. The UN in this case was instrumental in making peace and facilitating the smooth and rapid transition of Namibia from a conflict-ridden de facto colony of South Africa to an independent state under an African-led government chosen in a free and fair UN-supervised election.

Namibia, formerly known as Southwest Africa, lies to the west of the Republic of South Africa. It is mostly arid and sparsely populated— 7 percent European, 93 percent African of several ethnic groups, the largest being the Ovambo. A German colony until 1918, it was awarded by the League of Nations to Britain as a mandate; Britain then assigned its mandate to South Africa for administration. South Africa gradually incorporated the territory into its pattern of rule. The more valuable lands and mineral resources were monopolized by the white minority, who also controlled all the political institutions, while Africans were mostly confined to reservations and thus available as a low-cost labor force for white-owned enterprises.

After World War II, South Africa refused to place the territory under UN trusteeship, arguing that with the demise of the League of Nations its responsibilities to any external authority had lapsed. South Africa then moved to annex the territory and, after 1948, to extend the practices of apartheid, including the establishment of eleven ethnically designated "homelands," one white and ten black.

The UN never recognized South Africa's control of Namibia, but it was originally inhibited by a decision of the International Court of Justice, which held that South Africa was not required to place the territory under UN trusteeship. Soon, however, the decolonization of Africa, which began in the mid-1950s, produced a bloc of African member states that could dominate voting in the General Assembly. Beginning in 1966 the assembly enacted annual resolutions revoking the mandate and establishing a UN Council for Namibia to administer the territory and, with full participation of its inhabitants, prepare for self-determination and independence. In 1973 the General Assembly recognized SWAPO (the Southwest Africa Peoples' Organization), an Ovambo-dominated nationalist organization with a Marxist ideology, as sole representative of the Namibian people. Meanwhile, the Security Council declared South Africa to be in illegal occupation of the territory and demanded free elections under UN auspices leading to independence. A tentative agreement for eventual South African withdrawal was negotiated by the Western powers and endorsed by the Security Council; it was to be implemented by a UN Transition Assistance Group (UNTAG). (Singham and Hune 1986).

With the Soviet invasion of Afghanistan in 1979 and the elections of Margaret Thatcher in Britain and Ronald Reagan in the United States, the cold war heated up. The Soviet Union expanded its activities in Africa, including the financing of Cuban forces to protect its client regime in Angola. Thatcher and Reagan viewed South Africa, with all its shortcomings in the area of human rights, as a bastion of anticommunism and capitalism, while the UN was controlled by an anti-Western, pro-Marxist coalition that could not deal impartially with South Africa and Namibia. They regarded SWAPO as a Soviet puppet that must not be permitted to take control of Namibia. The United States and Britain vetoed several Security Council resolutions condemning South African incursions into Angola and other frontline states to punish and deter the use of these sanctuaries for African National Congress raids against South Africa and for SWAPO operations against Namibia. Encouraged by the United States and Britain, South Africa saw no reason to compromise with the UN on Namibia. It became clear that the stalemate could not be resolved outside the context of the global cold war; South Africa would not withdraw from Namibia unless Soviet-financed Cuban contingents were to leave Angola.

The emergence of *perestroika* and *glasnost* in the USSR and Mikhail Gorbachev's decision to cut back Soviet commitments in Africa, including the financing of Cuban forces in Angola, provided the basis for breaking the stalemate on Namibia. The high costs of military operations in Angola, the prospect of Cuban troop withdrawals, and pressure from the United States persuaded the South African regime that it could safely coexist with an independent and neutral Namibia. In an atmosphere of unprecedented good will, negotiations were initiated in 1988 to implement Security Council resolution 435, which had been enacted ten years earlier; arrangements were completed for the phased departure of Cubans from Angola and of South Africans from Namibia. The UNTAG was activated, charged with ensuring free and fair elections in Namibia. Its military component was to monitor the cease-fire, disarm irregular militias, maintain surveillance over the borders, and ensure the scheduled dismantling of South Africa's military presence. The police component was responsible for strengthening the capabilities of the Southwest African police establishment and ensuring that they maintained law and order efficiently and impartially. The civilian component was charged with changing the laws, establishing the apparatus for elections and ensuring that they were conducted honestly and fairly. To that end, fifty-six pieces of legislation that would have restricted democratic participation in the elections were repealed or rescinded, a vigorous voter education campaign was launched, and a corps of election officials was mobilized and trained. The civilian component also monitored an amnesty and the repatriation of forty-two thousand political exiles.

In November 1989 in a peaceful election conceded by all parties to be free and fair, SWAPO won 41 of 72 seats in the new constituent assembly, short of the two-thirds needed to write a constitution. A constitution that protected the rights both of individuals and of ethnic minorities was negotiated and duly enacted early in February 1990. On March 21, Independence Day, the UN secretary-general administered the oath of office to President Sam Njuoma, leader of SWAPO. Its mission accomplished, the UNTAG was rapidly disbanded. Though the UN's interest in Namibia extended over four decades, once a peace-making formula had been accepted, the operational phase, though costly, was completed in less than eighteen months. The UN proved itself capable of managing a difficult and complex situation efficiently, impartially, and with dispatch (Sparks and Green 1992, UN Department of Public Information 1990).

The Conference on Security and Cooperation in Europe

The CSCE is a regional international organization expressly concerned with defending and vindicating the collective human rights of ethnic minorities. It originated in 1972 in an agreement between the superpowers, the United States and the USSR, to provide an ongoing forum for ventilating and achieving cooperation on issues of common concern. The USSR was interested in gaining formal recognition by the Western powers of the post-World War II borders in Eastern Europe. The West was interested in opening the Soviet Union and Eastern

Europe to economic, intellectual, and scientific exchanges and in promoting human rights, hoping to broaden detente by involving the Soviet satellites in a network of relationships with the West. The Helsinki Final Act of 1975, enacted by the thirty-two European members of the CSCE, plus the United States and Canada, contained, among others, three important "principles."

Principle 7 proclaims the rights of individual members of national minorities to equality before the law and full opportunity to enjoy human rights and fundamental freedoms, regardless of race, sex, language, or religion—in effect, to nondiscrimination.

Principle 8 requires participating states to respect the equal rights of "peoples," including the right to self-determination in relation to their internal and external political status.

Principle 6, however, reaffirms the traditional proposition that participating states must refrain from intervention "direct or indirect, individual or collective," in matters falling within the domestic jurisdiction of another participating state.

These principles, presumably of equal validity, illustrate the classic unresolved dilemma facing IOs: internationally recognized norms asserting the human rights of individuals and the collective rights of peoples confront the sovereign immunity of states from external intervention on matters falling within their "domestic jurisdiction."

Despite severe tensions between the Soviet Union and the West, including the 1979 invasion of Afghanistan, the CSCE survived. During the next decade follow-up meetings were deadlocked by confrontations between the United States and its allies and the Soviet Union. The United States emphasized violations of the rights of dissidents, and persons desiring to emigrate. The Soviet Union countered with charges of violations of economic, social, and cultural rights by capitalist regimes. The deadlock was first broken in the late 1980s after Gorbachev had come to power. The Vienna Concluding Document in 1989 focused on human rights, freedom of information, acknowledgment of religious and political pluralism, and the legitimacy of international discussions of human rights violations. Most significant was paragraph 19, which called on participating states to "protect and create conditions for the promotion of the ethnic, cultural, linguistic, and religious identity of national minorities on their territory." (Bloed, 1990, Lehne 1991).

This breakthrough was followed by a flurry of activity, including the Copenhagen Meeting in 1990, which took place in the wake of the collapse of communist regimes in Eastern Europe; demands for independence for the Baltic states; and the onset of the Yugoslav crisis. Emphasis was on the collective rights of national minorities, including the use of "mother tongues," freedom of religion and other forms of association, and effective participation in public affairs, including local and autonomous administration. The Paris Summit later in 1990 called for the establishment of permanent administrative structures for the CSCE, including a Conflict Prevention Center in Vienna. At the Geneva Conference on National Minorities in 1991, the concluding document further committed participating states to recognize and protect the rights of national minorities and specifically asserted that "issues regarding national minorities do not constitute exclusively an internal affair of the respective state", but could legitimately be addressed by IOs (CSCE 1991a-c). Minority rights appear to encompass not only cultural pluralism—religious, language, and educational rights—but also political pluralism—regional autonomy and proportionality in representation and in government employment. Participating states were not able, however, to agree on procedures to protect minorities whose rights are endangered or violated, except by good offices and publicity, by "mobilizing shame."

At the CSCE meeting at Helsinki from March to June 1992, the number of participating states had grown from the original thirty-four to fifty-two, all the ex-Soviet states, including those in the Caucasus and Central Asia, and a number of Balkan states having joined. At this meeting the CSCE declared itself a "regional organization" under the provisions of the UN charter, so that henceforth it could relate its own efforts to those of the UN. It would not maintain or raise its own peace-keeping forces but would send good offices and reporting missions to troubled areas and provide humanitarian assistance. A high commissioner for national minorities was to work on preventing as well as moderating and terminating ethnic violence. (CSCE 1992).

CSCE doctrine has moved farther than that of any other IO on two themes: recognizing the collective rights of ethnic minorities to cultural and political expression, including self-determination, and declaring that state sovereignty must at times yield to international intervention when basic human rights are violated. Thus in its short history the CSCE has given new weight to the normative statements of IOs on the collective rights of ethnic minorities, the obligation of governments to protect them, and the duty of IOs to intervene when minority rights are abridged. The CSCE has organized and dispatched more than a dozen fact-finding, monitoring, and reportorial missions to hot spots in the Balkans and the former Soviet states.

Beyond good offices and publicity, however, the CSCE has been powerless to prevent or moderate any of the many violent ethnic conflicts that have broken out within or between its member states. Decisions to act require full consensus of all members except a state charged with gross violations of CSCE norms; thus, the Yugoslav government succeeded in vetoing a CSCE initiative to inquire into violations of the rights of the Albanian majority in the Serbian province of Kosovo. Except for good offices, the organization possesses no mechanisms for effective intervention—no authority, no funds, no forces. Its inability to contain ethnic violence in the Balkans or the former Soviet republics means that it has added no resources to those already available to the European Union or the UN. Progress in norm setting may be a useful, even necessary role for IOs, but norms do not readily displace interests. They become institutionalized only with the passage of much time, and they are seldom self-enforcing. Without the capacity to implement its stronger norms, the "mobilization of shame" has been ineffectual and the CSCE's performance has been marked by frustration.

Conflicting Norms, Limited Capabilities, Selective Interventions

An optimist might regard recent developments in the international system as favorable to an expanded and more productive role for IOs in regulating ethnic conflicts. The collapse of the bipolar confrontation between the superpowers has freed the UN from some inhibiting deadlocks and has made possible some productive interventions, for example, the Namibia settlement, which would previously have been unlikely. IOs have gained useful experience in addressing ethnic conflicts, often combining several of the methods available to them as circumstances permit. When civil war was reignited in Angola in October 1992 in defiance of the results of a UN supervised election, the secretary-general appointed a special representative to attempt to broker a cease-fire and reactivate the reconciliation process. The Security Council imposed an arms embargo and economic sanctions on the party responsible for the hostilities. A major humanitarian effort was reinstituted. A renewed verification mission and peace-keeping operation ensued resulting in the achievement of a cease-fire.

These hopeful signs must, however, be evaluated in light of continuing institutional realities in the international system. IOs remain political bodies in which member states, though influenced by international norms, pursue their own interests. These interests exclude some ethnic conflicts from the agenda of IOs—Tibet because of a Chinese veto, Corsica because of a French veto, East Timor because states friendly to Indonesia agree to turn a blind eye to its brutal treatment of an ethnic minority, Sudan for reasons already explained. The doctrine of state

sovereignty and nonintervention is still normative; the presumption
continues to run against external intervention. New norms regarding
human rights are unlikely to be institutionalized unless they can be
reconciled with the interests of member states.

Compounding the disjunction between human rights norms and
state interests are the limited capabilities of IOs. Their administrators
enjoy no autonomy, either of action or of access to resources. IOs remain membership organizations in which member states, particularly
the more influential, must specifically authorize every intervention and
must agree to provide the material, financial, and manpower resources
needed to implement them. Mandates tend to be narrowly defined,
usually authorizing peace-keepers to use force only in self-defense.
The financing of interventions by the UN has proved to be a chaotic
combination of obligatory assessments, some of which remain unpaid,
voluntary contributions to peace-keeping contingents, and accumulat-
ing debts.

All these factors create a pattern of cautious reaction to crises rather
than anticipatory action, very deliberate behavior, limited expectations,
and selectiveness about when to intervene. IOs are reluctant to act
when the state on whose territory the conflict occurs is unwilling to
accept intervention or when the parties on the ground decline to
cooperate. The reasons are juridical—deference to state sovereignty;
political—disinclination to censure an established government; and
practical—the high risks to peacekeeping and peace-enforcing manpower and the heavy financial cost of operations that may be resisted
violently by one or more of the parties. IO interventions have been
most effective when the have been accepted as useful by all the concerned parties and when those parties have been able to impose compliance on their partisans. When the time has been ripe, the UN
has proved an impressive implementor—keeping the peace in Cyprus, providing humanitarian assistance for displaced Palestinians,
and making peace, including the organization and supervision of free
elections in Namibia.

The more difficult question is what IOs can and should do when
good offices fail and violent conflict persists. By what criteria can an
IO justify overriding state sovereignty or putting itself into opposition
against one or more parties to the conflict?

The most persuasive and most legitimate argument for intervention
remains the threat to international peace. This elastic concept is likely
to be invoked by partisans of any intervention. Its validity must be
judged in every instance by the members. The danger that a domestic
ethnic dispute may embroil neighboring states and escalate into a regional conflict may be compelling and call for urgent action by an IO.

Recognizing, for example, that if ethnic tensions in Macedonia should explode into violence, Bulgaria, Greece, Albania, Turkey, and Serbia might soon be drawn in, precipitating another Balkan war, the Security Council early in 1993 deployed a small observer force in Macedonia as a deterrent.

IOs may also find the large-scale suffering of innocent victims of violent conflicts persuasive. They may act when the lives of tens of thousands of refugees are threatened by displacement, starvation, disease, and exposure, though the injuries involved in their original displacement are seldom addressed by humanitarian diplomacy. IOs tend to focus only on salvaging disrupted lives and helping people to rebuild their livelihoods in new locations. Parties to disputes may, however, regard humanitarian efforts as impeding their operations or favoring their enemy. Consequently, humanitarian operations may need military muscle for extended periods of time to protect them from violent or predatory disruptions. Yet, as in Somalia, governments may withdraw their forces once they sustain casualties.

IOs may also be moved to intervene when there are flagrant violations of the human rights of ethnic communities. A current example is the UN-sponsored, United States-managed operation to protect the Kurdish minority in northern Iraq. This operation, a consequence of Iraq's defeat in the Gulf War, enforces a UN mandate in defiance of the express opposition of the state on whose territory it is operating. For this very reason, however, it barely escaped a veto in the Security Council by China, which decided only at the last moment to abstain. The human rights criterion may some day become normative, but there are so many real or alleged violations of the collective rights of ethnic minorities that IOs could not consider becoming involved in all of them. The most compelling cases would be violations that are flagrant, sustained, and highly publicized as in South Africa or that threaten genocide as in northern Iraq.

Interventions, whatever their motivations, are likely to require costly measures for long periods of time—peace-keeping forces, infrastructure for delivering humanitarian services, and military protection for humanitarian operations. "Peace enforcement," coercing factions that resist international intervention, as in Bosnia, could involve large-scale high-risk operations for years. Members of IOs are especially reluctant to take on such dangerous open-ended military commitments that might jeopardize the lives of peace enforcers unless the more powerful members are willing to take the lead. Intervening against the will of local forces, an IO could be accused of favoring one party and unwittingly become embroiled in ethnic violence. This has been the fate of the Economic Community of West African States which intervened in a failed attempt to terminate the brutal civil war in Liberia.

The sheer number of ethnic conflicts in the modern world, the passions they release, the modest conflict-management capacities of IOs, and the reluctance of their members to intervene virtually ensure that many such conflicts will follow the tragic course of violence, destruction, and human suffering. Interventions by IOs are likely to remain selective, constrained by the perceived interests of member states and by limited resources. Yet, as the number of ethnic conflicts grows and ethnic minorities demand international protection in the name of human rights, requests for help have soared. During the early 1990s, the UN has been overwhelmed by demands that it intervene to control ethnic conflicts. Its financial commitments have expanded tenfold and its manpower requirements sevenfold, even though it acted on only a fraction of the ethnic conflicts brought to its attention.

Interventions in conflict situations are inherently problematic; neither their scale nor their duration can be predicted in advance. Even when the parties agree to the terms of IO interventions, they may later change their minds or be confronted with irregular forces they cannot control. Because of limited capacity and a limited mandate, twenty-five hundred peace-keepers in Rwanda were compelled to stand aside in April 1994 while tens of thousands of civilians were slaughtered by armed ethnic mobs.

Nevertheless, some practical steps might be taken to expand the capabilities of IOs to respond to ethnic conflicts, similar to those advanced by Secretary-General Boutros Boutros-Ghali (1992). First, the burden might be shared more effectively. Regional IOs might take more initiative and equip themselves to play a more active role. Thus far, they have not possessed the authority, the political will or the resources to intervene, and they have been even more deferential than the UN to the absolute sovereignty of member states. Equipping the regionals to upgrade their performance would require major efforts in institution building.

Second, the UN could be given authority to intervene before conflicts turn violent. The secretary-general could set up early-warning systems that would enable the UN to initiate good offices and mediation procedures while there is still time to preempt the outbreak of hostilities. In the past the UN has reacted only after damage was done. The Security Council has been reluctant to endow the secretary-general with the initiatives that a preventive posture would require, such as the authority to send small observer units to potential trouble spots to attempt timely mediation. Some governments would reject such overtures as encroachments on their sovereignty; others, as in the recent Macedonian deployment, would welcome them.

Third, the UN might be endowed with more adequate and more reliable resources for effective intervention. Observer and mediation missions consume modest resources that are already affordable. When other operations are required, the UN must use ad hoc methods to mobilize manpower and money. Effective humanitarian assistance and peace keeping in major conflicts such as Rwanda, Bosnia, Angola, and Nagorno-Karabakh would require substantial forces for extended periods. When military units are needed, the secretary-general and the Security Council should be able to draw on standby national contingents earmarked and committed by member states for this purpose and whose members have volunteered for such service.

Nor should the UN be forced to beg, borrow, and steal to finance such operations. In addition to such assessments as member states will tolerate and to voluntary contributions, the time has come to endow the UN with autonomous sources of funds earmarked for humanitarian and peace-keeping purposes. Royalties on minerals extracted from the deep seabeds, small surcharges on international telephone messages or on petroleum moving in international commerce, for example, could help to finance the unavoidable costs of the expanded UN role. Without a more stable financial base, the UN will be compelled to limit its operations even when the members agree that intervention is indicated. (To keep the financial dimension in perspective, costs of UN peace-keeping operations in 1993 totaled about $3.5 billion, less than 2 percent of the U.S. military budget for that year. Cumulative unpaid assessments for such operations amounted to $1.4 billion. Annual sales of the Coca Cola Corporation exceeded $9 billion.)

The failure of the UN and the EC in Bosnia—elaborated in Chapters 7, 8, and 9—has impaired their moral authority and undermined respect for IOs. Yet, as the survey in this chapter demonstrates, the historical record includes several successes, none of which was assured when operations were initiated. Normative expectations seem to be shifting in favor of limiting absolute state sovereignty when international peace and stability are threatened, human rights are flagrantly abused, and humanitarian disasters are created by ethnic conflict. Ethnic conflicts continue to impose imperative demands on the conflict management function of IOs. The international community and its leading member states will be pressed to conform to these emergent norms by increasing the capabilities of IOs to respond to these growing demands.

2

The Past, the Present, and the Future Prospects

Jack Donnelly

The disintegration of Yugoslavia has given ethnic conflict greater prominence on international agendas than at any time since the creation of Bangladesh. Furthermore, the problems of the former Yugoslavia often seem part of a broader pattern of resurgent ethnic conflict which includes Kurds in Iraq, any number of minorities in the states of the former Soviet Union, Karen in Burma, the partition of Czechoslovakia, genocidal violence in Rwanda, and a general resurgence of ethnic political activity in Africa as one-party states are forced to liberalize.

The so-called new world order, whatever its attractions, is marked by a very unattractive streak of often virulent ethnic conflict. But it is also marked by an unusual degree of activity by international organizations. This chapter attempts to survey and assess past and present efforts by international organizations, particularly the United Nations, to resolve or ameliorate ethnic conflict.

At the outset, however, it must be noted that ethnic conflict is inherently resistant to multilateral resolution in a world of sovereign states. Ethnic groups have no special status or standing in international law or politics. Decolonization, collective security and peace keeping, refugee and humanitarian assistance, and human rights activities have all led to multilateral involvement in ethnic conflicts, but international organizations have no clear mandate to deal with ethnic conflict per se. It is not even clear that they have any special substantive skills or competence. And I maintain that this state of affairs is not likely to change soon.

A Typology of IO Involvement

Contemporary international politics, for all the talk of the decline of the nation-state, remains structured around sovereignty. International (intergovernmental) organizations in particular, being creations of states, tend to be solicitous of the sovereign rights of their creators. If an ethnic (or other) conflict crosses state boundaries, sovereignty may not pose a serious impediment to IO involvement, but if the conflict remains within state boundaries, international organizations must contend with the powerful principle of nonintervention.

"Intervention," however, can be a slippery term. Unauthorized coercive interference in the internal affairs of another state —the threat or use of force, short of aggression or war, in ways that infringe state sovereignty —clearly is intervention. Definitional controversies arise, however, if the interference is authorized or does not involve force (cf. Haas 1993, 65-68). For example, were the security zones and the restrictions on Iraqi armaments following the Gulf War "intervention"? Although they involved coercive interference in matters that ordinarily would be considered internal affairs of Iraq, they were authorized by the United Nations, and the Security Council (e.g., resolution 687, paragraphs c and f, and resolution 688, 7th preambulatory paragraph) went out of its way to emphasize that its actions respected the sovereignty, territorial integrity, and political independence of all states, including Iraq, and thus did not involve intervention (cf. Malanczuk 1993, n. 35).

So long as we somehow distinguish between authorized and unauthorized coercive interference, whether we do so in the definition of intervention is largely a matter of stipulation. Here, I use "intervention" to mean any coercive interference in the internal affairs of a state. As I use the term, intervention involves an infringement of or restriction on the liberty of a state, but only a *prima facie* violation of sovereignty.

A more substantial definitional controversy concerns noncoercive interference. Some commentators define intervention as any interference in the internal affairs of another state (Beyerlin 1981, 211-12; cf. Damrosch 1989). Most of international relations, however, involves attempts to influence the behavior of states (and other relevant actors), often by "interfering" in domestic political processes. But the concept is of little interest if we consider even diplomatic expressions of concern as "intervention," as, for example, many governments have alleged in response to international human rights criticisms. Only when the interference is coercive but still short of aggression or war do we have a type of activity (intervention) that can be usefully distinguished from the rest of international relations.

"Coercion," in its core sense, involves force. The principal definition of *coerce* in the *Oxford English Dictionary* is "to constrain or restrain by force, or by authority resting on force." But "coercion," in an extended sense of the term, may exist even in the absence of the threat or use of force. For example, an economic boycott may be as "coercive" as a naval demonstration or even a limited reprisal bombing.

A considerable range of activities short of the threat or use of force seek to exercise influence not by rewarding cooperation but by sanctioning uncooperative behavior. Rather than attempt to find or create common interests, one party seeks to subordinate the other to its will through injury or punishment. For lack of a better term, I call such activities, which fall between intervention and clearly noncoercive forms of diplomatic influence, quasi intervention.

Below the level of quasi intervention we can further distinguish policies that actively support, oppose, or seek to change the internal behavior of another state from those that ignore or are indifferent to its internal politics. I call such activities positive nonintervention. Foreign aid and diplomatic protests are common examples.

One final distinction needs to be drawn. Intervention is an unusual or irregular event, external interference in a realm of activity ordinarily governed by the rules of sovereignty. Even authorized intervention, such as the security zones in northern Iraq, occurs with respect to behavior that would ordinarily be a matter of sovereign prerogative. Such actions differ fundamentally from those that rest on a permanent transfer of authority to an international organization.

If a state no longer possesses sovereign authority —most notably, where a strong international enforcement regime has been established —there can be no intervention, because the matter is no longer essentially one of domestic jurisdiction. The state, although still sovereign, is no longer protected from (at least certain forms of) external interference in this domain of multilateral authority. Such transfers of authority, although of great importance, differ both conceptually and in practical political ways from intervention.

This continuum of means gives us one half of a typology. The other half is provided by the kinds of situations that have typically led to IO involvement in ethnic conflict.

Aggression and war provide a clear mandate for UN involvement. Collective security and peace-keeping operations are thus one important motivation for involvement in violent interstate ethnic conflicts. Collective security (although not peace keeping) is also conceptually important because it is the one domain that can plausibly be said to involve multilateral enforcement based on a transfer of authority to the United Nations.

Decolonization has been a more common cause of UN involvement in ethnic conflicts, in cases including India, Palestine, Congo, Cyprus, and Namibia. Involving the creation of a new sovereign state, decolonization provides a particularly appropriate occasion for multilateral management of structural change. It also allows the UN to respect the principle of sovereignty and yet act relatively unconstrained by any state's sovereignty.

Because ethnic conflict often involves or arises out of discrimination and other human rights violations, human rights would seem to be another important cause for IO involvement. For our purposes here we can divide such violations into those that involve large-scale killings of a significant proportion of a target population (genocide or politicide) and those that do not. Such a distinction should not be taken to suggest any moral priority for the right to life. Nonetheless, beyond the obvious finality of death, genocide and politicide do often evoke a qualitatively different emotional response.

It is also important to emphasize that human rights violations, as they are understood in contemporary international law and politics, ordinarily involve actions of a state against its own nationals. Although a wide range of individuals and organizations may prevent people from enjoying life, liberty, equality, and other goods, services, and opportunities, "human rights" are usually taken to have a special reference to the ways in which states treat their own citizens in their own territory. For example, domestically we distinguish muggings, private assaults, and ransom kidnappings, which typically are not considered to involve human rights violations, from police brutality, torture, and arbitrary arrest and detention, which are. Internationally, we distinguish terrorism, war, and war crimes from "human rights" issues, even though they also lead to denials of life and security.

Human rights violations, in this strict sense of the term, can be distinguished from what I call humanitarian crises, in which great numbers of people suffer as a result of extraordinary circumstances that are *not* the result of direct actions of the government. Consider, for example, the difference between the human rights violations in Somalia under the regime of Siad Barre, when the problem was the actions of the government, and the humanitarian crisis into which factional warfare had plunged Somalia by 1992, when the problem was the absence of government. Massive breakdowns of authority, however,

	Transfer of Authority	(Military) Intervention	Quasi Intervention	Positive Non-intervention
Collective Security				
Decolonization				
Genocide/ Politicide				
Human Rights				
Humanitarian Crisis				

Figure 1. International Organization Involvement in Ethnic Conflict

are rare. Civil wars, in which much (although not necessarily all) of the suffering comes as an indirect and largely unplanned consequence of fighting, are a more common cause of humanitarian crisis.

External involvement in humanitarian crises often will be less coercive. Furthermore, the targets of coercion are more likely to be private individuals and groups rather than the government itself. Therefore, the infringements on sovereignty caused even by interventions involving the use of military force are likely to be substantially reduced.

Combining these sets of means and issue areas yields the typology of international organization involvement in ethnic conflicts summarized in Figure 1.

The United Nations and Human Rights during the Cold War

The League of Nations, as noted in Chapter 1, dealt in a limited way with minority rights, but not with human rights issues more broadly. Human rights are not even mentioned in the Covenant of the League of Nations. They are, however, among the principal concerns of the United Nations, as specified in the preamble and article 1 of the charter.

Ethnic conflict often involves or arises out of discrimination and other human rights violations. Thus, it would seem to be a natural part of the human rights work of the United Nations. Such an expectation seems to have been shared by those involved in the early work of the Commission on Human Rights, as reflected in the creation of the Subcommission on Prevention of Discrimination and Protection of Minorities, as the successor to the League's Minorities System. In fact, however, ethnic conflict has been a minor concern in the UN's human rights work. Perhaps, the most vivid illustration has been the rapid transformation of the subcommission, despite its name, into a general purpose body that has devoted only slightly more attention to the treatment of (nonracial) minorities than its parent commission.

In the Commission on Human Rights, as elsewhere in the United Nations system, racial discrimination has been a major concern. Nonracial ethnic discrimination, however, has been largely ignored, as is evident in the use of meeting time in both the Commission on Human Rights and the Third Committee of the General Assembly (Donnelly 1988b, tables 2, 5). It is apparent as well in work on international human rights instruments. The first single-issue human rights treaty of any sort was the 1964 Convention on the Elimination of All Forms of Racial Discrimination. In 1979 the Convention on the Elimination of Discrimination against Women was opened for signature and ratification. Work on a declaration of freedom of religion began in 1962 and was completed 1981. But even today, there has not been serious discussion of a declaration (let alone a treaty) on ethnic discrimination. Scarcely greater attention to ethnic discrimination is evident in the list of particular countries that received special UN human rights scrutiny during the 1970s and 1980s, most notably South Africa, Israel, and Chile. Although Israeli practices in the Occupied Territories do involve serious issues of ethnic discrimination, the ethnic dimensions of the conflict have received surprisingly little emphasis in the United Nations.

This neglect of discrimination not based on race or gender (or religion) reflects political considerations rather than the frequency or severity of violations. This pattern is clear even in the relative balance between racial and gender discrimination in the United Nations' human rights work.

Racial discrimination undoubtedly merits extensive international concern and action. Discrimination against women, however, is a much more pervasive problem. The UN's rapid and relatively aggressive response to racial discrimination largely reflects the political interests of Third World states, as does the tardy and still not entirely enthusiastic response to discrimination against women. Almost all the states of Asia and Africa suffered under white colonial domination and thus have been particularly sensitive to issues of racial discrimination. It was also an issue with which they could embarrass their former colonial masters and their allies. Furthermore, few of these states had sizable racial minorities. By contrast, most had (and still have) serious problems of discrimination against women.

Similar political logic helps to explain the disregard for issues of ethnic discrimination. Although not as pervasive as gender discrimination, nonracial ethnic discrimination is much more common than racial discrimination. It is therefore potentially embarrassing to more states, and thus less likely to be a high priority at the UN. In addition, ethnic discrimination is a serious problem in much of the Third World, whereas the most prominent cases of racial discrimination have been in the West. Racial discrimination thus helped to cement Third World solidarity, which would have been undercut by a focus on ethnic discrimination.

There is also a more subtle basis for slighting issues of ethnic discrimination. Ethnicity is a less powerful source of transnational political identification and mobilization than either race or gender, which by their very nature transcend national boundaries. Blacks or Asians can relatively easily identify with discrimination anywhere based on color. Much the same is true of women. Ethnicity, by contrast, is much more particularistic and inward looking.

Members of ethnic minorities usually must make a more active effort to identify with distant victims of ethnic discrimination. They must abstract from the particularities of discrimination against, say, Kurds, Tamils, Quiche, Tuaregs, Croats, or Bengalis. These particularities and cultural differences, however, often not only shape the forms that discrimination takes but also separate different ethnic minorities.

Ethnicity distinguishes, and thus separates, at times even estranges, different victims of ethnic discrimination. Race and gender, by contrast, tend to unite victims of discrimination across national boundaries. Racial minorities and women who are victims of discrimination typically have "natural" allies in other states who often will press the issue of their suffering. Ethnic solidarity, by contrast, tends to be subnational. And when it does acquire a transnational political character, it tends to be restricted to a relatively small group of foreign co-nationals. For example, in the United States, Irish, Italian, Greek, Polish, and other (white) ethnic organizations, usually have been actively concerned with issues of discrimination only in the case of co-nationals, the American Jewish community being the principal exception that proves the rule.

Finally, we need to note that even should ethnic discrimination become more prominent on international agendas, the powers of international human rights regimes remain extremely circumscribed. The mere existence of international norms and obligations does not imply that any international actor is authorized to implement or enforce those obligations. Much as national legislatures are free to adopt legislation with extremely weak implementation measures, or with none at all, states are free to create and accept international legal obligations that are to be implemented entirely through national action. And this is close to what states have in fact done in the field of international human rights.

The 1948 Universal Declaration of Human Rights and the 1966 International Human Rights Covenants today are generally accepted as authoritative international human rights norms. But no multilateral human rights treaty obligations may be coercively enforced by any external actor. The task of implementing, let alone enforcing, international human rights norms is largely left to sovereign states.

International human rights treaties typically require state parties to submit periodic reports on their practices with respect to the rights recognized in the treaty. The typical supervisory committee is authorized to study these reports, question state representatives about their contents (including omissions) in public, and make comments. But once the review of a report has been concluded, the state in question remains free to do as it sees fit. The obligation to submit a report is the *only* international implementation obligation a state accepts by becoming a party to most international human rights treaties (see Hannum 1992, chap. 3, 10; Donnelly 1993, chap. 4).

Many treaties do include optional provisions that allow supervisory committees to receive complaints from individuals. These procedures, however, typically apply to only about half the parties to the treaty and in any case are rarely used. For example, the most active supervisory committee, the Human Rights Committee (established under the International Covenant on Civil and Political Rights), has registered fewer than 600 communications in more than fifteen years of work. Furthermore, even if a supervisory committee determines that the treaty has been violated, it has no legal authority to implement or enforce its findings.

Elsewhere as well, we see a similar pattern of largely hortatory international implementation of human rights norms. The UN Commission on Human Rights, which has been the principal forum for the development of international human rights norms, has no coercive enforcement powers. It relies almost exclusively on the power of persuasion, backed principally by the force of international publicity. The UN Security Council may take binding enforcement action. In practice, however, it has done so on human rights grounds only in southern Africa.

Regional human rights regimes are both substantially stronger and weaker (cf. Hannum 1992, chap. 7-9). The Council of Europe has established an effective system of regional human rights enforcement, which includes binding judicial decisions by the European Court of Human Rights. Furthermore, Greece and Turkey have been suspended from membership in the Council of Europe for systematic human rights violations. But no other regional system even approximates this European transfer of authority to regional institutions. The Inter-American Court of Human Rights has decided only three contentious cases and issued a handful of advisory opinions, and the Inter-American Commission of Human Rights has been far less effective than its European counterpart. The African Commission on Human and Peoples' Rights has had no discernible effect on state practice, and there is no regional human rights court. And in Asia and the Middle East, not even weak regional regimes have been established.

International human rights supervisory bodies (except the European regional regime) are essentially restricted to using the powers of persuasion; in other words, to positive nonintervention. Viewed historically, even this modest ability represents real progress: before World War II even noncoercive involvement was, with a few very limited exceptions, precluded. In addition, although the means available to most international human rights bodies are unlikely to be of much value in cases where ethnic discrimination is severe enough to merit the label ethnic conflict, they may have some influence where violations are less gross, persistent, or systematic. Nonetheless, the fact remains that international organizations have played an extremely limited role in dealing with the human rights dimensions of ethnic conflict. And in the most severe cases of genocide/politicide the UN, at least during the cold-war era, was particularly noteworthy for its failure to attempt to exercise even its limited powers and authority. No case of genocide—not Bangladesh, Uganda, Cambodia, Burundi, or East Timor—was even the subject of a public human rights resolution by either the UN Commission on Human Rights or the General Assembly.

Decolonization, Peace-Keeping, and Humanitarian Assistance

The United Nations has become involved in ethnic conflicts in the pursuit of decolonization, collective security, and humanitarian objectives. Here too, however, involvement has come irrespective, rather than because, of the ethnic dimension of the conflict.

One might argue that my account of the human rights activity of the United Nations ignores one of the most important and most successful areas of activity, namely, decolonization, which implements the right of peoples to self-determination (recognized in article 1 of both International Human Rights Covenants). The right to self-determination, however, is not included in the 1948 Universal Declaration of Human Rights. And self-determination became a major item of concern in UN human rights bodies only after 1965—that is, well after the process of decolonization had achieved a full head of steam. In fact, authoritative international recognition of a right to self-determination was more a result than a cause of decolonization. Furthermore, within the UN (and other international organizations) self-determination has been interpreted largely as a right of (Western-held) colonial territories to become states. Although eminently defensible from a practical political point of view, such an interpretation, from a human rights perspective, amounts to a perverse confusion of the rights of peoples with the rights of states. For such reasons, I view decolonization, as it has been treated in multilateral diplomacy, as a separate issue area, rather than a part of the broader issue of human rights.

Decolonization, however, has brought the United Nations into recurrent involvement with ethnic conflicts. In the late 1940s the decolonization of Palestine and India brought about UN involvement that continues today in both the Middle East and Kashmir. Ethnic conflict was at the heart of long-running UN decolonization efforts in Cyprus and Southern Rhodesia (Zimbabwe) which began in the 1960s. The UN was also at least partly involved in decolonization operations in the Belgian Congo (Zaire), Dutch New Guinea (Irian Jaya), Ruanda-Urundi (Rwanda and Burundi), the Cameroons, and Togoland in the late 1950s and early 1960s.

In none of these cases, however, did the UN act *because* the conflict was ethnic. UN involvement rested on either an explicit decolonization mandate as in Palestine, Cyprus, or the trust territories, or a more general mandate to protect international peace and security. The ethnic nature of the conflict may have helped to create the internal political conditions that led to international involvement. It was, however, neither an explicit nor even an implicit basis for that involvement. Such extensive UN activity instead reflected the political interests of parties with otherwise often very different views.

The interests of the emerging Afro-Asian bloc were obvious. The Western powers as well, especially the US and Britain, found the United Nations a convenient mechanism to help to manage a process of decolonization that they were coming to view as inevitable, and perhaps even desirable. There was something approaching cross-bloc consensus on the utility of a formally neutral third party to help to manage some of these difficult transitions. Decolonization was one of those rare issues in which both the structure of the international system and the typical interests of the parties involved often combined to facilitate UN involvement.

UN involvement included not merely the development of very strong norms, codified in General Assembly resolution 1514 (the 1960 Declaration on the Granting of Independence to Colonial Countries and Peoples) but also the use of relatively strong implementation procedures. The Special Committee on Decolonization (the Committee of Twenty-four) became the focal point for an aggressive program of mobilizing international public opinion against the maintenance of colonial rule anywhere in the world. And in southern Africa in particular, the UN was even willing to resort to very strong measures, including a mandatory economic embargo on minority-ruled Southern Rhodesia, and numerous forms of legal and political pressure on South Africa to relinquish control over Namibia (Southwest Africa).

The temporary ambiguity in authority during the period of devolution, especially when the transition was troubled, raises the specter of a vacuum of power and authority, a moment of potential disorder in an international political system structured around sovereign states. Where powerful external actors do not wish to take advantage of such opportunities to intervene, or where they have strong incentives to seek to forestall intervention by others, UN involvement may be actively sought. In addition, the ambiguous status of the governing power largely removes arguments of sovereignty and nonintervention as impediments to UN involvement.

Such political conditions simply were not replicated even in other issue areas that were substantively closely related, especially human rights. As we saw, human rights activities did not extend to the most modest monitoring. And UN involvement in cases of ethnic conflict under a decolonization mandate did little or nothing to spur direct efforts to deal with the issue of ethnic conflict. When the wave of decolonization ran its course, so did the IO activity it provoked. Instead of spilling over into other issue areas, decolonization became a largely encapsulated issue area.

Although analytically distinct, there was a substantial overlap between UN peace-keeping and decolonization activities during the cold war. The decolonization of Palestine and India led to the first two major peace-keeping operations, the UN Truce Supervision Organization (UNTSO) and the UN Military Observer Group in India and Pakistan (UNMOGIP). In the 1960s, peace-keeping operations in the Congo (UN Congo Operation), West Irian (UN Security Force), and Cyprus

(UN Force in Cyprus-UNFICYP) were largely decolonization missions. The UN Emergency Forces, the UN Disengagement Observer Force (UNDOF), and the UN Interim Force in Lebanon (UNIFIL) were outgrowths of the still-unsettled decolonization of Palestine. In the late 1980s, the UN Transition Assistance Group in Namibia was engaged in a fairly conventional decolonization mission. Even the collective security operation in Korea arose out of a contested decolonization. The only peace-keeping missions of the cold-war era that were not also decolonization operations were the UN Observer Group in Lebanon (UNOGIL), the UN Yemen Observer Mission, and the UN Good Offices Mission in Afghanistan and Pakistan, which arose out of more conventional civil wars, and the tiny UN Mission to the Dominican Republic in the aftermath of the U.S. invasion in 1964.

Ernest Haas's set on collective security and peace keeping by international and regional organizations reveals a record of considerable success in situations involving decolonization and in conflicts without a strong cold war dimension (Haas 1983, 1986). I have already discussed the political logic of UN involvement in decolonization. The importance of insulation from cold-war conflict is obvious. Here, I simply want to note that in the case of peace keeping, as with decolonization, the UN has never become involved in an ethnic conflict because of its ethnic dimension. Its mandate has instead rested on a threat to international peace and security. The same is true of broader "peacemaking" efforts to mediate conflicts in locales including the Middle East, Kampuchea (Cambodia), Central America, Afghanistan, and the Persian Gulf.

Even if the mandate should change, the inherent limits of peace keeping must be noted. Peace keepers are neutral intermediaries operating with the consent of the parties to a violent conflict. Although they have occasionally been drawn into active involvement in violent conflicts, most notably in the Congo, typically their role is to monitor compliance with truce agreements or at most to serve as a buffer to dissuade the parties from resuming active hostilities. Peace keeping is a multilateral supplement to, not as a substitute for, the efforts of the parties. When the parties no longer desire a state of active war but lack the ability, resolve, or trust to end the conflict, peace keeping becomes a plausible option. Until that stage has been reached, peace keeping is an inappropriate instrument.

Collective security enforcement largely escapes such strictures. During the cold war era, however, coercive UN involvement in a conflict was the rare exception rather than the rule, and I can point to not one case of coercive involvement in an ethnic conflict.

I have distinguished human rights violations, in the strict sense of infringements of internationally recognized human rights by one's own government, from humanitarian crises, understood as systematic but extraordinary threats to subsistence, security, or liberty arising from sources other than one's own government. Natural disasters present perhaps the clearest examples of humanitarian crisis (although they typically have little relevance to ethnic conflict). Humanitarian crises are also often caused by war, either international or civil. As I use the term, however, although famines typically are humanitarian crises, the sort of ordinary malnutrition that is the lot of hundreds of millions of people is not. This distinction is not intended to suggest any moral or even political priority for situations of humanitarian crisis. My point is simply that when such suffering is extraordinary and systematic, it often receives different treatment in both bilateral and multilateral international politics.

Natural disaster, violent conflict, or massive human rights violations in one country may lead to refugee flows that create a humanitarian crisis in another country. In a world of sovereign states, refugees present an inherently international issue. Furthermore, host governments often have special incentives, including financial ones, for seeking external multilateral assistance. The United Nations has thus been especially active in attempting to meet the humanitarian needs of refugees.

In 1946 the first General Assembly established the International Refugee Organization, a successor to the wartime UN Relief and Rehabilitation Administration. The General Assembly also established the UN International Children's Emergency Fund to provide emergency aid to European children suffering because of the devastation of World War II. In 1949 the UN Relief and Works Agency for Palestine Refugees in the Near East was established to deal with the humanitarian crisis of Arab refugees following the violent decolonization of Palestine. And in 1951 the United Nations created the Office of High Commissioner for Refugees, which has become the focal point for dealing with humanitarian needs of refugees and even some internally displaced persons.

Again, though, even where such efforts involved the organization in ethnic conflicts, the justification for and direct aim of the enterprise was something else—in this case, humanitarian. Furthermore, humanitarian assistance typically deals only with the symptoms of the conflict. Where the causes of suffering are transitory (after natural disaster for instance) or have for some other reason disappeared, nothing more is required. But where the source of the suffering is ethnic conflict, humanitarian assistance is unlikely to have any significant influence on the long-run prospects for conflict resolution. Relieving suffering is an important and valuable achievement. Its limits, however, must also be recognized.

We should also note that the multilateral delivery of humanitarian assistance, at least during the cold war era, depended almost entirely on the voluntary consent of the governments in question. If a government was unwilling to acknowledge the crisis, as in the early stages of the Ethiopian famine, the UN, in deference to sovereignty, was unwilling to attempt to deliver aid. A government's failure to accept aid for starving people might transform a humanitarian crisis into a case of direct human rights violations as well. As we have already seen, however, such violations provides no additional authority for even quasi intervention on behalf of the victims.

IOs and Ethnic Conflict after the Cold War

Our brief post-cold-war experience contains nothing that indicates the development of a direct UN mandate to deal with ethnic conflict. Nonetheless, activity continues, and in many cases seems to be intensifying in the areas relevant to ethnic conflict. The question I want to address is the extent to which the so-called new world order—characterized by a largely tripolar military world, an increasingly multipolar (or at least tripolar) economic balance, and an ideology of political democratization and financial liberalization—implies a fundamentally enhanced role for international organizations in these issue areas.

I am particularly interested in what I will call strong (or structural) and weak (or incremental) arguments for an enhanced UN role in international relations. The strong (structural) argument (e.g., Chopra and Weiss 1992) holds that sovereignty is undergoing a fundamental erosion; authority is being transferred from states to the international community as represented by the United Nations and other multilateral organizations. We would expect to find an increase both in the frequency of UN involvement and in the strength of the means used. The weak (incremental) argument (e.g., Gordenker 1991) holds that there is no systematic or structural alteration in the place of international organizations in world politics, but that recent political changes have increased the opportunities for significant UN initiatives. We would expect some increase in frequency but no clear pattern of change in the means used and certainly no discernible trend toward a transfer of authority to the United Nations.

There are many reasons why a militarily dominant but economically ailing United States would prefer to act through multilateral channels. More generally, a trend toward multipolarity suggests increasing multilateralism, at least while the multipolar powers remain political allies. But nothing in the post-cold-war environment suggests a serious challenge to the continuing primacy of states in international relations, and the resulting secondary role for international organizations. International organizations will have increased opportunities for greater and more effective involvement in a wide range of international issues, including issues intimately connected with ethnic conflict. But these undeniably important changes, I maintain, are not harbingers of a qualitatively different era.

In assessing such changes it is essential to distinguish between norms and implementation. As we have seen in the case of human rights, it is entirely possible to develop strong, fully internationalized norms that are widely accepted by states but are not supported by strong implementation procedures. Although normative changes may be harbingers of increased powers for supervisory institutions, I believe that they are leading only to incremental strengthening of multilateral implementation procedures.

Past experience suggests that the end of the cold war should permit a significantly enhanced role for the UN in issues of international peace and security. During the cold war, superpower involvement usually prevented multilateral action. This situation began to change in the late 1980s, with UN involvement in Afghanistan, Cambodia, and Central America. Today, not only is the UN no longer precluded from acting by superpower rivalry, but the United States and Russia have become major supporters of multilateral action. There has thus been a renaissance in peace keeping.

In 1992 there were twelve active peace-keeping operations. Five of these were begun before the end of the cold war: UNTAC and UN-MOGIP from the 1940s, UNFICYP from the 1960s, and UNDOF in the Golan Heights and UNIFIL from the 1970s. Seven, however, were established in 1991 and 1992: the UN Iraq-Kuwait Observation Mission, the UN Angola Verification Mission, the UN Observer Mission in El Salvador (ONUSAL), the UN Mission for the Referendum in Western Sahara, the UN Transitional Authority in Cambodia (UNTAC), the UN Protection Force in the former Yugoslavia, and the UN Operation in Somalia. These operations represented an annual expenditure of about $3 billion. Furthermore, UNTAC was the largest and in some ways the most ambitious peace-keeping operation ever undertaken.

Does this dramatic increase in the level and intensity of peace-keeping activity reflect a fundamental transfer of authority from states to the international community or a more incremental response to new political opportunities? A brief examination of UN operations in Iraq, perhaps the paradigmatic case of post-cold-war multilaterialism, suggests a weak (incremental) interpretation of these changes.

Although hardly collective security in a strong sense of the term, the international response to the invasion of Kuwait was in sharp contrast to the cold-war pattern of superpower unilateralism. The international response was genuinely multilateral, in recognition of the decreased international political freedom of action of the United States. Although the Gulf coalition was dominated by the United States, the Bush Administration exerted intense diplomatic pressure to involve Russia, Europe, and Japan, and to neutralize China, Israel, and Syria. Policy was coordinated through the United Nations. And other countries covered much of the bill, reflecting declining U.S. economic power.

The end of the cold war undoubtedly facilitated a massive, multilateral response. The war against Iraq is thus a fine example of the new opportunities for strong multilateral action. But at stake was the very old principle of territorial integrity. Questions can be raised about the connection between many targets of U.S. bombing and the expulsion of Iraq from Kuwait. Nonetheless, soon after the Iraqis were expelled, the fighting did halt. The Gulf War was principally about restoring the territorial status quo ante. In addition, the war was fought principally by the world's dominant military power. It also served the economic and geopolitical interests of the United States, Europe, and Japan.

Iraq, by violating the fundamental legal norm of territorial integrity, subjected itself to multilateral enforcement action. In the aftermath, during an extremely unusual period of punitively restricted sovereignty, Iraq was forced to accept certain multilateral humanitarian guarantees. (The situation is analogous to the League of Nations Minorities System, which imposed limited supervision of minority rights in countries defeated during or created in the aftermath of World War I, but left other countries untouched.) No general conclusions or broader precedents can be drawn from this very exceptional case. There is no evidence of willingness even to give serious consideration to the use of multilateral force to protect other ethnic groups facing comparable or even worse attacks at the hands of their governments. Consider, for example, the persistent refusal of the international community to intervene in the civil war in Sudan, which since 1988 has killed over half a million people and has taken on near genocidal proportions, and the capitulation to ethnic violence represented by the internationally sanctioned partition of Bosnia. The tepid international response to genocide in Rwanda in 1994 further underscores the exceptional nature of the Iraq operation.

Although perhaps not, strictly speaking, instances of decolonization, the dismantling of the Soviet Union and Yugoslavia, which have often involved ethnic tension or conflict, are very closely analogous situations. Multiethnic empires are being dismantled, largely (at least in the first instance) along the often arbitrary territorial lines established by the dominant central power. Other multiethnic states may disintegrate as well. After the tumult of recent years, who will confidently predict the fate of, say, Nigeria or India? But any involvement such cases may provoke, provides reason to expect spillover into other issue areas.

As in the past, decolonization is a special case with few, if any, broader structural implications. Decolonization does not challenge a state-centric order; it reinforces and reaffirms it. Decolonization is about creating new states, not alternatives to states. And new states tend to be particularly deeply committed to the principle of sovereignty, precisely because of their relatively fragile hold on it. Consider, for example, Croatia's reluctance to accept international monitoring of its own human rights practices, which in areas such as freedom of the press are among the worst in Central and Eastern Europe. Groups seeking to acquire or defend a state of their own are often very willing to ask for multilateral assistance. Once their power is secure, though, their emphasis tends to shift quickly to (their own) sovereignty.

More interesting possibilities are suggested by the recent UN involvement in political transitions following internationalized civil wars in Afghanistan, Angola, Cambodia, and El Salvador. The transformation of the UN operation in Somalia from an exercise in humanitarian assistance to one of assistance in state and nation building is also in many ways very similar. Although not really decolonization operations, they are sufficiently analogous to merit the label "quasi decolonization."

Quasi decolonizations involve troubled political transitions in which both the deeply involved external power and the principal indigenous political forces have accepted the value of a neutral third party in achieving a relatively smooth and rapid devolution of power. Multilateral action is further facilitated by the ambiguous political, legal, or moral status of the government in power and by a perceived need for international recognition of the legitimacy of the existing or soon-to-be-created government. For our purposes it is also interesting to note that the conflicts in Angola and Somalia have a significant ethnic dimension, and even in Afghanistan there was a dimension of regional/ethnic conflict.

The operations in El Salvador and Cambodia are especially interesting. Although there was little ethnic dimension to the civil war in El Salvador, ONUSAL operated with an unusually broad mandate, including the authority for extensive-on-site human rights monitoring.

UN mediation and transitional assistance may even have helped to create a new political order in which the prospects for systematic human rights violations in El Salvador are at an all-time low. The Cambodia initiative was even more ambitious. The UN effectively took over the civilian administration of the country, engaged in a partially successful effort to disarm the various factions, and organized new elections. When the UNTAC forces finally withdrew in the fall of 1993, then left in power a freely elected civilian government. Again, there was no significant ethnic dimension to the conflict, but the authority and impact of UN forces were notable.

ONUSAL and UNTAC were authorized interventions involving a temporary, yet significant transfer of authority to the international community. We should be careful, however, about overgeneralizing or treating these operations as signs of a broader trend. In each case, UN involvement was voluntarily accepted. Acceptance did not make the authority of the forces on the ground any less real. It was, however, contingent on an unusual configuration of national and international political forces. There is no indication that other states will choose to allow similar interventions.

In addition, these operations were only temporary measures, agreed to as part of a broader political settlement, intended to help smooth the transition to a new government. The political dynamics that facilitated UN involvement in such transitional situations are almost certain not to be replicated after an internationally supervised devolution of power has been achieved. Just as the UN acquired no special authority in recently decolonized states in the 1960s and 1970s, an active transitional role implies no augmentation of UN powers over even newly established governments that owe their position to UN operations. For example, it is highly unlikely that comparable interventions could be mounted today in post-election El Salvador or Cambodia.

A similar distinction between "normal" and transitional or other extraordinary situations helps to explain the interventions of the UN and the United States in Somalia. These efforts came in a situation in which the Somali state had largely disintegrated into warring clans and factions. Rather than a transfer of authority to the international community, or even multilateral intervention, they represented an international response to a breakdown of national political authority. Although the result is the same—the UN achieved extraordinary authority in Somalia—the political processes by which this authority was obtained are unlikely to be replicated in more settled situations.

Where sovereignty or international legitimacy has become problematic, the UN may even have an opportunity to intervene coercively. We should not belittle the importance or local impact of such interventions. But what has changed is not so much the balance of power between states and the international community as the opportunities for action.

The end of the cold war has made it possible for (states to allow) the UN to act in such former areas of superpower rivalry. These cases, however, do not provide significant precedents for action in more settled cases. It is not even clear how much of a precedent they provide for action in other troubled transfers of power. Is it a coincidence that Afghanistan, Angola, Cambodia, El Salvador, and even Somalia were all conflicts with a substantial cold-war component? In each case, a substantial part of the reason local factions were willing to accept international intervention was the withdrawal of superpower support from one or both sides in the conflict. These withdrawals themselves reflected the desire of the superpowers to reach regional accords and, if necessary, to use the UN to extricate themselves from situations where they no longer wanted to compete.

In other words, we can conclude there has been a substantial increase in UN activity and authority in the field of "decolonization," very loosely defined to include devolutions of power following internationalized civil wars. Where comparable situations recur in the next few years, we are likely to see relatively strong multilateral responses— at least until disillusionment with the costs or outcome of such operations sets in. But like earlier decolonization efforts, such initiatives are likely to remain encapsulated rather than to spill over into similar kinds of activities in more settled circumstances. And nothing in these cases provides evidence of a new mandate to deal with ethnic conflict.

If we look at international human rights regimes in the past five years it is hard to see even incremental change. For example, the UN Commission on Human Rights, the body with the fewest formal constraints on rapidly developing an expanded role, has not launched a single qualitatively new initiative. In fact, during the 1990 session, the first in decades in which the clear majority of delegates were from countries with more or less freely elected governments, proposals from the Third World caucus to eliminate the existing independent thematic procedures and replace them with politicized working groups of professional diplomats was narrowly defeated. The commission and the treaty-based supervisory committees, most notably the Human Rights Committee established under the International Covenant on Civil and Political Rights, do seem to be functioning more smoothly as a result of the end of the cold war. But we are seeing a bit more, and perhaps more effective, action under already well-established mandates, rather than the emergence of new mandates.

On further reflection, this is perhaps the best description of the changes in collective security, peace keeping, and quasi decolonization as well. There has been a significant increase in the frequency of use of the most forceful instruments previously available in a given issue area but no qualitative augmentation of available means. The collective security operation against Iraq was largely comparable to the Korean operation of the 1950s. The operations in Cambodia and Somalia have been roughly comparable to the earlier Congo operation, which until the 1990s was the most ambitious peace-keeping/decolonization operation undertaken by the United Nations. In a few years we have thus come close to matching in frequency the cold-war record that spanned decades. But the post-cold-war world seems to be one of (quantitatively) greater activity for international organizations, not (qualitatively) enhanced powers and authority.

There are three possible exceptions in the areas of human rights and humanitarian politics which are worthy of careful consideration. The first is genocide/politicide, which as we have seen, was almost completely ignored by the United Nations during the cold war. The international response to Bosnia has given considerable attention to ethnic cleansing. One might even suggest that without that dimension, even the humanitarian response of the international community might have been less vigorous. The proposal for an international war crimes tribunal also suggests a declining international toleration of genocide. Bosnia, however, remains but a single case. It is an intriguing possible precedent, but we will require more examples before we can say confidently that there has been a fundamental change in international responses to genocide. The failure to respond forcefully in Rwanda suggests a return to old patterns, rather than a building on the Bosnia precedent.

Another possible qualitative change involves regional human rights regimes. There has been real progress in the inter-American system. The forceful, united, and sustained hemispheric response to the September 1991 coup in Haiti is a heartening change from the early 1980s, when the Organization of American States General Assembly refused even to comment on the well-documented excesses of the military regimes in Central and South America. It is particularly significant because these same Latin American governments still often oppose more forceful action on behalf of human rights by the United Nations. The rapid response to the suspension of parliamentary government by President Alberto Fujimori in Peru in 1992 also suggests both greater vigilance and significantly diminished organizational self-restraint. Although such actions were always possible in principle, there seems to be a new willingness to make use of previously almost entirely neglected options. And the continued, at least grudging respect for electoral mechanisms throughout the continent suggests that such a willingness is likely to persist for at least the next few years.

But the African Commission on Human and Peoples' Rights remains a low-profile organization with few formal powers and even less political impact, and Asia and the Middle East still lack regional human rights regimes of any sort. (The Council of Europe system has not been significantly enhanced, but that is largely because there has already been a substantial regional transfer of authority to the European Commission and Court in Strasbourg.) Regionalism as a mechanism of fundamental change, as we have seen in the area of economic integration as well, is subject to extreme local variation. There simply is no evidence for convergence towards strong regional human rights regimes.

The third area of possible qualitative change is humanitarian assistance. In fact, the United Nations is pushing aggressively at the limits of its existing humanitarian authority. In Bosnia humanitarian assistance has been provided to both Sarajevo and outlying areas, against the express wishes of those controlling military power on the ground. Perhaps even more significant, because it involves action in the face of resistance by an internationally recognized government, is the pressure that has been applied on Sudan to allow humanitarian assistance to reach civilians in the south of the country. Aid has even been provided in some instances without the consent of the government in Khartoum. These examples, along with the initial humanitarian intervention in Somalia, do seem to suggest the emergence of a new international norm, very close to a right to humanitarian assistance. They also suggest a new willingness of the international community to press hard against the limits of sovereignty in responding to humanitarian crises. Even in Rwanda, where the United Nations refuses to deal with the politics of genocide, efforts are being made to provide at least modest armed humanitarian assistance to some of the survivors.

But humanitarian crises, especially famines, have always provoked an unusual degree of international concern and activity. In Europe immediately after World War II, in Biafra twenty-five years ago, during the Sahel drought of the mid-1970s, in Ethiopia in the mid-1980s, and in many other cases, substantial outpourings of humanitarian assistance in response to well-publicized mass suffering have been a recurrent feature of postwar international relations. Such efforts, however, have not spilled over in the past. The conceptual distinction between humanitarian crises and both human rights violations and other kinds of substantively similar suffering (for example, malnutrition after a famine has passed) has been deeply embedded in international practice. And I can see no evidence that this point of view is changing.

More aggressive humanitarian initiatives simply do not suggest more aggressive IO activities under different mandates.

My account has stressed incremental growth in international organization activities related to ethnic conflict. In the post-cold-war era we have seen more activity, but under well-established organizational mandates. Both the progressive nature of this change and its limits need to be emphasized.

The issue-by-issue discussion I have presented may subtly understate the nature of the change, however. The overlap between peace keeping and decolonization activities even during the cold war has already been noted. One of the more interesting aspects of UN operations in the post-cold-war era has been a tendency to combine old mandates in creative new ways. In Bosnia and Somalia in particular, and to a lesser extent in Cambodia, Angola, and El Salvador, peace keeping, decolonization, humanitarian assistance, and even human rights concerns have been combined into wide-ranging operations that had few parallels during the cold war. These integrated operations are likely to have more substantial effects in the target country than more fragmentary efforts. Humanitarian assistance operations that simultaneously address, even if indirectly and with limited impact, the underlying political causes of the humanitarian crisis are likely to be particularly effective.

Nonetheless, we should be careful about overgeneralizing from humanitarian assistance. Humanitarian crises—massive suffering independent, or at worst as an unintended consequence, of government action are relatively amenable to effective outside intervention. The costs may be high, especially if the crisis is the outgrowth of civil war, but the task is largely one of delivering goods and services to the needy. Private and multilateral agencies have substantial, and improving, capabilities in this area.

As I have noted, however, ameliorating a humanitarian crisis is largely a matter of treating symptoms. Even famines almost invariably arise at least as much from political and economic problems of maldistribution as from drought or other natural causes. When the crisis arises from civil war or a more radical breakdown of authority, as in Somalia, the problem is almost certain to recur unless authority is reestablished. Ethnic conflicts are likely to present this more difficult type of international undertaking.

International agencies can bring in and distribute massive quantities of food, medicine, and other supplies, but they have no special competence in state building, let alone nation building, which, by their very nature must be left largely to local actors. International agencies can subsidize start-up costs and provide limited technical assistance. A functioning system of government, however, must be created and maintained by the people who will operate and live under it. This is especially true if we want that government to respect internationally recognized human rights, that is, if we do not want the new government itself to become a potential source of crises that require humanitarian intervention.

As I have said elsewhere at some length, "human rights are ultimately a profoundly *national*—not international—issue" (Donnelly 1988A; 259). The causes of human rights violations are largely national (especially where governments do not owe their power to external intervention). The solutions must also be largely national. Foreigners simply cannot be expected to have the information, knowledge, skills, resources, or ultimately even the desire to engage successfully in the daily work of maintaining limited government. Stable regimes that protect internationally recognized human rights over the long run almost always have arisen, and must arise, from sustained national political struggle and vigilance.

External actors often do have the capability, through humanitarian intervention, to remove an offending regime from power (although, as we have seen, they rarely attempt to exercise it). But unless there are profound domestic political changes—changes that are largely beyond the power of external actors to control—only the worst symptoms, not the disease, will have been treated. For example, Milton Obote's second regime in Uganda, installed after the overthrow of Idi Amin, was guilty of human rights violations fully comparable to Amin's in scope and severity.

Multilateral (and bilateral) action can provide transitional assistance and continuing financial and political support, which can increase the chances of new governments. If they are vigilant and respond with firm measures of positive nonintervention whenever backsliding appears, external actors may have a very important humanitarian impact. But these efforts are supplemental to national efforts.

We return, in a somewhat different form, to my initial observation that ethnic conflict by its very nature is poorly suited to multilateral resolution. This does not mean that international organizations should not do what they can. Quite the contrary, they should continue to work to enhance their ability to provide the kind of support they are well suited to provide. Although peace-keepers can play only a supplemental role in resolving a conflict, sometimes that can be of considerable value. Humanitarian assistance may deal only with the symptoms of conflict, but treating symptoms is an important and worthwhile task. Even limited human rights monitoring, without coercive enforcement, may subtly influence the behavior of even the most repressive regimes.

We must, however, have reasonable expectations about what international organizations can achieve. Without clear and reasonable objectives, disillusionment is likely, as can be seen in the evolving American assessment of the operation in Somalia. And disillusionment with one instance or form of multilateral involvement can easily spread, making it more difficult to use other opportunities for constructive action. If the new opportunities that are available for more frequent multilateral action are not to be squandered, the initiatives that are undertaken must not be oversold.

The world is in many ways a better place after the end of the cold war. But it is still a world where IO involvement in ethnic conflicts is largely incidental and peripheral, although not without interest or significance.

3

Anomie, System Reform, and Challenges to the UN System

Raymond F. Hopkins

Rising ethnic conflicts pose a serious challenge to the world's international organizations in the late 1990s. Public agencies created to articulate and implement multilateral policy, especially the principal one, the United Nations, have inadequate capacity to ameliorate such conflicts. The civil strife and killing in Somalia, the former Yugoslavia, and the Israel-Lebanon-Occupied Territories complex and the continuing conflicts in Cambodia, Sudan, Afghanistan, Rwanda/Burundi, Sri Lanka, and many other countries are not, or at least have not been, resolvable by the intervention of one or a few outside allied states. With support from many states the UN secretary-general himself called for a "wider mission," the imposition of global authority to resolve such conflicts (Boutros-Ghali 1992b, 8). Though the possibilities for intervention have increased since the end of the cold war, however, the UN cannot meet new responsibilities in this area without substantial reform.

Two institutional reforms are required. First, conflicts among basic principles and norms guiding international action need resolution, particularly the conflict between state sovereignty principles and human rights principles. These must be reconciled in ways that give legitimacy to expanded action by IOs in cases of state failure. Second, the capabilities of IOs, principally the United Nations, need expansion. In the early 1990s as the UN undertook broader responsibilities in southern Europe, Southeast Asia, and Africa, it was critically short of coercive capability, basic humanitarian supplies, intelligence and communications, and managerial competence. Without greater external resources and internal management changes, the current challenges cannot be met. Worse still, the UN and perhaps IOs more generally will suffer a decline in respect and authority.

In the post-cold-war era international organizations, particularly the United Nations, are experiencing irreversible incremental changes. The challenge of intervening to ameliorate violence and innocent suffering engendered by ethnic conflicts is but one of several increased demands on IOs, and the important role of UN agencies in the former Yugoslavia, Somalia, and Cambodia represents not merely an episodic or "transitional" phase but a real, however modest, step-level change in the functions of IOs.

This chapter does not assess the intriguing question of how the end of the cold war has affected the strength or weakness of the state system. In fact, it does not even challenge the centrality of states in contemporary international politics, although it is clear from the collapse of states such as Somalia and Yugoslavia that the system faces difficulties. For example, consider the dilemma of how states can intervene to preserve a state without violating the historical norm of noninterference. One result of such post-cold-war dilemmas is a change of attitude about international politics, a growing confusion and disagreement about traditional norms, i.e., a case of "anomie" in international affairs. This anomie, as discussed later in this chapter, creates conditions conducive to incremental change in the structure of IOs.

In this chapter I focus almost exclusively on the UN system. The effects of ethnic conflicts on other international organizations is less clear, I believe, in part because regional IOs are even weaker than universal ones and their features vary widely. Consider, for example, the variety among non-UN IOs, including regional bodies such as the Organization of American States, the Arab League, the Association of Southeast Asian Nations, and nonregional bodies such as the World Trade Organization (WTO).

This chapter argues two theses: first, that the normative order has declined and, second, that one result has been the overburdening of the United Nations. Elaborating briefly, I contend that the cold war provided international norms based on structured antagonisms. In the absence of these antagonisms, the norms have weakened, and anomie has increased. It has become more difficult for states and IOs to recognize their interests and pursue them through prudent action. In this situation ethnic conflicts and other dangers, including weakened control over nuclear weapons, pose increased threats to peace and stability in the international system. With declining domestic support and unclear interests, however, states are less able to take unilateral or common state-level action against these threats. The result is that more states expect IO intervention to solve problems related to international public goods. For example, the dominant impulse is to work through the IOs, especially the UN system, to resolve ethnic conflicts in Bosnia, Rwanda, and Somalia. The expectation of the IO role is far greater in the 1990s than any time since the months following World War II. Resources and revised normative underpinnings to equip IOs for an expanded role have failed to emerge, however. Thus we have a danger-ous situation. Until an adequate intellectual and financial base is estab-lished, the UN's response to these shifting demands and expectations is likely to be judged a failure.

Anomie and a New International Order

Anarchy, the key element in international politics, reflecting the ab-sence of a hierarchical order and the relative independence of like nation-state units (Waltz 1979; Oye 1986), continues largely unaffected by the end of the cold war. What changed was ideology. Polarized belief systems collapsed, and when they did, the attitudes of millions of people about paths towards modernization, the virtues of technol-ogy, and the legitimacy of democratic practices for exercising author-ity changed.

Emile Durkheim described "anomie" as a kind of moral turbulence. In illustration, it is the loss of her/his moral anchor which a peasant feels upon entering urban life. The morality of village society, with its fixed categories for gender and age relationships, for linkage to work, and for conferring worth, enables a person to succeed by doing what is expected. In the post–World War II global society, bipolar solidarity provided such guiding norms. At the international level it reinforced norms of state sovereignty, limited UN actions, and gave a reasonably clear rationale for multinational policy coordination. Indeed, the states of the West and the Soviet bloc, by performing expected tasks, "saw" rewards for their actions (George 1983). In current global society, as for the peasant entering the city, however, things have "fallen apart," and the old normative order has lost relevancy, engendering a search for new ways of doing things and a new set of moral and practical rules. One key issue is how existing identities and moral systems relate to the global spread of liberalism. The individual freedom to act celebrated by the liberal political and economic order contains an invitation for ethnic groups to assert claims.

The future of IOs and the resolution of ethnic conflicts will be shaped by consequential changes occurring in the 1990s in the subjective realm. Identities, expectations, demands are in flux—far more so than the distribution of power among major states. There have been attitude shifts regarding animosities and threats across borders, most clearly in Europe and the Middle East following German reunification in 1991 and the 1993 Israeli-Palestinian accord and in Africa following state failures in Liberia, Sudan, Somalia, and Rwanda. The identities and goals of peoples within many states have also shifted: witness changes inside the states of the former Soviet Union, of Eastern Europe, and of South Africa. Theorists, recognizing this shift in subjectivities around the world, interpret it differently. One vision sees communal-oriented conservatives, in the guise of Islamic fundamentalists, neo-Nazis, neo-Stalinists, or the religious right (as in the United States), pursuing various forms of international xenophobia. Such groups mobilize fears of disadvantaged peoples as a way to counter threats they see in an approaching consensus on "liberal" norms, which are diffusing through non-Western cultures. Because these norms challenge traditional values, they are rejected by anachronistic minorities. Norms of exchange and trade based on reciprocity and rationality, for example, while consistent with both capitalist and Marxist economic ideas, are anathema to some communal or nonsecular traditions. International agreements, whether they be free-trade or Israeli-Palestinian accords, are seen as dangerous, for they push pragmatic action and greater foreign involvement in local problems. Foreigners proposing global solutions under an IO banner, therefore, are distrusted, even hated. Realist theorists are particularly sensitive to this post-cold-war phenomenon. For them, narrow solidarity groups, demanding to be organized within effective new state structures, are the basic new property in world politics (Moynihan 1993), and they greet the rise of communal, particularistic sentiments with special pessimism.

At the other extreme are theorists, usually liberal optimists, who see the current era principally as an opportunity to revitalize world federalism. This group finds in the collapse of the cold war the prospect for greater international harmony, a new order grounded in coherent, inclusive, and increasingly effective international regimes. According to this interpretation, as these regimes expand, particular issue areas will be governed more effectively because of greater international policy coordination, especially through existing (or occasionally new) international organizations (Young 1989b; Wendt 1992). This governance will often occur within the United Nations but not exclusively so. WTO, the European community, Organization for Economic Cooperation and Development, the World Bank, and International Monetary Fund, and other organizations are expected to play an important role in international affairs (Ruggie 1992). The renewal of the Nonproliferation Treaty (NPT) in 1995, for example, is predicted to be a major advance, consolidating already strengthened NPT norms and enforcement mechanisms. Such "regimes", as the one represented by the NPT, will perform an "agency" function, acting as entities to express behaviorally an underlying structured complementarity of norms and principles—orientations that are emerging as part of the new post-cold-war order.

The liberal view is premature. The evidence is mixed that stronger norms of world order now exist or that democratic values, including human rights, are in the ascent. In fact, regimes such as those regulating trade and nonnuclear violence seem to have been stronger in the cold-war era than they are in the 1990s. International diplomatic norms, flouted only on occasion in earlier years by Libya and Iran, appear (in the 1993–1994 era) to be readily and flagrantly violated by Serbian nationalists, Iraqi expansionists, or North Korean iconoclasts.

Both views face a problem. They ignore the growth of normative confusion. Instead, each falsely assumes the existence of a key ingredient for their diagnosis, that is, that consensus on principles, norms, and expectations has become more widespread among the world's populace. The struggle over the meaning of sovereignty and the significance of ethnic conflict exemplifies this problem. While violation of human rights within a state is now less tolerated, norms for action are in disarray. Confusion over what norms govern behavior undercuts the view of pessimistic realists who see new cleavages between cultures (Huntington 1992) and also that of idealist reformers who see the approach of an orderly new world system.

Thus with the decline of the ideological antagonism between the United States and the USSR and the rise of "liberal" views (Doyle 1986), roles for states have become less clear. Improvisation is common in international behavior or in mediating ethnic rivalries. This decline in clear norms for state policy has led to an increase in the demand for international institutions to undertake or legitimate conflict resolution among groups. Strategy calculations have become less certain; nation-states' "interests" are less easy to discover in the absence of bipolar cold-war rivalry. Thus, the UN is more readily perceived as the agent for defining the interests of its members. It can respond, many believe, to the felt obligations of individuals and nation-states to protect individual human rights *and* group ethnic rights. In doing so it can reject constructions of pluralist states that violate them (e.g., as in apartheid South Africa or the occupied lands of Israel). Thus states and groups reasonably turn to the United Nations as a vehicle for addressing such issues and as a way to clarify, through multilateral processes, their

own interest in intervention, the promotion of peace, and the maintenance of sovereignty.

Sovereignty Reconstruction and the UN

Can the United Nations serve such ends in the 1990s and beyond?
The anomie condition of international society does provide an opportunity for institutional development of the United Nations. It can be
the arena for reworking conflicting historic norms, of sovereignty and
justified intervention to empower the UN to develop operational procedures for managing ethnic conflict. The capacity of the United Nations
itself to deal with weakening norms, however, is problematic. Evolving
identifications among peoples within state borders have bred greater
intrastate disaffection and mutual antagonism. Perceived injustices
and the competing demands to which they give rise have created an
epidemic of ethnic conflicts. More established nation-states are understandably ambivalent about taking action in these cases, especially outside the framework of an international organization.

Sovereignty has been anchored in established identities of people
and has shaped the provision of human rights by defining the role of
the state. Now that these and other important social constructions in
international politics are in flux, peoples' degree of security and their
sense of community (see Lasswell 1935; and Deutsch 1966) have been
stirred up. Previously, these were subordinated to such global constructs as revolution, but the removal of cold-war requirements has
liberated them. Ethnic conflict is basically a product of differential ego
identifications. Rooted historical antagonisms emerge as the basis of
hostility among differentiated groups whose belief systems are mutually exclusive. Such conflict is particularly intractable because there is
an absence of inclusionary norms allowing for mutual accommodation.

When new conflicts arise for which historical norms prove inadequate to help develop accommodation, anomie is the consequence.
Consider the "nation-state" dilemma. At least a minimal degree of
shared global identity is necessary for each state to exist successfully.
One cannot imagine a world of successful states in which the exclusivity of each state leads to total anarchy and their roles derive solely
from domination by force (Kaplan 1957). Thus, conventions, norms,
and international principles all provide a social context within which
different peoples, acting through various collectivities, particularly
states, shape international affairs through various historical cycles (Puchala 1994). Grand schemes of thought, for example, Western liberalism, diffuse around the world to provide the intellectual milieu within
which peoples and their agents construct new organizational patterns

and undertake productive or destructive actions (see Bull 1977; Keohane 1984; Haas 1990; Ruggie 1992). In this milieu, changes in the
firmness and clarity of norms affect the relative strength and in-
novativeness of international institutions. That is, it is not strategic
calculation among power holders that inhibits otherwise effective UN
interventions to minimize ethnic combat or prevent its spread to
others. Rather, it is the absence of structured complementarity among
belief systems and attitudes about what procedures and methods are
appropriate.

Changes in identities and "interests" attached to shared identities
are bringing pressure to reconstruct principles of sovereignty. The formulation of this social construct, embracing peaceable order, property
rights, self-determination (identity rights), and universal principles, is
under challenge. In its "normal" application, the sovereignty principle
has sanctioned a secular state system, autonomous from religious
claims (Ruggie 1993, 163). This secular system, however, was maintained particularly by cold-war bipolarity. Recently, newer "interests,"
discovered by peoples released from this crumbled structure, suggest
that sovereignty rules need reworking. As Alexander Wendt notes,
"Sovereignty norms are now so taken for granted, so natural, that it is
easy to overlook the extent to which they are both presupposed by
an ongoing artifact of practice" (Wendt 1992). For example, territorial
divisions, many artificial—as between North and South Korea, Somalia and Ethiopia, or Lebanon and Israel—have been seen as nonnego-
tiable aspects of sovereignty for much of the postwar era. Now,
however, the UN is involved in territorial discussions to create new
boundaries (in the case of Bosnia) or negotiate new formulas for rule
within older ones (in the case of Somalia).

Norms of sovereign independence are evolving, under the impetus
of pressure to contain the violence of ethnic conflicts and the loosening
of cold-war ideas. External actors, seeking to alleviate the negative
consequences of ethnic conflicts, have sought to modify norms to better justify intervention (Reed and Kaysen 1993). Responsibilities of UN
organs have also expanded. Territorial adjustments, once within the
purview of the UN only in decolonization cases, are now subject to
UN review. The UN also has a larger role in protection of basic needs—
promoted for example by UNICEF's "Adjustment with a Human Face"
campaign and reflected in the Department of Humanitarian Affairs.
Finally, the UN's World Court (at the Hague) has taken on the authority
(analogous to the Nuremburg trial authority) to identify and prosecute
individuals for crimes against humanity. These new responsibilities
are indicative of changing demands on the UN and more generous
expectations about its ability to play a constructive role in human af-

fairs. They also show growing anomie in international affairs as realist assumptions about states as units and the legal principles of sovereignty are challenged (Reisman 1990).

External Intervention to Support Sovereignty

As norms are challenged, it is proposed that domestic autonomy, supported by the sovereignty principle, does not always override global humanitarian standards. Marc Trachtenberg, for example, concludes that "the great powers, having ended the dispute that effectively neutralized their collective force, can now set the norms that not only govern the nature of international conflict but also set limits to what sovereign states can do within their own borders" (Trachtenberg 1992, 228).

The establishment of human rights has grown since World War II, sanctified in countless declarations and resolutions by the United Nations and other international bodies. After the Persian Gulf war against Iraq, UN resolution 688 authorized humanitarian intervention to protect Kurds in northern Iraq. In light of this precedent, former secretary-general Manuel Perez de Cuellar asked whether the sovereignty-preserving intent of article 2 of the UN Charter, which prohibits intervention in domestic affairs, was to be superseded by humanitarian concerns. He asked in particular whether "the Universal Declaration of Human Rights, do[es] not implicitly call into question the inviolable notion of sovereignty" (cited in Lewis 1991, 16).

Sovereignty provides fundamental advantages to people. It creates a presumption about noninterference from people outside the state unit, thus enhancing the safety of people's lives and property from "foreign" interference. It also presumes a single authoritative body or procedural code for establishing rules over the people and territory. It is expected to protect against crime, enforce contracts, and secure the rights of individuals and groups (families, religious associations, ethnic groups). Sovereignty assures people that the relationships into which they enter will endure for a long time and that expectations of outcomes will be less problematic. Markets should flourish under sovereignty, and incentives should be improved for sharing the burden of the cost of collective goods and for the more effective provisioning of these goods. Political and legal philosophers have long noted these properties. When the government of a sovereign state effectively delivers such advantages to people, the "inviolability" of the government, people, and territory defining the sovereign state commands the recognition and acceptance of other actors in international affairs.

When, however, a state fails in these "duties," the socially constructed mandate of sovereignty becomes increasingly problematic. Ethnic conflicts give rise to such questions. Property rights and individual rights of a legal and social nature, when extended to some but not all ethnic groups within a state, is a systematic source of tension among people. In such cases the writ of the state to control property, to allocate resources, to impose obligations on people is challenged by "entrepreneurs" representing the interests of disadvantaged groups. As these claims are contested, they become associated with protest and eventually, if unresolved, with violence. This in turn undermines the very rationale for the existence of the mandated sovereignty. Thus, states that systematically discriminate against groups within their borders, as South Africa did for decades against its nonwhite populations, give rise to widespread external condemnation and the withdrawal of some privileges of sovereignty. Economic sanctions against South Africa were imposed in the 1980s, for example, precisely for its failure to fulfill sovereignty mandates regarding the protection of individual and group rights, property, and lives for *all* its population. Legal explorations and explications of human rights doctrines since World War II have heightened sensitivity to and collective consciousness of the rights it is believed sovereign states are obliged to protect and uplift. By nurturing and promoting recognition of such rights, international organizations, particularly the United Nations, have helped construct a status for individuals and, with less clarity, for groups (see the problem of less-developed rights for groups as discussed by Milton Esman, Chapter 1) which, in ideal circumstances, can be "nested" within principles of sovereignty.

The "sovereignty regime," therefore, accommodates and embraces an unfolding and expanding set of purposes and obligations for maintaining the sovereignty of a particular government, territory, and people (Krasner 1988; Wendt 1992). These obligations are a nested subregime within the concepts and empirical activity of a sovereign state. Their shaping, however, derives from lateral pressure exercised by other sovereign states and through multilateral bodies that formulate and refine the meaning and obligations of sovereignty (see Ruggie 1992). The rise of counterclaims within "sovereign" states from groups claiming discrimination and seeking relief may lead to the division of a territory into two or more distinct sovereign entities, as for example the division of Czechoslovakia into two states in 1992. Peaceful devolution, in the extreme case into separate sovereign entities, is one way to resolve an ethnic conflict, a solution not likely to provoke calls for external assistance or intervention. Other "peaceful" transformations of sovereignty have occurred in the breakup of the Mali Federation, which existed for only a few months before it became two states, Mali and Senegal, the dissolution of the Malaysian Federation into Singapore and Malaysia, and the emergence of an independent Eritrea in 1993, separating from Ethiopia. When, however, group rights have been violated for a long period and when state leaders bring issues to an international forum, such as the United Nations, seeking resolution of the internal contradictions in a sovereign state—usually other than their own—the proper, initial goal for intervention is not to eliminate or violate sovereignty but to uphold and recreate the conditions that justify sovereignty.

This argument, put forward by many analysts (see Reed and Kaysen 1993), calls for an examination of competing impulses of external states regarding the affairs of countries fraught with internal conflict. Consider the parallel to the principle of colonialism, an accepted principle of international affairs in earlier centuries, which was proscribed only in the twentieth century (see Puchala and Hopkins 1983). The Trusteeship Council of the United Nations has the mandate to oversee twelve trust units and to further the elimination of colonialism. Its concern to protect and establish sovereignty for peoples previously subjugated by foreigners has principally focused on ending intervention by powerful states in the affairs of people separated geographically, linguistically, and ethnically from the colonial power (UNA/USA 1992). The anticolonial theme has been aligned with the principle of noninterference or nonintervention in the domestic affairs of sovereign states, which has been a major bulwark and justification for the decolonialization work of the UN. The virtual elimination of trust units and formal colonial relationships (perhaps the return of Hong Kong to China after 1997 will mark the last vestige of colonialism) allows for a shift of the pendulum in the UN toward protecting rights of groups within states. Although some theorists see "humanitarian intervention" as a dangerous principle and many representatives of recently independent states resist or oppose such intervention, the trend is unambiguous.

It may be necessary to specify a variety of conditions and tests for discussion and debate. An organization such as the UN would need to review evidence in a particular context before authorizing intervention over "domestic" objections, as it did in Haiti in 1994. Nonetheless, I propose these key conclusions: first, sovereignty is not inviolate; second, violations of human rights (whether defined by local or global standards) provide a basis for intervention; and third, intervention can be considered legitimate only after multilateral consideration of the specific case and a formal resolution through the procedures of that body.

What options can the United Nations exercise which would alter the forces that increase the frequency of ethnic conflict and demands on

IOs to intervene? Basically, as I have said, reconstruction of sovereignty principles to make the requirement to protect human rights more explicit could improve the UN's ability to reduce ethnic tensions. Ethnic conflicts that arise from constricted identifications and competing demands of people could be defused by reworking basic constitutional formulas, altering territorial boundaries, and creating new, separate states. In addition the UN could monitor state-society interactions and the treatment of people. Altered sovereignty norms would allow states to cooperate with the UN in gathering information and exposing problems.

Reconstruction of state system norms to relax the strictly dichotomous view of sovereignty would also make it easier for parties to negotiate. Moreover, reconstruction would make humanitarian intervention a norm consistent with other sovereignty norms. The UN already recognizes the right, even duty, of international personalities to intervene for humanitarian causes, as in the work of the Red Cross or bilateral nongovernmental organizations. UN humanitarian assistance, even if it were delivered by force, similarly would be considered not interference or infringement on sovereignty (the domestic jurisdiction principle) but "an expression of that sovereignty" (Schachter 1991, 469). Already chapter 7 of the UN Charter specifies enforcement mechanisms for preventing threats to peace. These have been used by the Security Council to justify the use of force to end threats that include human rights violations, notably the failure of a state as in the case of Somalia.

Legitimizing humanitarian intervention, even when military force is necessary, is consistent with the goal of developing tolerance across competing identity groups. The prospect of this action is, in turn, a basic incentive for pluralistic states to maintain accommodation arrangements. Nevertheless, changing international norms is likely to be a slow process (Reed and Kaysen 1993), proceeding step by step. In Somalia, for example, UN agencies might adopt the strategy of encouraging mutually profitable trade. In Bosnia any peace is likely to require UN efforts to ensure fairness in legal decisions regulating key elements of human life, including property rights and distribution of resources. The UN could also legitimately undertake efforts to prevent ethnic conflicts, monitoring antagonism between groups and suggesting formulas for reducing conflict. This sort of role would entail a UN presence among antagonistic groups, for example, Armenians and Turks, Kurds and other Iranians, Palestinians and Israelis, Tamils and Sinhalese, Chinese and Malays, Hausas and Igbos, Hutus and Tutsis, and Indian and Spanish descendants in Latin America.

Of course, structured antagonisms often produce latent rules for collective resistance, which imply conformity by all group members. Thus ethnic conflicts can promote intragroup solidarity at the same time as they create greater divisions between segregated communities. From a global perspective, the expression of such antagonisms usually erodes universal principles. Liberal norms asserting universal individual human rights become subordinated to attitudes asserting a particular group's rights. Terrorism and torture become legitimate. Universal norms are weakened and anomie rises, especially among individuals who have multiple ethnic identities.

Asserting "sovereignty" for each group could reduce these ill effects, but only if property rights and other goals are divisible. The redefinition of goals by Israel and the PLO in September 1993 illustrates this distinction. An intractable conflict becomes tractable once claims over divisible goods, such as land, became negotiable. This redefining of sovereignty issues could relieve the frustration of external brokers in dealing with peoples who hold fairly deep, irrational mutual animosities. Once sovereignty is seen as a relative, less absolute condition, IOs have a resource for driving bargains.

In contrast, the all-or-nothing element of absolute sovereignty exacerbates the situation and limits what IOs can do. Such norms are no longer appropriate for a changed global society. Global anomie, exacerbated by liberalism, could be tempered by making the obligation to protect citizens primary and subject to external evaluations. Reducing sovereignty rights in this way would make it easier to construct a set of accommodation rules for collective action by rival ethnic groups. External norms are needed to steer those who have been born, raised, acculturated, and elevated to positions of leadership in these communities. Without the continuing pressure of norms and rules from a higher, external organization it is no wonder that hostility among confessional communities in Lebanon led to communal violence or that in 1991–1994 efforts to reconcile groups that lived at peace for decades in the former Yugoslavia have been relatively unsuccessful. As in Africa these "states" were artificial constructs, subject to fragmentation. A secular, unified nation-state was not acceptable as a solution; other forms of social organization, however, were not available. Softening sovereignty principles could make internationally sanctioned reconstructions of territorial and property rights part of solutions to ethnic conflicts.

Thus, altering sovereignty could reduce anomie. Neither of these concepts, of course, is a static phenomenon in the social order. In recent centuries, rival ethnic groups overcame antagonisms largely by constructing arrangements that met principles and norms for the primary acceptable political organization, that is, the state (Kratochwil

1989). Conflicts rooted in history and tradition have proven long-lived, however, and when secession is the only option, they have become deadly. The effort by external forces to redesign Serbia and Bosnia in such a way as to leave but minimal basis for conflict, exemplifies a trend toward a larger role for outsiders in promoting peace.

Ethnic Conflicts and IO Capabilities: A Precarious Balance

The proposed role for IOs in reducing and ending ethnic conflict remains problematic. Ethnic conflict in the 1990s between communities with "distinctive collective identities" (as Milton Esman and Shibley Telhami note in the Introduction) in their competition for scarce public or private goods, including sovereign independence, has increasingly resulted in violence. I said earlier that such violence calls for international response especially when warring groups violate global norms regarding the basic rights of "innocent" people and threaten the "peace" among other states. In these circumstances demand rises for IO-sanctioned "humanitarian intervention" and "peace-making" efforts by outside agencies (Weiss 1990; Johanssen 1990; Lewis 1991).

My focus on the United Nations as the subject for addressing such conflicts is narrower than the general scope of this volume. Esman and Telhami discuss international organizations that are both public and private, global and regional, diffuse and narrowly functional. As noted earlier, I believe the universality of the United Nations gives it unique authority to address ethnic conflicts. Regional organizations such as the OAU or the Arab League are less able to be neutral in a "neighborhood" dispute. The UN brings other strengths to the management of ethnic conflict as well. Through its legislative organs, for example, it is able to define the character of conflicts. As a practical matter, the UN was the logical agent for judicial action on crimes against humanity committed in former Yugoslavia. Another strength is coordination. The UN in 1991 established the Department of Humanitarian Affairs to coordinate worldwide deliveries of relief supplies to conflict victims.

Capabilities are limited, however. The UN has few regular financial resources for humanitarian or peace-keeping missions, and no military arm of its own with which to apply force. Paradoxically, this organizational impotence often makes the UN more acceptable as an outside broker by parties in conflict, at least in certain circumstances.

The political role of the UN was largely marginal during the cold war. Though it was founded in 1945 to further global peace and economic prosperity, its institutional value in assisting cooperation and coordination among states was vitiated by deep ideological divisions (both East-West and North-South) and military conflicts outside its purview (in Europe, Vietnam, the Middle East, and Afghanistan). By the end of the 1950s, with the admission of a growing number of impoverished but newly independent countries, the role of the United Nations increasingly shifted to development. Efforts to settle purely ethnic conflicts were largely relegated to ad hoc interventions by individual states (Syria in Lebanon in 1975 or India in Sri Lanka in 1989) and to very "careful" diplomacy including indirect intervention by the super-powers (the Yom Kippur War of 1973, the Ethiopian-Somalian War of 1977–1978). Other cases, such as Czechoslovakia (1968), Vietnam (1961–1975) and Afghanistan (1979–1988)—to the extent they involved ethnic conflict—went beyond indirect intervention but illustrate the exclusion of the UN. The Cyprus peace-keeping effort, which did involve the UN, was a major exception. In general, then, ethnic conflict, as it broke out in Africa and Asia and even among Latin American groups (through the assertion of demands by Guatemalan and Peruvian Indians, for instance) was contained or marginalized by super-power impacts.

Since 1990, demands for action by the UN have grown (Bread for the World 1992), far outpacing its capacity. Clearly the United Nations cannot intervene in every ethnic conflict, but it cannot ignore conflicts as it could, or even had to, before the end of the cold war. Either a new and stronger formulation for addressing these problems must be developed, including reforms that empower the UN to act effectively, or its powerlessness in these crises will breed disillusionment and contempt. Indeed, speeches and "programs of action" are the established forte of the United Nations, and not only on security issues.

To solve ethnic conflicts, especially those that have grown in recent years, their sources must be understood. Some of these, rich, complex, and often intractable, lie deeply imbedded in the history of the area being contested (Horowitz 1985). Others, however, are to be found in changing external circumstances, and these account for much of the increase in recent years. Effective techniques to reduce conflicts, at least as provided by external actors, particularly international institutions, will likely have to be different from the external techniques used by the protagonists of the cold war. Certainly the UN cannot employ such superpower techniques as military aid, covert action, and ideological alignment. Further, at present the UN is not constructed in a way to exercise significant moderating influence on contestants, even when it is presented with a mandate to do so, as in Somalia from 1991 to late in 1992 and early 1993 to 1994. When the initial UN effort proved ineffectual, the U.S. government offered to send military troops under

UN auspices and without a Somali invitation—thus creating new precedents. Similarly in the Bosnian conflict, NATO forces, with U.S. backing, were added to UN resources in 1993. Such novel action suggests that support exists for new UN modalities that might match the "power vacuum" created by the end of the cold war.

Cold-War Containment of Ethnic Conflict

During the cold war, at least within their respective realms of influence, the United States and the Soviet Union constrained ethnic conflict. Limits on ethnic rivalry were imposed by support for the coercive capabilities of a central government authority. Such external support helped suppress discontent (for example, separatist tendencies or demands for rights by minorities in the former Soviet Union, the Kurds in the Middle East, the Somalis in Ethiopia, the Slovaks in Czechoslovakia, and the Chinese in several Asian states). In addition, the rivals in the cold war provided a universal ideology that denied legitimacy to ethnic rivalry. The tenets of Marxism and liberal capitalism legitimated the actions of the two powers and of governments aligned with them, while their universalist tenets delegitimated separatist claims of ethnic groups. For example, the liberal emphasis on individual liberties provides no basis for group rights.

The alignment structure of the cold war had a pervasive influence. For example, secessionist movements in Eritrea, Mozambique, or Sri Lanka (among the Tamils), though recognizably sui generis often turned to outside "allies" for material support. In addition, some adopted models for national political order were provided by the Soviet Union, the United States, or other sympathetic states. The weaker the "state," or the more an issue crossed state boundaries, the more likely it was that external assistance would be used to repress or ameliorate the conflict. In many cases where a state could manage the situation, whether in Burma between the Karens and Burmese, in India, Pakistan, and Bangladesh between Muslims and Hindus, and in various Asian countries between overseas Chinese communities and a larger dominant population (Philippines, Indonesia, Malaysia, etc.), the resolution of conflict was seen to be the responsibility of the accepted and "legitimate" nation-state. Sovereignty exercised by a government with recognition by and representation at the United Nations was respected. The possibility of superpower involvement also encouraged "domestic" solutions to ethnic conflict, for it was often feared as likely to be detrimental to all parties. Such calculations alone, it seems, inhibited ethnic community members from committing resources to the assertion of rights or to demands for a separate political entity. The authority structure of territorial units created by European or American colonialism remained intact, for the most part, among the new states of the post–World War II age.

The strong ideological antipathy and security strategies of these two most powerful countries created the overarching structure within which ethnic rights in world politics were protected or marginalized from the end of World War II until the end of the 1980s (Waltz 1979; Mearsheimer 1990). The dissolution of imperial relations within opposing blocs has overturned long-held expectations and abrogated reward systems that had come to seem routine. In many former communist states, particularly in Eastern Europe and the former Soviet Union the changes seem deep and irreversible. Without bipolar structures, existing solidarities and rules of conduct for the governments of "nonaligned states," for example, or "Western Europe," are challenged. Many rules and identities even seem anachronistic. Richer states have less incentive to provide military and economic assistance to developing countries. Virtually all normative views about world affairs have been affected. The collapse of the Soviet Union has created enormous changes in the structure of influence bearing on various regional and ethnic hostilities, creating a "space" for the promotion of competing ethnic claims and the use of force to advance them—actions that previously were held in check by the anticipation that they would prove unsuccessful (Moynihan 1993). Thus, while the end of the cold war did not create ethnic rivalries, it did open new space for them to be played out.

External pressures worked in many ways. Many ethnic groups forged coalitions based on anticolonial nationalism in opposition to the colonial power (Emerson 1960; Rustow 1967). The two "sides" of the cold war diminished internal conflict in multiethnic states by providing material support to dominant but weak groups, as, for example, when the United States lent its support to suppress "rebellions" (Leites and Wolf 1970; Rothchild and Olorunsola 1983). Ideological principles of the superpower contest also denied legitimacy to particularistic partisanship during the cold war. Thus many states—especially those closely controlled by one or the other superpower—had support in containing ethnic rivalries and bolstering central authority. Ethnic separatism was silenced by coercion. The former Soviet Union helped the government of Ethiopia to repress dissident ethnic groups in the late 1970s and 1980s; the United States supported the Peruvian government in its effort to restrain Indian demands. Authoritarian order was assisted, when necessary, over democratic movements. In addition to direct repression, communist and capitalist ideologies, as noted, provided support for political institutions that opposed secession or the expression of ethnic culture in the form of political demands. Their universalism marginalized the validity of claims based on "subnational" or separate identities. Such subordinated groups, however, often carried "hidden scripts" about the evilness of the "other," allowing feelings of discontent and hatred to fester while group members practiced a variety of noncompliance and opposition behavior (see Scott 1985, 1990). The recent break-up of Yugoslavia exposed many such hidden views or "scripts" among its several ethnic minorities.

Collective scripts of ethnic antagonism, therefore, whether of Palestinians in Israel or Sikhs in India, were partially repressed, subordinated to global nuclear rivalry between the superpowers. Major industrial states aligned themselves to protect peoples within their sphere of influence from the horrific prospect of nuclear war and, to varying degrees, the penetration of opposing ideologies. Some newly independent states—Guinea, Somalia, Cuba, for example—seeking industrialization, aligned themselves with the "communist bloc," selecting a Leninist rationale for centralized rule. Certainly, a number of states developed authoritarian rule. Many newly independent states bolstered the solidarity of their order through a strategy of trade with Western industrial states and economic assistance from them, and this formula aided the political security and economic capacity of the central state (Jackson and Rosberg 1982). By and large the 1945–1989 world was one of "sovereign" nation-states making foreign policy decisions in light of the cold war; ethnic conflicts were secondary concerns. The problem is that many of these states, especially in Africa and the Middle East, are fragile, rather artificial constructs (Jackson 1990). With external props removed, internal conflicts are less readily managed by existing arrangements, as is most dramatically evident in the breakdown of the Somalian state.

UN Containment of Ethnic Conflict

Have the recent interventions by IOs, particularly of the United Nations, created new roles for IOs in international order? Is resolving ethnic conflicts likely to be an important task for international institutions, particularly the United Nations? And can universalist international bodies provide effective external resources to mitigate conflict, sufficient to replace the kind of structure and inducements supplied during the cold war?

Before these questions can be probed a review of the demands on the UN and IOs to help mitigate ethnic conflict is in order. Cold-war factors kept demands on UN involvement modest in marked contrast to the surge of interventions since 1990. Demand for containment, as in former Yugoslavia, has outpaced physical and organizational capacity, generating high probability of institutional overstretch and even failure. The transformation of the UN over the last fifty years from 50 to over 180 members contributed to this expansion in the scope of responsibilities while attenuating capacity for decisiveness on issues of sovereignty and treatment of nationals in pluralist states.

The limited capacity of the United Nations in the 1990s to contain ethnic conflicts is also partly a legacy of the cold war. Historically, UN action was predicated on principles of nonintervention and the application of self-determination "rights," especially with regard to ending "colonialism" by Western states. As a consequence, the UN has limited capacity to provide good offices (for example, in Liberia and Lebanon), virtually no ability to send in an effective peace-keeping force when invited by protagonists (for example, in Angola and the former Yugoslavia), or to intervene without an invitation when human rights are violated even when there is support by an international public to end such abuses (as in Somalia). The scope of action supported by member governments has been relatively limited.

Perhaps the most unsuccessful UN effort to intervene in a situation of ethnic conflict under crumbling state authority was the intervention in the Congo (now Zaire) in 1960. After three years of continuing strife, the death of the secretary-general, and its own near bankruptcy (see Franck 1985), the UN pulled out. This fiasco disinclined future UN executive leadership to promote intervention. It also discouraged support from key countries on the Security Council to commit resources to such undertakings.

Another factor leading to a decline in willingness to intervene, in addition to the UN's own institutional legacies, is the orientations of members from less-developed countries. Intervention, even to bring about peaceful resolution of ethnic conflict, is frequently perceived by new states—those recently gaining independence under the self-determination element of sovereignty—as a threat to the force of sovereignty principles. Proposals in the United Nations to condemn violence in Cambodia or human rights violations in Chile or to call for an end to ethnic or religious conflict in Lebanon or Sri Lanka have been opposed by some or many developing countries, which have been leery of establishing a dangerous precedent for undermining their newly won sovereignty.

From the 1960s to the 1990s, to the extent that leaders in Western industrialized countries or the Soviet Union felt an interest in or an obligation to address problems of ethnic conflict, they did so on a bilateral basis or through regional organizations they largely controlled such as NATO or the Warsaw Pact. In fact, very little effective *interna-*

tional intervention occurred, whether in the form of good offices, resources to induce negotiations, or outright threats to deter aggression and violation of state system rules. The case of Idi Amin, who came to power in 1971 in Uganda, is instructive. This pathological personality was at once a world-class buffoon and a source of extreme internal terror (see Southall 1980). Initial supporters of Amin's government, such as many Arab states (with the exception of Libya and perhaps Saudi Arabia) withdrew support and assistance by the mid-1970s. Most of the world viewed the regime with considerable repugnance. Many states accepted political refugees. Nonetheless, neither the Organization of African Unity, the United Nations, nor even major states, acting unilaterally or with independent but coordinated policies, took serious steps to end transparent violations of the basic norms that provide the very justification of a nation-state. Amin's brief 1979 invasion of a strip of land between Uganda and Tanzania provided the catalyst for a counterinvasion organized and largely supplied by Tanzania. Although the invasion was condemned by the OAU as violating principles of sovereignty and nonintervention, a number of Western states, particularly the Netherlands and Scandinavian countries, provided resources (on the order of a million dollars a day) to assist the Tanzanian government and its military in a successful effort to overthrow the Amin regime and disband state terrorist organizations. The Tanzanian intervention also allowed approximately two thousand Libyan troops that had been sent to support the regime to fly home with their weapons. Once a semblance of order was restored, albeit with considerable turbulence, Tanzanian troops withdrew. Since 1979, or more clearly since Yoweri Museveni took power in the mid-1980s, Uganda has reestablished its character as an independent state with diverse populations and an effective central government. Respect for law, reasonably sane leadership, and some semblance of national unity exists in most of that country. Throughout this episode, inhibitions kept out interventions by regional organizations, the UN, and the superpower rivals in what, it became increasingly clear, was a case of a minority—Nubian—ethnic group terrorizing other groups.

In 1994 the atmosphere has changed. Somalia, Liberia, Rwanda, Angola, and Mozambique are among the major IO intervention responding to a breakdown of civil order in Africa. Yet in the former Yugoslavia, divided into separate states by rising ethnic "nationalism," the dominant Serbs have redrawn boundaries by force. UN efforts did not prevent thousands of innocent deaths and brutal violations of human rights. In Somalia an even more chaotic and capricious decay of political institutions has occurred. By 1991 clan factionalism and governmental anarchy had appalling consequences for the lives and property of Somali citizens. Among other things, the collapse of national institutions meant that relief efforts by international groups, both private and governmental, were rendered ineffective by extortion and robbery carried out by rival political leaders and their largely unpaid but heavily armed supporters. In this context, the UN withdrew in February of 1991 after failing in the initial objective; it then hoped for military forces of the United States and other states to enter Somalia with the UN-authorized goal of creating a more "secure environment." This devolved as the only way to allow emergency relief operations to proceed (see Branigin 1992). Prodded by the United States and others in November 1992, the UN returned to Somalia in May 1993 with the more ambitious goal of establishing a coherent Somali nation-state by 1995. Attempts to negotiate among the factions a pact for reestablishing the Somali state largely failed and the negotiations required the UN to oppose the declaration of independence by leaders of the former British Somalia seeking recognition of a new country, Somaliland. Thus, no state or international body has recognized this claim from the most stable area of Somali territory (although the British government quite seriously considered doing so [Samatar 1992]).

In the face of such rising demands for intervention the United Nations, as noted already, is resource weak. Not only does it lack finances, but it lacks administrative capability to deal effectively with ethnic conflicts. Thus it is being asked to do something of which it is now incapable. The situation is much like that facing the nation-states of Africa in the 1960s. There seemed great promise for these "new" institutions; expectations of their ability to solve problems were high. Yet after thirty years many have proven to be failures, owing in part to the overextension and subsequent collapse of the state (see World Bank 1989; Chazan et. al. 1992). Analogously, the United Nations, pressed to meet rising expectations, may find itself overextended and behaving counterproductively.

The UN requires greater information, relief, logistical, and military resources if it is to be effective in addressing and defusing international ethnic conflicts. Its budget for peace keeping and peace making is limited. Their costs were about 5 percent of the UN budget at the beginning of the 1990s (Branigin 1992a), but such activities are expensive, and more money will have to be found if the UN accepts this role. In 1993 the budget for regular operations was strained; hopes to pay UN bills through donations were described as "financial bungee jumping" ("As Ethnic Wars Multiply UN Struggles to Meet the Challenge," *New York Times*, February 7, 1993, pp. 1, 14). The costs of peace keeping nearly tripled in 1992 from the previous year, and in each case the UN relies on special assessments and emergency appeals (Lone 1992). The amounts needed are enormous compared to historical expenditures. In Cambodia, for example, the UN spent over $1.3 billion on peace-keeping operations in 1992–1993, more than all the funds used for peace keeping in its previous forty-six years. This amount, in turn, is swamped by the off-budget costs of operations authorized by the UN, as in the Persian Gulf in 1990–1991 (over $60 billion) and Somalia in 1992–1994.

Regular financial resources are also a major issue. In the mid-1980s the new budget committee began to enforce a no-growth rule on the Secretariat, the central leadership, in exchange for the promise to pay delinquent assessments. Thus, even as the Secretariat has been expected to undertake many new and critical tasks, its budget has been flat (Branigin 1992a). In spite of the procedural compromise on budget issues between major contributors and poorer states, which have a majority in the General Assembly, UN finances remain fragile. Unpaid assessed UN dues are over $1 billion with the United States and Russia having the largest delinquencies (Ogata and Volcker 1993, 8). Nonassessed or voluntary contributions, based on pledges (usually paid), make up nearly half the UN system costs. Of the relief and other resources available for intervention in ethnic conflicts, almost all are from voluntary contributions. UN appeals for emergency relief totaled nearly $3 billion dollars in 1992. These appeals, met by a multitude of voluntary donations, have grown dramatically as popular opinion inside states has supported efforts to assist innocent people trapped in disintegrating states. Funds flow both through the UN and through bilateral national arrangements, including overseas nongovernmental organizations. The 1992 appeal for Somalia, for example, was met by resources from thirty-two states and international organizations. Only a portion of these relief resources appeared in the UN budget.

Another costly capability, military force, is nonexistent, aside from building guards. There are proposals to extend the voluntary provision of national troops to the UN. Indeed, some implementation of these proposals has begun. Training programs have been developed, for example, in the United States, so that designated units of the American military could receive training appropriate for performing multinational military tasks, that is, develop skills appropriate for serving with troops from various countries—for example, learning rules for serving within a multinational common command. Such "callable" military resources, similar to callable pledges for food aid, are widely envisaged, but the methods and commitments are as yet lacking. Thus in 1990–1994 when the UN has authorized sending coercive force into another country, leadership has been decided by ad hoc national coalitions. Creating a truly multinational force remains a great challenge to contemporary norms and practices. Another challenge is combining relief work and military force, especially sending troops into areas without the explicit permission of a "sovereign" government; recent "experiments" in Rwanda, Somalia, and parts of Iraq have created the precedent.

Another resource problem is the arcane bureaucratic structure of the UN organization itself, a nest of specialized agencies, which often compete for jurisdiction or credit. In ethnic conflict situations they have exhibited their rivalry, jockeying for position with one another and debating procedure and responsibility. Infighting among semiautonomous, almost feudal organizations, is an important barrier to effective action by the Secretariat. Moreover, even the Secretariat has familiar aspects of bureaucratic weakness—budget protection, inertia, avoidance of tasks for which failure is possible. In addition, the UN is far less disciplined as an organization than most national governments.

In spite of the complicated bureaucracy, the UN does adapt to achieve effectiveness. Consider its institutional performance in providing food to victims of ethnic conflict. As with most cases, UN procedure calls for mobilizing food and other resources from donors: the World Food Program has the prominent lead to do this. Relief supplies are then provided to the legal authorities of a state. In the case of conflicts such as Ethiopia (1980s), Liberia, Sudan, Bosnia, and Somalia this formula is not effective since recipient governments often allocate supplies in ways that vitiate their intended purpose, or worse, no effective government exists to which supplies can be given for distribution. In Somalia the UN surmounted this problem by working through overseas nongovernmental organizations. The secretary-general appointed the president of one of the largest such organizations, Philip Johnston of CARE, as a special representative and gave him the job of coordinating all relief activity among UN agencies and dozens of nongovernmental organizations in 1992 and early 1993. In general, the UN lacks competency in on-the-ground operations. Following experiences in northern Iraq among the Kurds and in Somalia, where effective relief efforts required coordinating the activities of foreign military forces and voluntary organizations, international bureaucratic capabilities have been developed to manage military interventions whose aim is to provide relief but this capability exists largely thanks to ad hoc efforts.

The UN also has weak intelligence capabilities. In the wake of the Persian Gulf War, for example, UN inspection/compliance teams had to create, virtually from scratch, the kind of information and control networks needed for coordinating and leading overseas operations, whereas such capability is well developed in national governments. The current cap on the budget of the Secretariat will prevent maintenance of these crucial control and intelligence features, although they are basic to operations needing round-the-clock command centers such as the UN has begun to undertake. Furthermore, the UN relies heavily on information supplied by national governments. In the past, some data, however suspect, have had to be publicly presented because of the UN's historical acceptance of the sovereign right of states to control information. In other instances, special UN efforts have developed independent monitoring (as the World Food Program has done for food aid) or special commissions have been sent to investigate questions, such as human rights in Chile or cases of murder during the civil war in El Salvador in the 1980s. Independent information gathering remains the exception, however, not the rule.

A final weakness in IOs, and certainly the UN, is that separate national identities of its personnel foster interpersonal and intergroup conflict. In considering how the external intervention of IOs, particularly the UN, can reduce ethnic conflict, it is germane to consider the degree to which ethnicity within the IOs themselves creates allegiances and rivalries. UN staff members have a national history. They carry a set of identifications, antagonisms, and ways of thinking developed from personal ethnicities and national identities. As a result, their ability to collaborate is far less than that of civil servants in most national governments. In the governments of most states, unlike the "government" of international institutions, role occupants share roughly the same heritage. The authority of state office, carrying the power to tax and punish, is supported by sovereignty norms. Accountability is bolstered by norms of civic duty and a common "we feeling" (Deutsch 1966) arising from loyalty to the nation. UN officials lack this common ground.

In the UN there are special linkages among peoples who are Arabs, for example, or Asians, Europeans, Americans, and Africans. Ethnic and regional ties facilitate quick easy communication; alliances form among "ethnic" officeholders to push policies for which they share a preference. This aspect of the UN should not be confused with the issue of subordination of UN duties to national obligations, which was common among Russians and others from the Soviet empire for many years. Often they controlled offices as an extension of their state's power, and their role was to serve their state, not defer to the norms of an international civil servant. Individuals could be rotated home while the office remained in the control of the same state. Much of this denial of role responsibilities to an international civil service has dissipated with the demise of the Soviet Union.

Regional organizations, as noted earlier, offer few solutions to weakness in the UN—either in financial resources or in management skills.

Consider the frustrated attempt of the Economic Community of West African States (ECOWAS) to intervene in the Liberian conflict in August 1990. A minority group, the Krahns, 4 percent of the population, held power by force and (electoral) fraud. They were challenged by other groups, notably the Gios and Manos. With backing by Libya and Burkina Faso, Charles Taylor led an uprising in 1990 which was fought to a bloody stalemate. After appeals to the OAU and several other parties to intervene went unheeded, ECOWAS sent troops to restore order, especially in the capital of Monrovia. After two years of intervention, principally by Nigeria and Ghana, the ECOWAS force had become one combatant in the internal struggle. While some ECOWAS members continue to support Taylor, ECOWAS troops support a designated new president, Amos Sawyer. The UN was initially blocked from considering action in Liberia by Ethiopia and Zaire (then dissenting members of the Security Council); the UN acknowledged the intervention only a year and a half later (Inegbedion 1992, 11–33). The Liberian case illustrates that ethnic and particularistic ties can be divisive in regional organizations and that regional sensitivities can block UN action. The prospects for successful intervention by regional organizations in cases of ethnic conflict seem even weaker than those of the UN, especially without greater resources than they currently enjoy.

With institutional reform, IOs could reduce the likelihood of ineffective and impotent undertakings. Furthermore, with clear, reconstructed norms that made the issue of sovereignty more pliable and subject to the collective decisions of UN members, the UN could participate in redrawing maps. Such participation would require more independent intelligence capability and appropriately skilled staff. Finally, reducing the feudal character of the UN, perhaps by altering the practice of providing separate funding to its specialized agencies, could create more productive relationships in the UN system. The resources and internal capabilities of IOs certainly must be brought closer to the levels needed to fulfill expected tasks if there is to be effective IO response to ethnic conflicts or other challenges in the future.

The weakening of international institutional order is the central issue of the 1990s, and rising ethnic conflicts are a particularly poignant and clear consequence of it. Another result is increased demand on the United Nations system to contain such conflicts. Arguably, the post-cold-war era of global politics may be best understood as the era of ethnic and cultural warfare.

Rousseau's proposal for social order is that people must be forced to be free. This is an apt description of the current paradox in international affairs. Liberal principles have gained ascendancy but fail to construct sufficient authority for their maintenance. Hence demands for new states by ethnic groups claiming overlapping territory for their nationhood cannot be settled, at least not peacefully or with hope of endurance.

A major tension exists between the historical principle of sovereignty and the call for international intervention on humanitarian grounds to end ethnic conflicts. This tension is resolvable, however, if parochial elements in the conception of sovereignty are abandoned. Intervention in a situation where violations of human rights indicate a lack of the guarantees justifying sovereignty does not violate the basic purposes of sovereignty. Once a government, although putatively having a legitimate monopoly of coercive power over a people and territory, fails to fulfill the basic purposes for its independence, to wit, providing safety and fundamental human rights to its population, then the principles that guarantee that state's immunity from intervention (under article 2, paragraph 1, of the UN Charter) are undermined.

The rise of ethnic conflict, in part "released" by an erosion of norms previously upheld by the cold war, has increased anomie in the international system. Freed from the normative constraints of competing ideologies, people have more forcibly asserted their demands for a variety of political "goods." In Korea and South Africa more democratic rule has been sought. In other, more extreme instances, such as the breakup of Yugoslavia, the Soviet Union, and the states on the Horn of Africa, demands for sovereign independence have been made. As cold war international norms have become less clear and binding, ethnic groups have had wider scope to press their claims.

At the same time, the end of the cold war has created new policy space for reconfiguring and strengthening the United Nations as an international institution. States and peoples are asking the United Nations and other IOs, to undertake new tasks, including intervention to manage ethnic conflict. The support for IO action is a reaction to the weakening of normative structures and the resources dedicated to upholding them—defense and foreign affairs budgets that for forty years propped up states allied in accord with cold war dynamics.

I believe that current shifts in demands and expectations point toward a new path for international organizations. Leaders of major states of the world and UN officials have urged changes to expand IO responsibilities (Boutros-Ghali 1992b). These include multilateral procedures for authorizing intervention, to be backed by additional resources for international organizations to use in managing ethnic conflicts. Concurrently, IO bureaucracies need reshaping to reduce internal organizational conflict. Such changes would begin to address the severe limitations of IOs, as presently constituted, in intervening in ethnic conflicts. Reconstruction of the meaning of sovereignty to incorporate toleration of humanitarian intervention and to recognize degrees of sovereignty (rather than a yes/no reality) is also recommended. This normative shift is inherent in the increased demand for IO intervention to bring peace in situations of violent ethnic conflict. Such reformulation would be one step toward filling the normative vacuum left by the decline of revolutionary communism and bipolar ideologies.

PART II

The Case of Lebanon

4

The Case of Nineteenth-
Century Lebanon

Samir Khalaf

There has been renewed interest, in recent explorations of the changing incidence and character of armed conflict, in mapping out the interplay between internal and external sources of political unrest. The demise or relaxation of the cold war and the disintegration of the Soviet empire and their tumultuous reverberations throughout the world have, among other things, brought about a perceptible decline in major wars between nation-states. These and associated global events—particularly reform and liberalizing movements in the former USSR and Eastern Europe and the presumed homogenizing influence of Western consumerism and popular culture—have reawakened the polemics over the nature and consequences of such transformations.

Lebanon's sanguinary history of protracted conflict epitomizes the predicament that other small, plural, fragmented political cultures, caught up in turbulent regional and superpower rivalries, are facing. Indeed, "Lebanization" has not only become an ugly metaphor indiscriminately employed in media sound bites to conjure up images of random and reckless violence elsewhere in the world, but has now entered the regular lexicon of social science terminology. Kumar Rupesinghe in fact employs it as a concept to describe "situations where the state has lost control of law and order and where many armed groups are contending to power" (Rupesinghe 1992, 26).

Such characterization is, in all fairness, too benign and generic to capture or do justice to some of the particular pathologies and circumstances associated with Lebanon's entrapment in that ravaging spiral of protracted hostility which characterizes its history. Nor is the blurring of boundaries between internal and external conflict of recent vintage, a portent, as some claim, of the new world order or a precursor of what is unfolding as the dominant pattern. Virtually all episodes of collective strife during the first half of the nineteenth century—recurrent peasant uprisings, sectarian rivalries, even petty factional feuds— were predisposed to being manipulated by external circumstances. Such internationalization of the conflict almost always contributed to the protraction of hostility. In earlier and more recent conflict, as Lebanon became increasingly embroiled in regional and superpower rivalries, it could not be sheltered from the destabilizing consequences of such struggles, even as the original issues provoking the conflict receded. Threatened and marginalized groups, victims of internal socioeconomic disparities or political neglect, sought external protection and patronage. Foreign powers, keen to gain inroads into the region, have always been eager to rush into the fray. Such intervention, solicited or otherwise, almost always further polarized the factions and deepened sources of hostility. In short, Lebanon again and again became an object and victim of this "inside-outside" dialectic.

Milton Esman in Chapter 1 maintains that during the past two centuries the dominant bias among ruling elites, particularly those confronting domestic ethnic pluralism, has been "assimilationist" in character. In other words, rather than oppress or discriminate against ethnic, sectarian, or communal entities, states have instead been inclined to encourage marginal groups to join the mainstream and assist in building a unified, "indivisible" nation. Assimilationism is predicated on the conventional assumption that policies or measures that recognize permanent collective rights or special status for minorities are impediments to the normal and desirable process of nation building.

The experience of Lebanon throughout its troubled history departs strikingly from this pattern. Rather, not unlike other plural and fragmented societies, Lebanon has displayed an aversion to homogeneity, anonymity, and all other forms of collective amnesia or "indivisibility." On the whole, foreign powers have recognized that reality. Rather than undermine the primordial sentiments underlying traditional identities, they have been predisposed to reinforce them. Both in their deliberate efforts and in their unintended consequences, the intervention of foreign actors has tended to sharpen and polarize the segmental character of society. Indeed, in foreign-brokered pacts and political settlements deliberate efforts were made to institutionalize confessional solidarities.

To assert that Lebanon's entrapment in protracted strife is largely a by-product of the interplay between internal dislocations and external pressures is, in many respects, an affirmation of the obvious. Yet, it is an affirmation worth belaboring, given some of its persisting complexities and disruptive consequences. The catalog of horrors of nearly two decades of bloody strife makes it abundantly clear that unless we consider alternative strategies for neutralizing external sources of instability and pacifying internal conflict, Lebanon's precarious polity will always be vulnerable to such pressures.

Since this "inside-outside" dialectic has been an inveterate feature of Lebanon's political culture, it is instructive to reconsider how earlier episodes of unrest reflected this disruptive interplay. Accordingly this chapter addresses three interrelated dimensions. First, an attempt is made to identify the nature and consequences of this persisting inside-outside dialectic. What form has foreign intervention assumed? How has it contributed to the protraction and escalation of conflict and the reassertion of communal solidarities? An effort is made here to document a few of the features that encourage communal loyalties, particularly those aspects of Lebanon's ubiquitous "retribalization" exacerbated by the inside-outside dialectic. How and under what circumstances are communal loyalties radicalized? By focusing on different episodes—ranging from peasant uprisings, factional feuds, "class" and ideological struggles to other intermittent incidents of civil strife—I elucidate how, regardless of their origins and overt manifestations, they are all transformed (or deformed) into sectarian hostility. Always, too, the conflict becomes bloodier and more tangled up with foreign intervention.

Second, since all political settlements in Lebanon—from the Règlement Shakib Effendi of 1843 to the celebrated Ta'if Accord of 1989—have been foreign brokered, it is pertinent to probe the factors associated with their success or failure. Again, what part did such efforts play in the institutionalization of communal identities?

Finally, since all forms of primordial loyalties, even the most ascribed and inviolable, are cultural constructs subject to being patterned in many ways, I consider how they could be restructured to become vectors for the articulation of a political culture of tolerance. Through rehabilitative programs and political resocialization, communal loyalties can be stripped of their bigotry and intolerance. They could also become, and the Ta'if Accord is a modest step in that direction, the bases for more equitable and judicious forms of power sharing. This, in fact, is the overriding premise of this chapter: that under the spur of enlightened leadership, groups can at least be resocialized to perceive inherited differences not as cause for distrust, fear, and exclusion but as manifestations of cultural diversity and richness.

The Inside-Outside Dialectic

Typical of small, communal, and highly factionalized societies, Lebanon has been plagued by intermittent outbursts of social and political violence. There have been dramatic episodes such as the peasant uprisings of 1820, 1840, and 1857; the repeated outbreaks of sectarian hostilities in 1841, 1845, 1860, 1958; and the latest prolonged hostilities—all of which have resulted from perpetual grievances within the country and pressures from outside.

Much of the early violence assumed the form of internal strife among factions and feuding families vying for a greater share of power and privilege. Little of it, at least until 1840, could be characterized as open confessional conflict. Nineteenth-century travelers and local chroniclers uniformly commented on the spirit of amity that marked confessional relations at the time.

There is no need here to review the complex and varied circumstances associated with the outbreak of protracted conflict. They have been amply and ably explored elsewhere (see Salibi 1965; Harik 1968; Polk 1963; Khalaf 1979 and 1987; Chevallier 1971). Four prominent factors, however, deserve to be underscored here. First, around the middle of the nineteenth century internal socioeconomic, political, and cultural disparities (both vertical and horizontal) were already becoming sharper. Second, despite all outward manifestations of secularization and social change, communal and primordial loyalties (particularly kinship, fealty, and sectarian ties) remained important. Indeed, they became the basis for the mobilization and radicalization of communal conflict. Third, the pattern of violence began to reveal a peculiar feature that became the hallmark of most subsequent episodes of armed conflict; that is, what began as predominantly nonsectarian, factional rivalries were almost always transformed into sectarian hostility. Finally, during this epoch, Western contact, foreign intervention, and diplomatic rivalry intensified. It is no accident that communal solidarity and the magnitude of belligerency intensified as well.

Naturally, foreign contact assumed many guises. First, many of the internal disparities were the unintended consequences of the disruptive force of Westernization already visible early in the nineteenth century: European industrialization, changes in patterns of world trade, the growing dependence of the local economy (particularly the burgeoning silk industry) on foreign markets, the role of foreign missions, and the like. More often, however, they were the result of deliberate efforts of foreign powers to privilege and assist their favored sects. Such shifting political clientelism was quite often dictated by regional and international rivalries. Third, and perhaps more damaging, foreign powers were also involved in successive efforts to consolidate and institutionalize confessional politics. Finally, their interventionism was most explicit in the role they played as prime architects of virtually all the peace treaties, political settlements, covenants, pacts, and rearrangements of Lebanon's political boundaries.

Let me elaborate on each of these points, albeit briefly and eclectically, from two epochs of the country's turbulent political history in the nineteenth century.

The Egyptian Occupation of Mount Lebanon, 1831–1841

Despite the confessional character of the hostilities that would follow the Egyptian occupation, it should be first remarked that they were neither motivated nor sustained by purely religious sentiments. There were socioeconomic disparities underlying the confessional enmity between Maronite Christians and Druzes. Furthermore, these disparities were of long standing. Christians in general had had a cultural and material head start over the other groups. Throughout the seventeenth and eighteenth centuries, they were able to maintain close cultural, commercial, and political contacts with Europe from which they had grown disproportionately richer and more influential. Political and socioeconomic developments early in the nineteenth century reinforced these imbalances.

More specifically, Christians, on the whole, were the main beneficiaries of the socioeconomic changes generated by the Egyptian presence. Several historians consider Ibrahim Pasha's ten-year viceregency in Lebanon as the beginning of the "modern" period, the dawn of a new era marked by the disintegration of feudal society and the so-called "opening" up of the country to foreign influence (see, for example, Polk 1963; Ma'oz 1968; Issawi 1967). The reforms introduced under Egyptian rule are seen as "bold" and "profound," transforming "almost every aspect of the old life" (Ma'oz 1968, 12). William Polk speaks of a "brief golden age which set in motion certain trends and movements which were to influence profoundly the future course of Middle Eastern history" (Polk 1963, 226).

A more realistic appraisal of the modernizing effects of the Egyptian occupation recognizes the positive transformations but also the tendency of these changes to generate communal conflict. The kind of political regime that Egypt's ruler, Muhammad Ali, envisaged for Mount Lebanon, which would permit a more efficient exploitation of the country's resources and maintain law and order, required a greater degree of government control over the movement of goods and the activities of people.

The Egyptians had every reason to be concerned. The people of Mount Lebanon, with their tradition of feudal autonomy and spirit of independence, have not been very hospitable to any system of centralized control. The rugged mountainous terrain and the isolation of villages put certain areas beyond the effective reach of any government authority. Many villages and towns levied their own tolls and duties, while cities prevented the entry and restricted the mobility of certain religious minorities.

Accordingly, early in the occupation, the Egyptian government determined to take the necessary steps to assert control. Hence, it resorted to such measures as conscription, disarmament, and the imposition of a more regular system of exactions, which became extremely unpopular. Moreover, they incited confessional jealousy and discord because they were not uniformly applied. Eager to win European good will, the Egyptians exempted Christians from many of the impositions levied on Muslims and Druzes. Likewise, in the imposition of personal or head taxes *(fardah)*, there is evidence that Muslims were paying higher rates than Christians (Polk 1963, 135; Ma'oz 1968, 16–18). Christians were also exempted from conscription and disarmament and permitted to hold responsible positions in government, to appear in public on horseback, and to wear a white turban—heretofore all exclusively Muslim privileges (Hitti 1957, 423). Writing from Beirut in December 1835, Eli Smith, an American missionary, observed: "The Christian community apparently escaped all of the fears of sudden arrest and conscription experienced by Muslims and Druzes. Indeed, there was a certain amount of conversion by the latter to escape conscription" *(Missionary Herald* 31 (1835): 92).

Of the extensive economic changes introduced during the Egyptian period, no factor had as much influence on the local economy as the change in the scale and pattern of foreign trade. This, too, widened the disparities between the religious communities. Muhammad Ali took a keen interest in encouraging and stimulating trade. Commercial treaties, intended as a compromise between the provisions of the old capitulatory privileges and modern requirements, were introduced to regularize custom duties and facilitate the circulation of goods. The opening of Damascus to Europeans, the transshipment of Western goods to the interior, growing public security and safety in the transport of goods and travels, growth of the foreign community, and freedom to expand missionary activities all helped to make Beirut into a major Mediterranean seaport. During the decade of Egyptian occupation, the city's population rose from ten thousand to nearly fifteen thousand and tax returns for the same period increased fourfold (Bowring 1840, 167).

The new cosmopolitanism and prosperity had compelling social implications. Some of the most visible consequences were the changes in tastes and life-styles. Travelers in the late 1830s and early 1840s were already describing Beirut as the "Paris of the East." As the seat of diplomacy, residence for consuls general, headquarters for French, American, and British missions, and a growing center of trade and industry, Beirut was "rapidly increasing in wealth, population, and dimensions. . . . Stupendous new mansions, the property of opulent merchants, were daily being built; beautiful country houses, summer residences of the wealthy; hotels and billiard rooms and cafes, elegantly fitted. . . . Everywhere utility was blended with magnificence" (Neale 1852, 209).

The economic and technological changes, particularly the upsurge in foreign trade and the consequential growth of Beirut, had other less favorable implications. To begin with, the stimulation and growth of commercial exchange with the more advanced industrial countries of Europe—France and England in particular—began to generate a chronic deficit in the balance of trade. Both French and British consuls of the period repeatedly noted the grave consequences of the trade deficit, which drained the country of its currency and precious metals (see Khalaf 1987, 52–55).

More important were the growing disparities in the relative positions of the various religious groups. The first symptoms of the uneven distribution of wealth and privilege—endemic to Lebanese society ever since—were becoming more visible, particularly in Beirut, where a small segment of the population enjoyed disproportionate prosperity. A new mercantile middle class—mostly Christian merchants and agents for European traders and firms—emerged as the most prosperous group. Foreign travelers who were so impressed by the conspicuous consumption, lavish display of wealth, and Parisian life-styles in Beirut at the time must have been observing the changes within this community. Other groups were largely excluded from the growing prosperity. The most prominent Druze feudal families were dispossessed and exiled by the Sunni Muslim Shihabi dynasty that ruled Lebanon from 1697 to 1842 with the support of Maronites. The bulk of the Druze middle and lower classes did not fully participate in the new economic opportunities. By virtue of their European predispositions and contacts and the security and privileges they were enjoying, Christian capitalists dominated the burgeoning trade network.

This disproportionate prosperity of Christians was achieved partly at the expense of other groups, particularly the Druze feudal lords. Indeed, Polk says it was possible to observe Christians "in the 1820s as serfs of such Druze shaikhs as the Abu Nakad and at the end of the Egyptian period as the chief moneylenders to the same Shaikhs" (Polk 1963, 137). Furthermore, Christians in general appear to have benefited considerably from improvements in public health, and their numbers grew relative to those of other religious groups (Guys 1850, 275–277).

Christian economic prosperity during the Egyptian period was not confined to Beirut. The town of Dayr al-Qamar, which at the beginning of the eighteenth century was no more than a "small straggling village inhabited by Druzes" (Churchill 1862, 104), came under the patronage of Amir Bashir, and with impetus from the silk trade, grew into a major town of nearly eight thousand, mostly Maronites and Greek Catholics. The same is true of other towns. Zahle, which formed a kind of federal alliance with the Christians of Dayr al-Qamar for the general protection of Christian interests, also rose "with astounding rapidity to a state of affluence and consideration" (Churchill 1862, 107). Its predominantly Greek Catholic population of about twelve thousand carried on a large trade with inland Syria and farmed the fertile land of the Bika (for other pertinent details, see Churchill 1862, 95–131).

By disrupting the delicate balance between the various communities, these growing disparities deepened confessional antagonisms between Christian and Druze and renewed hostilities between peasants and feudal lords. The economic transformations also helped generate a group of commercial capitalists able to threaten the wealth, power, and prestige of the traditional elite.

The new pattern of trade produced further dislocations within the rural economy. The village was no longer a self-contained economic community. The peasant and village craftsman became increasingly dependent on urban creditors and entrepreneurs, and their economic well-being was now linked to fluctuations in the world market. The primitive methods of local production could not face competition from European products. Even silk, Lebanon's major cash crop, suffered from native reeling methods. Furthermore, some of the new laws were not to the advantage of the villagers or the products of their labor. The commercial treaties of 1838 were designed, after all, to favor foreign trade.

During the last few years of the Egyptian occupation, conditions worsened. Some of the favorable aspects of the Egyptian presence were wearing off, and the population—both Christian and Druze—was growing increasingly restless. Disenchantment with the despised measures of conscription, corvée, and stringent taxation was more widespread. As early as 1834, there were uprisings in Palestine, Tripoli, and Lattakia against the imposition of such measures, and in each case, Ibrahim Pasha managed to subdue the insurrections. He then turned to Mount Lebanon and requested from Bashir II, the Shihabi prince who had ruled Lebanon for half a century, the conscription of sixteen hundred Druzes to serve for the regular fifteen-year term in the Egyptian army.

This request was unprecedented in the history of Mount Lebanon, where a sort of peaceful confederacy had evolved between the various communities, preventing any direct clash between them. The internal strife had heretofore been between factions and feuding families. Little of it took the form of religious rivalry. The conscription of Druzes and exemption of Christians was bound to arouse bitter confessional hostility.

In 1840, however, Muhammad Ali reversed his decision and insisted on disarming all Christians of Mount Lebanon. They correctly perceived this step as a prelude to general conscription. Even in normal times, mountaineers are generally reluctant to abandon their rifles. Indeed, a village proverb has it that "the Lebanese would rather part with his wife than with his rifle" (al-Halabi 1927, 2:6).

By then Bashir II had been reduced to a mere instrument of his Egyptian masters. Despite his initial reluctance, he had no recourse but to comply with Muhammad Ali's commands. Accordingly, in May 1840 he summoned the Druzes and Christians of Dayr al-Qamar to surrender their arms. The outcry, this time, was total. It spread to other towns and villages, and the call for armed struggle became more audible. Christians, Druzes, Sunni Muslims, and Shi'ites temporarily suspended their differences and acted collectively to resist Bashir's orders.

From the beginning, it was apparent that the insurgents were not acting alone. Indeed, however restive the population, much of the impetus for the uprising came from superpower rivalry. The British, at the time, were still convinced that an Ottoman-controlled Syria (of which Lebanon was then a part) would be a better safeguard for their trade routes to India. Lord Palmerston had therefore forged a delicate alliance among Britain, Russia, Austria, and Prussia to rescue Syria from its Egyptian occupiers. Russia, eager to widen the rift between France and Great Britain, endorsed Palmerston's plans. So did Metternich. All the major powers, except France, believed their national interests would be better served by evicting the Egyptians from Syria.

None, however, was willing to commit the necessary forces to engage Ibrahim Pasha in battle. Inciting local insurgents, already outraged by the abusive policies of the Egyptians, seemed a less hazardous course. Certainly it was less costly to the European powers.

This was clearly not the first or last episode in which local feuds and genuine grievances were manipulated by and deflected into international rivalries. Indeed, from then on, this became an inveterate feature of the inside-outside dialectic.

The Ottoman Reforms of 1839 and 1856

The end of the Egyptian occupation and the consequent collapse of the Shihabi dynasty marked a significant turning point in the political history of Lebanon, a serious challenge to the traditional Lebanese privilege of autonomy under hereditary rule. The Egyptian threat and the growing recognition of Western superiority prompted the Ottomans to advance a new ideology of reform. Traditionally, the Ottomans, as far as possible, recognized the autonomy and importance of various millet communities. Accordingly, the scope of the reforms was limited to military and administrative changes. Matters such as health, education, social security, communications, and the promotion of industry, trade, and agriculture remained within the scope of local religious authorities. Care was taken, in other words, to preserve the old institutions even when they were being superseded by new ones.

The edicts of 1839 and 1856 marked a fundamental departure from the traditional system: rather than sustain the autonomy of the millets, the Ottomans sought to introduce new institutions and to extend the scope of the central government by increasing autocracy and centralization. More important, the secular tone of the edicts, particularly in their promises of religious equality, generated considerable unease.

The Druze notables bore a good deal of resentment toward Bashir II for undermining their feudal authority and privileges. They had been dispossessed and forced into exile, and then Bashir had assisted Ibrahim Pasha in suppressing a Druze uprising in Hawran. During the Egyptian interlude, the Druzes enjoyed none of the preferential treatment accorded to Christians and were subjected to the hardships of conscription and disarmament. When they returned from exile in 1840, they were embittered further by the heightened prestige and prosperity of Christians and the comparative destitution of their own communities.

The downfall of Bashir II and the appointment in 1840 of an incompetent cousin, Bashir III, as his successor gave the Ottomans a welcome opportunity to undermine the local autonomy of Lebanon's feudal

chiefs. Upon the insistence of the Ottoman authorities, Bashir III organized a council, or *diwan*, of twelve men (two from each of the dominant sects—Maronites, Druzes, Greek Orthodox, Greek Catholics,
Sunni Muslims, and Shiʿites)—to assist him in the administration of
justice. Both Druze and Christian feudal sheikhs believed this arrangement encroached on their traditional authority and refused to cooperate. More provocative was the circular issued by the Maronite Patriarch
Yusuf Hubaysh and signed by leading Maronite families, calling on
their coreligionists in the Druze districts to assume the judicial authority traditionally held by the feudal chiefs. "This was tantamount to an
assertion by the Patriarch of the power to withdraw authority from the
Druze shaikhs" (Kerr 1957, 4).

Following a dispute in October 1841 over the distribution of taxes, a
party of Druzes attacked Dayr al-Qamar, set the town on fire, pillaged
Christian homes and besieged Bashir III. The incident touched off
other sectarian clashes throughout the Shuf, Bika, and Zahle. This was
the first sectarian outburst, and it left a staggering toll: a loss of about
three hundred people, the destruction of half a million dollars' worth
of property (Churchill 1862, 63–64), the dismissal of Bashir III under
humiliating conditions, the end of the Shihabi dynasty, and a large
residue of ill feeling and mutual suspicion. (For further details, see
Churchill 1862, 46–62; Hitti 1957, 434–435). The animosity was further
aggravated by the complicity of the Ottoman authorities. Eager to undermine the autonomy of Mount Lebanon, the Ottomans supported
the Druzes in an effort to disrupt or discredit the Shihabi regime. Not
only were they suspected of having been involved in the initial Druze
plot against the Christians (Salibi 1965, 50; Hitti 1957, 434–435); there
were instances in which Ottoman troops participated in the plunder-
ing. Such instances gave rise to the saying common then among Christians: "We would sooner be plundered by Druzes than protected by
Turks" (Churchill 1862, 52).

By 1842 an irreparable breach was becoming apparent between the
religious communities. The Maronite-Druze confederacy, which had
sustained Lebanon's autonomy for so long, suffered its first serious
setback. The Ottomans, eager to step in and impose direct rule over
Mount Lebanon, appointed Umar Pasha "al-Namsawi" ("the Austrian") as governor.

Umar Pasha's main concern was to demonstrate to European powers
that direct Ottoman rule enjoyed wide support in Lebanon. To this
end, agents were hired to circulate petitions and secure signatures—
a sort of plebiscite by coercion—in favor of direct Ottoman rule. He
resorted to bribery, entreaties, false premises, threats, intimidation,
blackmail, and "every species of personal indignity" (Churchill 1862,

66–75) to procure the necessary signatures. So flagrant was the extortion that European consuls in Beirut collectively protested and declared the petitions to be "completely unrepresentative of true Lebanese opinion" (Salibi 1965, 55).

Incidentally, no stretch of imagination is required to discern the close parallel between these events and those surrounding the shifting political fortunes of the Syrian "occupation" or presence in Lebanon in the 1980s and early 1990s. Much like the Egyptian and Ottoman occupations, Hafiz al-Asad's guileful statesmanship has been largely dictated by regional and global considerations and his desire to ingratiate himself with the powers that be and carve for himself a prominent role in the region. Of course, as in earlier episodes, his maneuvers have also been made possible by the furtive but willful cooperation of embattled factions within Lebanon.

In the mid-nineteenth century, as now, internal alignments within Lebanon were being swiftly redefined. The petitions had hardly been circulated when the Druzes had serious afterthoughts about direct Ottoman administration and their place within it. They had considered themselves responsible for the collapse of the Shihabi regime and the establishment of direct Ottoman rule, and were therefore reluctant to make themselves subservient to the arbitrary dictates of Ottoman officials. Confronted with Druze intransigency, Umar Pasha, in desperation, turned to the Maronites for support and started his policy of ingratiation, which succeeded only in arousing the suspicion of the Maronites and the bitter resentment of the Druzes. So intense was Druze opposition that Umar Pasha was forced to arrest seven of their prominent sheikhs. The outrage was instantaneous. An open Druze rebellion was declared demanding the immediate dismissal of Umar Pasha, immunity from conscription and disarmament, and a three-year tax exemption (Salibi 1965, 62). After strong resistance, Druze leaders finally surrendered to a joint Turkish-Albanian force.

The rebellion, nonetheless, was a clear indication that direct Ottoman control was disagreeable to both Druzes and Maronites. In the face of such opposition, the Ottomans were forced to dismiss Umar Pasha before he completed his first year in office. The most important effect of this brief interlude with direct Ottoman rule was that it had intensified the enmity between the religious communities. The Ottomans had used the time-worn ploy of inciting sectarian suspicions and hostility.

European intervention—particularly by France and Britain—prevented the Ottomans from imposing firm control over Lebanon but failed to reconcile the Druzes and Maronites. Consequently, the five powers and the Porte agreed in 1843, as will be seen, to an ill-fated partition scheme.

It is within this context that the Ottoman reforms should be viewed and interpreted: growing social and political unrest generated by the perennial problems of taxation, feudal authority, disarmament, and conscription; the rather fluid state of affairs existing after the expulsion of the Egyptians and the demise of the Shihabs; growing disparities between religious communities; increasing foreign intervention in the internal affairs of Lebanon; and the eagerness of the Ottomans to impose direct rule on Mount Lebanon and to undermine all vestiges of local autonomy.

It is not within my scope here to elucidate the underlying objectives, ideology, and specific circumstances that led to the promulgation of the two edicts, the Hatti-i Sharif of 1839 and the Hatti-i Humayun of 1856. It is sufficient to note that they were both inspired by the belief in the need to treat people of all creeds equally within the empire. They were also motivated by the desire to introduce order into government, to enhance the role of ministers, and to safeguard the bureaucracy against the arbitrary whims of the sultans (Davison 1963, 37).

The principle of religious equality was implicit in the adoption of mixed tribunals, secular education, and Western law. But these provisions were for foreign consumption—to win the good will of Western powers or to stave off European intervention—and did not reflect a genuine desire for reform. Indeed, many were never implemented (Hurewitz 1956, 113; Ma'oz 1968, 25–26). Muslims were unwilling to accept Christians as officers, and Christians were reluctant to serve in the army at all, preferring to pay the traditional exemption tax (Davison 1963, 45).

The socioeconomic changes observed during this period did not act evenly upon the various elements of the population. Once again, the urban middle class—mostly Christian merchants and agents for European traders—continued to prosper. The rest of the society, particularly craftsmen, artisans, peasants, and small traders, were adversely affected by the growing dependence of the Lebanese economy on European production and trade. The new trading patterns deprived a large portion of the rural society of its traditional sources of livelihood and rendered the economy sensitive to external circumstances. Any disturbance in the European economy had its reverberations within Lebanon.

More damaging were the widening religious cleavages and confessional hostility. The two edicts that espoused the principle of equality between Christians and Muslims in fact achieved just the opposite: a complete rift between the two dominant groups, which ultimately provoked the massacres of 1861. It is instructive that the two decades of the worst civil and confessional turmoil in Lebanon's history should have coincided with the epoch of Ottoman reforms. The liberal policy of Ibrahim Pasha, the egalitarian provisions of the edict of 1856, and the efforts of the Ottomans to subject Lebanon to more intensive centralized rule brought forth a large measure of confessional hostility. Muslims, on the whole, found the secularism inherent in the reforms repugnant, and they resented the educational and judicial reforms introduced by the Ottomans, which undermined rather than reinforced traditional systems (Tibawi 1969, 132–34). They were also jealous of the religious liberties and economic prosperity the Christians were generally enjoying. Just as Christians were the main beneficiaries of the socioeconomic changes generated by the Egyptian presence, so they had most to gain from the Tanzimat, the Ottoman reform movement. Indeed, Christians in Lebanon, as elsewhere in the Ottoman Empire, welcomed the egalitarian provisions of 1856 with much exuberance. Church bells rang in the countryside, and in some instances, the French flag was hoisted above churches and monasteries and religious processions were held in public, often in open defiance of Muslims and Druzes (Ma'oz 1968, 203). Gradually, however, Christians began to doubt the motives behind the reforms; the Ottomans, they came to believe, remained steadfast in their desire to reinforce the predominance of Islam.

Around the middle of the nineteenth century, to speak broadly, Mount Lebanon had all the ingredients of a fractured social order: factional and family rivalry, a bit of "class" conflict between the feudal aristocracy and Maronite clergy, on one side, and the mass of exploited peasantry, on the other, determined to challenge the social and political supremacy of feudal authority. Tensions were often deliberately incited by Ottoman pashas playing one faction against another or by the intervention of Western powers eager to protect or promote the interests of their own protégés.

The interplay of all these forces was apparent in the early phases of conflict. The Khazins, as feudal masters of Kisrwan, were outraged by the appointment of a member of a competing Maronite family, the Abillama Bashir Ahmad, as Christian qa'immaqam (subgovernor) of the north. To cope with the growing challenge and displeasure of the feudal families, the qa'immaqam turned to the Maronite clergy and peasants for support. Encouraged by the French and Austrians, he posed as the champion of Roman Catholics. He also incited a number of intersectarian conflicts between Maronites and Greek Orthodox Christians. The British, aware of the support of the French and Austrian consulates, threw their weight on the side of another Abillama, Bashir Assaf, who was making a bid for the post of qa'immaqam. This support persuaded other feudal families to back Bashir Assaf. With this conflict in mind, the townsmen of Zahle were encouraged to form a village council and elect a *sheikh shabab* (a village strongman) to manage the public affairs of the town. This open defiance of the authority of the *qaᵓimmaqam* was emulated elsewhere. In some of the towns the uprisings, which first took the form of mass agitations and public rallies, openly challenged the supremacy of feudal families. Petitions were drafted and public assemblies were organized to articulate the grievances of commoners against feudal injustices and oppression.

In short, by the spring of 1858, the Christian districts in the north were in a state of total disorder bordering on anarchy. At both ends of the social hierarchy, there were growing signs of unrest. Feudal families, jealous of their feudal privileges and kinship consciousness, managed to destroy the authority of the *qaᵓimmaqam* over their districts. Meanwhile, the peasant protest against feudal abuses was also beginning to gain considerable momentum.

Successful as the peasant revolt in Kisrwan had been in raising the hopes of other peasants throughout Lebanon, the movement remained predominantly a local upheaval. Druze peasants were apprehensive about taking similar action against their own feudal sheikhs. The sheikhs muted and deflected the grievances and discontent of their own peasants by provoking sectarian rivalry, particularly in the religiously mixed communities of the Shuf and Matn, where confessional enmity was already seething and required little provocation. After the first clash of 1841, both Druzes and Maronites continued to rearm themselves. The supply of arms and ammunition that cleared Beirut customs in the years preceding the war was voluminous (Tibawi 1969, 123). The two communities had also been preparing for the confrontation, although Christians went about it much more openly and with greater deliberation and boasting, often taunting their adversaries. Several of the Christian villages, for example, were in a state close to actual mobilization. Units of armed men, with special uniforms, led by a *sheikh shabab*, were organized in each of the villages, and then placed under the command of higher officers. In Beirut the Maronite bishop himself organized and headed such an armed group, and wealthy Maronites competed with one another in raising subscriptions for the purchase of arms and ammunition.

Once again, the parallel with recent events is obvious. In an already explosive situation, only a spark was needed to set it ablaze. With every renewed confrontation, the ferocity of the fighting intensified, and the magnitude of damage to life and property swelled. Although the Maronites, with an estimated force of fifty thousand men, were expecting to overwhelm the twelve thousand Druze soldiers quickly (indeed, they often boasted of exterminating their adversaries), the Druzes proved to be superior fighters. In one battle after another, they defeated and humbled the Maronites.

Sometimes within hours entire villages and towns would fall, often with little resistance. Townsmen, seized with panic, would abandon their villages, leaving their homes to be plundered, pillaged, and burned. Fugitives on their way to Beirut or Sidon were often overtaken, robbed, and killed indiscriminately by their assailants. Even Christian strongholds were not spared. In fact, it was in these towns (for example, Dayr al-Qamar, ʿAyn Dara, Babda, Jazzine, Hasbayya, Zahle) that the worst atrocities were perpetrated. Sometimes, an Ottoman commander would offer the Christians asylum in the local serai, request the surrender of their arms, and then stand idly by watching the carnage.

In the short span of four weeks—from mid-May until late June of 1861—an estimated twelve thousand Christians lost their lives, four thousand perished in destitution, a hundred thousand became homeless, and about four million pounds' worth of property damage was done (Churchill 1862, 132; Hitti 1957, 438; Salibi 1965, 106). A worse residue was the legacy of confessional bitterness and suspicion. Lebanon was clearly in urgent need of swift and sweeping measures to pacify, rehabilitate, and reconstruct the fabric of a dismembered society. It was also clear, as we shall see, that a mere restoration of order and tranquility would not be sufficient. Once again the future of Lebanon was at the mercy of foreign powers.

Foreign-Brokered Settlements

Without exception, all pacts in Lebanon, particularly those coming in the wake of armed conflict, were brokered by foreign governments. Nor, as noted, were ill effects only the unintended consequences of well-meaning foreign intervention. Foreign powers, often for considerations unrelated to internal crises, also widened or accentuated the gaps and disparities between the various communities. Their direct involvement, often as principle architects of covenants and pacts or in negotiating terms of settlement on behalf of their client groups or protégés, carried intervention to its ultimate degree.

Despite their own sharp differences, all the foreign powers involved in the various settlement schemes ended up, willfully or otherwise, consolidating the confessional foundation of the political order. Of the two schemes I discuss here, the Règlement Organique of 1861 was comparatively more successful in limiting hostilities, largely because it recognized confessional affiliation but encouraged sufficient secularism to permit harmonious coexistence between the various confessional groups. In short, the outside powers made efforts to transform some of the more divisive and pathological features of confessional hostility into a more enabling and constructive system.

Let me elaborate by reviewing the record of two landmarks in the political history of Lebanon, namely, the règlements of 1843 and 1861. Both came in the wake of bitter communal hostility. Despite their mixed record, they offered Lebanon, relatively early in its political history, opportunities to experiment with different forms of representative government. More vital, perhaps, they also dealt with the more vexing issues of confessional balance and national identity.

The Règlement Shakib Effendi of 1843, as the plan is dubbed by historians of the period, was largely a reaction to problems of Ottoman centralization and growing sectarian tensions in Mount Lebanon. European intervention—particularly by France and Britain—prevented the Ottoman government from imposing direct control over Lebanon but failed to reconcile the Druzes and Maronites. Consequently, the five powers and the Porte agreed in 1843 to partition Lebanon into two administrative districts: a northern district under a Christian qaʾimmaqam and a southern under a Druze qaʾimmaqam. The Beirut-Damascus road was used as an arbitrary line of demarcation. The partition scheme was a compromise plan—advanced by Prince Metternich—between the French and Ottoman proposals. The French, supported by the Austrians, continued to hope for a restoration of the Shihabi Emirate; the Ottomans, backed by the Russians, insisted on the complete integration of Lebanon into the Ottoman Empire and opposed any reinstatement of Lebanese autonomy.

The plan was doomed from the day of its inception. The partition was an artificial political division that aggravated rather than assuaged religious animosity. In the words of a contemporary observer, "It was the formal organization of civil war in the country" (as quoted by Salibi 1965, 64). According to the scheme, each qaʾimmaqam was to exercise authority over his own coreligionists. Because the religious composition of the two districts was far from homogenous, however, the partition created the problem of how to treat those who belonged to one religious community but happened to be living under the political authority of another, especially in such areas as the Shuf, Gharb, and Matn.

To overcome the jurisdictional problems created by the mixed districts, the Porte decided to limit the authority of each qaʾimmaqam to his own territory, thus denying Christians in the Druze districts the right of appealing to a Christian authority in judicial and tax matters. As usual, European powers intervened on behalf of their protégés.

France, as the protector of Maronite and Catholic interests, opposed the Ottoman plan and encouraged the church to remove Maronites from the jurisdiction of the Druze *qaᵓimmaqam* and to place them directly under the Christian one. Britain, eager to safeguard the prerogatives of the Druze feudal sheikhs, approved the revised scheme. In the meantime, Russia maintained that the Greek Orthodox community of 20,500 was large enough to justify the creation of its own *qaᵓimmaqamiyyah* (for further details, see Salibi 1965, 63–66). Out of such conflicting expectations, the parties created an arrangement whereby a Christian and Druze deputy would be chosen in each district, each with judicial authority over his coreligionists and responsible to the *qaᵓimmaqam* of his sect. Mixed cases, involving Christians and Druze, would be heard jointly by the two deputies. Each was also empowered to collect taxes from his own sect on behalf of the feudal chief (Salibi 1965, 66–67).

A fresh outbreak of hostilities in the spring of 1845 finally convinced the Ottomans of the inadequacies inherent in the double *qaᵓimmaqamiyyah*. Nevertheless, the Ottomans avoided a thorough reorganization of Mount Lebanon. Instead, they modified the existing arrangement by settling the jurisdictional problems of Christians living in Druze districts. A review of the articles and provisions of the règlement reveals that over all it reinforced rather than undermined the prevailing social and political power of the feudal families. (For further details, see Chevallier 1971, 174–179). Thus, the *qaᵓimmaqam* was to be appointed from princely families (Arslans in the case of the Druzes and Abillama in the case of the Maronites). An elected council of twelve members (two from each of the major six religious communities) was to be selected at large from the people without restriction to birth and status, yet the Christian clergy had the strongest voice in determining the election of Christian members and the Muslim members were appointed by the Muslim *wali* of Saida (Harik 1968, 273). Furthermore, in the event of vacancies, the heads of the religious sects were to appoint the new members.

Feudal families throughout Lebanon recognized Shakib Effendi's règlement as a direct threat to their status and traditional privileges and did their utmost to resist its application. Shortly after his departure, both Christian and Druze feudal sheikhs began "to resort to the old ways and to revive old fiscal abuses, much to the distress of the peasants" (Salibi 1965, 73). The abuses, exacerbated by the dislocations generated by the disruptive impact of European industrialization on the local economy, finally culminated in the outbreak of sectarian hostilities.

The massacres of 1860 were so devastating that they drew the attention of the international community. France in particular, as a leading

Roman Catholic power, had for a long time considered itself the protector of the Maronites. To ward off European intervention, the Ottomans were eager to dismiss the crisis as a purely internal affair. Accordingly, Khurshid Pasha, the governor of Beirut, succeeded in drawing up a peace settlement between the warring factions, which, among other things, gave the Ottomans increased control over the country. The crisis was almost settled when, only three days after the Druze-Christian peace convention in Lebanon was signed, the Christian quarter in Damascus was attacked and set on fire, without any provocation. About eleven thousand lost their lives. Foreign intervention became unavoidable and imminent.

Through French initiative, Great Britain, Austria, Russia, Prussia, and Turkey convened and decided on intervention. An international commission was created to fix responsibility, determine guilt, estimate indemnity, and suggest reforms for the reorganization of Lebanon.

The political settlement was complex and problematic. Internal divisions and a growing polarization between Christians and Druzes were compounded by the divergent plans and intentions of foreign powers. France advocated restoration of an autonomous Maronite principality much like the Shihabi Emirate of the pre-1840 model. Russia mildly supported the French proposal, but Britain, Austria, and Turkey bitterly opposed it. Britain, it seems, wanted to transform all Syria into a vice-royalty similar to the Egyptian khedivate, or to partition Lebanon into three qaʾimmaqamiyyah—Maronite, Druze, and Greek Orthodox. After eight months of extensive discussion, agreement was reached on June 9, 1861, on the Règlement Organique, which reconstituted Lebanon as an Ottoman province or mutasarrifiyyah (plenipotentiarate) under the guarantee of the six signatory powers.

At least on paper the règlement called for some radical reorganization of the country's political, administrative, and institutional structures, along with its geographic boundaries. A Catholic governor (an Ottoman subject but non-Lebanese), designated by the Porte with the approval of the signatory powers, was now to govern Lebanon, assisted by a central administrative council of twelve elected members representing the various confessional groups. Each of the major six sects (Maronite, Greek Orthodox, Catholic, Druze, Shiʿite, and Sunni Muslim) claimed two seats.

The provisions of the règlement also called for a new geographic delimitation of Lebanon. The country was now stripped of its three major coastal cities (Beirut, Tripoli, and Sidon) and its fertile regions of Bika and Wadi al-Taym, and divided into seven districts (qadaʿ), each under a qaʾimmaqam with further divisions into small counties (mudiriyyat).

All members of the administrative council, judiciary councils, and smaller counties were to be, according to article 11, "nominated and chosen, after agreement with the notables, by the leaders of the respective communities and appointed by the government." Likewise, the adjudication of minor local cases was left in the hands of government-appointed or popularly elected sheikhs. Ecclesiastical jurisdiction over cases in which only clergy were involved was maintained.

Other than the geographic rearrangement of Lebanon's boundaries and the formal abolition of feudalism, which continued to survive in other forms, the règlement did not involve a radical redefinition or a qualitative transformation of the social order as is often suggested. In fact, it reinforced the provisions of Shakib Effendi's règlement of 1843, as is apparent in its explicit avowal of confessionalism as a basis for distributing seats within the administrative council. The architects of the règlement had no other option at the time. Given the mutual confessional bitterness and suspicion generated by decades of civil unrest, they tried to generate a modicum of harmony among the various sects by seeing to it that none was placed in a position of dominance over another. Hence, in its original form, the règlement favored straightforward sectarian representation over a more territorial, proportional or "democratic" representation.

This disregard of the proportional principle of representation was not enthusiastically received by the Maronites and was a source of unrest and agitation during the formative years of the mutesarrifate. As the most populous group, the Maronites favored a system of representation that reflected their numerical or territorial distribution. The designation of an Armenian Catholic (Dawud Pasha) as the first mutesarrif was intended as a compromise appointment. By 1864 it was apparent that the règlement needed drastic revisions if the growing tension between the mutesarrif and the Maronite community of the north was to be mitigated and controlled. Once again, the signatory powers intervened, each advancing a proposal intended to give its favored protégé or client group added advantage. The French sought a reconsideration of the confessional formula and proposed the allotment of seats in the administrative council on a territorial basis giving one seat for each of the seven districts. By outwardly opting for more "democratic" representation, the French were hoping to grant the Maronites more seats on the council.

The British and the Russians were not eager to endorse the French scheme. The British recognized that territorial representation would give their Druze clients only one more seat in their stronghold of the Shuf. The Russians saw that their Greek Orthodox clients were also not likely to gain more than one seat in the Kura district. Strong opposition and months of debate persuaded the French to modify their proposal of territorial divisions and to accommodate a greater measure of sectarian representation. The formula that emerged embodied both these principles and proved instrumental in shaping the political life of Lebanon. The council was now to be composed of twelve members: four Maronites, three Druzes, two Greek Orthodox, one Greek Catholic, and one each from the Sunni and Shiʿa communities.

This compromise arrangement was acceptable both to the signatory powers (particularly France, Russia, and England) and to their confessional protégés in Mount Lebanon. It maintained a delicate balance among the Uniate, Muslim, and Druze representatives, and gave the Greek Orthodox, in the event of a sectarian split, the decisive votes; something Russia was angling for. Confessionalism, in short, became firmly rooted in Lebanon's political system.

The Règlement Organique had recognized the confessional and pluralistic realities of Mount Lebanon but carefully worked out a formula that avoided the political subordination of one sect to another. In doing so, it promoted sectarian coexistence, but it did not dilute confessional loyalties. In fact, religious sentiments assumed a more important role in sustaining identity and communal solidarity. Other than the growing disparities in wealth and life-style, which accentuated the differences among the various communities, there were at least three major manifestations of the persistence and growing dominance of confessionalism.

First, both in its original and revised forms, the Règlement Organique had confirmed the sectarian foundation of society by institutionalizing confessional representation on the administrative council. More important, perhaps, the broad religious conflict was compounded by a more diffuse, often pernicious intersectarian rivalry, as each sect sought a greater share of power and privilege. Such conflict, however, rarely degenerated into belligerence or erupted into collective violence.

Second, the Maronite community in the north maintained the communal consciousness awakened earlier in the century. In a sense, the Maronites never ceased to recognize Mount Lebanon as their national home. Accordingly, they longed for a greater measure of autonomy and independence, and on several occasions, they attempted to reawaken Maronite nationalism. Several attempts were made in 1873, 1874, 1875, and 1877, to liberate the Mountain. French political circles and the Maronite clergy encouraged the resurgence of such sentiments.

Third, the forces of secularization which often accompany urbanization, growing literacy, and exposure to alternative sources of socialization, did not detract from the dominance of the church and growing influence of prelates. It should be remarked here that both Catholic and Ottoman theories of government legitimated and reinforced the exertion of church influence.

Not only was the church gaining increasing recognition as the protector and promoter of Christian autonomy in the Mountain, it reinforced and extended the multi-faceted roles it had initiated earlier. Church-affiliated schools and colleges of the various monastic orders became more widespread. Enterprising monks maintained their position as a major source of agricultural and industrial employment. The ubiquitous village priest dominated the everyday life of his community as much as he did at the turn of the century.

In fact, the mutesarrifate evolved into a sort of "confessional sectocracy" (Corm 1988, 338). Though the country's economic development became more subordinate to European market forces and there was a massive demographic hemorrhage in its manpower resources, on the whole, this special political arrangement managed to contain internal sources of instability and usher Lebanon into its longest interlude of guarded coexistence. Except for minor revisions introduced in 1864, the règlement remained in effect until the State of Greater Lebanon was established in 1920.

Lessons and Future Prospects

The inside-outside dialectic throughout Lebanon's eventful political history has clearly not been an auspicious or neutral phenomenon. Western incursions and exposure to the mobilizing effects of advanced technology and liberal thought associated with such contacts have not always been sources of regeneration. Willfully or otherwise, they have also contributed to asymmetry, socioeconomic dislocations, political instability, and discord between communities. Ironically, this influence was most visible in the diplomatic role of foreign powers and in their efforts to formulate successive settlement schemes, peace accords, and political covenants.

The same pattern that informed the dynamics of nineteenth-century conflict—that is, protracted and unresolved strife, multiplicity of warring factions and shifting targets of hostility, disjunction between the initiation of violence and the sources that sustained and escalated its intensity, relatively large proportion of surrogate victims, and the propensity of Lebanon to become a proxy killing field for other peoples' wars—was still in evidence during the civil disturbances of 1958 and the wars of 1975–1990. Here as well, the resort to collective violence was initially rooted in legitimate socioeconomic and political grievances. The issues underlying the conflict were nonsectarian. So were the composition and motives of the main adversaries. For example, in 1958 both insurgents and loyalists were broad, loose coalitions of religiously mixed groups. Yet, fighting soon assumed a religious character. Indeed, leaders on both sides used religious affiliation to consolidate communal solidarities and extend the basis of their mobilization.

The internationalization of the conflict in 1958 also contributed to the protraction and escalation of hostilities. Events outside Lebanon (the Suez Crisis of 1956, the formation of the United Arab Republic in February 1958, and the Iraqi revolution in July 1958) threatened Western interests in the region, raised the specter of growing Soviet influence, and legitimated the internationalization of Lebanese politics. Heated debates in the Arab League and the UN Security Council and the ultimate landing of U.S. troops did little to address or assuage the internal sources of discord. The intervention, as was the case in earlier and subsequent instances, only polarized the factions and deepened paranoia and hostility.

Many of the internal contradictions, as we have seen, were exacerbated by unresolved regional and international rivalries. When external sources of instability were contained and neutralized, various Lebanese communities were able to evolve fairly adaptive and accommodative strategies for peaceful coexistence. The last and, perhaps, most successful of these was the National Pact of 1943, which survived for over thirty years. The ideology or philosophy that inspired it perceived Lebanon as neither a society "closed against the outside world, nor a unitary society in which smaller communities were dissolved, but something between the two: a plural society in which communities, still different on the level of inherited religious loyalties and intimate family ties, co-existed within a common framework" (Hourani 1976, 38).

A critical question asserts itself. How much, after all, can be done to reverse deeply embedded cultural antipathy or geopolitical realities, particularly in the face of retribalization and protracted hostility? The Lebanese have been predisposed, and for understandable reasons, to reinvent their communal and spatial identities. In unsettled times, especially in cultures averse to propinquity, traumatized groups are inclined to reconnect with family, home, and community for security and shelter.

The point I wish to advance is that pathological as they may seem at times, communal solidarities need not be sources of paranoia and hostility. They could be extended and enriched to incorporate other more secular and civic identities. Stripped of bigotry and intolerance, they could also become the bases for more equitable and judicious forms of power sharing and the articulation of new cultural identities.

Here lies the hope, the only hope perhaps, for an optimal restructuring of Lebanon's pluralism.

This is not another elusive pipe dream. Just as enmity has been socially constructed and culturally sanctioned, it can also be unlearned. Group loyalties can be restructured. Under the spur of visionary and enlightened leadership, individuals can be resocialized to perceive differences as manifestations of cultural diversity and enrichment, not as dreaded reasons for distrust, fear, and exclusion.

Lebanon has already tried nearly every experiment possible. Of all the attempted solutions—coexistence, guarded contact, compromise, partition, and integration—the political management of separate, exclusive, and self-contained entities has always been the most costly and short-lived. If it has been difficult for the Lebanese to live together, it is extremely unlikely that they can live apart. The calls for cantonization, federalism, or other partitioning and dismantlement schemes, like earlier such experiments are products of xenophobic fears and vengeful impulses. They are impelled by a merger of parochial interests and short-term political expediency.

Such appeals, though understandable in view of widespread fear and distrust, are not and cannot become viable sources of socioeconomic and political mobilization. Nor can they inspire any cultural rejuvenation. Monolithic and cloistered communities can only inculcate further dogmatism and intolerance. More disquieting, they are inclined to stifle cultural and intellectual experimentation and lead to the spiritless, joyless life-styles symptomatic of all closed and homogeneous societies. Pluralism is, after all, an antidote to collective amnesia.

It is also vital to recognize that Lebanon is a small, fragmented state in a turbulent region, and it will always be vulnerable to forces beyond its borders. Like many such tiny republics, Lebanon is destined to remain at the mercy of its neighbors' good will and the compassion of international organizations. Nevertheless, the Lebanese can do much to benefit themselves. Furthermore, tasks of reconstituting or reconstructing a society are much too vital to be left to local politicians and embattled groups or to the imperious whims of officious international organizations. The former are much too vengeful, the latter too distant and often obsessed with intricate diplomatic haggling over matters such as bilateral or multilateral agreements, constitutional reforms, demilitarization, peace keeping, border controls, and the like.

The Lebanese can at least begin by putting their internal house in order. There are measures and programs, already proved effective elsewhere, which might do much to immunize them against the disruptive consequences of external destabilizing forces. Two basic objectives are paramount: first, to encourage the participation of seemingly indifferent and lethargic groups in society and, second, to consider alternative dimensions thus far overlooked or dismissed as irrelevant.

Peace in Lebanon, though difficult to achieve, is not impossible if the Lebanese can be made to realize that disengaged, isolated, and indifferent groups must transcend their parochial loyalties and reconnect with the maligned and neglected symbols of their national heritage. In the post–Gulf War context, such reconstruction programs could at least provide opportunities to experiment with new modes of guarded coexistence among fractious communities embittered by protracted strife. This would reduce the need and the pretext for outsiders to intervene.

5

The Domestic Context and Perspectives in Lebanon

Michael C. Hudson

A country whose very name has become an adjective for communal conflict and whose modern history is laced with external interventions should in theory offer important lessons for a world facing a virtual epidemic of ethnic strife and in which international organizations are growing stronger even as states grow weaker. The applicability of the Lebanese experience, however, depends on the extent to which it fits the definition of ethnic conflict put forth in the Introduction. It is also important to distinguish between the interventions of international organizations and those of ad hoc alliances or of individual states. Lebanon doubtless is an appropriate case to study, but we should bear in mind that not all conflict in Lebanon is ethnic conflict and not all external interventions are carried out by international organizations.

How then might we learn from the Lebanese experience? I propose first to examine the terrain of Lebanese politics, with an eye to identifying the principal actors, issues, and behavior patterns and, in so doing, to highlight the ubiquitous involvement of external players. Then I focus on the two major twentieth-century conflicts in Lebanon—the crises of 1958 and 1975–1990—with particular attention to domestic Lebanese perspectives on the external interveners. What were the perceived purposes of the interveners? How did they interact

I acknowledge the research assistance of Margaret Zaknoen, a student in the Master of Arts in Arab Studies Program at Georgetown University.

with various local actors? What were the perceived results of their interventions? I conclude with an attempt to ascertain the "lessons" to be learned not only by those intent on offering advice to future interveners but also by those "on the ground" in the conflicted territory. It is perhaps only natural for analysts viewing ethnic quagmires from afar to seek to provide roadmaps for high-minded IO interveners, but one should not neglect the perspectives of those actually caught in the quagmire. If the Lebanese experiences are any guide, domestic players rarely see external interveners (even IOs) as neutral, benign, and competent—and for good reason. If IO interveners are some-times—often?—unsuccessful in conflict resolution, let us reflect before we put all the blame on the local "fanatics."

The Lebanese Context

Lebanon is, perhaps, the most extreme case of a general phenome-non in contemporary Middle East politics—the feeble legitimacy of the territorial nation-state. With the waning of the Arab "nation-building" project in the 1970s, scholars have turned to the surprisingly persistent building blocks of collective identity—tribe, sect, ethnic group, reli-gious community. For students of Lebanon, of course, there was less surprise. This new "nation," stitched together by the French govern-ment and Maronite leaders after the defeat of Turkey in World War I, was an unhomogenized mixture of unruly communities (Zamir 1985). Had France, its Maronite collaborators, and a compliant League of Nations not decided to graft the adjacent mainly Sunni and Shiʿa terri-tories onto historically Christian and Druze Mount Lebanon to create the State of Greater Lebanon in 1920, perhaps a more coherent national identity could have taken root. The new state was born in a climate of communal conflict, and international organizations—the principal Allied powers and then the League of Nations—were not only present at the creation but midwives as well (Longrigg 1958).

Given these origins, it is understandable that Lebanese politics from that time to the present has generally been analyzed in terms of sec-tarian rivalries. The founders of Greater Lebanon insisted that the fundamental problem—and mission—of the new republic was the maintenance of sectarian harmony. Memories of the "time of troubles" in the mid-nineteenth century, marked by sectarian massacres, were still fresh. Yet, the founders were also influenced by European liberal-ism. The Constitution of 1926 reflects the contradiction: article 7 states that all Lebanese are equal before the law and shall enjoy equal civil and political rights, and article 12 states that "every Lebanese shall have the right to hold public office, no preference being made except on the basis of merit and competence," but article 95 states: "As a provisional measure and for the sake of justice and amity, the sects shall be equitably represented in public employment and in the composition of the Ministry" (*Lebanese Constitution* 1960).

Most writers on contemporary Lebanese affairs point to the National Pact of 1943 (the year of Lebanon's independence) as a political invention of the highest order which created the relative stability that lasted until 1975. The National Pact extended and deepened commitment to the "provisional measure" of institutionalized sectarianism in article 95. Although it still left the Maronites as the most powerful community, it brought the non-Christian sects, especially the Sunnis, into a more prominent position. It stipulated that the powerful president of the republic would be a Maronite Christian, the prime minister a Sunni Muslim, the chairman of the Chamber of Deputies a Shi'ite Muslim, and the deputy chairman a Greek Orthodox Christian. By custom, the smaller but influential Druze community would usually be given the defense portfolio. Parliamentary seats and government jobs were meticulously allocated on the basis of sectarian proportionality, with an overall Christian to Muslim ratio of six to five. Thus, the "provisional" measure of sect-based representation was continued for the sake of amity, if not justice. As a further measure to ease sectarian suspicions and insecurities, the National Pact stipulated that Lebanon would abjure entangling alliances with either East (meaning Syria and the Arab-Muslim world) or West (meaning France and the Christian powers).

It was axiomatic to the French and to Lebanon's political elite that ethnic (read, sectarian or "confessional") pluralism was the defining characteristic of Lebanese political culture and also its principal political problem. This is a valid and perhaps sufficient reading for the nineteenth century up through the French mandate, but it has become increasingly incomplete since independence in 1943. And the "cure" for this problem—institutionalized political sectarianism—has proven to be not only incomplete but seriously counterproductive. Such is clearly the lesson of the crisis of 1958 and the civil war (with its deep regional entanglements) of 1975–1990. When the key sectarian elites and their followers came to regard the fixed sectarian proportions as illegitimate, conflicts over *other* issues began to take on dangerous sectarian coloration. In postindependence Lebanon, "sect" should not be considered the only unit of analysis, nor does ethnic pluralism sufficiently describe Lebanese political culture, let alone Lebanese political behavior. Sectarian harmony is a necessary but not sufficient requisite for political stability. Measures adopted to promote sectarian harmony cannot succeed if they do not take account of change in the social, demographic, and political environment or if they generate "side effects" that create or exacerbate other conflicts.

Sectarianism, of course, remained a building block of Lebanese political culture after independence, but it was not the only one. Sectarian leaders such as the Maronite patriarch and the Sunni grand mufti were not the only players on the field, and not the most important ones either. As important were the traditional notables, or *za'ims*, whose extended families and clans provided an independent power base and whose wealth and prestige enabled them to dispense patronage to various clienteles through a system of intermediation known as *wasta*. The za'ims and a supporting elite of landowners and merchants stood at the top of a segmented, quasi-feudal socioeconomic structure with a highly skewed distribution of wealth and prestige. Lebanese presidents relied on key notables from each of the country's provinces (Beirut, Mount Lebanon, North Lebanon, South Lebanon, and the Bika) to share in the running of the country and provide a winning coalition (Hudson 1985). These coalitions of necessity were multisectarian, as were the opposition coalitions, and the notables themselves did not derive their power and influence solely or even mainly on the basis of sect. For them the "unit of analysis" was primarily family, clan, and tribe. There has been a tendency among some writers on Lebanon and on ethnicity in general to conflate tribe with sect or ethnic group (Horowitz 1985), but such conflation dilutes the specificity of the term "ethnic group" and can lead to analytical errors. In Lebanon, at least, it makes it hard to explain why there was probably as much intrasectarian as intersectarian conflict during the long civil war (Tibi 1990).

These historically rooted structures have been subjected to massive and accelerating socioeconomic change since World War I. French colonialism, the economic stimulus of World War II, the development of a service-oriented economy with strong finance and tourism sectors, the expansion of the educational system, the spread of the mass media, and the effect of the oil boom all contributed to political ferment. By the 1950s Lebanon was experiencing the growth of parties and movements, labor unions, and mass protest. Some traditional za'ims found themselves leading or being led by constituencies of the "deprived." Sunni leaders in particular took up populist positions that seemed quite different in tone and substance from the elitist sectarian consociationalism of the founders of the new republic. The 1958 crisis revealed the extent to which Lebanese politics had become an unstable hybrid of the old feudal-sectarian structures and the new populist ideologies and groupings. The Druze za'im Kamal Jumblatt symbolized the uneasy, sometimes incongruous juxtaposition, as he utilized his traditional status to promote socialism, democracy, anti-imperialism, Arabism, Gandhian nonviolence, and an end to political sectarianism (Jumblatt 1982).

Compounding these internal tensions still further was the enormous volatility of the region. In the aftermath of World War I not only Greater Lebanon but an entire new state system had replaced the four-hundred-year Turkish administration. Indigenous nationalist pressure and postwar fatigue at home dislodged France and Britain from their mandates, protectorates, and spheres of influence in Syria, Egypt, Iraq, and Jordan, but the establishment of the state of Israel in Palestine generated a powerful and virtually unending current of anti-Western sentiment. After their brief failed experiments with Western parliamentary government, Egypt, Syria, and Iraq were taken over by Arab nationalist, military-led movements espousing a kind of state-directed socialism. Radical Islamic movements and, to a lesser extent, communist parties also emerged as important political forces. On the broader international stage, the cold-war antagonists competed for ideological and political position throughout the region, and the United States came to look upon the Arab nationalism of Gamal Abdel Nasser in Egypt and the Baʿth party in Syria and Iraq as a cat's paw for Soviet and communist influence. Ruling elites and public opinion in the region viewed the United States as an enemy, largely because of its support for Israel. Surrounded by this turbulence, Lebanese leaders found it increasingly hard to convince their constituencies that they were observing the injunction of the National Pact to avoid siding with either the Arab East or the American-dominated West.

All these factors—sectarianism, "feudalism," social change, and regional/international turbulence—played a part in igniting and fueling the crises of 1958 and 1975–1990. In both crises, regional and international organizations intervened with little success. Even before we examine each case in more detail, it should be clear that we cannot fully understand what happened if we adopt a reductionist model of Lebanese politics which focuses only on religious and sectarian cleavages. These conflicts were much more than a fight between Christians and Muslims or even among Maronites, Sunnis, Shiʿa, and Druze. The Arab League and the United Nations, which intervened in both, found themselves embroiled in a far more complex situation.

The 1958 Crisis

What Lebanese call the "events" of summer 1958, in which perhaps 2,000–4,000 Lebanese died, was a mere shadow of the 1975–1990 conflict, in which the death toll probably exceeded 120,000 (Hudson 1985;

[Nasr et al.] 1991). Its origins were primarily domestic although not fundamentally sectarian. But it quickly took on a regional dimension as President Camille Chamoun and his foreign minister Charles Malik sought to attribute their growing problems to the expansionist activities of the allegedly procommunist, pro-Soviet nationalist regime in Egypt led by the charismatic Gamal Abdel Nasser, which had lately absorbed Syria into "the United Arab Republic." Chamoun, who had been elected in 1952 as a reformist candidate, made it clear from the beginning that he was determined to be a strong, even authoritarian president. He set about building his own multisectarian coalition. He excluded his main parliamentary rivals in the 1957 elections by forcing passage of a controversial electoral law. He was the only Arab leader to accept the 1957 "Eisenhower Doctrine," a step seen by the Lebanese opposition as a violation of the National Pact. Arguably, the trigger for the 1958 civil war was Chamoun's plan to amend the constitution to remove the prohibition on presidential succession so that he could be reelected when his term expired in 1958. In the process he alienated the commander of the army, General Fuad Shihab (a Maronite Christian), as well as a number of traditional politicians (including several Christians) and—most important—the mostly Muslim urban masses who strongly supported Nasser's pan-Arab, anti-Zionist, anti-Western ideology (Kabbara 1988; Qubain 1961).

The 1958 civil war was a struggle between the pro-Western, anti-Nasser regime of President Chamoun and a coalition of rebellious notables, most of whom had served as government ministers, and whose influence rested on their traditional social status, their sectarian affiliation, and their reformist, pro-Nasser, and anti-Western ideological positions. The murder of a pro-Nasser but Christian newspaper editor in May initiated the rebellion, which within a few weeks split the country into government and rebel-held territory. President Chamoun urgently sought help from the Arab League, the UN Security Council and the United States, claiming that Nasser's United Arab Republic was trying to undermine the legitimate government and bring Lebanon into this union. The two international organizations proposed conciliation but offered little else, as we shall see. The U.S. government temporized, not seeing Lebanon as a vital interest in itself; but when a nationalist coup toppled the pro-Western monarchy in Iraq on July 14, President Eisenhower suddenly acceded to Chamoun's entreaties and intervened with twenty thousand army troops and marines. At the same time he dispatched his diplomatic troubleshooter, Robert Murphy, who expeditiously ended the civil war in a manner most satisfactory to Nasser but bitterly disappointing to Chamoun by arranging for General Shihab to be elected president. The last American troops were on their way home by October 25. The only overtly sectarian fighting during the civil war occurred after the formal settlement had been reached: in the period from September 20 to October 14, Christian factions led by the Phalangist party and other supporters of Chamoun protested the composition of Shihab's proposed government, dominated by "rebel" notables, and there was a surge of kidnappings and killings with clear religious motivation (Qubain 1961, 157–59). This "counterrevolution" was settled with the appointment of a more balanced cabinet.

One can reasonably argue that the American intervention led to the resolution of Lebanon's 1958 crisis. Clearly, no international organization intervened directly, nor was the 1958 crisis essentially "ethnic." Nevertheless, it would be a mistake to say that the case sheds little light on the role of IOs in ethnic conflict. Among the important cleavages in Lebanon were ethnic divisions, even though unmistakable ethnic strife occurred only at the very end of the 1958 "events." Notwithstanding the crosscutting sectarian composition of the government and rebel forces, the communal mythologies of Christians and Muslims sharpened the political clash over Lebanon's foreign policy orientation. And two international organizations did try at the onset of the troubles to avert the civil war. That the efforts of the Arab League and the United Nations failed is no reason to ignore them; indeed, their failure perhaps reveals the limitations of IOs in dealing with deep and complex conflicts.

Let us recount briefly the involvement of the Arab League and the United Nations. As the crisis deepened, Chamoun's government, on May 21, requested an urgent meeting of the Arab League regarding its complaint against the United Arab Republic for interfering in Lebanon's internal affairs. A day later Lebanon filed a similar complaint with the UN Security Council, apparently not expecting much help from the Arab League. On June 4 the Arab League issued a draft resolution offering conciliation but not condemnation of the UAR. This resolution was approved by all the delegates present at the meeting in Benghazi, including the representatives of Lebanon and the UAR. Two days later the Lebanese government—to the "dismay and consternation" of the League Council—rejected this resolution on the grounds that its "overall approach was conciliatory rather than adjudicatory" (Hassouna 1975). Then the Security Council began its debate on the matter and on June 11 resolved to "dispatch urgently an observation group . . . to ensure that there is no illegal infiltration of personnel or supply of arms or other materiel across the Lebanon borders" (Khalil 1962). The United Nations Observer Group in Lebanon (UNOGIL) stated in its first report on July 3 that it had observed "substantial movements of armed men within the country . . . yet it had not been possible to establish where the arms seen by the observers had been acquired from, or whether any of the armed men observed had infiltrated from outside." The UNOGIL observers were nevertheless convinced that the majority of these armed men were Lebanese (Hassouna 1975). The secretary-general accordingly asserted that there was no substantial evidence to warrant Lebanon's charge against the UAR, and the Lebanese government in turn rejected UNOGIL's findings. In the weeks following the U.S. military intervention and the process of replacing President Chamoun with General Shihab, UNOGIL continued to operate and to insist that no infiltration was taking place from the UAR (Syria). On August 21 a common Arab draft resolution was submitted to the General Assembly very similar to the Arab League resolution rejected by Chamoun's government in June. By this time, however, the crisis had essentially been resolved with the election of Shihab as president on July 31; and so Lebanon joined with the Arab states and the rest of the General Assembly in its unanimous endorsement of a resolution notable mainly for its blandness and absence of finger pointing, whether at parties to the Lebanese conflict, at regional neighbors, or at the United States (Qubain 1961).

How did the Lebanese actors perceive the purposes of the Arab League and the UN? How did they react to and interact with these two IO efforts at conflict resolution? And how did they evaluate the results of these efforts? Oversimplifying matters a bit, we may identify two principal "players" in the Lebanese crisis: the government of President Chamoun and the opposition movement known as the United National Front. The Chamoun government seems to have expected little from the Arab League, for it speedily turned to the Security Council—and for good reason. The league had always been dominated by Egypt. Moreover, the Arab states in early 1958 were divided into "pro-Western" and "Arab nationalist (and pro-Soviet)" camps. Jordan, Iraq, Saudi Arabia, Libya, and Lebanon leaned toward the West, whereas Egypt, Syria, and Sudan were pursuing a "revolutionary" course. In addition, significant elements of public opinion in the pro-Western states sympathized with Nasserite Arab nationalism, particularly following the merger of Syria with Egypt in February 1958. That the Arab League states could reach agreement on a brotherly, if anodyne, resolution was perhaps all that the Chamoun government could realistically expect, but Chamoun demanded a condemnation of the UAR, which was politically impossible for the league. Chamoun quickly became disenchanted with the UN as well, bitterly condemning Secretary-General Dag Hammarskjold for preparing "a new Munich for Lebanon" and allowing Nasser to extend his imperialist reach over a small, defenseless country. As for UNOGIL, Chamoun expressed only contempt, charging that the observers spent most of their time at the beach and attending receptions (Chamoun 1963).

The Lebanese opposition insisted, on the one hand, that Lebanon's problems were internal and that Chamoun was trying to international-ize the crisis to his advantage. On the other hand, they could not have found the league's resolution objectionable, nor could they find fault with UNOGIL's inability to uncover evidence of UAR intervention. At the UN, the UAR's representative was effective in challenging Leba-non's accusations and in arguing that the conflict was essentially among Lebanese (Agwani 1965). Nevertheless, it is true that some leaders of the opposition, notably several Muslim politicians from Bei-rut, Tripoli, the Bika valley, and south Lebanon, had good relations with Nasser and sympathized with his Arab nationalist orientation. It is probable that the Lebanese opposition did receive weapons, funds, and other kinds of aid from the UAR-Syrian intelligence services, al-though there was no intervention of military forces; and UNOGIL was, especially at the beginning, a very small and poorly equipped organi-zation, insufficient to monitor the long and rugged Syrian-Lebanese border (Pogany 1987). For the opposition, therefore, a weak IO inter-vention was not much of a problem and perhaps even an asset.

The 1958 crisis was, essentially, a nonethnic conflict in an ethnically divided society. Had it been clearly a struggle between Christians and Muslims perhaps Chamoun's government could have elicited more helpful IO involvement. As it was, however, the conflict was seen as a dispute between rival politicians in multisectarian alliances. The gov-ernment side enjoyed stronger support among Christians than Mus-lims; yet it still had important Muslim members. If the opposition could be described as mostly Muslim, it still had the active or tacit support of prominent Christian figures, including the Maronite patri-arch. The Arab League involvement proved insignificant owing to the divisions within the Arab states and the league's inability to do any-thing but offer diplomatic good offices. The UN's capabilities were somewhat greater, allowing the dispatch of an observer group; but this initiative too was ineffective. It took muscular American intervention to break the Lebanese impasse, and the Americans at that time were adroit enough to avoid being sucked into the conflict on one side or the other. When an outbreak of clearly sectarian violence did occur (between September 20 and October 14), as President Shihab was be-ginning his term, neither IOs nor the United States had much to do with its resolution. Instead, President Shihab and the Lebanese no-tables themselves settled the matter by installing a "no-victor–no vanquished" cabinet less dominated by the former opposition members than the one he had first proposed.

The 1975–1990 Civil War

The period from March and April 1975 through December 1990 is in all probability the most blood-drenched episode in the history of Lebanon, surpassing even the violence and massacres of the mid-nineteenth century. *Grosso modo*, the conflict over these fifteen years, unlike the 1958 crisis, may be designated as "ethnic" in terms of the definition proposed earlier in this volume. The sectarian-driven violence over these years was more sustained and intense than anything before.

Nevertheless, we should guard against sectarian reductionism in analyzing this catastrophe. The Lebanese political sociologist Salim Nasr has "disaggregated" the period into three levels of intensity ([Nasr et al.] 1991). The first level he describes as periods of generalized and intense confrontation (the 1975–1976 "two years' war" marked by Christian-Palestinian and Christian-Muslim battles; the Israeli invasion and siege of Beirut, June–October 1982; and the confrontation between General Michel Aoun's forces and the Syrian army and then the Lebanese Forces militia, 1989 through December 1990). The second level involves hostilities in only some parts of the country and involving only some of the actors, including the Syrian army against the Lebanese Forces militia in the spring and summer of 1978 and in the summer of 1981; the Druze against the Maronite militia in 1983 and early 1984 in central Mount Lebanon; the "war of the camps" between the Amal Shiʿite militia and Palestinian forces in south Beirut and south Lebanon in 1985–1987; and the battles between Syrian and Palestinian forces in Tripoli in the summer of 1985. He identifies a third level of "low-grade, intermittent fighting," localized and small-scale, carried out by "various armed gangs, militias, and other irregular forces against civilians, both individually and collectively," during which, he believes, perhaps 60 percent of the fatalities occurred.

Whereas the conflict as a whole was suffused with sectarian (ethnic) antagonisms, it is clear that several of the major actors were nonsectarian and non-Lebanese, and some of the multiple struggles that we lump under the "civil war" rubric were either not sectarian at all or not "purely" sectarian in nature. Non-Lebanese (and nonsectarian) combatants included the governments of Israel and Syria, the Palestinian organizations, and, one might also add, "reluctant" international actors such as the United Nations Interim Force in Lebanon (UNIFIL) and the 1982–1984 Multinational Force (the United States, France, Italy, and Britain). Nonsectarian Lebanese actors included the Lebanese army (arguably), secular movements and militias such as the Syrian Social National party and the Communist party, as well as some local gangs and individuals acting on criminal or personal motivations. Furthermore, it is important to note that the stated motivations of key actors cannot plausibly be reduced to pure sectarian hostility. Granted that formal goals may mask atavistic intentions, one still must acknowledge that the Shiʿite Amal organization, for example, was fighting for socioeconomic gains and an end to political sectarianism, and that the Lebanese forces were trying to expel "foreign" Palestinian organizations and not just promote "Maronitism" against "Islamism." The raison d'être of Hizballah after 1982 was to resist Israeli occupation of south Lebanon as much as to promote an Islamic government in Beirut.

While it is impossible precisely to quantify the "ethnic" content of Lebanese violence, one can obtain a rough idea by examining the twenty-four "major battles and campaigns" delineated by Nasr in his careful study of the conflict ([Nasr et al.] 1991). Nineteen of them involved at least one ethnic (sectarian) Lebanese actor, such as a Christian or Muslim militia, but only five were "pure" ethnic battles, that is, between ethnic antagonists exclusively. An example is the "Black Saturday" massacre in December 1975 when Christian Phalangist militiamen killed two hundred Muslims. Another five are intrasectarian battles, in which militias loyal to rival leaders of the same sect fought each other. An example is the battle between the Lebanese forces and another Maronite Christian militia in July 1980, or the 1988–1990 "Shiʿite civil war" between Amal and Hizballah. But more than half of the battles (thirteen) involved nonethnic actors—governments (armies)—either against each other or against a Lebanese sectarian militia. Examples include the Syrian army's clashes with Christian militias in 1978 and 1989 and the Lebanese resistance forces' attack on Israeli occupation forces in 1984–1985. Many "games" other than the ethnic kind were being played throughout the civil war, and the "international" dimension of the conflict was particularly striking. Israeli, Syrian, and Palestinian vital interests made Lebanon too important to be left to the divided and squabbling Lebanese. Another striking characteristic was the relative absence of the Lebanese government and army in much of this fighting, owing to the historical weakness of the state and to sectarian cleavages within the military. As in 1958, this lack of "stateness" posed a major problem for those trying to organize a successful IO intervention.

During the fifteen years of conflict, there were (according to Nasr) fifteen major agreements and attempts to settle the fighting, many of them by Lebanese and some by outsiders (*Conference on Lebanon* 1991). Of the external initiatives some were purely diplomatic and others involved direct intervention by "peace-keeping" or other kinds of armed forces. Of these interventions, the most significant (as in 1958) were by individual governments or movements—Israel, the Palestinians, Syria, and Iran—and by an ad hoc alliance, the 1982–1984 Multinational Force (MNF), which consisted of the United States, France, Italy, and Britain. (Although the MNF does not qualify as an IO under the Esman-Telhami definition because it did not meet the "organizational" criterion, I nevertheless discuss it briefly for comparative purposes). Only three external involvements would seem to qualify as IO interventions: the Arab Deterrent Force of 1976–1979, UNIFIL (1978–present), and the Arab League–sponsored mediation that led to the Taʾif Accord of 1989. Neither of the first two succeeded in its primary mission: the ADF failed to keep or restore peace among Lebanese factions, and UNIFIL failed to persuade Israel to withdraw entirely from Lebanon or to serve as a transition/buffer force pending the reestablishment of de facto Lebanese sovereignty there. But the third project did in fact lead to a cessation of internal violence and it set in motion a project for restoration of state authority.

The Arab Deterrent Force

From June 1976 until its formal dissolution in September 1982 the Arab Deterrent Force represented the first of two efforts by a regional international organization—the Arab League—to solve Lebanon's internal problems. To understand why the ADF failed requires (among other things) an examination of its composition and its relations with the several contending parties in Lebanon (Pogany 1987; Haddad 1985). The initiative began in June with the dispatch of a symbolic force, organized by the Arab League secretary-general, soon comprising around twenty-five hundred troops from Syria, Libya, Sudan, and Saudi Arabia; but it was not until after the Riyadh Arab Summit Conference in October that the force really took shape, expanding to thirty thousand. Syria, which had already intervened unilaterally to prevent the Lebanese Muslim and Palestinian forces from overrunning the Christian militias, emerged as by far the main contributor to the ADF, making up around 80 percent. When newly elected president Elias Sarkis authorized a Syrian commitment of twenty-five thousand, the "international" character of the ADF faded, notwithstanding the symbolic presence of around five thousand soldiers drawn from Libya, Saudi Arabia, Sudan, the United Arab Emirates, and South Yemen. Almost immediately these non-Syrian contingents began to drop out, as they perceived the intractability of Lebanon's factional conflicts, and by April 1979 the ADF consisted entirely of Syrians (Pogany 1987).

From the start, major players in Lebanon regarded the ADF not as an impartial peace maker but as just another partisan; and as alliances shifted and circumstances changed, so did local attitudes toward the ADF. To be sure, the ADF had been placed under the command of the Lebanese president, but Sarkis soon realized that he lacked real control over it. When the Lebanese parliament called for repositioning the ADF in April 1978, its resolution was ignored. Initially, the Palestinians rightly felt that the Syrians were trying to curb them; but following Anwar Sadat's 1977 trip to Jerusalem to break the psychological barrier between Arabs and Israelis, Syria's relations with some Palestinian groups improved. In June 1976 Christian militias had welcomed Syrian support against the Lebanese National Front–Palestinian threat; but by late 1977, as some Christian leaders began to develop contacts with Israel, they discovered that they were on a collision course with Damascus. Syria, after all, was in Lebanon to preempt Israeli inroads. ADF (Syrian) forces fought a series of major battles against Christian militias between 1977 and 1980. Only the mostly Muslim-leftist Lebanese National Front gave more or less support to the ADF. It should be noted as well that Syrian (and ADF) forces were deterred by Israel's unilaterally declared "red line" from deploying in south Lebanon.

After the ADF became totally Syrian by May 1979, it lost any resemblance to an international organization. Christian politicians, and some Muslims, repeatedly called for the withdrawal or redeployment of ADF forces and their replacement by the Lebanese army, while the Lebanese National Movement and the Palestinians insisted that such moves would harm the legitimate presence of the Palestinians in Lebanon as guaranteed in the Cairo Accords of 1969. When ADF forces actually did withdraw from the Beirut-Saida area early in 1980, the Palestinians took over (in the absence of an effective Lebanese army), thus strengthening their capabilities vis-à-vis Israel. But these advances alienated the Palestinians' erstwhile allies, the Lebanese Shi'ites of the Amal movement. Syria found it expedient to support Amal in order to contain (but not eliminate) the Palestinians. ADF forces also withdrew from Christian east Beirut, in favor of the Lebanese army, but Syrian-Christian hostilities intensified as the Christian militias were forcibly "unified" under the tough leadership of Bashir Gemayel. By the spring of 1981 the Lebanese government, as well as the Christian militias, was trying to get rid of the ADF. President Sarkis enlisted the help of an Arab follow-up committee, but Syria resisted the pressures from Saudi Arabia and Kuwait to pull back. President Hafiz al-Asad presumably felt that Syrian vital interests required continuing involvement in Lebanon, for two reasons: the growing polarization between Israel and the Palestinians in south Lebanon, which had already triggered a temporary Israeli occupation in 1978; and the need to offset the influence of Syria's longtime rival, Iraq, which was trying to make trouble for Syria in Lebanon to punish Syria for supporting Iran in the Iraq-Iran War, which began in 1980. Fulfilling the ADF mandate for Lebanon—restoring its security, sovereignty, and unity—was not Syria's highest priority.

The ADF, already effectively moribund, disappeared entirely in the wake of Israel's invasion of Lebanon in June 1982. With Syrian forces bloodied and in retreat, President Asad accepted the termination of the ADF's mandate at an Arab summit conference in Fez on September 6, 1982. Although in its early stages—in 1977—it did succeed in collecting some heavy weapons from contending militias and reducing tensions, it soon became crippled. One reason was the growing differences between Syria and other Arab governments, notably Saudi Arabia. Inasmuch as contending Lebanese parties also were affected by inter-Arab divisions, the ADF could not command general respect as an impartial actor. With the increasing "Syrianization" of the ADF, only Syria's closest allies in Lebanon—the Lebanese National Movement, the pro-Syrian notables of north Lebanon and the Bika, and the Amal movement—would cooperate with it. Meanwhile, Syria's many enemies—the Christian militias, the mainstream Palestinians, the Christian-run enclave in south Lebanon—resisted its efforts. When the ADF mandate ran out in 1982, Lebanon found itself split into eight fairly distinct jurisdictions (Haddad 1985) and thus was even more divided than it had been in 1976.

UNIFIL

Ever since the reemergence of the Palestinians as an independent political force in the mid-1960s, Lebanon had been a major theater in the Arab-Israeli conflict. The war between Israel and the PLO took on new intensity after the expulsion of Palestinian guerrillas from Jordan in 1970–1971 and the Arab-Israeli War of 1973. Initially most Lebanese, regardless of sect, supported the Palestinian guerrillas, and in 1969 the Lebanese government signed the Cairo Accords, which allowed the Palestinian guerrillas limited freedom of action in Palestinian refugee camps and against Israel from south Lebanon. Later, however, the Palestinian presence began to polarize and poison Christian-Muslim relations as Israeli reprisals escalated against Lebanese as well as Palestinian targets. Israel invaded south Lebanon on March 15, 1978, and the Lebanese government appealed to the UN Security Council. The Security Council, with strong American support, responded with resolution 425 calling for Israel's unconditional withdrawal, the restoration of peace and security, and assistance to the Lebanese government in restoring its authority in south Lebanon. To monitor Israeli compliance, a UN force (UNIFIL) was established (Skogmo 1989). Although Israel formally withdrew from south Lebanon in June, it left in place a surrogate Lebanese militia, trained and supported by the Israeli army, in a "security zone" along the international frontier. UNIFIL lacked the mandate and the necessary force to compel Israel's complete withdrawal from the security zone or to curb the incessant low-level hostilities with Palestinian and, later, Lebanese guerrillas. Israel's far more massive invasion in 1982, which carried it all the way to Beirut and central Lebanon, lasted four years; but when it completed its withdrawal in 1986 the "security zone" remained intact, run by an Israeli-backed "South Lebanon Army." And UNIFIL remained too.

Unlike the ill-fated ADF, UNIFIL enjoyed "international" status and "organizational" coherence, but UNIFIL shared a key weakness of the ADF: it was not accepted as authoritative by several of the major local actors. The PLO viewed UNIFIL as an impediment to its own operations against Israel. Inasmuch as the PLO had not been recognized as a party to resolution 425, it felt no obligation to submit to UNIFIL monitoring. PLO fighters forcibly resisted UNIFIL efforts to deploy around Tyre and other PLO strongholds. To be sure, PLO chairman Yasir Arafat pledged to cooperate with (but not submit to) UNIFIL; yet occasional clashes continued. UNIFIL lacked the manpower and firepower to suppress Palestinian guerrilla activity substantially. It could prevent the movement of armed Palestinians through its scattered checkpoints, but it could not effectively curb the movement of unarmed Palestinians, nor could it prevent the influx of arms by other routes. UNIFIL and the Palestinians reached an uneasy modus vivendi and tried to keep clashes to a minimum.

UNIFIL's relations with Israel and its Lebanese surrogates in the "security zone" were also marked by distrust. Even though UNIFIL managed to negotiate a substantial Israeli withdrawal in 1978, the Israelis refused to abandon the border area to UNIFIL; and when Israel invaded again in 1982 it advanced right through UNIFIL-held areas. During the Israeli occupation, UNIFIL units were able only to monitor Israeli behavior and, occasionally, to prevent Israeli mistreatment of the population. In the chronic clashes between Israel or its Lebanese surrogates and Lebanese resistance forces or Palestinian guerrillas, the five-thousand-man UNIFIL force often simply found itself in the middle. Between 1978 and 1993 it suffered 190 killed and 250 wounded. Israel frequently complained that UNIFIL condemned Israel more harshly and frequently than it criticized Amal or Hizballah. "Israel views UNIFIL militarily as weak and undependable, politically as disjointed and inconsequential," wrote one observer (Heiburg 1991). Accordingly, the Israelis, who regarded their "security zone" as highly successful, had no incentive to withdraw and turn over this sensitive area to such an inadequate body.

Relations between UNIFIL and the de facto local authorities in the "security zone" were no better. During the early stage of UNIFIL's mission, the local Lebanese commander, Major Saʿd Haddad, refused to honor his commitment to facilitate UNIFIL's mission. Haddad's forces actually prevented UNIFIL efforts to deploy into the "security zone," and there were a number of clashes between his militia and the UNIFIL forces, in which the UN forces suffered deaths and injuries. Relations deteriorated further after 1984, when Major General Antoine Lahd (another renegade Lebanese army officer) succeeded Haddad and transformed his rudimentary militia into a more disciplined force known as the South Lebanon Army. Since UNIFIL officers believed that Israel commanded these Lebanese militiamen, they declined to deal with the SLA leadership directly and instead made representations to Israel; but Israel always insisted that it had no control over them. For their part, the SLA leaders nurtured distrust toward UNIFIL because of its "working relationship" with their sworn enemies, the PLO and Lebanese resistance fighters.

After the forced withdrawal of PLO forces in 1982, the "Lebanese resistance" became the main antagonist of the SLA and the Israelis in and around the "security zone." The Lebanese resistance consisted mainly of the Shiʿite Amal organization, but another more radical—and rival—Shiʿite organization, Hizballah, began to play an increasingly effective military role. UNIFIL had no mandate to interfere with Lebanese groups engaged in legitimate resistance to foreign occupation and so developed, at first, a good working relationship with Amal. Hizballah, however, regarded UNIFIL as an obstacle to its activities, accused it of cooperating with the Israelis, and resented its coordination with Amal (Skogmo 1989). From the mid-1980s onward there were sporadic clashes between Hizballah (and occasionally Amal) fighters and UNIFIL soldiers. While the Taʾif Accord of 1989 paved the way for an end to most of the intra-Lebanese fighting, it had little effect on the situation in south Lebanon. UNIFIL continued to patrol a swath of territory in central south Lebanon but could do little except monitor the regular and quite destructive encounters between the SLA-Israeli forces and the Lebanese resistance. Even with the weakening (but not the disappearance) of PLO authority, the Lebanese government was able to make only a partial advance into the south, partly because of the intrinsic weakness of the Lebanese army and partly because Syria did not wish to allow Christian-dominated Lebanese military units to constrain the Lebanese resistance organizations. Syria actively supported Amal, and it tolerated the Iran-backed Hizballah. UNIFIL thus was unable to accomplish its primary mission.

The UN peace-keepers, however, found themselves performing another, largely unintended function: governance and dispute resolution among the battered civilian population in its south Lebanon enclave (Thakur 1987). But UNIFIL was ill-equipped for such activities, much as they were appreciated by some of the Lebanese inhabitants. There were reports of some UNIFIL personnel getting caught up in the inevitable corruption to be found in a region lacking effective law and order or administrative stability. By 1990 morale within UNIFIL was said to be poor: personnel from some of the nationalities represented were reported to be profiteering and taking kickbacks. UNIFIL's limited mandate and its manifest military weakness prevented it from implementing resolution 425, as it was instructed to do. UNIFIL found that it too had become "just another player" in the Lebanese morass.

In 1979 Lebanon's ambassador to the UN, the noted journalist Ghassan Tuéni, wrote presciently about the difficulties: "UNIFIL was given a *dynamic* role with a *static* description . . . it was given a mandate, but not the power to exercise it . . . UNIFIL further has to act as a *united*, or 'integrated force' (to quote its very terms of reference) for a *disunited* Security Council . . . 'Force without the use of force' is the name of the game, which can only work if the peace-keepers are interposed between 'state-parties', equally committed to the fulfillment of the peace-keeping mandate and not acting in defiance of its objectives . . . In Southern Lebanon, the implicit and silent mandate was to interpose the Force between parties that deny each other even recognition, and will therefore hardly tolerate the most neutral course of action" (Tuéni 1979). Over a decade later, although the demise of the Soviet Union brought more unity to the Security Council, Tuéni's analysis of the contradictions facing UNIFIL within Lebanon remained valid.

A Note on the MNF Intervention, 1982–1984

The Multinational Force in Beirut, as Richard Nelson has observed, "had a violent beginning and a humiliating end" (in McDermott and Skjelsbaek 1991). As noted, the MNF does not meet the criteria for an international organization. Nevertheless, its sad experience does throw some comparative light on the analysis of IO interventions in Lebanon and elsewhere. Indeed, the fact that it was not an international organization probably contributed to its failure. The MNF was put together in haste, as Israeli forces advanced through Lebanon toward Beirut in

June and July 1982. An American diplomat, Philip Habib, was trying to avert an all-out Israeli Defense Force attack on Beirut and the PLO forces entrenched in its southern districts. The Israelis, long suspicious of the UN, were resisting proposals to interpose a UN force (drawn from UNIFIL), and so the United States, France, and Italy—at the invitation of Lebanon's hapless government—intervened, first, to arrange the withdrawal of Palestinian leaders and forces, second, to ensure the protection "of persons in the area," and third, to further the restoration of Lebanese government control over the Beirut area. The first contingents of the MNF arrived toward the end of August, expecting to remain for one month. But having achieved the first objective, the evacuation of the PLO forces, the MNF departed around September 10—two weeks ahead of schedule—without having attended to the other two. The massacre of eight hundred to a thousand Palestinian civilians in the Sabra and Shatila refugee camps by Lebanese Forces militiamen (acting without hindrance from nearby Israeli units) brought the MNF contingents back again at the end of September—too late to protect the luckless "persons in the area" of Sabra and Shatila and with too little force to extend the authority of the Lebanese armed forces and government throughout Beirut.

MNF II, as it came to be called, was the victim of an ill-considered mandate, the conflicting priorities of the United States, French, Italian, and token British components, and above all, a fatally oversimplified understanding of the Lebanese environment. Of the three major interveners, only the Italians succeeded in pursuing the MNF's humanitarian mandate in a nonpartisan way: it helped the frightened and desperate Palestinians without antagonizing any of the Lebanese parties. The French found themselves drawn by their own history and mythology into helping primarily the Christians. The Americans, having unaccountably elevated Lebanon's importance as a U.S. national interest, seemed to believe that the Lebanese government was fundamentally legitimate, needing only a little time and some technical military assistance to expand its authority beyond the presidential palace and the Maronite enclave of east Beirut and the adjacent mountain districts (Fisk in McDermott and Skjelsbaek 1991). They appeared to think that Israel's military presence and Syria's retreat had cut the Gordian knot of the Lebanese conflict, making possible the restoration of a government dominated by the Christian forces and ready to make peace with Israel basically on Israeli terms. This view reflected an inadequate comprehension of both the grievances and the capabilities of the non-Christian Lebanese elements. As Phalangist units swept into traditionally mixed and Druze areas of the Shuf, the Druze began to regroup. As the Israelis began to outlive their welcome in southern

Lebanon, the Shiʿite organizations began to organize resistance. When the U.S. government helped broker an unequal peace treaty between Israel and Lebanon in May 1983, the Syrians—now resupplied by the USSR and resupplying the Druzes, Shiʿites, and other Lebanese allies—moved to reverse the adverse political tide. The American and French MNF units soon became the targets of sniping incidents and several devastating terrorist bombings. Spectacular but clumsy retaliation by American warships only intensified the cycle of violence. Having misread the political equation and the balance of forces, the MNF—now viewed as a pro-Christian, pro-Israeli presence by virtually all the Lebanese parties—had become "just another player," and by February 1984 it was ready to make a humiliating departure.

The Taʾif Accord and the End of the Civil War

On October 23, 1989, after three weeks of negotiation in a luxurious palace in the Saudi Arabian resort town of Taʾif, the sixty-two surviving members of Lebanon's ninety-nine-seat parliament (elected in 1972) reached agreement on a National Accord Document for Lebanon. The Taʾif Accord remains highly controversial in Lebanon, where many Christians feel it brought peace at the price of independence (Maila in Collings 1993). There is general agreement, however, that Taʾif did bring the long civil war to an end. The full story of Taʾif has yet to be written, and when it is, a great deal of credit will go to the Algerian diplomat Lakhdar Ibrahimi, to whose tireless professionalism all concerned attested. The Taʾif process was an IO intervention that worked. It was a diplomatic—not military—initiative organized through the Arab League at the May 1989 Arab summit meeting in Casablanca under the leadership of a tripartite committee consisting of the leaders of Algeria, Morocco, and Saudi Arabia. Formal ratification of the accord did not immediately bring peace. Indeed, there was an explosion of new fighting between Christian General Michel Aoun, who claimed to be head of state, against his rival Samir Jaʿjaʿ, head of the Christian Lebanese Forces militia. But a year later, Aoun had lost that battle and was forcibly ousted from the presidential palace by Syrian army forces and a coalition of Muslim and Christian Lebanese militias. The Taʾif-mandated constitutional reforms had been enacted, a "greater Beirut security plan" was being implemented, and preparations were being made for new parliamentary elections in 1992. Although several major Maronite Christian leaders and parties boycotted the election in their areas, the new parliament was generally accepted as legitimate. A new government was created, headed by a strong Sunni prime minister,

Rafic Hariri, and it energetically set about the enormous task of reconstruction.

What accounts for the relative success of Taʾif compared to earlier interventions? For one thing, the Arab League was less divided than it had been. Syria was mending its fences with Egypt and Saudi Arabia as its Soviet patronage withered away and after rival Iraq's semivictory in its eight-year war with Iran. Indeed, it appears that Syria was a silent partner with the Arab League tripartite committee, notwithstanding its public criticisms of the Taʾif negotiations. Another silent partner was Israel—or, if not a "partner," at least not an obstructor. The United States is thought by some observers to have played an important role in enlisting Syria and Israel at least as "nonobjectors" (Salem 1991).

The importance of such a relatively broad and minimally homogeneous international grouping lay in its ability to influence the contending Lebanese parties. To be sure, a group of the more militant Muslim militias did gather defiantly in Teheran while the Taʾif conference was under way, but their opposition was oblique, directed more at General Aoun than at the Taʾif process per se. Moreover, their ire was tempered by Syria's unspoken interest in Taʾif. For relatively centrist Christian politicians, the presence of Saudi Arabia and Morocco as negotiators perhaps eased their fears about Syria's power. In any event, General Aoun ended up the odd man out, supported only by some army loyalists and a broad but unorganized segment of Christian public opinion. Ranged against him were the major external players, especially Syria and the United States (which Aoun had gratuitously antagonized). His major regional supporter, Iraq, dropped out in August 1990 after its invasion of Kuwait and its subsequent encirclement by a U.S.-led international coalition that included Syria. Aoun therefore was largely unable to intimidate those Christian leaders who had accepted Taʾif to defect later on.

If Taʾif succeeded in part because Muslim militias and movements more or less dependent on Syria could be brought into line, it was also aided by the wave of intrasectarian fighting that broke out following the agreement. A long-simmering cleavage between the army units of General Aoun and the Lebanese Forces of Samir Jaʿjaʿ split Christian ranks. At the same time, the violent rivalry between Amal and Hizballah helped weaken the opposition of the Shiʿites as a community—an important factor in advancing Taʾif since it did not confer very much new power on the Shiʿites. One should note the absence of the Palestinians as an influential organized force. Long-term fatigue was also taking its toll on the Lebanese militias. The collapse of oil prices had reduced some of the external financial aid of some of these organizations. Iraq, Iran, Saudi Arabia, and Libya, all of which at times had supported one faction or another, were in somewhat straitened financial circumstances. Nor was the fast-fading Soviet Union interested in stirring up the Lebanese pot or encouraging Syria to do so. Israel, chastened by its unpopular and unsuccessful intervention of 1982, preferred to "play Lebanon as it is"—but mainly in the "security zone."

Finally, one might observe that there had been an accretion of tacit consensus (or at least familiarity) over the substance of a solution based on many (failed) conflict-resolution projects dating back almost to the beginning of the civil war. The "Constitutional Document" proposal put forth by President Suleiman Frangieh and the Syrians in February 1976 had called for an adjustment of sectarian representation rather than a full abolition of sectarianism. The 1984 meetings of some major Lebanese leaders in Geneva and Lausanne ultimately failed but still showed that agreements between Muslims and Christians on certain reforms were theoretically possible (Faris in Collings 1993). A Syrian-sponsored "tripartite agreement" in 1985 among the Druze, Shiʿite Amal, and Christian Lebanese Forces militias prefigured Taʾif in several respects but collapsed after a coup in the Lebanese Forces leadership. These projects had called for incremental adjustments favoring greater Muslim representation and the eventual gradual abolition of political confessionalism. They had also advanced electoral reforms and some kind of "special relationship" with Syria. These were among the principal features of Taʾif. Familiar old ideas finally found a space. And as Joseph Maila has ironically observed, that space existed in part because of three past failures: the failure of General Aoun's war against Syria, the failure of Syria to impose a solution unilaterally, and the failure of previous international interventions to resolve the conflict (Maila in Collings 1993).

Lessons

The Lebanese experience shows, if nothing else, the difficulties and limitations of IO intervention in complex conflicts in which ethnic cleavages are a key but far from exclusive element. Here are some possible lessons.

First, the duration of the IO intervention should be as short as possible. Diminishing returns set in as time goes on, and the IO risks becoming just another player.

Second, the IO should be cohesive, determined and broad based. If the IO is a regional organization such as the Arab League, the interests of some of its members in the ethnic conflict are likely to differ from or to clash with the interests of other members. Such was the case with the Arab League in 1958 and in 1976–1982. In the Taʾif process, only by skillful diplomacy were these conflicting interests subordinated in a common project, which ultimately achieved considerable success.

Third, non-IO, that is, alliance or ad hoc, interventions would seem to require an overwhelming military presence in order to achieve success. This was the case with the successful U.S. intervention in 1958, and it was clearly not the case in the failed MNF intervention in 1982–1984.

Fourth, IO interventions stand the best chance of success if they occur either at the very beginning of a crisis or after a long period of conflict when the local actors are becoming exhausted. Had the ADF been deployed in the spring or summer of 1975 instead of a year later, perhaps it could have headed off the deepening internal conflict. The Taʾif process succeeded in part because after thirteen years the Lebanese parties could see more clearly the virtues of peace over their diminishing capabilities to make progress through violence.

Fifth, successful IO interventions require a minimum of acceptance on the part of the principal antagonists, domestic and external. Accordingly, diplomacy must be given the highest priority in organizing an IO intervention. Among other things, the objectives of the intervention must be not only clear and limited but also acceptable in principle to the local actors. If a military intervention is contemplated, there needs to have been prior diplomatic negotiation between the IO representative and key players. In 1958 the Lebanese government refused to accept the Arab League conciliation plan, and it had no confidence in UNOGIL. The Lebanese opposition was either noncommittal or indifferent. The unilateral American intervention succeeded not only because it was backed by impressive firepower (which did not have to be used) but also because the U.S. special envoy was able to win the confidence of the army commander, the opposition, and even (reluctantly) the government that had implored the United States to intervene. In the 1975–1990 civil war the ADF, UNIFIL, and MNF interventions did not meet this criterion; only the Taʾif intervention came to be accepted as legitimate (or at least not intensely objectionable) by nearly all the major players.

6

How Peace Keeping Becomes Intervention: Lessons from the Lebanese Experience

Naomi Weinberger

The end of the cold war opened new frontiers for international peace-keeping forces. Five operations were deployed by the United Nations in 1987, but seventeen missions fielding seventy thousand soldiers were in place in 1994. More impressive than the number of forces was the diversity of their missions. While UN peace-keepers continued to carry out traditional tasks, such as patrolling buffer zones between former belligerents, "second-generation" forces often undertook more ambitious mandates. They were called upon to disarm rebel movements, organize elections, and deliver humanitarian relief in hostile situations (Weiss 1993; Boutros-Ghali 1992c; Coate and Puchala 1990; Mackinlay and Chopra 1992; Anderson 1992).

In its classic conception, peace-keeping is the antithesis of intervention. Peace-keepers are supposed to be strictly neutral in their behavior toward parties in a conflict, whereas intervention aims either to alter or to preserve the authority structures of a target state. Moreover, peace-keepers adhere to highly restrictive rules of engagement, using force only for self-defense, whereas interveners have recourse to military means to assist the party they favor in a conflict (James 1990; Rikhye and Skjelsbaek 1991; Skjelsbaek 1989; Diehl 1988; Rosenau 1973; Little 1975; Weinberger 1986).

By these criteria, peace-keeping has been most successful in cases of interstate hostilities, where former belligerents have consented to the deployment of international forces after achieving a diplomatic agreement. Examples include the United Nations Emergency Force in the Sinai Peninsula (UNEF I from 1956 to 1967 and UNEF II from 1973 to 1982) as well as the United Nations Disengagement Observer Force on the Golan Heights (from 1974 until the present). Similarly, the Multinational Force and Observers deployed in the Sinai under American initiative since 1982 has followed the traditional model and performed its mission unchallenged.

More problematic are cases in which international forces are interposed in the midst of a civil conflict. Where civil conflict persists, efforts to adhere to peace-keeping norms are necessarily strained. Impartiality is virtually impossible, for the international force is generally identified with central authorities rather than insurgent forces. Restrictive rules of engagement are breached when "peace-keepers" resort to enforcement measures, whether to fulfill their designated mandate, to restore stability, or to fill the vacuum of authority in the troubled state. Even if those who sent the international force or those participating in it wish to maintain neutrality and avoid the use of force, the environment militates against these intentions.

As a result, to fulfill their mandate international forces may easily be drawn into enforcement actions better labeled as "collective intervention" (Luard 1984). Tensions and ambiguities may arise when the authorizing mandate of the force does not anticipate such eventualities, and when there is insufficient political will on the part of troop contributors and interested parties to broaden the terms of the force's mandate. In the first such instance, the Congo mission deployed by the United Nations in 1960-1964 aroused intense controversy between the superpowers and engendered wariness about deploying international forces in civil conflicts (Hoffmann 1962; Lefever 1967; O'Brien 1962).

Nonetheless, in the wake of the Lebanese civil war that began in 1975, unilateral interventions by neighbors were followed by the deployment of two distinct international forces. The experiences of the United Nations Interim Force in Lebanon (deployed from 1978 to the present) and the Multinational Force in Beirut (1982-1984) reveal many of the potential pitfalls of collective intervention and provide lessons that may be usefully applied to the new challenges facing peace-keepers in the post-cold-war era.

Choice of Auspices

One reason that the Lebanese case is so interesting to students of international organization is that the modalities of intervention in this conflict varied in accordance with regional and international trends. The first instance of unilateral intervention in the civil war that began in 1975 was initiated by Syria and subsequently gained the regional sanction of the Arab League. The loose bipolar system of the mid-1970's was permissive of intervention by aspiring regional powers, especially in areas marginal to superpower interests. Accordingly, Syria could intervene in Lebanon in 1976 without significant constraints by either its Soviet patron or the United States.

Syria's motives for intervening in Lebanon were both bilateral and transnational. On the bilateral level, Syria wished to ensure that Lebanon would emerge from its civil conflict with a government that was congenial and deferential to Syria, avoiding the dangers of victory by either the Lebanese right (which might partition the country along ethnic lines, prompting contagious ethnic unrest in Syria) or by the Lebanese left (which might trigger an unwanted confrontation with Israel through its support for the Palestine Liberation Organization). On a transnational level, Syria sought to assert its own dominance over the PLO, which was using Lebanon as its major base of guerrilla operations against Israel. Syria demanded that the PLO sever its identifications with the goals of the Lebanese left. The PLO's refusal to comply led to an all-out military conflict between Syria and the PLO from June to October 1976.

Until June 1976, the Arab League, as the regional organization authorized to express consensual Arab goals, neither sanctioned nor condemned Syria's unilateral intervention in Lebanon. Implicitly recognizing the paramountcy of Syria's claim as the regional power with the deepest interests in Lebanon, other Arab states advanced support for contenders in the Lebanese conflict but did not challenge Syria's initiative. Only after Syria launched its attack on the PLO did the Arab League respond to a plea by Chairman Yasir Arafat, deciding in June on "the formation of symbolic Arab security forces under the auspices of the Secretary General of the Arab League . . . to replace the Syrian forces," (Khywayri 1977, 2:369–71). Yet only token forces from several Arab states were deployed alongside the thirty thousand Syrian troops then in Lebanon.

The cease-fire agreement mediated by the Arab League in October 1976 called for a cessation of Syria's onslaught against the PLO and a reaffirmation of the right of the guerrilla organization to operate in southern Lebanon. Syria's forces in Lebanon were now designated as part of an Arab Deterrent Force, which was supposed to have other Arab troop contributors and to be funded by the Arab League. The practical effect of this decision was to grant Syria's unilateral intervention the imprimatur of regional legitimation, as well as financing. In fact, troop contributions by other Arab states were limited and short-lived, whereas Syrian forces continued to be deployed in a "peace-keeping" capacity in Lebanon (primarily in the eastern Bika and the north) in the mid-1990's.

The second unilateral intervention in Lebanon's civil conflict was initiated by Israel in 1978 and precipitated the deployment of UNIFIL. Israel's motives for intervening in Lebanon were transnational, responding to guerrilla raids launched by the Palestinian Resistance (the PLO and associated guerrilla groups) against northern Israel. The Litani Operation conducted by Israel in March–June 1978 was the culmination of a long-standing reprisal policy against Palestinian raids, which had intensified with Syrian encouragement in early 1978.

The decision to create UNIFIL was taken by the Security Council on March 19, 1978, four days after the Israeli invasion began. Resolution 425 defined UNIFIL's objectives as "confirming the withdrawal of Israeli forces, restoring international peace and security and assisting the government of Lebanon in ensuring the return of its effective authority in the area." The United States took the initiative for UNIFIL's creation for reasons UN undersecretary-general Brian Urquhart characterized as follows: "When UNIFIL was put in in 1978, why was there this wild enthusiasm on the part of the United States? . . . Because they were bang in the middle of the Camp David process, . . . and the process could not go ahead if nothing was being done about the Israelis in south Lebanon" (interview with author, January 20, 1983).

The introduction of United Nations peace-keeping forces as a mechanism for reversing unilateral intervention by an external power had many precedents. Indeed, Israel's occupation of the Sinai in 1956 was reversed through the deployment of the first UN Emergency Force (1956–1967). Its reoccupation of the Sinai in 1967 was partially reversed after the October 1973 war with the introduction of UNEF II (1973–1982). Then, Israel withdrew from a segment of the Golan Heights, occupied in 1967, and the UN Disengagement Observer Force was created in 1974.

Ostensibly, therefore, in deploying UNIFIL the United Nations was acting within a long tradition of using a buffer force to separate former combatants in an interstate conflict. The critical difference was that Lebanon was still immersed in civil conflict. The absence of central government authority, especially in southern Lebanon, presented special dilemmas that were not adequately anticipated by the framers of resolution 425. When the Security Council indicated that one of the UNIFIL's objectives was "assisting the government of Lebanon in ensuring the return of its effective authority in the area," it woefully underestimated what the fulfillment of that condition would entail.

Why, after Israel again invaded Lebanon in 1982, was the UN by-passed in favor of a multilateral peace-keeping force? This decision reflected a broader trend toward multilateralism during the 1980's, rather than a specific reassessment of the peace-keeping mechanism. The United States especially was disenchanted with the United Nations and other intergovernmental organizations and therefore had increased recourse to multilateral diplomacy to tackle security dilemmas and seek international economic cooperation. This trend was reflected, for example, in the formation of the Namibia Contact Group and in the Contadora peace process in Central America (Karns 1986 and 1987). The American renunciation of UN leadership need not be attributed to an overall decline in American hegemony, but rather to a calculated preference for mobilizing more congenial groups to address specific issues (Haas 1986).

In a departure from previous practice, the United States recruited ten national contingents to participate in the Multinational Force and Observers (MFO) in the Sinai, as part of the 1979 peace treaty between Israel and Egypt. In this case, multinational auspices were chosen by default, in view of the threat of a Soviet veto in the Security Council for establishment of a UN peace-keeping force. American decision-makers viewed the smooth initiation of the MFO as an auspicious precedent when they decided, in the aftermath of Israel's 1982 invasion of Lebanon, to send a multinational force to Beirut in cooperation with Italy and France. Yet the Sinai precedent was actually irrelevant because of fundamental contextual disparity between the MFO buffer operation and the Beirut civil strife arena.

In a decision to deploy an international force, context—that is, the nature of the conflict environment, whether interstate or intrastate—is the critical variable in determining whether the operation will be able to adhere to traditional peace-keeping norms of neutrality and restrictive rules of engagement. United Nations buffer forces, such as those in the Sinai and the Golan Heights, lived up to these criteria throughout their deployment. The Sinai MFO, too, adhered to the same model. By contrast, UNIFIL, the UN operation in the Congo, and to a lesser extent the UN Force in Cyprus (1964–present), deviated from peace-keeping ideals because of the troubled circumstances of civil strife in which they were deployed.

Yet the choice of auspices may independently affect the capacity of international forces to conform to peace-keeping norms, especially in a context of civil strife. Indeed, multinational auspices accentuate the propensity to become embroiled in collective intervention. An ad hoc operation lacks the restraints imposed by international organizations through adherence to precedents or established decision-making mechanisms. An absence of precedents may allow greater flexibility to a multinational force, but it also permits partisanship and fosters an impulse toward military engagement.

In Lebanon's civil conflict, the composition and mandate of the Multinational Force in Beirut (in its two incarnations, August–September 1982 and September 1982–February 1984) reinforced its tendency to identify with incumbent Lebanese authorities and increasingly to act in their behalf. A contrast between the missions and conduct of UNIFIL and the Beirut MNF underscores the relative effects of the auspices of peace-keeping operations.

The missions of UNIFIL and the MNF, though both served in Lebanon, were not symmetrical. The distinctions were already evident in the circumstances leading to the creation of each force. For one thing, Israel's objectives in invading Lebanon in 1982 were much farther reaching than those of the Litani Operation in 1978. By 1982 the security threat posed by the PLO stemmed from its buildup in conventional capabilities to the north of UNIFIL's area of operation. Moreover, Israel now had a second, bilateral goal: to influence the outcome of Lebanon's imminent presidential elections to bring to power Bashir Jumayyil, who had vowed to curb PLO influence in the country. This time, Israel was an overt intervener, intent on transforming the authority structures of the Lebanese state. A third objective of the Israeli invasion was to challenge and possibly remove Syria's sphere of influence in Lebanon (Schiff and Yaari 1984; Rabinovich 1984; Yaniv 1987).

In pursuit of these objectives, Israel exceeded the scope of its 1978 march into southern Lebanon, proceeding north to the outskirts of the Lebanese capital. It was Israel's siege of Beirut in August 1982 that precipitated the American efforts to create the MNF. U.S. special envoy Philip Habib negotiated agreements leading to the introduction of American, French, and Italian forces to oversee the evacuation of Palestinian guerrillas from the capital. The precipitous withdrawal of these peace-keepers sixteen days later was followed by massacres in Palestinian refugee camps, and a second Multinational Force was hastily introduced.

By virtue of its presence in the capital, the Beirut MNF was more inclined to become embroiled in Lebanon's civil conflict than was UNIFIL. UNIFIL's mission was restricted to southern Lebanon, which had long been removed from central government control; whereas the second Beirut MNF sought to help the Lebanese government repossess its fundamental sphere of authority. Thus, it was more likely to become engaged in enforcement actions on behalf of the central government against its domestic opponents.

Moreover, the auspices of the MNF predisposed it to greater inter-

ventionist tendencies than a UN force would be expected to display.
Aside from the greater partisanship that Western states contributing
troops might display, the operational guidelines of the force allowed
greater discretion to individual unit commanders than would be possible under the unified command structure typical for a UN force. Moreover, once the MNF came under challenge, the military capabilities
available to the great powers could be called upon, as opposed to the
meager capacities of most UN forces.

Given that a multinational force is more prone to collective intervention and less likely to conform strictly to traditional peace-keeping
norms, intervention is not necessarily harmful in a given context. If a
state is unable to resolve civil strife on its own and the combatants
prove unreceptive to IO peace-keeping, collective intervention may be
preferable to unilateral intervention. As opposed to unilateral interveners, which often act without invitation or authorization, collective interveners gain legitimacy through invitation by recognized authorities
in the target state. Further, a general preference for United Nations
rather than multinational auspices arises from the greater legitimacy
associated with the decisions of a universal international organization
(Thakur 1987).

The critical issue, therefore, is not so much whether an international
force ought to intervene in civil conflicts but whether the sponsors of
the force adequately anticipate the challenges inherent in its mission.
What must be assessed is the effectiveness of peace-keeping operations—that is, the ability of an international force to carry out its assigned mission in conformity with its mandate. In a civil conflict
environment, troop contributors need consensual rules of engagement
and predictable mechanisms for coordination, to be able to respond to
dynamic circumstances. Neither UNIFIL nor the MNF was able to perform effectively, largely because the framers of the mandates for each
force underestimated the challenges posed by Lebanon's environment
of civil strife.

Determinants of Effectiveness

The highly variable scenarios encountered by international forces—
in terms of both context and auspices—impede systematic comparison
and analysis. Nevertheless, I believe it is possible to predict or assess
the effectiveness of any international military operation by identifying
five critical variables. Hypotheses may be advanced about the circumstances that would maximize force effectiveness with respect to each
of these variables.

One set of determinants is contextual. They define the environment within which a military operation functions and the magnitude of its task. The first and most important is consent of the parties. The degree of cooperation advanced by the host state or states (in an interstate conflict) is a major determinant of force effectiveness. Where civil strife is still intransigent, the parties (incumbents and insurgents) necessarily have different stakes in cooperating with, or undermining, an international military operation. In these circumstances, force effectiveness may be correlated with the legitimacy and relative strength of the incumbent authorities, as well as the degree to which the international force is identified with the central government. For example, if the host government is weak and its legitimacy contested and the international force is heavily committed to its support, insurgents will have a strong incentive to undermine the force mission.

The second contextual variable is the degree of peace-making that occurs prior to the introduction of the force and during its deployment. Without preliminary diplomatic efforts, an international force cannot be created and from this perspective, peace-making is a precondition to peace-keeping or collective intervention. Ultimately, success in peace-making terminates the need for the military operation, whereas a breakdown in diplomacy undermines the minimal consensus necessary for sustaining the mission of the force.

There are, in addition, three operational variables relevant to the assessment of an international military operation. Definition of the mandate is vital, and one may postulate that peace-keeping norms are more readily applied to static than to dynamic mandates. Insofar as a mandate is dynamic, effective implementation requires consensual and predictable means for interpretation and possible redefinition.

Second, there must be mechanisms for coordination among troop contributors. On an operational level, coordination is maximized by formation of a unified command structure. Several subordinate hypotheses specify conditions promoting cooperation in an international military venture, including a unified command structure; balanced distribution of influence and political heterogeneity among force contributors; compatible foreign policy interests in participating in the operation; and equitable sharing of costs and casualties.

Finally, the capabilities of an international military operation should be sufficient to ward off challenges to the integrity of its area of operation. For peace-keeping missions, adequate capabilities should be coupled with strict and restrictive rules of engagement. If troop contributors choose to redefine their mission and pursue enforcement actions, they will require precise consensual rules of engagement in order to pursue collective intervention with maximal effectiveness.

One might argue that instead of looking for determinants or measures of effectiveness, one should ask what variables will determine the outcome of the operation, its success or failure. Enormous subjectivity is involved in the interpretation of outcomes, however. Some mandates are far more ambitious than others. Comparison requires us to examine initial expectations and how these expectations evolve during the life cycle of a force.

An emphasis on vantage point—generating subjectivity in the assessment of international military operations—stems from the question of *who* is assessing performance, with what expectations and what stake in the outcome. A variety of perspectives must necessarily be taken into account: first, the parties to the (interstate or civil) conflict; second, other regional actors, as well as interested superpowers; third, troop contributors, whose impact scholars consistently underrate; and fourth, the sponsoring international organization or multinational group. Success in the eyes of one may spell failure for the other. Another problem is that the outcome of the mission is usually judged according to the success of peace-making diplomacy. If stability is achieved, observers tend to say that the international force succeeded because its presence provided the conditions for the fortunate diplomatic outcome, implying a causal connection that may not necessarily exist.

Another methodological dilemma surrounds the differential effects of context and auspices on force effectiveness. The problem here is that the choice of auspices may itself be conditioned by perceptions of the setting in which the operation will take place. An IO such as the United Nations may be precluded from involvement in an interstate or civil conflict if an enabling resolution is blocked by the veto of a member of the Security Council (as in the case of the threatened Soviet veto of a United Nations force in the Sinai to monitor the Egyptian-Israeli peace treaty) or by the unwillingness of parties to a conflict to submit the issue for consideration by the international organization (as is often the case when Third World states experience civil conflicts and as also occurred for much of the duration of the Iran-Iraq War). Once the UN has authorized creation of an international force, however, there has rarely been difficulty in recruiting troop contributors, subject to the organization's guidelines for geographic diversity and screening by the host state. Even in the case of the Congo, where the UN force engaged in heavy-handed enforcement actions and sustained heavy casualties, a wide variety of troop contributors participated without protest.

By contrast, perceptions of physical and political risk appear to weigh more heavily in decisions to participate in a multinational undertaking. In view of pervasive Arab criticism of the Camp David accords and the resulting Egyptian-Israeli peace treaty, the United States had great difficulty recruiting participants for the Multinational Force and Observers, even among its European allies. For this buffer force, according to Scott Gudgeon, legal adviser to the MFO, risk perceptions declined as the peace process stabilized and no challenge was mounted its presence (interview with the author, November 1984).

In the Beirut Multinational Force, on the other hand, risk perception grew dramatically as the force came under challenge. The MNF troop contributors—the United States, France, Italy, and subsequently Britain—clearly underestimated the dangers. Although there is no basis for concluding that the choice of multinational (rather than UN) auspices was made in anticipation of higher risks, one may argue that once a commitment to participation has been made, troop contributors are more prone to engage in intervention under multinational auspices (James 1984).

Contextual Variables

It is worth making a general observation, however simplistic, that the easier the task assigned to an international force, the greater the chance of performing that task effectively. Contextual variables define the setting within which a force functions and the magnitude of the task it must perform. In addition to the type of conflict in which it is interposed (whether interstate or civil), the magnitude of a force's task is determined by two other parameters: the intensity of the conflict and the stage of combat (which affects the will of combatants to persist).

The two contextual variables—consent of the parties and the degree of progress in peace-making—may be viewed as preconditions to the creation of an international force. As dynamic factors, these variables continue to be redefined throughout the peace-keepers' mission, down to the moment when their contingents withdraw.

Consent of the Parties

Consent of the parties is the paramount determinant of effectiveness as well as the prime distinguishing characteristic between operations. Who are the parties to an agreement to deploy an international force? When the parties are states, as in the case of former belligerents, the degree of cooperation advanced by the host state or states is crucial. For example, as long as Egypt and Israel supported the mission of UNEF I in the Sinai, the operation performed flawlessly; conversely, the withdrawal of Egyptian support in May 1967 doomed the peace-keeping effort (Elaraby 1983; Comay 1983).

Amid civil strife, by contrast, an international force rarely enjoys the support of all parties to the conflict. If incumbent authorities request the deployment, insurgents may view the force as partisan and seek to undermine it. This polarization of attitudes is more likely if the operation is committed to support the host government and to perform functions (for example, army and police functions) that the challenged authorities cannot. The more contested the legitimacy of the central government, the more the outsiders' commitment negates the appearance of neutrality between the parties to civil strife. This condition is unique to civil conflict; for a buffer force, neutrality connotes impartiality between former belligerents, rather than between actors within one state (Forsythe 1969).

Who were the relevant parties in Lebanon whose consent was necessary for UNIFIL and the Multinational Force to carry out their tasks effectively? One must emphasize that by 1978, Lebanon was not merely a state in which insurgents were challenging the legitimacy of incumbent authorities. In effect, Lebanon had experienced a total collapse of state authority, including the complete disintegration of the army, during the 1975–1976 civil war. After the October 1976 cease-fire took hold, the authority of the central government was primarily confined to the vicinity of Beirut, and even there it was beholden to the backing of Syria's Arab Deterrent Force. In the rest of the country, partisan militias exercised control in diverse spheres of influence. When one refers to the consent of Lebanon's central government to the deployment of either UNIFIL or the Beirut MNF, therefore, it is important to bear in mind that the government was merely one among many players, and in each case it viewed the introduction of the international force as a means of strengthening its own position vis-a-vis a variety of domestic contestants.

The weakness of Lebanon's central government was less critical to the functioning of UNIFIL than to the operations of the Beirut MNF. After all, UNIFIL was initially deployed to facilitate the withdrawal of Israeli forces from southern Lebanon and, in that sense, resembled the classic interstate or buffer forces previously deployed by the United Nations. UNIFIL then evolved into a hybrid interstate-intrastate force, insofar as its ability to carry out its functions was impeded by the environment in which it served. Yet because its mission was not intrinsically linked to the fate of the central government, there was no strong incentive for opponents of the regime to target UNIFIL. Instead, UNIFIL faced the challenge of coping with the efforts of local actors within southern Lebanon to circumvent or undermine its authority within its own sphere of influence.

From the outset, geographic contraints impeded the mission. Israel refused to permit its deployment up to the international border, having embarked on Operation Litani with the declared intention of setting up a six-mile-wide "security belt" to prevent terrorist infiltration. At the end of its phased withdrawal from the Litani, Israel turned over the border enclave not to UNIFIL but to a renegade Lebanese officer, Major Sa'd Haddad. Further geographic limitations were posed by the UN decision to restrict UNIFIL's area of operation to positions that had been occupied by the Israel Defense Force. The coastal city of Tyre, which had not been penetrated, remained a PLO stronghold, and most subsequent attempts at guerrilla infiltration through UNIFIL lines originated in the "Tyre pocket." By the same principle, seventeen PLO and Lebanese National Movement emplacements were permitted to remain within UNIFIL's area of operation.

In this geographic environment, the parties whose consent UNIFIL needed in order to perform its mission effectively were not states but nonstate actors—either subnational (such as Haddad's militia) or transnational (such as the PLO). Each, in turn, was linked in a network of relationships with interested regional powers. Major Haddad served as an Israeli proxy, depending on Israel for economic, military, and logistical support. Yet he insisted that his militia was protecting the local population in the south from PLO raids, rather than providing a "security belt" for the Israeli north (interview with author November 29, 1982). On several occasions, Haddad tried to enlarge his enclave, and his militia often harassed UNIFIL soldiers.

The PLO, in turn, received Syrian acquiescence and at times encouragement for its operations in southern Lebanon. After the Syrian-PLO confrontation in 1976, the October cease-fire confirmed Palestinian freedom of operation in the south, an area understood to be off limits to Syrian forces as a result of a tacit agreement on "red lines" between Israel and Syria. Syria actively supported Palestinian guerrilla activities after a Syrian-PLO rapprochement, which followed the Egyptian president Anwar Sadat's diplomatic overtures toward Israel in 1977.

When Palestinian infiltration occurred through UNIFIL lines, the peace-keeping force was limited in its ability to respond. Timur Guksel, a UNIFIL spokesperson recalled:

> We kept catching the same guys in most cases. . . . You are risking your life in a way. . . . it's risky at night; you can get shot easily, a lot of people did get shot. So you catch this guy, take his gun away and take him out of the UNIFIL area. . . . But the thing is, your

hands are tied. . . . I don't assert the sovereign powers of the country. I catch him, there's nobody to turn him over to, I take him out of UNIFIL area and let him go. . . . I usually give him a ride back. It became so ridiculous, the morale of [the]soldiers was being affected. (Interview with the author, October 26, 1982)

Guksel's complaint that "there's nobody to turn him over to" captured the essence of UNIFIL's dilemma. Faced with an impotent central government, UNIFIL became locked into a static conception of its role, as a buffer between Haddad's enclave to the south and a PLO-controlled zone to the north. In effect, the most significant Palestinian military emplacements were not within the UNIFIL area—where no artillery was permitted—but in a zone north of the Litani River virtually controlled by the PLO. Palestinian guerrillas and their leftist allies in the Lebanese National Movement also controlled a series of checkpoints leading to Beirut, site of the PLO's political headquarters.

If UNIFIL was primarily a buffer, the mission of the Beirut Multinational Force closely linked its fate to the viability of the Lebanese central government. In this case, a peace-keeping operation in a weak state extended a broad commitment to assisting the government in restoring stability within its capital. The Lebanese army was clearly not prepared to undertake this task; so MNF contingents undertook to train the Lebanese army. Ultimately, the MNF was drawn into serving as a substitute army in combat against the regime's opponents. Even before this process came to full fruition, opponents of the regime were challenging the basic mission of the force, which was so closely identified with the regime. At first the aim was to discredit it totally, and finally it was targeted directly.

Undoubtedly, the erosion of domestic Lebanese consent for the deployment of the Beirut MNF was related to its auspices as an operation composed of Western contingents whose governments supported the regime of President Amin Jumayyil. It is important to emphasize that disenchantment with the MNF was not manifested until months after its deployment. Initially, the operation appeared to be popular, according to Ghassan Tuéni, former Lebanese ambassador to the United Nations: "People seem to be agreeable to an American-sponsored force, and tend to trust it more. Even the so-called enemies of America—I mean the leftist parties and the Palestinians—seem to be very agreeable to having American guarantees and assurances. They think the multinational force is more credible and they think the Americans will be fair and will protect them, even against a Lebanese army that is, in all candor, still debatable." (interview with author, November 8, 1982).

Why did the MNF's honeymoon end? The cause may be traced to the increasing unpopularity of the government it supported. The near-unanimous election of Amin Jumayyil to the presidency by the Lebanese parliament, shortly after the assassination of his brother in September 1982, created an illusory image of consensus. Over time, it became clear that many elements in Lebanese society viewed the president as a minoritarian figure. Ruling through the Maronite-dominated Kataʾib (Phalangist) party, Amin Jumayyil perpetuated a regime based on Christian privilege and avoided serious efforts at national conciliation.

In these circumstances, opponents of the regime in the Druze and Shiʿa communities became increasingly disenchanted with Jumayyil, and they received strong regional backing from Syria and Iran. The Druze community, more homogeneous and more geographically concentrated, also had more definable leadership in the person of Walid Jumblatt. Jumblatt was primarily supported by Syria, but he kept channels of communication open to Israel as well.

The Shiʿa, by contrast, posed a more fundamental threat to the regime because they were less homogeneous than the Druze and there was no single person to talk to in seeking their cooperation. Not only did the Shiʿa lack a unified leadership, but their grievances in different geographic sectors—be it the Bika or the south or Beirut—were different grievances. This community was mobilized in a way that was potentially dangerous both to the regime and to the Multinational Force because its members engaged in less conventional tactics of opposition, including terrorism. Shiʿa dissidents were also supported by outside actors, including Syria as well as Iran.

As dissent against the Jumayyil regime increased, Lebanese authorities hoped that the MNF would be willing to engage in enforcement actions, ultimately including combat with the regime's opponents. The more President Jumayyil came under challenge, the more he tried to use the Multinational Force in this way and the more he succeeded in getting the MNF to act in this way. In the escalation that ensued, the MNF's mission could no longer be defined strictly in peace-keeping terms. In the fall of 1983, when the American battleship *New Jersey* provided artillery backing for the Lebanese army in its fight with the Druze, this could only be construed as intervention.

Progress in Peace Making

Progress in peace making is the key to determining the life cycle of an international force. Such ventures cannot be initiated unless some peace making has already occurred—the consent of key actors won and a lid placed on the intensity of the conflict. The degree of peace making which precedes deployment of an international operation determines how difficult the mission will be. In the absence of sufficient peace making to secure the consent of all relevant parties—that is, those capable of disrupting the mission—one may expect enforcement measures to be required eventually.

Yet, if peace making were fully successful, the international force would be unnecessary, its presence superfluous. In theory, at the point that peace-making succeeds, the force should be withdrawn. One rationale for introducing an international force into a conflict (whether interstate or civil) is that its very presence will facilitate the resolution of underlying conflicts. Ironically, however, in the case of buffer forces, there is inevitable tension between a static force mission and dynamic diplomacy. If the presence of peace-keepers engenders a tolerable status quo, the incentive for aggressive diplomacy declines. A frequent critique, for example, of the United Nations Force in Cyprus, is that its effect has been to freeze the conflict between Greeks and Turks, rather than resolve it (James 1989).

What are appropriate expectations for diplomacy during the tenure of an international force? Who is best suited to conduct the diplomacy—the sponsors of an international force (providing parallel diplomatic auspices) or an alternative negotiator? It seems to me that it is desirable to separate the auspices of peace making from those of peace keeping. If the identity and sponsorship of the peace-keepers is distinct from those of the mediators charged with resolving underlying disputes, there is a better chance of insulating the one from a negative outcome to the other.

The two multinational operations under American sponsorship in the Middle East reveal the pitfalls of parallel auspices for peace-keepers and diplomats. On the surface, the success to date of the Multinational Force and Observers in the Sinai may seem to vindicate parallel auspices, since the framers of the Camp David accords for peace between Israel and Egypt also negotiated the MFO's mandate. In the event that anti-American (or broader anti-Western) dissent became pervasive in Egypt or led to a change of regime, however, the status of the American-dominated MFO could well be jeopardized.

The Beirut Multinational Force was also a product of American diplomacy. As usual, the expectation was that the peace-keepers' presence would facilitate further negotiations, ultimately creating a situation in which the MNF would no longer be needed. Instead, what actually transpired was that the American-negotiated accords of May 17, 1983, between Lebanon and Israel called into question the neutrality of the American-dominated Beirut MNF. Conversely, participation in the MNF, whose activities were viewed as progressively more partisan in favor of Lebanese incumbents, weakened the ability of the United States to pose as an honest broker.

In the case of UNIFIL, it is curious that the customary expectations of a link between peace keeping and peace making were not raised at the time of deployment. The twin expectations of Security Council resolution 425, that Israel would withdraw its forces to the international border and that the Palestinian resistance would cease its guerrilla attacks against Israel, were both unfulfilled. Yet the United Nations did not activate a diplomatic response as long as the level of violence in southern Lebanon remained at a tolerable level and UNIFIL performed its buffer function relatively well.

It was only in spring 1981, after violence escalated in Lebanon, that mediation was tried. The United States responded to a "missile crisis" prompted by Syria's introduction of SA-6 missiles into the Bika, by sending Special Envoy Philip Habib to dissuade Israel from carrying out its threat to remove the missiles by force. Then, in July 1981 violence in southern Lebanon rose when the PLO unleashed artillery and rockets from north of UNIFIL lines against Israeli settlements in Galilee. Israel responded with unprecedented air strikes along the Litani and Zahrani rivers and in Beirut. Diplomacy then occurred under dual auspices, when a July 24 accord was concluded by Philip Habib with Israel and by Secretary-General Kurt Waldheim with the PLO. This device was necessitated by the absence of U.S. diplomatic relations with the PLO. Although the accord was not a formal cease-fire agreement, it endured remarkably well, and in the eleven months prior to the second Israeli invasion, the UNIFIL commander, General William Callaghan, reported, "incidents were minimal in UNIFIL's area of operation, infiltration was minimal, and the incidents from Lebanon into Israel that year were none" (interview with author, November 9, 1982).

UNIFIL's record reveals the pitfalls in relying on a peace-keeping force as a stopgap when the underlying conflict is unresolved. Once Lebanon's two powerful neighbors contested each other's spheres of influence in the strife-torn country, negating the "red lines" agreement that had tacitly governed their conduct since 1976, southern Lebanon was an easily available playing field for their competing ambitions. More fundamentally, as long as Lebanon's civil conflict simmered and the country lacked the institutions (army and police) vital for asserting the central government's authority, the peace-keeping force was operating in a vacuum that invited penetration by external interveners.

Operational Variables

Defining the Mandate

The mandate of an international force is defined by the sponsoring intergovernmental organization or multilateral group. Mandates may be differentiated in terms of their clarity and precision and the expectations of parties to the conflict and troop contributors when they embark on the mission. Interpretation of an operation's mandate depends in part on whether it is static or dynamic. In a dynamic environment, there must be consensual and predictable means to interpret and modify a mandate once a mission comes under challenge.

In this respect, conventional IO auspices present considerable advantages. The means for interpretation of United Nations force mandates reflect consensual organizational procedures. After an initial mandate is set through a resolution of the Security Council (or, occasionally, the General Assembly), a decision to redefine the mandate or provide new instructions requires a new enabling resolution.

In UNIFIL's case, the peace-keepers settled into a static conception of their role, and no initiatives were taken to modify the original mandate. Yet Security Council resolution 425 did include a dynamic component charging UNIFIL with assisting the government of Lebanon in restoring its authority in the south. In one serious effort to implement this responsibility, UNIFIL attempted to incorporate units of the Lebanese army into its area of operation. It did so pursuant to a new Security Council resolution authorizing the pursuit of this objective. Ultimately, two Lebanese battalions did reach the south, although their incorporation in UNIFIL's operational command rather than in an autonomous zone reduced their effectiveness as a symbol of the reconstruction or empowerment of the Lebanese army (Weinberger 1983, 350–54).

For an ad hoc multilateral operation, the means of interpreting or revising a mandate are rarely clear-cut. The definition of the mandate of the Beirut Multinational Force was encumbered by the peculiar circumstances at the force's inception. MNF I performed its task expeditiously in supervising the withdrawal of PLO fighters from West Beirut in the wake of the Israeli siege of August 1982. Despite written American guarantees for the security of non-combatants remaining in Palestinian refugee camps, this responsibility was never publicly acknowledged as part of the mandate of MNF I. When the peace-keepers withdrew after sixteen days, they declared that they had successfully performed their mission, but withdrawal created a legacy of bitterness among the Lebanese when the Sabra-Shatila massacres rapidly followed. Former Lebanese prime minister Saʾib Salam charged: "Without any formal notice, they [the Americans] withdrew against the engagement they gave us and they gave the Palestinians. . . . They left too soon and they were responsible no doubt for those massacres, horrible massacres" (interview with author, November 9, 1982).

The fatal flaw in creating the reconstituted Multinational Force was that it was introduced in a crisis atmosphere right after the massacres. The contributors simply resurrected the framework of MNF I, superimposing it on the new situation without redefinition. Using the same basic diplomatic instruments—bilateral exchange of letters between troop contributors and the Lebanese government—the new mandate envisioned a vague function of helping the Lebanese government restore "sovereignty and authority over the Beirut area." As opposed to the firm end point of thirty days originally designated for MNF I, no target date was set for its successor's departure and there was no criterion by which to determine when the mission of the force was complete. It was entirely open-ended.

The MNF had no mechanism analogous to Security Council resolutions for redefining its mandate. There was much ambiguity, yielding a progression from naive optimism at the beginning that the MNF could maintain a low-profile commitment to a situation in which, as civil strife in Lebanon rose, a new level of commitment could not be defined. Since the existing level of commitment was not viable, each individual troop contributor was faced with a stark choice: either to withdraw or to escalate. They could not maintain their existing positions, and they had no systematic mechanism for redefining their commitment.

A fundamental characteristic of the Beirut Multinational Force was its dynamic nature, its progressive redefinition. Although turning points may be identified, they were defined by the outside environment, by diplomatic and military developments in Lebanon and in the region which were not intrinsic to the Beirut force but affected its capacity to function. The first, a diplomatic development, was the May 17, 1983, accord negotiated by the United States between Israel and Lebanon, which was unpopular in Lebanon and opposed by Syria. The accord clouded the environment in which the MNF functioned. The second, and critical military development, was the unilateral Israeli withdrawal from the Shuf mountains in September 1983. Although this occurred south of the Beirut locale where the MNF was deployed, it changed the perception of Lebanese parties toward the Multinational Force. Renewed civil strife in the Shuf strained the resources of the Lebanese army, and American backing of the Lebanese army in its combat with Druze dissidents undermined the MNF's posture of neutrality. A final development, decisively wounding the already weak force, was the attack on the American and French compounds in October 1983. It was then only a matter of time before the MNF withdrew.

The mission of the MNF was dynamic because diplomacy had failed, and the consequences of this failure were reflected in the deteriorating environment for the international operation. Yet diplomatic success might also have led to an expansive, dynamic mission. As proposed by the Lebanese government and backed in principle by the United States, a diplomatic agreement for the withdrawal of Syrian and Israeli forces from Lebanon would have led to an enlargement of the Multinational Force and its area of deployment. In many ways, the dynamism of a mandate for collective interveners directly responds to the outcome of the civil conflict they aspire to contain.

Coordination

Coordination is the variable for which the choice of auspices of a peace-keeping force makes the greatest difference. To understand why, it is necessary to distinguish between operational factors promoting effective coordination within a force and factors promoting an image of neutrality.

On an operational level, coordination is maximized by formation of a unified command structure. In theory, a force under either IO or multinational auspices could fulfill this requirement. In practice, UN forces have consistently imposed a joint command; multinational forces have not always done so. Other relevant operational variables are the distribution of influence among troop contributors; willingness to share costs and casualties; and compatibility of foreign policy objectives.

The image of neutrality fostered by traditional peace-keeping forces is best promoted by political heterogeneity among troop contributors. The United Nations has pursued this goal through the principles of balanced geographic distribution among troop contributors and the conscious exclusion of great powers and states with a direct foreign policy interest in the outcome of a given conflict. The geographically balanced force, however, may suffer somewhat in its operational effectiveness because of differences in military traditions and training among units.

UNIFIL's experience substantiates these generalizations. UNIFIL benefited from a clearly defined chain of command. The commander of each contingent reported to the force commander, who in turn reported to the UN secretary-general. Any major dispute over how the mandate should be interpreted or proposal for redefining it required a decision by the Security Council.

Nonetheless, variations among contingents selected on the basis of balanced geographic representation led to considerable diversity in practice. The French battalion, which became involved in intense clashes with Palestinian guerrillas, was deemed "overqualified" for its peace-keeping duties and left within one year. A French logistical unit was subsequently invited to guard UNIFIL headquarters, which had come under attack by Major Haddad, after which Haddad never again ventured to attack the site. The Fiji battalion, stationed alongside the Tyre pocket, earned a reputation for toughness in dealing with guer-rilla infiltrations and suffered many casualties as a result. By contrast, the Senegalese were known to be lax in supervising the PLO, and the Nepalese became quite cozy with Haddad's militia. Thus, unified command did not always translate into standardized practice.

On the surface, it may seem that whereas the political homogeneity of the Beirut MNF detracted from an image of neutrality, the compati-bility among Western-trained military units should have enhanced op-erational effectiveness. There are several reasons why it did not, the most important of which was the absence of a unified chain of com-mand. The MNF was really three (and, once a small British contingent joined, three and a half) forces, each essentially making its own strate-gic decisions. Whatever mechanisms there were for cooperation—such as daily liaison committee meetings—were merely tactical. The lack of strategic coordination reflected disparity in the objectives that led each of the countries to contribute its forces to the MNF.

Several subordinate hypotheses may be advanced to account for the diversity of incentives and mechanisms for coordination in an interna-tional venture. First, asymmetry of influence among troop contribu-tors, especially domination of a force by a single country, is antithetical to effective coordination, unless there is consensus on a unified com-mand structure led by the dominant state. For the MNF, asymmetry was reflected in American domination of the mediation setting the initial frame of reference for the operation. Over the longer term, the United States had disproportionate influence over the regional actors, and therefore local parties turned to the United States to resolve the conflict. The French were sensitive about American domination, con-cerned that France might be seen as following the American lead. In the Italian case, this concern was most pronounced among the Com-munists (then members of the ruling coalition), who were uncomfort-able about participating in an American-dominated force.

Second, incentives for coordination are determined by whether troop contributors have compatible foreign policy interests at stake in an international operation. Do all participants see the host state as intrinsically important? In this case, Lebanon was not intrinsically im-portant, but the outcome of the Lebanese conflict would tangibly affect the regional policies of the Americans and, to a lesser extent, the French. Is participating in peace-keeping operations considered valu-able in its own right (as, for example, among Scandinavian nations, which have a tradition of contributing to UN forces)? This perception was not manifested either in the United States or in France. The Italians, for their part, indicated that participating in the MNF was important because they were being taken seriously and consulted by NATO allies and because it furthered the recent emphasis in Italian foreign policy on a more active Mediterranean posture (interviews with Egidio Ortona, former Italian ambassador to the United States, November 8, 1984, and Dr. Maurizio Cremasco, Istituto Affari Internazionali, November 7, 1984). None of these incentives had anything to do with the intrinsic value of peace-keeping.

Finally, coordination is promoted if troop contributors are willing to share costs and casualties fairly evenly. This factor depends primarily on domestic decision making in each contributing state. On an operational level, one relevant question is who serves in the international force. Are they conscripts? Are they volunteers? Are they professional soldiers? Are they Foreign Legion? All these factors influence sensitivity to casualties. For example, if troops are derived from the French Foreign Legion, not only are they professionals, but they may not even be French. Obviously, if an eighteen-year-old Italian draftee is killed, public reaction is different than if a French Foreign Legion soldier is killed.

In addition, how do the professional military personnel in each country feel about the value of the peace keeping? Do they think the experience is useful, for training purposes? There is quite a variation in attitudes among contributors, based in part on what their other opportunities are for training in a foreign environment. Finally, how important is the professional military in domestic decision making? To illustrate, the record shows that the American military consistently opposed participation in the MNF. By contrast, the Italian military was very enthusiastic, seeing the venture as invaluable training and as an opportunity to raise the institutional stature of the Italian army.

The policy implications of willingness to sustain costs and casualties for a force with a dynamic mandate boil down to a question of whether each contributor is willing to take risks. The Lebanese government continually urged that the MNF be expanded to be sent to the Shuf, to the Beirut-Damascus Highway, to any areas from which Israeli or Syrian forces might depart. It was clear that if any of these developments came to pass, the French were more likely to go than the Americans or the Italians.

Would the coordination problems have been resolved by introducing a unified command? Neither French nor Italian spokespersons showed any enthusiasm for a joint command structure as long as the force served under multinational auspices. As a French official at the UN declared, "The best solution is if you have one commander for all the forces under the umbrella of the UN. . . . I cannot imagine the MNF under one commander. Impossible. . . . The only obstacle is the Americans; they can't go to the UN umbrella" (interview with author, March 1983). At issue was the traditional policy of the United States barring participation in military operations under foreign command.

Capabilities

A final determinant of effectiveness is capabilities. In optimal circumstances, an international force has sufficient capabilities to ward off challenges to the integrity of its area of operation, coupled with restrictive rules of engagement for the use of those capabilities. UN forces have frequently been derided for lacking heavy weapons, that is, "teeth." A multinational force, by contrast, especially with great power contributors, has greatly enhanced capabilities. The relevant question is whether superior military capabilities play a deterrent or provocative role.

One may note that UNIFIL's image of weakness did not primarily stem from a lack of adequate military capabilities. The reason, instead, was the ability of both Palestinian guerrillas and Haddad's militia to encroach on UNIFIL's area of operation with relative impunity. The restrictive rules of engagement by which UNIFIL was bound, permitting soldiers to fire only in self-defense, prevented them from taking the initiative in pursuing encroachers.

UNIFIL's reputation was further undermined when it failed to resist the Israeli forces that overan its positions on June 6, 1982. Hasan ʿAbd al-Rahman, director of the PLO Information Office, declared: "They should have employed their capabilities in trying to stop the Israeli invasion. Whether they would have succeeded or not, that's a totally different question. But at least they should have made that effort" (interview with author, March 9, 1983). But Timur Guksel of UNIFIL objected that any attempt to resist the Israelis would have led to heavy casualties: "So you're losing [many UNIFIL] soldiers, for what? For delaying the Israelis fifteen minutes? Symbolically, I wish there was more we could have done, but militarily speaking, it's suicidal" (interview, October 26, 1982).

Undoubtedly, UNIFIL's image of weakness explains the Lebanese government's advocacy of multinational auspices for the new peace-keeping force deployed in the wake of the Israeli invasion. President Jumayyil hoped that the Western troop contributors would possess greater deterrent capabilities. Ultimately, Bassam Torbah, political counselor to the Lebanese Embassy in Paris, reported, Lebanese officials were disappointed and bitter that the MNF contingents were unwilling to escalate their military backing for the Lebanese army (interview with author, December 14, 1984). Nevertheless, the possession of heavy weapons, coupled with inconsistent rules of engagement for the MNF, became a recipe for escalation. Arguably, possession of visible military capabilities in the field, as well as heavier offshore weapons at the disposal of the Americans and the French, made the Multinational Force "vulnerable to attempts to provoke retaliation" on the part of dissident groups eager to disrupt the status quo (Heilburg and Holst 1986).

Inconsistent rules bred disparate behavior among contingents. For example, when the Italians were asked to join the Lebanese army in house-to-house searches in west Beirut in October, 1982, they refused because, said General Franco Angioni, former force commander of the Italian contingent, they were unwilling to seize weapons from Muslims but not from Christians, as was the Lebanese army plan (interview with the author, November 5, 1984). The French, by contrast agreed to participate in searches. An official of the French Foreign Ministry later indicated that local commanders had acted without consulting the ministry, that they had been reprimanded for insubordination and never did it again (interview, December 1984). The fact remains, however, that the French did participate. The lack of clear rules of engagement help explain why a local commander could agree to a request of this sort from the Lebanese army.

Another issue was the difference in retaliatory measures by the French and the Americans after their MNF contingents came under attack in summer 1983. French spokespersons insist that when they bombed Syrian forces in the Bika, they did so in direct retaliation for attacks upon them; whereas when the Americans unleashed the battleship *New Jersey*, they were inappropriately intervening in civil strife. The Lebanese did not always see these fine distinctions. In both cases, it looked like intervention to those on the other side of the barricades.

The experience of the Beirut MNF reveals that an emphasis on capabilities—insofar as it focuses on the availability of weapons—is a spurious issue in predicting the effectiveness of an international force. The relevant issue, instead, is the willingness of troop contributors to engage in enforcement actions in implementing their mandate. In cases of civil strife, nonetheless, the impression of military strength may affect the perceptions of those with an interest in disrupting the force—tending either to deter or to provoke.

Lessons for a New Era

At the time that UNIFIL and the MNF were deployed, Lebanese civil strife appeared to be an aberration. The degree of fragmentation in

Lebanese society, featuring conflict among seventeen recognized sects as well as within individual sects, was unusually complex. Moreover, the internationalization of the conflict, precipitating unilateral interventions by both neighbors and collective intervention by extraregional actors was rare for such a small country, especially one that was not considered strategically vital in the cold war.

Yet the patterns of instability unleashed in many parts of the world once the cold war ended make the lessons of the Lebanese experience more relevant than ever. Lebanon seemed to be an extreme example of Third World conflict in the 1970s and 1980s, but developments in the early 1990s provide ample analogies not only in the Third World but in Europe and the former Soviet Union. Ethnic particularism has intensified both in habitually fragile states and in states previously considered viable which have recently disintegrated (Helman and Ratner 1992; Ryan 1990b; Goodby 1992).

Simultaneous with these manifestations of disorder, an increasing consensus arose that the United Nations should be empowered to cope more effectively with civil conflicts as well as international disputes. The remarkable popularity of the peace-keeping mechanism in the years since 1988 gave rise to an unprecedented number of new operations. Whereas some resembled traditional buffer forces, the prevalence of ethnic strife bred conditions whereby international forces increasingly engage in collective intervention.

Secretary-General Boutros Boutros-Ghali, in *An Agenda for Peace*, suggested an ambitious set of guidelines for the new generation of peace-keeping forces, the most ambitious of which he described as "peace-enforcement units:"

> The mission of forces under Article 43 [of the United Nations Charter] would be to respond to outright aggression, imminent or actual. . . . This task can on occasion exceed the mission of peace-keeping forces and the expectations of peace-keeping force contributors. I recommend that the [Security] Council consider the utilization of peace-enforcement units in clearly defined circumstances and with their terms of reference specified in advance. . . . They would have to be more heavily armed than peace-keeping forces and would need to undergo extensive preparatory training within their national forces. (Boutros-Ghali 1992a, 26–27)

Indeed, Boutros-Ghali portrays missions entailing different degrees of risk which might oblige United Nations troops to engage in enforcement actions. These include the provision of protection to humanitarian relief, military assistance to civil authorities, and maintenance or restoration of cease-fire agreements that may be breached by the signatory parties.

Such diverse and complex peace-keeping missions will have to modify both the contextual and the operational premises of traditional operations if they are to function effectively. In the context of civil strife in a fragmented society, it is not possible to assume or rely upon consent of all the relevant parties, either at the time of deployment or during the life cycle of the force. If peace-keepers are invited by incumbent authorities, they may be asked to neutralize the opposition of insurgents to their mission, and they must determine what kinds of enforcement actions may be undertaken in those circumstances. Moreover, identification with one side in a civil conflict will engender an image of partisanship that makes it impossible to serve as an honest broker in mediating the underlying conflict (Weiss 1993, 58–59).

On an operational level, undertaking missions that may require escalation under challenge gives rise to heightened demands for dynamic mandates, consensual mechanisms for coordination, and adequate but discreetly deployed capabilities. In the assessment of Thomas Weiss, such missions will "require a level of military professionalism and discipline not commonly found in previous UN peacekeeping operations. They would necessitate participation by the armies of major powers. Accomplishing the tasks in these operations would go far beyond both the expectations and the capacities of most countries that have contributed troops to UN peacekeeping operations during the Cold War" (Weiss 1993, 61).

The perceived necessity of including the forces of major powers in peace-keeping efforts raises the issue of the auspices under which they might serve. Even as the United Nations becomes more favorably disposed to the inclusion of great power troop contributors than it was in the past, the willingness of these states to serve under UN command is still questionable. The traditional policy of the United States, of allowing its forces to serve only under American command, was reaffirmed after its bruising experience of peace keeping in Somalia (Peck 1994).

Of the "second-generation" peace-keeping missions, the United Nations Operation in Somalia (UNOSOM) most closely resembled the experience of the Beirut Multinational Force. As in the Lebanese case, peace-keepers entered a turbulent civil conflict with an open-ended mandate to assist in the reconstruction of the country. After displaying a similar pattern of escalated commitment followed by abrupt withdrawal of troop contributors, UNOSOM was no more able than its Lebanese predecessor to address the fundamental causes of the Somali conflict.

The peace-keeping operation in Somalia experienced a curious switch from multilateral to United Nations *auspices* in mid-course. The Bush administration initiated the operation as an emergency relief mission in December 1992. After three years of civil war in which over 500,000 Somalis died in combat or from famine, the United States mobilized a multinational force to provide security so that relief agencies could supply food to starving people. President Bush announced, however, that the United States was willing to command the force for only a short time, and the United Nations assumed command of the operation in May 1993 with a Turkish commander in charge. The United States retained a logistical unit of twenty-seven hundred persons under United Nations command. Since this was not a combat unit, the UN command was not considered a departure from traditional practice. The deputy commander of UNOSOM was an American, moreover, and a Quick Reaction Force of thirteen hundred was attached to UNOSOM, while remaining under exclusive American command.

The unusual arrangements whereby the United States achieved a prominent role in a UN force reflected the enthusiasm of the newly elected American president Bill Clinton for participation in UN peace-keeping, under a policy of "assertive multilateralism." Yet the image of an American-dominated force quickly became problematic in the Somali civil setting, for reasons analogous to the image of partisanship of the Beirut MNF.

One comparable problem was the ambiguous *definition of UNOSOM's mandate*. Just as the MNF mission evolved from a clear mandate for the evacuation of Palestinian guerrillas from Beirut to a far-reaching pledge of restoring stability in the capital, UNOSOM found its mission changing from humanitarian relief to active military enforcement. When the United Nations assumed control from the Americans, the Security Council embraced an open-ended commitment to the reconstruction and rehabilitation of the war-torn country, which was to culminate in the supervision of democratic elections in 1995. Yet once UNOSOM's expanded mission came under challenge, it quickly sought to enforce its mandate by military means.

Upon entering Somalia, UNOSOM could neither seek nor achieve *consent of the parties* to the local conflict. By the time of its deployment, Somalia did not possess even the meager trappings of central government authority that Lebanon could boast in 1982. In conditions of political anarchy, rival clan leaders with small local followings battled each other. The multinational and UN forces that entered Somalia, therefore, did so without a local invitation, on the grounds of humanitarian intervention. As long as the peace-keepers' efforts were concentrated on supervising relief efforts, they enjoyed local popularity. Only when the UN declared that reconstruction required active efforts to disarm the supporters of rival warlords did the climate change.

At this point, a confrontation evolved between one prominent clan leader, General Mohammed Farah Aidid, and the United Nations force. Aidid, who commanded a mere three hundred to five hundred lightly armed fighters in the capital city of Mogadishu, resisted the UN efforts to disarm them. In June 1993, Aidid's fighters ambushed and killed twenty-four Pakistani peace-keepers, and the United States responded with strikes by its Quick Reaction Force, supported by air power, against Aidid's positions. In a report to the Security Council in August, Secretary-General Boutros-Ghali declared that responsibility for growing hostilities against UN troops "rests squarely with the faction leaders, in particular Mohammed Farah Aidid." He asserted that disarmament of the various clan-based factions "is indispensable for the establishment of peace and security in Somalia" (*New York Times*, August 19, 1993, A3).

A lack of consensus about the redefinition of UNOSOM's mission gave rise to serious problems of *coordination among troop contributors*. Despite the existence of a unified command over the twenty-three-nation force, disagreements over objectives led to cases of insubordination. The most serious incident involved the dismissal in July 1993 of the commander of the Italian contingent after he insisted on waiting for instructions from Rome rather than obey the United Nations commander. The underlying issue was Italy's objection to what its defense minister described as the "Rambo tactics" of the UN in targeting General Aidid. Italy feared that these moves would widen the war and turn the local population against UNOSOM. As the former colonial power, Italy claimed to possess greater insight into Somali politics and society and advocated continued negotiations with Aidid and renewed emphasis on the humanitarian relief effort (*New York Times*, July 12, 1993, A5, July 15, 1993, A8, August 15, 1993, A12).

Nonetheless, over the coming months the Clinton administration expressed determination to continue the pursuit of General Aidid. In so doing, the United States drew upon its superior military *capabilities*. That the Quick Reaction Force operated outside of UNOSOM's chain of command increased the temptation for the United States to take unilateral measures. The use of American forces in targeting Aidid's positions in Mogadishu in July 1993 was followed by the introduction of an elite unit of Army Rangers whose mission was to target the Somali warlord. Yet on October 3, a disastrous raid against Aidid's top aides led to heavy American losses, with eighteen dead and seventy-five wounded. This turning point, analogous to the bombing of the American marine barracks in Beirut in October 1983, led to a change of heart by the Clinton administration. Under heavy congressional pressure, the president announced a phased withdrawal of American forces over the next six months, which was completed by March 31, 1994.

This tale is sadly reminiscent of the demise of the Beirut Multinational Force. Because Somalia, like Lebanon, was not considered vital to the strategic interests of the United States, once the risk of casualties became high and the mission began looking like an indefinite quagmire, it was likely to be terminated. Yet because of its choice of auspices, UNOSOM was not immediately doomed by the American departure. Although other Western troop contributors left along with the United States, a force of nineteen thousand remained in place, drawn from Third World countries.

In its latest incarnation, UNOSOM reverted to its initial emphasis on safeguarding the delivery of humanitarian relief in Somalia. Secretary-General Boutros-Ghali announced that the force would continue to serve until March 1995. The long-term contribution of UNOSOM to stability in this troubled country would ultimately depend on the link between *peace-keeping and peace making*. The United Nations made many attempts to foster reconciliation among Somalia's competing warlords and to negotiate arrangements for a transitional government and national elections. On March 22, 1994, the leaders of all fifteen Somali factions, including General Aidid, signed a Declaration of National Reconciliation agreeing in principle to the formation of an interim government. The declaration did not spell out the distribution of power for a new government, however, and there were grounds for pessimism that a viable agreement would emerge.

In retrospect, UNOSOM erred in striving to foster Somalia's reconstruction without an adequate commitment by troop contributors or reliable partners within Somali society. The cases of Lebanon and Somalia illustrate the perils of introducing peace-keepers in ongoing civil conflicts. Nations that send their forces into a strife-torn society had best be prepared to sustain the costs of collective intervention, or else refrain from participating in such missions in the first place.

PART III

The Case of Yugoslavia

7

Historical Roots of
the Yugoslav Conflict

V. P. Gagnon Jr.

Because protagonists in Yugoslavia themselves refer to ethnic differences to justify their resort to warfare, it is perhaps understandable that at first glance the conflict would seem to be the result of such differences, especially inasmuch as outside observers, and IOs in particular, did not turn their attention to Yugoslavia until fighting had already broken out along ethnic lines. But the Yugoslav conflict, far from being an outburst of "ancient ethnic hatreds," was the purposeful creation of specific sectors of the country's political elite, which provoked conflict along ethnic lines (Žižek 1993; Cerović 1993; Banac 1992a).

This strategy was employed by those parts of the elite most threatened by social, political, and economic trends within Yugoslavia which were militating toward radical restructuring of the political and economic system. By diverting political discourse away from the issue of reform toward alleged threats posed to the "nation" (in an ethnic sense) and by provoking violent conflict along ethnic lines, these conservative forces managed to overcome the opposition of liberals within the Communist party and then opposition forces outside of it (Gagnon 1994).

Of course, the nature of the party-state system, the depth of the

Research for this paper was funded by the Social Science Research Council-MacArthur Foundation Fellowship on Peace and Security in a Changing World.

social and economic crisis, and the alternatives being proposed by reformers all ensured that any radical change would be fiercely contested. Moreover, several characteristics of the Yugoslav system made compromise very difficult, exacerbating the contest and allowing conservative forces to push the country toward violence along ethnic and national lines.

First, the concentration of power in and the relative autonomy of the local (commune)-level apparatus gave elites there great influence in the republics. At the same time, the structure of economic and political power at the local level and the nature of that power (bureaucratic position rather than "ownership" of property) meant that radical economic and political reform was most threatening to those local elites.

Second, the confederal structure of the country, virtually without an autonomous center, meant that conflict resolution depended on the willingness of republic-level elites to reach consensus and to abide by joint decisions.

Third, the "national" character of the federal units meant that conflicts among and between republic-level elites could be portrayed in "ethnic" or "national" terms.

Fourth, the special role of the JNA, the Yugoslav People's Army (Jugoslovenska Narodna Armija), in the Yugoslav system, in particular its privileged position, its active participation in political issues, and its stated role as defender of the internal "socialist order" put it on the side of those most opposed to change.

These characteristics, taken together, created a dynamic that enabled conservatives to respond to the threat of radical change with a strategy of ethnically based violent conflict.

Setting the Stage

Since the very concept of a Yugoslav state has been at the center of the current conflict, a review of the first Yugoslav state, the Kingdom of Serbs, Croats, and Slovenes, founded in December 1918, provides some insight into the political currents that helped shape the structures I have outlined. The main axis of conflict in this first Yugoslav state was between political elites in Croatia (including both Croats and, after 1927, Serbs) and in Serbia, and it was the result of different conceptions of what the new joint state of South Slavs should be.

Prior to World War I the lands that came to make up Yugoslavia were divided between the Kingdom of Serbia and the small independent Kingdom of Montenegro, which together included only 35 percent of the total population of the future Yugoslav state (and whose joint population was only 65 percent Serb); and lands inhabited by South Slavic peoples in the Austro-Hungarian Empire (divided between Croats, with 37 percent of the population in the Habsburg lands; Serbs, with 26 percent; Slovenes, 13 percent; and Slavic Muslims, 8 percent). These included the Slovene-inhabited provinces in Austria, Dalmatia, the provinces of Croatia-Slavonia and Vojvodina, and Bosnia-Herzegovina, a former Ottoman province that had been occupied by Austria in 1878 and annexed in 1908. All these lands had been parts of two empires that based political participation and representation on principles of nationality: language in Austria-Hungary, religion in the Ottoman lands. Since political elites had, prior to the formation of Yugoslavia, operated on the basis of these national distinctions, both in the Austro-Hungarian Diet and in Serbia and Montenegro, the political relevance of national sentiment did not disappear in the new state.

As it became clear near the end of World War I that the Austro-Hungarian Empire (which, along with Germany, had fought against the Allies, including Serbia) had disintegrated, its South Slavic population faced the likelihood that Italy would seek to annex formerly Austrian lands. Drawing on the nineteenth-century romantic Illyrianist or Yugoslavist ideal of a state of all South Slavs, representatives of the empire's Croat, Serb, and Slovene elites agreed to join the Kingdoms of Serbia and Montenegro to form a new South Slavic state. In Serbia itself, the ruling Radical party had sought as its main war aim unification of lands with significant Serb populations, in particular Bosnia-Herzegovina and Vojvodina, and an outlet to the Adriatic. With the loss of its tsarist patron to the Russian revolution, however, and under pressure from the Western allies, Belgrade reluctantly agreed to the creation of a state that would also include territories inhabited by Croats and Slovenes.

Yet although the principle of a joint state was accepted, its form and essence were unresolved at the moment of unification. This disagreement over the nature of the new state, not its multiethnicity, was the main reason for the conflict between Belgrade and Zagreb. The Habsburg Slavs, especially the Croats, saw the new state as an equal partnership with the Serbian kingdom. In contrast, the Serbian Radicals and much of the political elite in Serbia, citing Serbia's enormous sacrifices during the war (including the loss of one-fourth of its population and 40 percent of its army) treated the new lands as conquered provinces annexed to Serbia. The Serbian regime's attitude also undoubtedly derived from the demographics of the new state, 65 percent of whose population was located in the Austro-Hungarian lands. A fear of being swamped by the more populous and economically developed Habsburg lands was thus not without foundation. The *conquérant* attitude was reinforced by the fact that the empire's South Slavs had fought in the Austro-Hungarian army against Serbia and the Allies during the war. Thus, for example, most officials and officers who had served Austria-Hungary were barred from serving the new state, and those who were allowed were accepted in a humiliating way (Banac 1984, 150–53). Such an attitude on Belgrade's part rapidly produced disillusionment and dissatisfaction among elites of the former empire.

Non-elites, too, quickly became dissatisfied, as Serbian army units were called in to put down peasant revolts in the chaotic days after the empire's dissolution and as unfamiliar Serbian laws and regulations were rapidly imposed on the Habsburg lands (Banac 1984, 129–32, 248–60). This non-elite sentiment was particularly important because the new Yugoslav state had extended universal male suffrage into the new territories. The political elites during the empire, and thus those who had arranged the Yugoslav union, had been selected on a very restricted basis of suffrage. Now, the new political importance of the peasantry strengthened the hand of the Croatian Peasant party (HSS), which had previously been marginal.

The HSS, which with universal suffrage became the largest single party in Croatia-Slavonia, had initially been the lone voice among representatives of the empire's South Slavs to raise objections about the rapid and unplanned unification. In particular the HSS had been a strong partisan of a peasant republic and had vigorously objected to imposing the Serbian monarchy. Now that the HSS had become a major factor in the political dynamic of the state, the Radicals' attempts to force through ground rules for drafting the new constitution, which included a pledge of loyalty to the monarchy, served only to further undermine support for the joint state among Croats. Indeed, the HSS boycotted the constituent assembly, which was therefore able to pass a centralist constitution. The HSS, which in both the 1923 and 1925 elections won the second largest number of seats in parliament (21 percent of the total), eventually accepted the Yugoslav state and even joined a Radical-led government. But the assassination of the HSS's founder, Stjepan Radić, on the floor of parliament by a Montenegrin deputy and the subsequent suspension of democratic institutions and imposition of a strong authoritarian dictatorship by the king in January 1929 marked a further deterioration of relations. Although the government, working with the HSS, agreed in 1939 to the formation of a separate Croatian federal unit (banovina) with a degree of autonomy, the onset of World War II and Germany's attack on Yugoslavia in the spring of 1941 deprived the new arrangement of a chance to overcome the past conflicts.

Although the main conflict in the first Yugoslavia could be described as a national one, between divergent social and economic interests of the elites of the two regions, it would be a mistake to describe it as being purely "ethnic," as Serbs against Croats. Indeed, the leader of Croatia's Serbs, Svetozar Pribićević, who in the first years of the new state had been one of the most outspoken and forceful advocates of a unitarist and centralist Yugoslav state, by the late 1920s was actively cooperating with the HSS and denouncing the Belgrade government for purposely inciting conflicts between Serbs and Croats and for labeling any Serb who disagreed with the government as a "traitor to the Serbian people" (Boban 1973, 36–38). Pribićević's Independent Democrats, the main political party of Croatia's Serbs, after 1927 formed with the HSS the Croat-Serb Coalition, running a single slate of candidates in the 1935 and 1938 elections against the official Belgrade-sponsored party. The Independent Democrats also as early as 1929 called for federalization of Yugoslavia, and in 1939 openly supported the creation of the Croatian banovina (Roksandić 1991, 129–32).

So while nationality politics and even differing national ideologies played a role in the conflict, it was not mainly an ethnic conflict. The weakness of the interwar Yugoslav state, and the main source of political conflict, was the disagreement over the nature of the state and the disregard by the center of the need to compromise and to integrate the 65 percent of the population in the Habsburg lands, especially its elite—Slovene, Croat, and Serb—into the joint state.

Thus when German forces entered the country in April 1941 and set up the Independent State of Croatia (which included Croatia-Slavonia, parts of Dalmatia and Vojvodina, and all of Bosnia-Herzegovina) many Croats saw it as liberation from Belgrade's dictatorial control. But when the HSS refused to collaborate with the invaders, the Germans and Italians installed in power a marginal political group, the Ustaše, whose leaders had been living in exile. The Ustaše pursued a narrowly chauvinist Croatian line that was strongly anti-Yugoslav and anti-Serb, and massacres of hundreds of thousands of Serbs (as well as Jews and Gypsies) followed. This reign of terror, along with harsh authoritarian rule, alienated much of their initial support among Croats (Jelić-Butić 1978).

The main opposition to the Ustaše was the communist-led multiethnic Partisan movement, which because of the massacres had a natural base of support among Croatian and Bosnian Serbs. But it also included large numbers of Croats and Muslims. Notably, Serbs in Croatia joined the multiethnic Partisans rather than the Serbian nationalist Četniks (who were loyal to the Belgrade regime in exile).

The Second Yugoslavia

The communist Partisans, under the leadership of Josip Broz Tito, were thus faced with a nationalities question that was as much regional as it was national. It had arisen out of the political dynamics of the previous twenty-five years and had been exacerbated and given an ethnic element by the Ustaše massacres and Četnik reprisals. The Yugoslav communists sought to resolve this question through economic growth and modernization and through repression of overt expression of narrowly chauvinistic nationalisms.

Yet national sentiment had in the past been central to political discourse, and it could not be ignored or changed overnight. Since the communist Partisan forces relied on the support of the wider population and drew its members from that population, these considerations were crucial to gaining and maintaining power. For example, given Croatia's experience in the first Yugoslavia (an experience shared to some extent also by other groups), the communists could not have gained the degree of support they did by calling for the renewal of a unitary, centralized Yugoslav state. The key challenge was to channel these national sentiments into an all-Yugoslav context.

In order to rebuild Yugoslavia, the Partisans stressed how the interests of each nation and region would be best met in a joint state, but a state radically different from the first Yugoslavia. Thus during the war, the Partisans were organized on regional lines, and each regional unit was led by local commanders (for example, see Irvine 1993). This basically local and regional character of the Partisan movement and the need to maintain genuine support were important factors in the federal structure of the new Yugoslav state, proclaimed in November 1943. The main concern of the new regime, however, was economic development, especially since economic growth was seen as the key not only to overcoming national and regional antagonisms, but to consolidating power domestically.

The Yugoslav communists, once in power set up an economic and political system closely modeled on the Soviet system. Its basic features were an economic model in which "social (the ruling class or group) and political (monopoly of power) considerations prevail over economic ones, forcing the economy to function according to vested social and political interests" (Brucan 1987, 91). This system "required an enormous political edifice to provide the decision making and the push, the regulation, supervision and coordination" of the economy (Bialer 1980, 19).

The 1948 excommunication of Yugoslavia from the Soviet bloc brought greater reliance on domestic popular support, which had begun to erode with the rapid introduction of the Stalinist economic system. Although this change necessitated a modification of the model (including a new ideological justification stated in terms of "workers self-management"), the main change was not in the political nature of economic decision making but in the location of that decision making. The central government stopped making detailed local decisions,leaving them to the republic or commune level.

The Yugoslav economy enjoyed tremendous rates of economic growth throughout the 1950s, when greater inputs automatically translated into greater output. Yet just as in the rest of the socialist world, this extensive growth model had begun to reach its limits by the end of the 1950s and indeed had begun to have a negative impact on economic growth (Bilandžić 1979, 305). The negative effects were exacerbated in the Yugoslav case by the tendency of decentralization to promote autarkic development at the republic level, a further drain on economic efficiency.

Yugoslav reformists believed these problems could be solved by shifting to economic criteria as the basis of economic decision making. If decisions were based on market signals rather than political criteria, resources would be used more efficiently, with an eye to the "profit" or return. This shift to economic criteria would also combat republic-level autarky, since market mechanisms, for example, in capital investment, would ignore political boundaries and help to integrate the entire country. This reform would also alleviate regional differences, which exacerbated interrepublic conflicts, and it would respond to the changing social structure of the country, with the growing number of workers with technical and other professional skills.

These policies were adopted by the party in 1964, and implementation began in 1965. But this apparent victory for reformists was actually the start of a deep-seated conflict between two visions of the Yugoslav political and economic system, which cut across national and regional boundaries—one based on the Stalinist command-economy model, the other seeking to alter that model radically. This conflict, which would continue for almost thirty years, was the main cause of the destruction of the Yugoslav state. Indeed, the conservative backlash against the 1960s reforms not only exacerbated economic difficulties and worsened interrepublic relations, it also set in place structures that made reform incredibly difficult at a time when the economic environment, including the global recession of the late 1970s (which hit Yugoslavia particularly hard because of its reliance on an export strategy and its large foreign debt), made radical reform even more urgent. Four factors in particular made change quite difficult and provided conservatives with the motivation and ability to respond with violent conflict along ethnic lines.

Local structure of power

Although resistance to change in both the 1960s and the 1980s was seen at all levels, the most vigorous opposition came from local-level party bureaucracies. The primacy of economic criteria over the previously dominant political criteria rendered many political decision makers at the local level irrelevant, especially since their main credential was often participation in the Partisan forces rather than any knowledge of economics. Indeed, reform posed such a great threat exactly because their source of power, prestige, and economic security came not from "owning" anything but rather from their position within the bureaucracy and their resultant control over resources. This threat held not only for local government and party officials but also for managers of enterprises that could not survive in a competitive market environment. Reform involved a transfer of power from elites whose power depended on political position to elites whose power rested on economic expertise. Losing the battle over reform thus meant losing everything. Those officials who had few qualifications other than ideological orthodoxy or party connections were therefore willing to fight vigorously against reforms that struck most deeply at the local structure of power.

In the 1960s the threat to conservatives was especially dangerous because the reformists who headed the republic-level communist parties were very popular among the wider party membership (and also among the wider population), and they moved to mobilize the party membership against the bureaucrats in attempts to deprive them of their institutional and ideological bases of power (Gagnon 1992, 467–74, 579–84). In the face of this threat conservatives in the party and the army successfully fought back by raising the specter of Croatian nationalism, thereby persuading Tito to crush the reformists. Despite strong resistance in all the republics' central committees, Tito purged the Croatian reformists, then the Serbian and other reformists, and reversed the very parts of the reform that were to provide the integratory mechanism: reliance on economic criteria and market forces. The result was the reentrenchment of local-level bureaucrats and the reinstatement of political criteria as the basis for economic decision making. Local commune (*opštine/općine*)-level bureaucrats gained enormous power: they chose enterprise directors, approved or denied expansion and investment plans, enforced ideological decrees, and collected all taxes.

When debate over radical reform again burst into the political arena in the early 1980s, the reformists once again took aim at exactly these powers. But unlike the 1960s focus on instituting economic criteria for decision making within a state socialist system, the early 1980s focus was the introduction of capitalist features, including greater reliance on private enterprise. The political reforms, which included multicandidate, secret-ballot elections for party and state positions, also resurrected the threat that reformists might oust conservatives through popular mobilization. When in 1990 multiparty elections were held, conservatives faced an even greater threat, as opposition parties and even some communist parties openly called for the full restoration of a capitalist system. Conservatives in Yugoslavia from the early 1980s onward were thus in effect threatened with the possibility of immediate extinction, and had a strong motivation to try to prevent such change. The confederal structure of the country and the "ethnic" character of the republics and provinces were the key factors that provided them with the ability to block these changes.

Confederalization

An integral part of the 1960s reform was decentralization of federal-level functions to the republics and provinces. Although conservative forces in the army and security services, along with local-level conservatives, rallied behind Aleksandar Ranković (Tito's second in command) and tried to sabotage the reform, these centralizing forces remained a minority, even in the Serbian party. Indeed, the outspokenly reformist leadership of the Serbian party, which had very strong support in the republic's central committee, argued just as strongly as the other republic leaderships for minimizing the role of the federal center and maximizing the power of the republics (Perović 1991; Burg 1983, 195).

The result was the 1971 constitutional amendments, which provided the six republics and two provinces with maximum autonomy. The federal organs became in effect a committee of republican representatives, with matters of federal jurisdiction decided by consensual agreement among the eight federal units. The center's role was to ensure the conditions for a single market, including enforcement of contracts, workers' rights, money supply, credit and banking, and ownership and property rights (Burg 1983, 205). This combination of federal-level ground rules for market relations and independent enterprises operating according to economic criteria was meant to integrate the country's republics and regions and to lessen regional disparities.

But, as seen, the purges of 1971–1972 attacked exactly this mechanism of economic integration, recreating and re-empowering local-level party organizations, and lodging local decision making with them. Yet the confederalization of the country remained and was included in the new 1974 constitution. The result was eight statist autarkic units with very limited interest in creating a common economic space or cross-republic economic activity beyond trade in commodities. Since decisions at the federal level required consensus, the success and stability of the state depended entirely on the sincere willingness and desire of the various republic and province leaders to compromise in order to reach solutions. It also required a common political language about the overall goals for the country as a whole.

As long as Tito was alive, his authority was an extrasystemic factor that could force actors to accept changes that were harmful to their interests. But the economic crisis that was triggered by the global recession of the late 1970s and Yugoslavia's huge foreign debt burden ($20 billion by the early 1980s) meant that at the very time this extrasystemic factor disappeared (Tito died in May 1980), the pressures for change were greatest. Especially given the chasm between conservatives, who argued for a return to Marxist orthodoxy and centralism, and reformists, who advocated further radical reform of both economy and politics, the consensual system soon ran into problems. Since each republic or province was in effect a unitary actor at the federal level, those interests that controlled a republic's communist party determined the express interests of the republic at the federal level. And among the constituents of the republican leaders were the local-level bureaucrats, whose attitudes toward reform were thus important in determining the balance within the leadership.

In the early 1980s reformists dominated in Slovenia and Vojvodina, which were the more developed regions, but also in Serbia, whose economy was very much split between underdeveloped regions in the south and more developed regions in the north, around Belgrade, and around other major cities in central Serbia. Conservatives dominated in underdeveloped Macedonia, Kosovo, Montenegro, and Bosnia-Herzegovina (Ramet 1987). But conservatives from underdeveloped regions of Croatia also dominated that developed republic's party, in large part because of the 1971 purges. Although reformists and conservatives existed in all republics, the republic as unit made it much more difficult to establish federal-level cross-republic alliances between reformist forces.

The confederal system, the very deep differences between reformists and conservatives, and the extreme difficulty in forging cross-republic alliances brought about deadlock at the center. Both reformists and conservatives debated within the common discourse of socialism and workers' self-management, defining their preferred policies as the best way to ensure these goals. But the conservatives' stress on Marxist orthodoxy endeared them to very few even within the party, whereas the reformers' stress on freedom of expression, tolerance of difference, and an economy based on market principles and their explicit contrasts of the crisis of state socialism to the apparent material successes of Western capitalism provided them with a clear advantage. So the debate was shifting in the reformists' favor between 1982 and 1985.

The deadlock, however, in conjunction with the growing economic crisis, provided party conservatives in Serbia with enough time to mobilize those constituencies most threatened by reform against the reformists who dominated the Serbian party. In particular they shifted the focus of political discourse away from the issue of the economy, where their ideological position had little popular support, toward the issue of how the reform threatened the interests of "the Serbian nation." Serbian conservatives, allied with nationalist intellectuals, pointed to alleged persecution and "genocide" against Serbs in the autonomous province of Kosovo. Kosovo, with a majority ethnic Albanian population of 80 percent, had been the heart of the medieval Serbian kingdom, and was thus central to the construction of the Serbian national mythology. The image of innocent Serbs being victimized and driven out of their own ancient homeland was reinforced with mass, mob rallies of Serbs from Kosovo and workers who would be most negatively affected by reform. These rallies, held in front of the Central Committee buildings while party meetings were in progress, were used as a means of pressuring the Serbian reformists, who were attacked for wanting a negotiated settlement of the Kosovo issue. After several years of such tactics, in September 1987 the Serbian party leader, Slobodan Milošević, managed to purge reformists and consolidate conservative control over the Serbian party.

But given the confederal structure of Yugoslavia, control over the Serbian party alone was not enough to ensure control of the federal party and thus the defeat of reformism in the country as a whole. Control of each republic and province party organization was necessary. Relying on strategies of intimidation and fear, Milošević first turned his sights on the party organizations of other federal units where Serbs were a significant portion of the party membership. As long as control over the communist party was sufficient to gain control over the republic and its vote in the center, Serbian conservatives could conceivably gain control of the federation in this way. These tactics succeeded in Vojvodina, Montenegro, and Kosovo, and were attempted in Bosnia-Herzegovina and Croatia. (In Slovenia the plan, which was uncovered before it was implemented, was for a military crackdown and imposition of a conservative centralist party leadership by force.)

This shift of political discourse away from economic reform toward the rhetoric of injustices and threats to Serbs marked a turning point in the dynamics of confederal relations. The common language of workers' self-management, although not completely jettisoned, took second place to this language of injustices against Serbs. Since Serbs made up 50 percent of the communist party members in all of Yugoslavia, such a discourse had the potential to gain their support; but it also, if undertaken in an aggressive way, would exclude and alienate the other 50 percent of party members, as well as the 60 percent of Yugoslavia's population which was not Serb.

In reaction to this shift, reformists made gains in other republics by associating conservative positions with Milošević's aggressive rhetoric. In March 1989 they managed to have a reformist, Ante Marković, appointed as federal prime minister. Marković (a Croat) sought to empower the federal government to impose radical reformist policies, and by spring 1990 he was more popular in Serbia than Milošević. In Slovenia, already reformist, Serbia's strategy served to radicalize the party and the republic, bringing calls for a multiparty system and political independence. In Croatia, a bastion of conservatism since 1971, reformists managed to take over the party and called multiparty elections. In both Slovenia and Croatia parliamentary elections in spring 1990 were won by noncommunist parties.

An important result of the elections was that although all the ruling parties in their political rhetoric accepted the need for market reform and privatization, in reality the stated goals of the new Slovenian and Croatian leaders (building a capitalist economy and integrating into Europe) were incompatible with the stated goals of the Serbian and Montenegrin leaders (retaining a basically socialist economy and opposing integration as a form of colonialism). In addition, the republics actively moved to sabotage Marković's reforms, which required strengthening the federal center in economic policy.

The reactions to Milošvić's strategy destroyed the organization that had held the country together, and with which the conservatives pursued recentralization: the communist party. Indeed, in a situation where legitimacy depended on electoral support from the majority of voters, the Serbian communists clearly could not succeed in taking power in all of Yugoslavia, where Serbs were only 39 percent of the population; nor would they succeed in any of the four republics they did not control (Bosnia as 33 percent Serb; Croatia 12 percent; Slovenia and Macedonia had negligible numbers of Serbs). The only option was a military intervention, but such a move would clearly create a very unstable situation.

The fall of communist parties in Eastern Europe and the growing pressure within Serbia itself for multiparty elections heightened the

Serbian conservatives' dilemma. The defeat of the communist (re-named socialist) party in Serbia would give noncommunists a clear majority in the federal institutions and thus bring the real possibility of rapid and radical changes in the political and economic system. The choice facing the Serbian conservatives was thus to accept defeat and the transformation to some form of Yugoslavia along capitalist lines or to fight to keep what they could. They chose the latter course, decon-structing Tito's Yugoslavia by means of violent warfare and provocation of ethnic conflict in order to rebuild a new Serbian-majority Yugoslavia. The result was the death of any possible common Yugoslav state, even in a confederal form.

Ethnic/National Bases of Federal Units

One of the reasons confederalism effectively blocked the formation of cross-republic alliances of reformists was that conservatives could claim the "national" interest of the republic or province was being threatened by any ceding of "sovereignty." But because of the "ethno-nationalist" bases of the federal units, the shift to a discourse of repub-lic interest, especially when framed in terms of fears and injustices, tended to become conflated with a discourse of ethnic interest. This discourse of ethnicity provided conservatives with an alternative to their unpopular Marxist rhetoric. The resort to "national" interest was a way of countering reformist appeals to liberal democratic values, and by focusing on injustices to their ethnic group, conservatives invoked a rhetoric of fairness that was not totally alien to socialist ideology.

This concept of ethnic injustice was effective exactly because Tito's Yugoslavia had suppressed aspects of national cultures and, while stressing the guilt of each group for the atrocities carried out in its name during World War II, refused to permit open debate or airing of these issues, further contributing to the impression that national sentiment was being suppressed. Although appeals to past injustices were insufficient to provoke the descent into warfare, once the wedge of "threats to the nation" was inserted into the party's agenda, conser-vatives drew on historical imagery and mythologies in order to com-pletely monopolize political discourse.

Thus it was no coincidence that the Serbian conservatives began their campaign by focusing on Kosovo, which has a tragic importance in the mythology of the Serbian past. By focusing on the demands of the ethnic Albanian majority there for a separate Kosovo republic, the Serbian conservatives stressed the danger that Serbs would once again lose their "Jerusalem" to Muslim aliens. Emphasis on alleged atrocities perpetrated by Albanians made the issue one of injustice rather than chauvinism.

These themes and ways of framing national questions were also seen in such forms as images that demonized Albanians, Croats, and Slavic Muslims by portraying them as viciously anti-Serbian (Banac 1992b). Critical to this instrumentalization of history was the Communist party's monopoly over mass media, especially television, which was divided along republic lines. Television allowed the creation of very threatening images of the outside world and was particularly effective in conveying the message that Serbs in other Yugoslav republics were facing a new genocide and in including these Serbs in the political discourse of threatened Serbdom (Bakić 1994). Through ethnic grievances the Serbian conservatives managed to create an identity between the Serbian people and the Serbian leadership. Indeed, the regime's statements all portrayed any criticism of itself or attacks on its actions as attacks against the Serbian people as a whole.

Of course this Serbian strategy brought backlashes in the other republics, where Belgrade's actions seemed threatening not only to the republic or province but also to non-Serbian populations. In the Croatian communist party this reaction was somewhat muted at first, because its membership included a large percentage of Serbs. The party denounced Milošević's policies and provocation of ethnic conflict, but it did not respond in kind. And although the Croatian party ran on a very reformist platform and called for formal confederalization of Yugoslavia, it received the large majority of Croatia's Serbian votes in the 1990 elections.

But when the Croatian party was taken over by reformists, conservative Croats left the party and joined the nationalist Croatian Democratic Union (HDZ), and conservative Serbs allied with the Serbian Democratic party (SDS), which was controlled by Belgrade. (A similar pattern was seen among Croat and Serb conservatives in Bosnia when that republic's party leadership was taken over by reformists.) Thus in Croatia, too, conservative communists, both Croat and Serb, shifted to a rhetoric of threats to the ethnic group in response to reformist success, though now in the guise of anticommunism.

Outside the Croatian communist party, of course, the reaction was much stronger, as intellectuals and nationalist-oriented conservatives responded in kind and demonized Serbs. Indeed, the HDZ, in the election campaign, made much of the Serbian threat and appealed to the injustices done to Croatia in 1971, cited the demonization of Croatian national sentiment in the entire postwar period, and even rehabilitated some aspects of the Ustaše Croatian state. Belgrade pointed to these actions as proof of its contentions about the renewal of genocide against Serbs and justified military occupation and expulsion of non-Serbs from areas of Croatia with significant Serbian populations.

The effect of this "ethnicization" of political discourse by conservative communists has been to ensure the continued existence of old structures of local power in both Serbia and Croatia. Indeed, in Croatia both the HDZ and the SDS (in areas under its control) strengthened state control over the economy, obstructed political pluralism and democracy, cracked down on the free press and open dissent, and continued to use enemy imagery defined in ethnic terms in order to marginalize reformist democratic forces. The dynamics in Bosnia were similar, although complicated by the existence of three major national groups (Slavic Muslims, Serbs, and Croats), two of which were "represented" by parties controlled by forces from outside the republic (Serbian and Croatian conservatives) and all three of which were, before the war, members of a coalition government.

Thus the ethnic/national basis of the federal units, although responding to the need of the Yugoslav communists for some level of popular support, when combined with a confederalized center with few integrating factors, meant that autarky in the realm of political rhetoric was a real possibility. As the reformists came to define self-management in terms of liberal values, conservatives attempted to shift the focus away from this universalist rhetoric toward a discourse of national and ethnic particularism. They did so first in Serbia mainly because they were most threatened there, but also because the Serbian party was one of the few that was relatively homogeneous (80 percent Serb). Once the discourse of ethnic injustice took root in Serbia, the dynamic of relations among the republics took a different turn and became an interaction of nationalist and ethnic claims and counterclaims, especially once the communist party was no longer relevant. This cycle of confrontation was possible mainly because of the republics' control over mass media, especially television.

The result of this dynamic was that even a renegotiated Yugoslav confederation based on liberal democratic lines became difficult to imagine. Once actual violence along ethnic lines was provoked, as a means of deepening the sense of victimhood and difference, such a joint state became almost impossible. This was a very important goal of conservatives throughout the country because one aspect of the ethnicization of political discourse is that it works only if a large majority of voters are of a specific ethnic group. Yugoslavia of course was a prime example of a multiethnic state, with many highly intermixed regions. But in order for this strategy to work the country had to be deconstructed into ministates where nationalist discourses could continue to dominate. Thus the most tragic result of this shift in discourse away from universalist rhetorics of self-managing socialism or liberal democracy toward ethnic particularism has been the attempts to create ethnically pure regions out of areas that had been highly heterogeneous for centuries.

The Yugoslav People's Army

The final, key factor in explaining the violence of the Yugoslav conflict, and thus one of the main ways in which it has threatened regional stability, is the Yugoslav People's Army (JNA). The Yugoslav communist party during World War II had been intimately interlinked with the Partisan forces that evolved into the JNA. Indeed, most of the early communist leaders had achieved prominence as a result of their military service in the Partisans. After the war the JNA leadership, although not directly involved in political decision making, was clearly a major factor in the overall federal leadership.

The army was, however, directly involved in the conservative backlash of the early 1970s. Indeed, parts of the army were instrumental in convincing Tito of the supposed danger to socialism posed by the policies of Croatian leaders, and the army's mobilization of veterans organizations was crucial to the ouster of liberals in all the republics in 1971–1972 (Remington 1974, 188; Johnson 1978, 31–33). Following the purges, Tito himself declared that the army "must participate" directly in political affairs and developments, and by 1974 army officers made up 12 percent of the central committee membership, up from 2 percent in 1969 (Dean 1976, 46). Indeed, the army's party organization, which was completely autonomous, became in effect the "ninth republic" in the federal party presidency.

Another legacy of the events of the early 1970s was that Tito stressed that the army's role was not only to defend the country against external aggression but also to ensure the domestic political order against external and internal enemies. The resulting ideological commitment to a specific conservative vision of the socialist system marked a natural alliance with conservatives in the party and explains in part the vehement opposition of the army leaders to the concept of multiparty elections contested by parties calling for restoration of capitalism. The conservative tendency within the army was reinforced by the fact that its officer corps drew heavily from economically underdeveloped regions of the country, especially Serbian regions in Croatia and Bosnia-Herzegovina. These regions had long-standing traditions of military service and were bases of the Partisan forces, but were also the site of massive Ustaše atrocities during World War II. Indeed, some of the army's top officers had lost family members in the massacres and were thus receptive to Milošević's arguments about the resurrection of fascism in Croatia.

This conservative ideological position was reinforced by the privileged position of the army in Yugoslav society. Army officers enjoyed levels of pay much higher than the average Yugoslav and also enjoyed housing privileges in a country with an acute shortage of housing. The JNA's budget was very high, and it had established its own domestic arms industry, 50 percent of which was located in mountainous Bosnia. Thus when the economic crisis hit in the early 1980s and the army's budgets were continually slashed, the defense minister criticized the reductions and called instead for more resources. As the reformist trend continued, one of the loudest demands was for further cuts in the JNA's budget as well as its privileges and its special role in Yugoslav politics.

Thus it was no coincidence that the army leadership allied with conservatives in the Serbian party who wanted to recentralize the country and remove the danger of radical reform. Although the army leadership, which revered Tito and was instilled with the ideology of Yugoslavism, may have been uneasy with parts of Milošević's Serbian nationalist strategy, it clearly supported his policy goals. Indeed, from 1988 on, the army actively cooperated with Milošević's attempts to subvert the republic and province communist parties (Bebler 1992).

The victory in Croatia of a noncommunist nationalist party, some of whose leaders explicitly and positively invoked aspects of the wartime Croatian state, marked the decisive shift in the JNA's stance. The defense minister and other top officers had been openly hostile to the HDZ, labeling it Ustaše and declaring that they would not allow it to take power. At this point their coincidence of interests with Milošević became almost complete. The socialist system was under attack as explicitly noncommunist parties had taken control of two of the eight federal units and demand for multiparty elections was increasing in the other republics as well. The prospect of a Yugoslavia ruled by liberal democratic (or at least anticommunist) ideology clearly frightened the army, as did the prospect of a confederal Yugoslavia with republic-based armies, since in either case, a massive reduction in its size and influence would be likely.

Indeed, the JNA's party organization, renamed the League of Communists-Movement for Yugoslavia (LC-MY) (whose chief ideologist is Milošević's wife, the academic Mirjana Marković), at the end of 1990 circulated a document that was more hard-line, anti-Western and Marxist-Leninist in its tone than anything seen under Tito (*Borba*, February 1, 1991, 4). Stressing that Yugoslav socialism was under attack by NATO, Germany, Hungary, and Austria, which were using nation-alists in Croatia and Slovenia to undermine the country, the document called for all "leftist forces" in the country to rally around the LC-MY. The JNA also had very close ties to conservative forces in Moscow which attempted to overthrow Mikhail Gorbachev in August 1991 (*Vreme*, September 23, 1991, 7).

By this time the JNA was clearly working with Milošević and the Serbian conservatives to reconstruct a new Yugoslavia. It took the side of Serbian guerrillas who were expelling non-Serbs first in Croatia and then in Bosnia-Herzegovina. The fact that 70 percent of the JNA's offi-cer corps was of Serbian nationality, although not in and of itself a sign of Serbian nationalist dominance (indeed the ideal of Yugoslavism lasted in the army far longer than anywhere else), allowed a relatively easy transition from the army of all Yugoslavia to the Serbian national army. Thus by the end of summer 1991 the JNA, the last bastion of Yugoslavism, had fully succumbed to the nationalist rhetoric. The final step, taken in the fall of 1991 and the spring of 1992, was a purge of non-Serb and Yugoslav-oriented Serb officers, which transformed Tito's JNA into a purely Serbian army under the tight control of Serbian leader Milošević.

Conflict along ethnic lines was due to a confluence of factors. Parts of the political elite at the central, republic, and local levels were moti-vated to resist radical reform and were willing to undertake costly strategies to prevent it. The institutional structure at the federal level prevented the reformists' popularity from translating into control over the federal decision-making organs and gave conservatives in Serbia time to undermine that republic's reformists. The national basis of the federal units provided an alternative ideology for political discourse, giving the conservatives the opportunity to appeal for mass support. The army's privileged position and its ideological and power interest in maintaining the socialist system gave it interests congruent with the Serbian conservatives, and the national makeup of its officer corps opened it to inclusion in the nationalist discourse. The war has thus been one between federal units, driven by conflict over the structure of power within each republic. To win the conflict and prevent radical change, parts of the elite have shifted the focus toward ethnic claims and have purposely undertaken strategies that created first the image and then the reality of an ethnic or national conflict.

In retrospect, an early intervention to prevent or moderate this con-flict would have had to deal with the fears of conservatives throughout the country about the effects of radical reform, as well as the concerns of the Yugoslav army. It would thus have had to address the most basic issues that arise when domestic structures are undergoing deep and rapid change. If this had been done, then the real grievances of Yugo-slavia's various nations could perhaps have been addressed without being instrumentalized, exacerbated, and cynically manipulated to the point of violent warfare.

8

Redrawing Borders in a
Period of Systemic Transition

Susan L. Woodward

Analysis of the role of international organizations in ethnic conflict for the purposes of helpful lessons and preventive diplomacy is put to a most severe test in the Yugoslav case. Foreign observers have viewed the dissolution of the country in 1991 and the wars over borders and citizens of new states in its former territory as an ethnic conflict. No matter that tens of thousands have died, millions have become refugees and displaced persons, and massive destruction of homes, cultural and religious monuments, infrastructure, and industry has occurred in the quest for international recognition of separate sovereignties—the conflict has been defined as an internal political quarrel. Yet actions of the international community contributed directly to the process by which internal conflicts in the 1980s became ethnicized. More properly seen as *national* conflict by 1990–1991, the Yugoslav case demonstrates the danger in many societies of economic and political disintegration in response to changes and uncertainty in their international environment. Under those circumstances, there is a powerful incentive and opportunity for politicians who can claim rights to national self-determination to choose political autonomy or independence rather than continue to share resources and compete with rivals.

The politics and social relations of multinational, multiethnic Yugoslavia have always included ethnic conflict. There were repeated warnings throughout the Tito period, 1945–1980, that conflict among its constituent nations would destroy the state. Nonetheless, the country managed to stay together until 1991 on the basis of a complex mix of constitutional guarantees and accommodations to its multinational character (Burg 1983; Cohen and Warwick 1983; Hondius 1968). Its disintegration in 1991 and the wars of Yugoslav succession which have followed and continue were the result not of ethnic conflict but of economic and political strains associated with reforming the domestic order (economy, government, and national security) in order to reduce foreign debt, reorient to Western markets, and adjust to the profound changes taking place in the European security order as the cold war ended. The failure of federal authorities to manage the process of change and the victory of politicians in the republics with nationalist agendas cannot be separated from the demands on the federal government from international organizations and the aid that foreign powers gave to some politicians who pursued national independence.

Contrary to the explanation that was popular in 1991–1992, it was not the papering-over or repression of ethnic conflicts under communist rule which prevented their explosion or their artificial containment by superpower rivalry and the unifying fear of external enemies. Instead, the constitutional guarantees that had worked to keep ethnic and national peace in Yugoslavia in 1946–1990 provided politicians with legitimate arguments on which to claim rights to economic resources and governmental prerogatives against the federal government and against other republics. With an opening of European borders, these claims to "sovereign" control within the country became claims to full national independence and to the breakup of the state. Only when that state ended with the assistance of European powers pursuing their separate national interests, however, did these constitutional protections become the source of the country's self-immolation. Then claims for political control over territory came up against the territorially overlapping character of those rights.

To evaluate the capacity of international organizations to ameliorate such conflicts and contribute to their peaceful resolution, one must first recognize their contribution to the origins, escalation, and continuation of such conflicts. Do the interests of states and the norms and capacities of international organizations privilege ethnic conflict over other forms, encourage nationalism, and diminish domestic capacities to counteract the interactive escalation of all ethnonational conflict? These questions took on a greater urgency in the Yugoslav case because of its location in Europe. The Yugoslav conflicts and outcome were inseparable from the process of international transition after the mid-1980s, which dealt primarily with the borders of Europe (the

"West") and the interests and primary bases of power of countries that would, after the cold war, define the norms of global governance.

The Yugoslav Conflict

The conditions leading to war in 1991 were created over the course of a decade, beginning with the onset of world economic crisis in 1979 (Woodward 1995). A balance-of-payments crisis and substantial foreign debt threatened a domestic economic crisis in Yugoslavia because of the very high dependence of domestic production on imports and the dramatic fall in monies to finance hard-currency trade due to changes beyond Yugoslavia's control in Western capital and product markets. The federal government was compelled to turn to international financial organizations for assistance, beginning with the International Monetary Fund. The terms required by the IMF initiated a decade-long effort at economic and political transformation, including a long-term, radical policy of economic stabilization, structural reforms to re-orient the economy toward exports in hard-currency (Western) mar-kets, and eventually a political reform aimed at making governmental macroeconomic policy more effective.

The program required severe domestic austerity and rising unem-ployment, and it resulted by 1985 in hyperinflation and increasing social polarization. About 20 percent of the population was able to maintain or improve standards of living, while 80 percent experienced increasing existential insecurity because restrictions on wages and in-comes, together with cuts in welfare, skyrocketing prices of basic goods, and unemployed family members, depleted household savings. Cuts in public investment and structural adjustments in production oriented to foreign trade affected some areas far more than others, so that the impact of declining industries, rising unemployment, auster-ity, and resulting welfare inequalities were not felt evenly across geo-graphic regions and administrative units of the federal system. In addition to a general rise in political conflict over shortages, the IMF program required cuts in public expenditures and recentralization of monetary policy and allocation of foreign exchange and led to higher tax assessments to balance budgets because tax revenues declined. The result was increasing conflict between the central government and the republican governments over rights to economic resources, govern-mental jurisdiction in the economy, and redistribution. Particularly contentious were the categories of the federal budget. Although the budget represented a very small portion of public expenditures and of interrepublican transfers, two categories—federal expenditures on economic aid to less-developed regions and the defense budget—became the focus of tax rebellions by parliaments in the richer republics. They asserted the right of republics to retain their earnings on the basis of their national rights to self-determination (embodied in the constitution). They also resisted the transfer of renewed power to an independent central bank and were joined by all republican governments except Serbia, where the fight for republican control of economic resources was aimed instead at reversing the independence of its autonomous provinces granted in previous constitutional reform in 1974. Radical youth also used nationalist arguments in independent protests against the army. In the public debate by economists and enterprises against economic redistribution nationalism was invoked because these were questions of federal-republican relations and because the one-party system permitted separate political organization at the level of the republics and provinces but not around ideological differences or class interests.

Conflict among representatives of the republican governments over federal legislation escalated during 1985–1987 from debate over the economic and political reforms required by the IMF program of stabilization and marketization into a constitutional crisis over the functions and jurisdiction of the federal government. This constitutional dispute was directly affected by the major changes taking place at the time in the international environment, which shaped the perceptions of threat and opportunity of the primary actors. Prospects of growing East-West cooperation within Europe arose from the renewal in 1985 of negotiations between the European Community and the Council on Mutual Economic Assistance (CMEA) and from the new stage of monetary integration begun by the EC (to be completed by 1992). The two military blocs of NATO and the Warsaw Treaty Organization revived talks about strategic and conventional arms reductions and confidence-building measures, and President Gorbachev also introduced Western-oriented economic reforms in the USSR. These developments intensified pressures within Yugoslavia to shift to Western markets, increased competition for market access, and reduced demand in Eastern markets. At the same time, U.S. security policy remained antagonistic ("Star Wars") and NATO intensified focus on the eastern Mediterranean.

For the two republics most engaged in Western trade (Slovenia and Croatia), these changes opened up opportunities, particularly through Austria and Italy, which were attempting to expand their economic prospects eastward. New cross-border cultural, tourist, and economic associations, the renewed activity of the Vatican in Eastern Europe, and the debate over Europeanization taking place in Central Europe and Russia added a layer of cultural and political significance to the debate over economic reform at home. The identification throughout the country of liberal economic policies and marketization with Western culture and Europeanization meant that the changing context of possibilities in Europe could not be separated from a cultural politics of identity reformation or reassertion of religious and cultural ties with Central Europe. In contrast to changing orientations and expectations, the continuing world recession and West European protectionism did not facilitate the export-oriented reform but made the federal government's task increasingly difficult. Producers and regions within Yugoslavia which were more linked to trade with the East had to shift from CMEA to Western markets and to world-market pricing, while the disruption in Middle Eastern trade from the Iran-Iraq War was costly to many regions and to the many bilateral trade contracts negotiated by the federal government. These factors exacerbated the industrial depression in areas undergoing structural adjustment away from infrastructure, mining and metallurgy, and capital goods in Bosnia-Herzegovina, Macedonia, Serbia, and the Croatian interior. On the security front, moreover, the federal army perceived a rising threat in NATO activity at a time when the army as an institution was already threatened by budget cuts, social change that required rationalizing reforms of its own, and Slovene youth and politicians (joined occasionally by Croatians) who insisted there was no more need for a standing army. As a neutral country, Yugoslavia was left out of the forums for East-West cooperation which were rapidly dismantling the security order that had defined the army's role and Yugoslavia's international position for nearly forty years.

Economic hardship and growing insecurity were reflected in growing social turmoil, manifest in a radical youth press, antinuclear and pacifist movements, workers' strikes, antifeminist and ethnic backlash, religious revivals, and mass demonstrations against governmental wage and price policies. Areas suffering the worst of the economic recession were particularly vulnerable to ethnic sensitivities over cuts in public employment in government and in industry because many (such as interior Croatia and much of Bosnia-Herzegovina) were ethnically mixed. The conflicts over public expenditures were already being expressed in the language of national rights; in addition, the constitutional protection of national equality included national proportionality in public employment. At the same time, in the republic of Serbia, a long-running incipient conflict between the republican government and ethnic Albanians in an autonomous province within the republic was escalating after 1981 into a social movement to transform that province into a separate (seventh) republic in the federation on the grounds of the majority's right to self-governance as a separate people.

The economic crisis and policies of liberalization engendered increasingly open political ferment among intellectuals, who blamed politicians (or the socialist political and economic system as a whole) for the economic crisis and began to organize protopolitical associations of liberals, nationalists, social democrats, clericalists, and others. Whether the language of these political conflicts was ethnonationalist, regionalist, generational, or anticommunist, however, the primary structuring issue was intergovernmental conflict over rights to economic assets and the authority to make economic decisions, phrased in the language of ownership and sovereignty over economies and territories.

With the exception of Slovenia, where full employment and relative prosperity had led to increasingly market-oriented and pluralistic politics, the consequence of the economic reform was a radical narrowing of the social basis for a liberal politics within the country. As insecurities rose and social and political tensions became more potentially destabilizing, politicians in the ruling Communist party tended to react with attempts to slow the pace of political change. As in many other countries at the time, economic liberalism was accompanied by political conservatism. Elections within the ruling party were won by leaders for whom the greatest threat to the system was independent intellectuals capable of attracting a popular following or organizing an opposition. Some leaders used political repression, others co-optation, but in either case, they slowed the development of independent political associations. While politicians in the republics began to campaign openly for popular support for their positions on constitutional and economic reform, federal politicians were too preoccupied with the need to stabilize and reform the economy and with the intense feuds over constitutional revision of the federal government and its budget. They seemed oblivious to the need to build a political base of support and loyalty independent of the republican government and party organizations.

The turning point of the old order came in 1988–1990. It began with the failure of a federal attempt in 1985–1986 to abandon the IMF program and revive economic growth so as to reduce political discontent. The growth in production increased the demand for imports, and the whopping trade deficit obliged the government to return to the IMF in 1987; its condition for new aid was radical surgery. The federal economic reform in 1988–1989 became a program of full marketization, dismantlement of the property rights and welfare basis of the socialist system, and the introduction of a "shock therapy" policy of macroeconomic stabilization for currency convertibility beginning January 1,

1990. At the same time, federal and republican legislatures debated political reform by constitutional amendment.

The change in superpower relations during 1988–1989 also radically transformed Yugoslavia's diplomatic and security environment. Both the Soviet Union and the United States announced in 1988–1989 that they no longer had a security interest in protecting either Yugoslav independence or Yugoslavia itself. Losing its guarantee of international financial assistance in exchange for neutrality and a well-armed defense in the Balkans, the federal government had no alternative but to push full speed ahead for full membership in Europe. Free from security constraints to focus on human rights, the U.S. ambassador began to demand greater conformity with Conference on Security and Cooperation in Europe (CSCE) norms in the case of Albanians in Kosovo. Although the Albanians were demanding the right of self-determination in an independent republic and federal troops (with contingents from each republic) had been ordered to impose martial law in the province in 1988, the U.S. position was that this was not a constitutional question but one of internationally protected rights of a minority against political discrimination and repression, which were being violated by the leadership of Serbia.

In the complex politics surrounding the constitutional reforms, two positions began to crystallize among the governmental participants in the debate. For Slovenia, the goal was full republican sovereignty within a confederation of independent republics. For the army, the federal government, the IMF, and many in Serbia, the goal was a more effective federal government. At the same time, in 1988–1989, there was a critical shift in the political tactics of republican leaders in Slovenia and Serbia. They began to use nationalist appeals to mobilize popular support for their constitutional positions, defining their programs as matters of "national interest" and linking the interests and security of individuals with the fate of their "nation" instead of the fate of the entire country. Under conditions of extreme austerity and an increasingly uncertain foreign climate, the leaders of these two republics portrayed themselves and their governments as "protectors" of their nations.

Slovene communist party leaders found that nationalism suited their increasingly open conflict with the army and their challenge against all federal and "Yugoslav" institutions and laws as interference with Slovene sovereignty. By openly criticizing repression in Kosovo as a more general threat by the Milošević leadership in Serbia to individual liberty throughout the country, the communist leadership sought to distance Slovenia from Yugoslavia, to win Western sympathy by asserting Slovene national interests in terms of "freedom" and "democracy," and simultaneously to win popular support within the republic in their contest with anticommunist challengers. For Serbian communist party leaders, mobilization of mass support on the basis of Serbian nationalism also served to undercut the popularity of anticommunist nationalists within the republic and, in the federal fight, to create a base of support in three other federal units where Serbs lived (the two provinces within Serbia—Kosovo and Vojvodina—and the republic of Montenegro) in hopes of shifting the voting balance in its direction. The consequence was increasingly open confrontation between leaders and opinion makers of Slovenia and Serbia. Like Slovene leaders, those in the republics of Croatia and Macedonia also began to use the language of national interests and national sovereignty more openly in their claim for republican economic powers and against recentralization of monetary policy and a restrengthened federal administration. Even though the Serbian government was campaigning on the side of republican sovereignty and there was political support for a more federalist policy in all republics and among people from all ethnic/national groups, the Slovene, Croatian, and Macedonian governments were able to form an alliance in favor of republican rights around the theme of "anti-Serbianism," by reviving historical allusions to Serbs as centralists and as the core of the army. This strategy then fueled reactive nationalism among Serbs, weakening the appeals of the liberal forces attempting to restrain Serb nationalism, and the political climate on all sides gave increasing permission to the expression of ethnic prejudice and nationalist competition.

The democratization associated with the year 1989 and political revolution in Eastern Europe was in Yugoslavia an extension of this constitutional politics to citizenship rights. The parliaments in the republics of Slovenia, Croatia, and Macedonia took the opportunity of constitutional revision to rewrite their republican constitutions along the lines of nation-state and republican (instead of Yugoslav) citizenship. Each republic was proclaimed the state of its dominant nation. Members of other nations in these republics were redefined as ethnic minorities, losing their previous status as constituent nations with equal rights in all previous constitutions since 1945. Brief but vicious flareups of ethnic discrimination against minorities ensued, particularly in Croatia (against Serbs, who formed 12 percent of the population) and in Macedonia (where Albanians, between 20 and 30 percent of the republic, began to lose their cultural rights as an ethnic minority). Alongside the ongoing internal war in Kosovo, now groups of territorially concentrated Serbs in poorer areas of Croatia began to organize self-protection and demand either the restoration of their rights or territorial autonomy. Eventually ethnic Albanians in Macedonia demanded political rights as a constituent nation. The revised constitution of Serbia took back the powers given to its autonomous provinces by the 1974 constitution, as approved the year before by the federal party, and joined the other republics (as well as states in Eastern Europe) in embracing the welfare of Serbs living elsewhere as part of its national interests. It thus seemed to provide the Serbian minority in Croatia, in particular, with a protector.

Political organizing among independent intellectuals in Croatia had begun to catch up with Slovenia and Serbia by February 1989, and the communist leadership there agreed to dialogue that led to the registration of political parties, round-table talks on political change, and multiparty elections set for April 1990. By September, however, the Slovene parliament had taken the final step in its attempts to remove federal authority from Slovenia. Declaring a policy aimed at "dissociation" (secession), it proposed that Yugoslavia be transformed into a confederation of independent states. Confrontation continued between Slovenia and Serbia, leading by the end of the year to economic warfare and prohibition of a caravan of Serb demonstrators in Slovenia. By January 1990, the Yugoslav Communist party dissolved when an extraordinary congress could not agree to Slovene demands for a confederal party or to continue proceedings once Slovenia walked out.

The politics of federal economic reform and constitutional revisions had thus led by way of republican fights over economic resources and constitutional authority to the collapse of the federal Communist party. Multiparty elections in the republics began in April 1990. In Slovenia, the Communist party leader, and in Croatia, a former communist turned anticommunist, interpreted their popular election—although neither obtained a majority—as a mandate for national independence. Even before the elections of November and December could be held in the remaining four republics, in July the two republics declared their intention to "dissociate." They proposed a confederation of independent Yugoslav nations based on the former republics and on economic links among them sufficient to meet qualifications set by the European Community for a transitional stage on the road to membership, which they intended to seek. Still committed to a revised Yugoslavia, the leadership in Serbia responded that if the country actually ceased to exist, it would demand that borders be "rectified" (redrawn to conform better with the pattern of Serbian settlements) to give Serbia its nation-state as well. As in Croatia, anticommunist nationalists won the elections in Bosnia-Herzegovina, but they were divided among three political parties corresponding to the three constituent nations of the republic (Muslims, Serbs, and Croats). They therefore created a power-sharing governing coalition patterned after the proportional distribution of offices and consensual voting of the multinational, federal government. In Serbia, Montenegro, and Macedonia the renamed communist parties won against opposition nationalists, although in Macedonia too a coalition was necessary to form a government.

Elections replaced the communist system with the first stages of a parliamentary democracy and market economy, but it did not resolve the constitutional dispute between separate nation-states in a transitional confederation, on the one hand, and a reformed federal state and Yugoslav democracy, on the other. The first casualty of this uncertain interregnum was the system of public security. Local and republican police either joined criminal syndicates or created paramilitary wings attached to political parties within the republics (and outside federal authority). Slovenia and Croatia began building independent armies during the summer and fall of 1990, in part with equipment of their territorial defense forces (the republic-level units of the combined armed forces) and in part with illegal purchases of weapons in Austria, Hungary, Germany, Belgium, and elsewhere. As Croatia moved to create a nation-state, nationalist fervor intensified discrimination against Serbs, and the new president's policy to replace all non-Croats in the police and security forces as unreliable encouraged militants among Serbs to mobilize in areas where they were territorially concentrated. Armed clashes and disruption of communications erupted in the *krajina* in August 1990. In Slovenia during the fall, the center-right coalition in the Slovene parliament, fearful that the nationalist momentum was losing popular support among Slovene citizens, declared a referendum December 23 on independence within six months.

In reaction to the formation of independent armies in Slovenia and Croatia, to growing armed clashes between the Croatian government and Serb autonomists, and to the Slovene referendum (approved by 88 percent), the newly elected federal presidency (one representative from each republic and province and from the army, responsible for constitutional order and internal security) began trying to restore order and the possibilities for political negotiation of the constitutional conflict. It called on all security and paramilitary forces to disarm, and it set up a series of consultations with republican leaders held (on Croatian demand) in different cities of the federation rather than the capital, Belgrade. The federal army in the military district of Slovenia and parts of Croatia began border maneuvers and, it is charged, redeployed equipment and communications to defend against secession. The federal cabinet was preoccupied with repairing the damage done to monetary discipline and its shock-therapy stabilization program by the spending and borrowing of new, elected governments in the republics. Federal elections were to follow those in the republics, and the prime minister expected a broad showing of support for his economic reforms, but they were not held because Slovenia refused to participate. While the presidency negotiated the fate of the country, the cabinet proceeded with radical economic reform.

International Intervention

Foreign offices and intelligence networks of Western countries, as well as academic specialists, had been warning of the potential for violent disintegration and civil war in Yugoslavia all during 1990 (and some before that), but the international community remained largely uninterested. The U.S. ambassador and visiting congressmen did react to developments in January 1991 with declarations of CSCE norms on human rights and inviolable borders, publicly warning the army to stop its maneuvers and not to use force in resolving the internal conflicts. They continued pressure on the Milošević government in Serbia to end its repression of Albanian civil rights in Kosovo. The failure of Western powers to do more was due, many argue, to overload and to preoccupation at the time with the Iraqi threat to world peace. (The Iraqis invaded Kuwait in August 1990, and the Persian Gulf War began on January 17, 1991.) But in fact, Western diplomats openly dismissed the Yugoslav case as insignificant to their security, national interests, and the new situation in Europe after 1989.

Explicit engagement by international organizations to mediate the domestic conflict grew, in fact, out of requests from Yugoslav actors to take sides in their domestic quarrels. During the fall of 1990, Slovene and Croatian authorities campaigned for support in Western capitals for their cause of independence, including discussions in Germany, Austria, Norway, and the United States. The first official action came only with the final denouement of the domestic crisis. On March 13, 1991, the European Parliament passed a resolution declaring the right of "the constituent republics and autonomous provinces of Yugoslavia . . . freely to determine their own future in a peaceful and democratic manner and on the basis of recognized international and internal borders" (European Parliament resolution on Yugoslavia, clause 8, cited in Gow 1991, 308). Several weeks earlier, Slovenia and Croatia had suspended all federal laws on their territory. At the same time, the army and the Serbian bloc within the federal presidency failed to win support for emergency rule within the country (in what those voting against considered an attempted coup), one branch of the army chose to support Serbian president Milošević against opposition demonstrations in Belgrade by moving tanks onto the streets, and the Croatian government officially paraded its new army. The resolution laid the basis for the emerging European acceptance, explicit by the fall, of the Slovene and Croatian confederation proposals and their argument that the republican borders of federal Yugoslavia were international ("Helsinki") borders.

Intervention also came as a result of the ongoing diplomacy of the federal prime minister, Ante Marković, and minister of foreign affairs, Budimir Lončar, to gain European support for the federal government and its economic reform and pro-Europe policy. Alongside trade negotiations with the European Community and European Free Trade Association (EFTA) and an application in 1989 to join the Council of Europe, they appealed explicitly for EC economic assistance and political mediation during the spring of 1991. In need of further financing for the economic reform, they also hoped that EC aid would send a political signal that would strengthen the federal cause and counteract foreign sympathy for Slovenia and Croatia. The preference of Marković and Lončar for EC intervention was in part a reaction to American indifference. The United States rebuffed their requests for economic assistance in late 1989 and declared that NATO should not become involved "out of area," including Yugoslavia. But the request for EC intervention also followed directly from their long-term strategy to join Europe. It played into the hands of Europeanists within the EC who seized on the Yugoslav conflict as an opportunity to demonstrate, in the face of the upcoming vote on the Maastricht treaty for full financial integration in December 1991 and the embarrassing show of disunity among members over the Persian Gulf operation, that the EC could develop a common security and foreign policy.

During May 1991, the EC began a series of fact-finding and good-offices delegations, including, at the end of May, one under the president of the EC Commission, Jacques Delors, and the president of its council, Prime Minister Jacques Santer of Luxembourg, with a commitment of $4.5 billion in credits (the amount requested by the Yugoslav federal government) in support of Yugoslav territorial integrity and its political and economic reforms (Dempsey 1991). At the same time, however, the United States did the opposite—withdrew economic assistance and promised to reinstate it only if the country remained together—and EC foreign ministers began to meet separately with leaders from Slovenia and Croatia.

On June 25 Slovenia and Croatia declared independence, and Slovenia sent troops to take over border controls and customs posts on its international border. On June 27 the Yugoslav People's Army (JNA [Jugoslovenska Narodna Armija]) moved to take back control. The next day, the EC mechanism for common foreign policy—the foreign ministers of the three governing states of the EC Council (the "troika")—arrived in the country to begin the EC's first attempt to negotiate a cease-fire by facilitating political dialogue among Yugoslav leaders to settle the crisis. At Austria's request, the newly established Crisis Prevention Center of the CSCE met on July 1 and called for an immediate cessation of hostilities. Its Committee of Senior Officials, chaired at the time by the German foreign minister Hans-Dietrich Genscher, joined its good offices to those of the EC mediation mission on July 3. On July 7 the EC negotiated a cease-fire agreement between Slovenia and the federal government on the Yugoslav island of Brioni, which cleared the way for eventual recognition of independence, although it obliged Slovenia and Croatia to stop that process for three months. The army was returned to barracks as a prelude to its exit from Slovenia (and, importantly, the Austrian border) into Croatia, and the EC sent observers under CSCE-defined terms of reference in its first such operation to monitor the cease-fire.

The EC mediation for Slovenia therefore opened the door to actual ethnic conflict. It set up the end of the state by declaring the actions of the army aggressive and requiring its return to barracks without discussing the implications for Croatia or the rest of the country. In Croatia approximately four hundred lives had already been lost in the conflict between the Croatian government and a Serbian minority in rebellion against the state's nationalist policies and plans for independence. Both Croat and Serb radicals had begun ethnically directed expulsions (later to be called "ethnic cleansing") in the ethnically mixed localities in the eastern areas of the republic bordering Serbia (Glenny 1992). The public declaration of the leadership in Serbia the previous July that if the country dissolved, the equal right of Serbs to national self-determination would require border changes with Croatia and Bosnia-Herzegovina, where Serbs lived in compact minorities ("Serb areas," in its view), still stood.

Paying no attention to these political conditions, the EC team ignored and interrupted the efforts by the federal presidency since January to restore order in Croatia and to resolve the constitutional dispute among republican leaders over the fate of their common state. The EC also ignored the compromise on confederation proposed by the presidents of Bosnia-Herzegovina and Macedonia to the federal presidency on June 6. It accepted the Croatian argument that the problem of Serbs (and other potential "ethnic conflicts" internal to other republics) was a matter of minority rights, whereas the source of the Croat-Serb conflict in Croatia was the insistence of the Serbs that they were not a minority and had been deprived by the amended Croatian constitution in 1989 and by subsequent decrees of their previous political equality. If Croats chose independence, they argued, under the constitution they had an equal right to be consulted and to exercise freely their will to remain within Yugoslavia. And although EC ministers continued to speak of the importance of guaranteeing such minority rights, their attention shifted entirely to the question of borders, subordinating human rights to the norm that borders could not be changed by force.

These two European decisions—that the republican borders were legitimate international borders and that the goal of mediation was to obtain cease-fires and ensure the acceptance of these new borders—thenceforth defined the relevant actors in the Yugoslav struggle. The EC would therefore negotiate with leaders of the republics but not with the army. It would be forced to recognize and negotiate with political leaders who claimed different borders on the basis of national rights and who were willing and able to field armies to achieve their projects. And it would refuse to hear nonnationalist voices within the former country representing political parties, civic groups, antiwar movements, or citizens in general because to do so would constitute interference in the internal affairs of sovereign units.

The three-month moratorium on Slovene and Croatian projects was also an instigation to violence, for it created another undefined interregnum, like that between July and November 1990, in which people had to begin to reassess and mobilize for several contingencies. Was there one country or many? Did the army have a state, or did it have to seek a new one? Was the rest of the country without Slovenia and Croatia expected to form one state, or were the republics all to become independent? Was it better to arm or to seek foreign support for their choice? While Slovenia bided its time and war began to rage in Croatia, people in the other four republics between July 7 and October 6 had to devise strategy and initiate separate tactical maneuvers to cover both assumptions—that there would be a Yugoslavia and that there would not. And although the federal authorities remained parties to negotiations until November, they were treated as ciphers, increasingly irrelevant to the EC-led process.

The nature of the conflict within Yugoslavia had also been transformed by the Slovene assertion of the sovereign right to control its borders militarily and by the Brioni Agreement. The constitutional quarrel over sovereignty in the respective powers of the federal and republican governments was replaced by conflict over the borders of new states. With the territorialization of national rights in a multinational environment of ethnically mixed populations, ethnic violence would surely follow. As political parties identifying in ethnonational terms began to mobilize local militias, paramilitaries, and armies to fight for national rights and as citizens had to choose political identities and loyalties on ethnonational terms, all other identities became secondary in the struggle for survival. Only in some parts of Bosnia-Herzegovina until August 1993, under the leadership of the Muslim party and the Bosnian government, was there an option of choosing a nonethnic or multiethnic identity.

The evidence of breakdown was clear in September 1991. Serbian paramilitary gangs crossed into Bosnia and terrorized towns along the Serbian border. The army revised strategy and began maneuvers to secure control of strategic territory for a smaller, rump Yugoslavia. Croatia declared open war against the army, and local skirmishes between Croats and Serbs in its eastern provinces of Baranja and Slavonia exploded into war. The Macedonian government declared independence. All three Bosnian communal parties prepared for war; the Bosnian Croat and Bosnian Muslim political parties ignored the power-sharing agreement of their ruling coalition in October when the three-month moratorium ended and jointly declared sovereignty, while the Bosnian Serb party declared it would remain within Yugoslavia if Bosnia seceded and left the government, setting up a separate parliament.

Already in early August, however, the German government began pressing more insistently to use recognition of Slovene and Croatian independence as a means to stop the war in Croatia. The idea was that if their borders were recognized as international, Serbian aggression—which they (and many others) called the cause of war—would have to cease. Britain and France opposed such recognition because of the implications for their own autonomist ethnic minorities and for the Soviet Union, and they tried to counteract German pressure by taking the case to the United Nations. France, in addition, having failed in July to gain support for sending European troops (of the Western European Union or a new Eurocorps), against U.S. opposition, sought a UN mandate for such interposition, or peace-keeping, forces. They succeeded only in obtaining a general and complete embargo on deliveries of weapons and military equipment to the country on September 25, but Secretary-General Manuel Perez de Cuellar did send an envoy, Cyrus Vance, on a fact-finding mission October 8. Disagreements within the EC over Yugoslav policy and instruments were temporarily quieted in September, moreover, by the initiation of a peace conference at The Hague under the chairmanship of the seasoned British diplomat, Lord Peter Carrington.

The Hague conference did recognize that the central issue was not ethnic conflict or military aggression but the need for a political settlement comprising all parts of the former country. But its premise was that Yugoslavia was finished. According to the conference's arbitration committee of international jurists, the Badinter Commission, it was, as of October 8, with the end of the three-month moratorium on Slovene and Croatian steps toward independence, a "state in the process of dissolution." In addition, the proposal for a constitutional settlement compiled by civil servants in Brussels, although an impressively reasonable document, also took sides in the political quarrel and was already out of date by the time it appeared in October. It accepted the Slovene and Croatian arguments that the republics were sovereign states and called for guarantees of minority rights and for disarming ethnic autonomists, thus ignoring Serbian (and eventually Albanian) objections and fears. With the prospect of full independence, its proposal for a "free association of republics with an international personality," had since been abandoned by its proponents, Slovenia and Croatia, and Slovenia refused to consider a customs union and programs for economic cooperation to make independent republics viable. Already, militant leaders from branches of the Serbian Democratic party in Croatia and in Bosnia-Herzegovina had declared their intention to join a new Yugoslav federation with Serbia and Montenegro, while the proposal for "special status" for Kosovo was acceptable neither to Serbia nor to Albanians. No pro-Yugoslav parties were represented in the formulation, nor were representatives of nonethnic parties, the civilian population, or the many civic groups mobilizing against nationally exclusive states and war consulted.

The parallel activities of EC and UN negotiators operated on a division of labor agreed between Carrington and Vance, that the EC would be responsible for a political settlement and the UN for a cease-fire sufficient to meet the conditions of sending a UN peace-keeping force. Although both Vance and Carrington objected publicly and vociferously to the damage that German insistence on early recognition of Slovenia and Croatia would do to negotiations and the prospects for peace, the Germans prevailed on December 16. Vance had obtained a cease-fire in Croatia in December (signed January 2, 1992), but it was predicated on an overall political settlement, which the German policy made impossible. As a result of the EC decision to ignore its own negotiations, a stalemate was left on the ground.

EC negotiations did proceed for a political settlement within Bosnia-Herzegovina during February and March 1992, but these were also interrupted by recognition. This time the pressure came from the United States, which wanted recognition of the independence of Bosnia-Herzegovina, so that it could restore unity with its European allies and its own influence on the issue by recognizing Croatia and Slovenia without abandoning its position that recognition must be given to all who sought it. Even before UN peace-keeping forces arrived in Croatia (after three months' delay in securing troop commitments and financial backing), therefore, the idea that establishing its headquarters in Sarajevo might prevent war from spreading was obsolete, overtaken by the speed of events. The demands on UN humanitarian agencies to expand from Croatia into Bosnia-Herzegovina to aid refugees and deliver relief began not only to skyrocket but also to require armed protection by a second UN force.

The failure of EC mediation to prevent and then to bring an end to the war in Bosnia-Herzegovina led the UN to join the EC negotiations by July 1992 (a decision influenced in part by U.S. pressure, working through the UN, and in part by the rotation of the EC chair from Portugal to Britain, whose prime minister, John Major, was seeking a foreign policy victory). Nonetheless, the prior division of labor between the UN and EC had already been institutionalized in decisions regarding the use of military force, substantially limiting the options for future actions and the effectiveness of those already adopted. Ground forces would be used for peace keeping, monitoring cease-fire agreements, and protecting those doing humanitarian work, but not to obtain the necessary prior peace agreements, for example, by giving negotiators a credible threat against those unwilling to cease hostilities, sign agreements, or honor those signed agreements. UN troops were, as a result, performing peacetime work in the midst of raging war without either mandate or rules of engagement and means appropriate to war. The use of force had to obey UN rules governing sovereign states, such as consent of all parties affected. Noninterference in the affairs of a sovereign state without its consent remained critical to China, the USSR (and then Russia), and until the autumn of 1992, the nonaligned members on the Security Council.

This original division of labor defining the use of force was prolonged by the continuing refusal of European nations to intervene militarily with separate forces. At the same time, the presence of European soldiers in the UN forces on the ground prevented a change in the UN mandate or new initiatives to end the war. A new U.S. administration in January 1993 attempted to change policy. During the spring, it pressured for an end to the war in Bosnia-Herzegovina and for protection of Muslim interests by the threat of NATO air strikes against military activity by Bosnian Serbs and against their interference with relief convoys, together with an end to the arms embargo on the Bosnian government: a policy called "lift and strike." The intention was to "level the playing field" militarily for those defending Bosnian sovereignty against those advantaged in the early distribution of heavy weaponry from the army and with support from outside the republic, with the aim of forcing Bosnian Serbs to sign a peace plan that would

return some land to the control of the Muslim-led Bosnian government. But this policy met consistent resistance from Canada, Spain,
Russia, Britain, France, and other countries whose troops on the
ground would therefore be at risk. Moreover, the Bosnian government
had no interest in negotiating a cease-fire and territorial compromise
from a position of weakness as long as it had hopes of retaking territory militarily under the cover of NATO air power.

The EC-UN concerted action had in the meantime produced another
peace conference, at London in August 1992; a restatement of the principles accepted the previous year; and a standing conference at Geneva
to negotiate a comprehensive political settlement—the International
Conference on the Former Yugoslavia (ICFY). But its proposal for
Bosnia-Herzegovina, called the Vance-Owen plan after its chief negotiators, Cyrus Vance and David Owen, was, like the Brussels document
of twelve months earlier, an eminently reasonable proposal that had
no support from any of the three warring parties and no input from
nonnationalist civic groups or persons from the republic. Negotiations
over this plan were also undercut by the United States in February
1993, when the Clinton administration moved from support for Bosnian sovereignty to a more assertive position in support of Muslim
victims in the war and the objections of the Bosnian president, Alija
Izetbegović, to the plan. The United States sided with President Izetbegović, who insisted on changes in the map drawn by negotiators, on
the grounds that it rewarded aggression by Bosnian Serb forces, and
U.S. support shifted from the Vance-Owen plan to what it called the
Vance-Owen "process." To reassure Izetbegović of its support and to
put pressure on the Bosnian Serbs, the United States insisted on adding its envoy and one from Russia to the ICFY negotiations. (German
patronage of Croats was presumed to continue.) But the result of this
U.S. policy was not to strengthen the negotiations but to weaken support for the one peace plan that held out any possibility of retaining a
multiethnic state. It also gave both the Bosnian Muslim leader and the
Bosnian Serb parliament an opportunity to refuse to sign the plan.
Alongside disagreements on military force among the United States,
Britain, and France, now a policy disagreement over the cause and
remedy of the wars was introduced. Russia was opposed to the U.S.
policy because it held Serbs to be the aggressors and singly responsible
for the war and it sought to make Serbia (and Montenegro) an international pariah through economic sanctions, diplomatic isolation, and
threats of air bombardment against Serbs in Bosnia-Herzegovina. This
Russian opposition could only water down or delay U.S. initiatives.
An alternative policy might have threatened Russia's special standing
among former socialist states, all seeking Western recognition and in-

corporation—the real issues at stake. The results were further disunity within the Security Council; an end to the post-cold-war honeymoon of Operation Desert Storm against Iraq with the renewed threat of a Russian veto; reduced UN forcefulness; and a growing crisis of confidence in the UN as a whole.

By June 1993 the Vance-Owen peace plan was dead. To get any political agreement that could bring a cease-fire and enforcement troops, David Owen and Thorvald Stoltenberg (the Norwegian diplomat who replaced Cyrus Vance on May 1) pushed indelicately for signatures on a new agreement worked out by the presidents of Croatia and Serbia, who had secretly agreed in a set of meetings from January to March 1991 to partition Bosnia-Herzegovina between them. Their proposal to make Bosnia-Herzegovina a confederation of three ethnic states acknowledged the fait accompli of military control by Bosnian Serbs and Bosnian Croats of substantial parts of the republic and of ethnic cleansing of ethnically mixed towns and villages. The plan delayed for two years the settlement of the contested status of its capital city, Sarajevo. A separate agreement among the warring parties for a referendum two years later on secession suggested that the Serbian and Croatian states would join their respective "homelands," leaving patches of noncontiguous territory under Muslim control to take the seat of Bosnia-Herzegovina in the United Nations. But this agreement was not signed by the Bosnian government and its parliament either, and the U.S. commitment to enforce the agreement with NATO ground troops appeared to vanish with congressional opposition to the U.S.-initiated UN action in Somalia in October 1993.

Thus, in the fall of 1993 France, which had the largest contingent of soldiers in the UN peace-keeping force, began to apply pressure to force a conclusion to the conflict and, through the vehicle of NATO, to oblige the United States to renew its attention. By February 1994, the United States had been midwife to a separate agreement between Croats and Muslims for a cease-fire between them, creation of a federation on the 30 percent of land the two former enemies held, and joint military operations against Bosnian Serbs, aided by alliance with Croatia. The threat of NATO air strikes against Bosnian Serbs, together with UN Protection Forces–sponsored negotiations, brought a cease-fire and withdrawal of heavy weapons under UN monitoring to Sarajevo as well. Russia was inveigled to put pressure on the Bosnian Serbs to comply with this withdrawal and to begin negotiations to join the federation or hand over substantial territory to it. The effect of the Washington framework agreement, however, was again to encourage Muslim-led Bosnian government forces to pursue their territorial goals militarily and to incite Bosnian Serb military response and moves to secure the borders and strategic routes of a separate state. It thus also revived conflict between the United States, which refused to accept a settlement it considered unjust toward the Bosnian Muslims, and the Europeans, particularly France, which demanded a political settlement by the end of 1994. Just as in May 1993, with the "joint action program" of the United States, Britain, France, Russia, Canada, and Spain, this quarrel was papered over in May 1994 with another declaration of unified policy (now including the ICFY negotiators) at Geneva. But this did not resolve the differences among them, except to insist that the Bosnian government and Bosnian Serbs sign a four-month cease-fire and work toward adopting the Owen-Stoltenberg plan of August 1993 and a distribution of land between the "federation" and Bosnian Serbs of 51 to 49 percent.

Like the intent of their original mediation in the Brioni Agreement, the primary concern of European powers was to contain the fighting within Yugoslavia. Thus, whereas Bosnia-Herzegovina was of little interest, the possibility that war might spread to the Serbian province of Kosovo and the former Yugoslav republic of Macedonia threatened to engage European powers or neighboring states and bring on a Balkan war. The CSCE therefore sent monitors to Kosovo, where Albanians had voted for independence and Serbian police had intensified its reign of political repression to prevent it. The monitors were withdrawn, however, after Serbia refused to renew their visas in the summer of 1993. Negotiators of one of the six ICFY working groups (on minorities) used shuttle diplomacy to keep some dialogue going between Belgrade and Priština as well as over national rights for the large Albanian minority in neighboring Macedonia. Viewing the problem of internal stability as a question of Albanian rights, the CSCE also set up a mission in Macedonia. Military troops from Scandinavia and the United States under UN authority were monitoring the Serbian-Macedonian border to prevent a Serbian invasion, while ICFY negotiators were also attempting to mediate the quarrel between Athens and Skopje over Greek objections to the country's name, which had stalled recognition of independence and left the status and stability of Macedonia uncertain.

Another ICFY committee was set up to negotiate questions of succession, but it was soon confined to the deep freeze by Slovene objections to any relations other than the disposition of economic assets and debts by international arbitration, and then by the war in Bosnia-Herzegovina and economic sanctions against the Federal Republic of Yugoslavia (Serbia and Montenegro). As negotiations regained momentum in early 1994, these talks also resumed, but this time the delegate from Serbia introduced a maneuver—that the value of all investments made from federal funds since 1945 be assessed in the pattern of assets and debts—which threatened to drag out the process of completing independence for many decades.

More than three years after the wars began in former Yugoslavia, foreign governments continued to speak about minority rights, the obligations of governments to protect these rights, and the so-called ethnic hatreds that had led to war. Having contributed to the breakup of the former state without defending their decision that the borders of the federal units were the legitimate international borders, Western states had helped create a self-fulfilling prophecy. It seemed in mid-1994 that ethnic identity and conflict had been implanted, perhaps irreparably, in the popular consciousness and in the political institutions of the new states that would emerge sometime in the future.

Observations and Analysis

International intervention in the Yugoslav conflict failed in its stated objectives—to prevent the spread of war, to stop the flow of refugees into Europe by providing assistance and safe haven in their localities, to enforce international humanitarian law against violations of the Geneva Conventions, to guarantee Bosnian sovereignty, to uphold international norms regarding the sanctity of borders and use of force, to deter the breakup of the Soviet Union, to reduce the threat to regional and global security of this and similar conflicts, and to create a new security regime in Europe. The prevailing explanation for this failure in the first year of the wars, 1991–1992, was that international attention was "too little, too late," despite sufficient information and warning in advance. And despite their unhesitating claim that international rules were at stake, Western powers were unwilling to commit military force to defend those rules against those willing to use military force to change borders. As a result, there was no deterrent to war, no credible threat that the norm on borders would be enforced, and none of the muscle necessary to back up international negotiators seeking a political settlement and cease-fires. The explanation for these mistakes in the external response to the Yugoslav conflict was a realist argument. Yugoslavia was of little strategic consequence or national interest to the major powers. No state, the United States asserted, should risk soldiers' lives in a foreign war that does not threaten its vital interests. This strategic insignificance was particularly important when there were so many other competing issues of greater importance. The period of transition in global order after the cold war had created an overload for major powers and the UN. And whereas some European powers recognized the need to act in the spring of 1991, they excused their inadequate response by saying that they too were in a transition, that Yugoslavs and outsiders distressed by the mounting numbers of dead, maimed, and displaced had unrealistic expectations of new European institutions (such as the emergency mechanism of the CSCE) which were not yet fully ready to undertake the task.

But if this explanation is sufficient, it revealed an abyss in world security in the 1990s, for many ethnic and national conflicts would fit the Yugoslav category. Moreover, acceptance of the realist explanation seemed to make this danger greater because it also dismissed any reason to draw lessons from the Yugoslav case.

In fact, the Yugoslav case posed a particularly severe test of the capacity of the international system to protect global security and threats to peace because it did fall outside the interests of major powers to prevent war, but not so far outside their national interests as to stand completely aside. It is precisely in such cases that multilateral organizations and mechanisms to enforce international norms are most necessary, as a safeguard of collective interests in security and a compensation for insufficient or partial national interest. Moreover, because international organizations as well as major powers did act, however inadequately, a realist explanation of failure is not sufficient. That explanation must be found with the particular order structuring their norms and interests at the time.

The primary problem of this structuring, as will be spelled out, was transition. It was not that institutions such as the EC and CSCE were untested, but that they were premised on the previous international order but nevertheless were acting to create new powers and jurisdictions. The Yugoslav conflict was an early and prime manifestation of the global crisis and transformation taking place during the 1980s and 1990s, variously called liberalization and westernization. The incorporation of formerly closed or developmentalist states into the order defined by the core powers—above all, the incorporation of formerly socialist states (the Second World) into the First World—was extremely problematic for those powers. The fine line between spheres of major power interest and spheres of international or regional organizations was disrupted because the question of membership itself and the corresponding principles of membership for an as-yet-undefined new regional and global order were at stake.

This situation was particularly stark because Yugoslavia was located in, but not a member of, Europe. Outside both cold-war and immediate post-cold-war alliances but on the European continent and at the physical crossroads of what is considered Western civilization, Yugoslavia could attract more attention and intervention than was ultimately justified by the national interests of the major powers. The invitation from domestic actors for outside intervention was a part of their political strategies to become accepted by Europe (Western European organizations) and to define their place in the new Europe. But for the major powers or regional and international organizations to have responded in kind, with reasoned, system-preserving collective security, their leaders would have had to accept that this question of membership in the "West" was already decided. Instead, the Yugoslav conflict was (as it had been in 1945–1949) a part of a larger struggle over the borders of Europe and, in turn, over the interests and primary bases of power of countries that define the norms of global governance. In such a case, realist and institutionalist explanations are not separable but interlinked parts of the same process of redefinition.

The Timing of Intervention

The issue of timing was less a matter of timeliness or lateness than it was of the kind of intervention that occurred at each stage in the Yugoslav conflict. The optimal moment for explicit intervention to mediate the domestic conflict so as to prevent either disintegration or war had long passed by the time the EC and CSCE began their mission on June 27, 1991, whereas less explicit intervention was actively part of the conflict by then. Some parties to the constitutional conflict within Yugoslavia successfully sought international support during 1990 and early 1991 for their domestic position so as to improve their chances of winning against domestic opponents: Slovenia gained support from Austria and the EC "troika," Croatia from Germany and Hungary, and the federal government briefly received the support of the United States and EC Europeanists such as Delors. Those who did not think that foreign support was necessary, who were preoccupied with domestic conflicts, or who felt confident that they commanded sufficient military power to win if the fight led to secession and the end of the Yugoslav state did not seek and did not receive support.

Uninvited intervention also occurred on behalf of international norms, but this followed the same pattern as invited intervention. Foreign condemnation of the treatment of Albanians in Kosovo began in early 1989, particularly from the United States, on the basis of the right under the Helsinki Convention to intervene to protect universal human rights. There was no condemnation, however, of discrimination in other republics against minorities and peoples placed in a minority position by the new laws, particularly in Croatia and Macedonia. Not only were international norms applied selectively, but they were also misapplied. In the case of Kosovo, outsiders were defending human and minority rights and freedoms for Albanians, whereas it was political rights to self-rule which Albanians claimed and which Serbs found threatening to the integrity of their republic. In other cases, such as increasing ethnic discrimination against individuals in Croatia and Macedonia, outsiders ignored developments that could have been solved at the level of guarantees to individual human rights and freedom had they been addressed at the time. The result was the escalation of individual discrimination to ethnic conflict and then to national conflict when the internal political balance swung to minority militants who demanded political autonomy and self-rule as the only means of protection for their people, who were willing to fight, and who could call on support from other parts of the country. In addition, the international community applied different standards to ethnic Albanians in Serbia from those applied to ethnic Albanians across the republican border in Macedonia.

Selective application of norms also fed the nationalist dynamic within the country. For example, by isolating the leadership in Serbia for condemnation, foreign powers and organizations inadvertently supported the nationalist case being built by Slovenia (and eventually Croatia) for secession, saying that their struggle was for freedom, human rights, and democracy, and that this was no longer possible in Yugoslavia. Because outsiders focused only on certain groups suffering discrimination and misunderstood the difference between individual and national rights, they did nothing to support the universal rules and institutional development necessary to protect human rights without violent conflict over territory. Although foreign governments said they supported the federal government and liberal reforms, they actually ignored the individuals and groups within the country who represented that alternative and were fighting against nationalism for civil liberties and democracy.

Justification for intervention in June 1991, when the act of secession by two of the Yugoslav republics actually occurred, was based on another Helsinki norm, that borders could not be changed by force within Europe. Yet this, too, was applied in support of those who chose to change the borders of Yugoslavia by declaring their independence and against those—primarily the federal army—whose task it was to protect existing borders. No attention was paid during the summer and fall of 1990 when Slovenia and Croatia were building up separate armies, with the aid of Austria, Hungary, Germany, and other European actors. Efforts by the federal presidency to maintain monopoly over the legitimate use of force and to negotiate Slovene and Croatian troubles after January were given no external support. No CSCE or EC good offices were volunteered when armed conflicts began in Croatia in August 1990 and when assertive diplomacy in defense of human rights and the democratic conditions of eventual European membership might have also helped to support moderates within the Croatian government, the Serbian minority within Croatia, and the federal government to find a peaceful solution.

The Instruments of Intervention

The second issue in standard evaluations of intervention in the Yugoslav conflict is that of instruments. From the moment the EC intervened, this became almost exclusively a question of the use of force: whether the use of military force was necessary, who would provide troops, and whether Western reluctance to place soldiers on the ground where casualties were possible made aggression more likely and ultimately successful.

There is much conviction, for example, that a credible threat of force in support of negotiations in July 1991 against those refusing to negotiate a peaceful political settlement on borders and interposition forces to separate warring factions while negotiations occurred (as was urged separately by the G-7 powers, France, and the Netherlands) would have had a very high probability of success in preventing further war. The refusal to do so, largely due at the time to U.S. objections both to the use of NATO forces "out of area" and to French alternatives for a European force, confirmed parties within Yugoslavia, so says this argument, in their reading of earlier U.S. statements and the lessons of the Gulf War operation. For the federal army leadership, for example, the lesson of Desert Storm was that U.S. leadership and Western consensus were necessary to UN action, and that the United States would act only when global strategic interests were threatened (Gow 1993, 69–92). Thus, the army was free to use military power in the territorial contests. Western military experts also cite moments when the threat of air strikes could have stopped the war in Croatia (for example, in September or October 1991 to stop the sieges of Vukovar and Dubrovnik, the latter a UNESCO-protected city) or in Bosnia-Herzegovina (also quite early in its war, such as the spring of 1992, when Bosnian Serb forces mercilessly bombarded civilians in towns in eastern Bosnia and in Sarajevo, using their advantage in heavy artillery). These moments had long passed by the time air strikes were seriously contemplated by the United States in the spring of 1993 and then finally threatened by NATO, as a result of U.S. and French pressure, to protect UN personnel on the ground in August 1993.

The refusal to use external military force to stop the war became an increasingly significant mistake as the wars continued, particularly when the simmering conflicts over independence within the tri-national coalition government in Bosnia-Herzegovina exploded into three-sided war after Western recognition of Bosnian sovereignty in April 1992. Mounting evidence of horrendous atrocities, mass rapes, butchery, and beatings and executions at detention camps in areas under siege by Bosnian Serbs, using heavy artillery left them by the former federal army, provided both humanitarian and military arguments for international military intervention. The objective of such intervention would be to defend principles of international humanitarian law, such as the Geneva Conventions on war, and to redress the military disadvantage of the Bosnian government forces. This summer campaign of 1992 was also the last moment, according to military experts looking backward, when air power could have been decisive and international intervention would not have become embroiled in the intricacies of three-sided ethnic war.

But the history of the conflict suggests that this emphasis on military power is misplaced. The problem by March–June 1991 was instead that the EC had broken its own norms on the sanctity of international borders and on noninterference in domestic affairs. The community took sides in the internal conflict over the reform of federal powers, over rights of self-determination, and over the location of national borders, and it accepted Slovene (and eventually Croatian) abrogation of the norm on the use of force to change borders. Yet EC member states were unwilling to take responsibility for the consequences, to enforce their own decisions against those within Yugoslavia who opposed the results. On the contrary, they were unwilling to acknowledge that they had made choices, continuing instead to insist that this was a civil war.

By accepting the position of nationalists that the fiscal and constitutional conflicts were a matter of sovereignty and rights to national self-determination, they prevented a domestic resolution of the conflict, ignored the federal government, and irreversibly transformed the conflict into one over borders and national states. And by accepting the Slovene and Croatian position that the republican borders were legitimate state (international) borders and that the conflict was therefore a result of the ambitions for a Greater Serbia of Serbian president Slobodan Milošević, the EC relieved them of any obligation to negotiate a peaceful exit, including delays until the status of all remaining republics was settled and believable guarantees to persons put in a minority position by their independence that they would be safe in their new states. At the same time, the EC gave no diplomatic options to those Serbs and army officers who opposed the secession of the two republics or the internationalization of existing republican borders and who were willing to use military force. Nor can ignorance be claimed, for political leaders from many communities—Serbia, Serbs in Croatia and in Bosnia-Herzegovina, the Bosnian president, Albanians in Kosovo, and others—had made the consequences of Western actions abundantly clear. Instead, external mediators refused to hear that in the event of the dissolution of Yugoslavia, there would be border conflicts and violent consequences for multiethnic communities and territories unless negotiators explicitly addressed the issue of borders and conflicting rights to self-determination on the same territory before granting recognition to some parts. The EC legitimated the breakup, left the rest of the country dangling, and opened the door to the resolution of conflicts over territory and international recognition of new states by those who had arms. It was at this point that it refused to commit troops to prevent war.

Even after the conflict had been allowed to deteriorate into a question of borders, international intervention could have formulated a strategy to guide the breakup peacefully. There were many groups within the former country who opposed war or who had an interest in a peaceful settlement and who, therefore, would have supported such negotiating efforts. Negotiations with the army (when it was being deprived of a state and its officer corps was torn between loyalty to a "Yugoslavia" and allegiance to new nationalist leaders according to their own ethnicity), either at the time of Brioni or before the moratorium ended October 7, held enormous possibilities for ending the clashes in Croatia and preventing war in Bosnia-Herzegovina.

Unwilling to give the army a neutral role in preventing the spread of violence and in support of negotiations, or to interpose external forces, Western powers instead sought an arms embargo from the United Nations. But this was singularly ineffective, in part because of the same international conditions feeding the Yugoslav conflict—a flourishing illegal arms trade exacerbated by the agreements negotiated between NATO and the former Warsaw Pact countries to reduce weapons stockpiles, and the desperate economic straits of arms producers in the former socialist countries. Moreover, governments in a position to enforce the embargo chose to defy it instead. Many were convinced that the former Yugoslav states had a right to national self-defense, and they had national interests in particular states. Most important, the embargo ignored the extensive defense industry within the country—a major cause of the actual fighting in Bosnia-Herzegovina—and that what remained of the federal army was being pushed by international action to ally with Serbs in Croatia and in Bosnia-Herzegovina, handing them military stocks and equipment. One partial exception to the embargo's ineffectiveness was the victim of containment, the landlocked Bosnian government, which had been led to expect international defense of its recognized sovereignty if it obeyed international norms and did not resort to arms in its own defense.

Thus, the EC decisions followed the same geographical line that was being drawn by the instruments of economic conditionality and moral pressure during 1989 and 1990. The EC and the United States treated the army as an aggressor in its own country and the rest of the country beyond Slovenia and Croatia as peripheral and "Balkan." Drawing a line between the West and the Balkans, they viewed the issue of force as one of containment, to be accomplished as during the cold war by economic and political isolation of those seen to fall on the other side of that line, as "renegade states" disobedient to Western norms. Western powers continued to declare the sanctity of the international norms they had broken, expecting the instruments of moral suasion and economic sanctions to do the job of resolving genuine political conflicts over territory. But these are instruments of enforcement which presume a community of mutual interest in the norms at stake, so that transparency and monitoring against occasional cheating are sufficient to protect security. This strategy was not only inappropriate to the circumstances of contested sovereignty but also contrary to the distinction being drawn by outsiders between those who were seen to belong to this community of norms but were not held to those norms, and those who did not belong but were held to them and labeled uncivilized, un-European, pariah nations and, in the case of leaders, war criminals.

The ineffectiveness of the instruments was compounded by the conservative impulse to protect their authority for use in other cases. The more suspect was international resolve to act and the more inadequate the measures used, the more major powers strove to erase doubts of their resolve by more forceful pursuit of these questionable instruments. Evidence that such measures as the attempt to end the war in Bosnia-Herzegovina by imposing an air exclusion zone over its territory, by economic sanctions against Serbia and Montenegro, and by publishing a list of accused war criminals to be prosecuted after the war were ineffective or even counterproductive appeared to matter little. Ignored by countries from Slovenia to Greece, the economic sanctions were even threatening to escalate war by contributing to conditions that exacerbated ethnic conflicts and the possibility of war in Serbia, Macedonia, and Montenegro. Nonetheless, they were progressively tightened and enforced to demonstrate (especially to countries of the Islamic Conference) that the West was acting decisively to end the war. Aware that the global order was changing but unable to formulate a common policy and appropriate response, major powers and international organizations resorted to norms and instruments that did exist, rather than risk demonstrating that they had no response.

According to Milton Esman's survey in Chapter 1,

> The presumption against external interference continues to govern the behavior of IOs; members are hesitant to establish precedents that might justify subsequent interference in what they regard as their internal affairs. Equally rigid has been the related principle concerning the inviolability of established international borders. There has been a strong presumption that any settlement of an ethnic dispute should respect this principle. The international system may yield to faits accomplis, such as the partition of Pakistan, . . . but IOs are not likely to promote such outcomes.

The EC unofficially overturned this historical precedent on July 7 and officially by December 16, 1991. Moreover, it did so despite the fact that it was usurping its own peace conference in session at The Hague, which aimed to negotiate a comprehensive political settlement with the aid of the collective authority of the EC and despite the very public pleading from President Izetbegović of Bosnia-Herzegovina with the German foreign minister to the effect that premature recognition of Croatia would ensure the spread of war to his republic.

In an attempt to resolve the EC's internal conflict over the question of recognition during the summer of 1991, between German pressure for unilateral recognition as an instrument of diplomacy to stop the war and British and French views that this would set a dangerous precedent and create more war if a comprehensive settlement did not precede recognition, Britain and France took the case to the United Nations. Once there no longer was a state and the conflict had become a contest for international recognition of rights to national self-determination and the borders of new states, the international organization most constrained by norms of sovereignty—not to interfere in the internal affairs of a state without explicit consent of all parties—and neutrality was drawn in to provide legitimacy and the military force the regional organization could not or would not provide.

The Role of International Organizations in Intervention

The third issue, after the timing and instruments of international intervention, is the role of international organizations. The EC decided to intervene in the Yugoslav conflict to seize the opportunity to create a capacity for common foreign policy and European security at the time it was completing financial integration, not because it had this capacity. Whereas its defenders could later excuse its failings as a result of this transition and others' unrealistic expectations, its member states in fact did the same as Slovene and Croatian leaders. Instead of feeling bound to work out their disagreements over recognition, military force, and independence with the United States and to create a common security policy, France and Britain turned instead to the United Nations. Similarly Austria and Hungary, as nonmembers of the EC but at the time nonpermanent members of the UN Security Council with active interests in support of Slovene and Croatian independence and against war on their borders, also turned to the UN when the Yugoslav federal government had vetoed the CSCE intervention they demanded.

By contrast, the United States and the UN, under Secretary-General Perez de Cuellar, had encouraged the EC to take on the Yugoslav conflict for financial reasons. The United States was in the course of a project to shift the burden of financing European security toward wealthier Europeans, while the UN was badly strapped for funds because the United States had refused to pay its past debts until the UN reformed and meanwhile demands for UN peace keeping were increasing in the post-cold-war turmoil. Both held to the belief that the end of the cold war would open an era in which threats to international peace and security would be more regional than global and that regional organizations were more appropriate to conflict resolution and crisis management. Yugoslavia, members of the U.S. Congress said repeatedly, was a "European problem."

The new UN Secretary-General, Boutros Boutros-Ghali, expressed this view of the importance of regional organizations even more assertively as he faced ever greater and more costly demands for UN peace-keeping services during the year. Rich Europeans, he felt, should be ashamed to demand UN action in Bosnia-Herzegovina when there were so many poor countries without rich neighbors which needed attention. At the same time his vision for this new regionalism, elaborated in his report of June 1992, *An Agenda for Peace*, and motivated in part by the experience of the Yugoslav case, was that the UN should delegate tasks to regional organizations, not the reverse.

The distinction between a regional organization and the UN is not so clear in the case of European conflict, however, for European powers form the core of the United Nations Security Council; yet their capacity to shift among organizations in their competition with each other was disastrous. Four members of the Permanent Five have direct national interests in European security. In addition, the United States could not be indifferent to the fate of European security arrangements as the initiator of those organizations in 1944–1949 and the mainstay of

NATO. Despite its early insistence that Yugoslavia was outside its area of interest, the United States could not leave the case alone, intervening with substantial effect but intermittently, so as to conserve its influence within Europe and the Atlantic alliance. Although a late entrant in the case because of the breakup of the Soviet Union, Russia, because of its interest in returning to the status of a major European power, became a major player as well by early 1993. In addition, there were in Europe several overlapping regional organizations whose memberships were not coincident and whose claims to represent European security were in competition.

The ability of European states to shift among organizations made it possible to avoid formulating a common policy and taking decisive action, while involving the United Nations in tasks for which its norms and organizations were unsuited. Although it promoted the dismemberment of Yugoslavia, the EC did so not by creating a set of neutral procedures and criteria for mediating national conflicts, for resolving conflicts over territory and the operative rights of self-determination, or for recognizing new states formed from one that has disintegrated without the need to resort to war. Instead of sharing the burden of global security with regional organizations, the UN was handed a mandate defined by the EC for which its entire history of peace keeping and neutrality was unsuited.

A reluctant Security Council entered the Yugoslav conflict slowly. The USSR, China, and nonaligned members were insistent in 1991 that this was a civil war, in which the UN should not become engaged. The UN adopted the arms embargo and sent a fact-finding mission to determine the possibilities for peace-keeping forces only with the approval of the Yugoslav delegate. It agreed to dispatch peace-keeping forces in Croatia to monitor a cease-fire agreement while political negotiations continued. Instead, UN headquarters in neighboring Bosnia became trapped in a war, and the assumption underlying its Croatian mission, that its peace keeping should not prejudice the final political outcome, was overturned because those negotiations were interrupted as a result of the internal politics of EC integration and the unilateral assertion of national power and interests over collective interests by Germany (over recognition of Slovenia and Croatia) and by the United States (over recognition of Bosnia-Herzegovina). While its troops in Croatia (UNPROFOR I) were caught between two parties that viewed the cease-fire agreement only as a way to gain UN legitimation of their (incompatible) claims to sovereignty over the territory under UN mandate, the General Assembly of the UN ratified the fait accompli by recognizing Slovenia, Croatia, and Bosnia-Herzegovina as member states and was left to find a solution to the conflict over Macedonian sovereignty which the EC created and then could not resolve. Accepting responsibility for humanitarian tasks in its division of labor with the EC, the Office of the UN High Commissioner for Refugees, the International Committee of the Red Cross, and a second military operation to protect them (UNPROFOR II) attempted to deliver aid and assist civilians so as to reduce the flow of refugees into Western Europe. Operating under rules of engagement defined by the norm of sovereignty—neutrality, consent, and lightly armed self-defense—in the midst of a raging war to *create* sovereignty by defining who among civilians had a right to live on particular territories, UNPROFOR II and the UNHCR were placed in the position of having to promote the combatants' military tactics of expelling unwanted or distrusted citizens if they were to protect civilian lives. Each warring party in Bosnia-Herzegovina saw UNPROFOR II as an instrument to legitimate and secure its territorial claims. When the terms of its mandate, such as neutrality and insistence on consent for the passage of relief convoys and agreements on the use of weapons, worked to the disadvantage of a particular combatant, UN troops were perceived as the enemy.

Both the specific mandate of the UN to serve its members' interests in the Yugoslav case and the general instruments of peace keeping were unsuited to the task of ending a war and enforcing a lasting peace. Were war to break out in Kosovo or Macedonia, its monitoring forces would be similarly ineffective. As a result, the authority and stature of the UN began to suffer. The Croatian government defied the cease-fire agreement it had signed in order to retake areas and attack the UN Protected Areas at many points during 1993, and in September 1993 it began to insist that UNPROFOR leave unless it could perform the task of restoring Croatian sovereignty to that land. Bosnian Serb military tacticians were particularly adept at getting UNPROFOR II to pacify an area they had seized once they were ready for a cease-fire. The Muslim party and the Bosnian government accused UNPROFOR of siding with Serbs (and at times demanded its withdrawal) because it did not act militarily to protect the Bosnian sovereignty declared in Security Council resolutions. UN Security Council resolutions during the first year of the Bosnian war, when news of atrocities was fresh and therefore most shocking, increasingly became symbolic expressions of outrage and international authority.

Commitments to deliver humanitarian aid "with all means necessary," to create safe areas around six Muslim-majority towns, and to prosecute war criminals, moreover, could not be implemented for lack of sufficient troops and financing. Continuing disagreement and competition among Western powers and the Permanent Five created delays and inconsistencies that were both embarrassing to the UN and useful to warring parties that needed time to regroup, rearm, or secure more land. When the Bosnian war was entering its second winter, European donors had committed only 20 percent of the food and funds necessary for the UNHCR to sustain the population.

The failure of international intervention to achieve its objectives in the Yugoslav case led observers to a realist conclusion. Without a triggering mechanism in the national interests of major powers, incipient threats to global security from ethnic conflict will be ignored until it is too late. The impetus to multilateralism will collapse if major powers, above all the United States, will not commit military forces, risk the political costs of casualties, and abandon the last prerogative of sovereignty by placing troops under UN or foreign command. Yugoslavs who expected international support were naive. The UN was being told to be more selective in its decisions to intervene and to transfer more responsibility to regional organizations and interests. Indeed, the policy of containing local wars by avoiding major power military involvement and relying instead on the imposition of economic sanctions to prevent aggression and to enforce international norms was hailed as effective in the Yugoslav case.

But this evaluation assumed that the interests of major powers and the distribution of power among them are stable. The disintegration of Yugoslavia and the new borders drawn within the country were part of a larger process of incorporation, and attempts at incorporation, of non-Western states into the West. Liberalization, export-orientation to Western markets, marketizing reforms under IMF guidance, cooperation on security in Europe between East-West blocs, and finally the complete collapse of socialist regimes had led by 1989–1990 to concrete questions of membership and new security regimes in Europe. Yugoslav parties requested European involvement, and the EC sought to intervene, as a part of this struggle for the redefinition of domestic orders, the borders and organization of regional security, and membership in Europe.

Within the country, the distribution of economic resources and power was such that Slovenia, as the wealthiest, most technologically developed, and largest earner of foreign exchange revenues, would take the lead in the conflict and would be the recipient of unquestioning Western patronage of its objectives and eventual easy inclusion. Similarly, in Western Europe, the reunification of Germany had led German leaders to assert what they and many others considered its natural dominance in the region on the basis of economic power and geopolitical position, including their role in EC actions toward Yugoslavia. Still constitutionally unable to use military power but acting in ways that suggested revanchist intentions, German support for Croatia and condemnation of Serbia fed nationalist emotions within the country as well as a belief on the part of those who controlled military resources, particularly Serbs, that a military fait accompli against the EC decisions would not be challenged and would eventually win.

The regional approach to conflict management was bound to fail in the Yugoslav case because there was no appropriate regional organization that did not have this internally divisive effect that made the conflict worse, rather than more susceptible to compromise. The desire for membership in the EC and differences among the republics in access to Western opportunities was one of the causes of the dissolution of Yugoslavia. The Yugoslav government invited the EC to mediate because it wanted to gain membership as a single unit and to make it impossible for Slovenia and Croatia to gain membership more rapidly as independent states than if they remained in Yugoslavia. The interests of the EC in resolving the conflict were limited by disagreements over the implications for the new frontier of European economic and security relations which might be drawn by its decisions. Individual European states could afford to dabble in the Yugoslav conflict, but the issues were too divisive for a collective Europe to formulate a policy.

At the same time, embodying the balance of power politics and the historical "fault lines" of the conflict itself, the EC exacerbated the conflict instead of contributing to its resolution. The benefit of familiarity had the cost of historical biases, abrogating the one essential axiom of conflict resolution and UN experience, that of neutrality. The resulting disputes among Western powers over which European organization would be responsible for European security (NATO, CSCE, EC, and WEU or a Eurocorps) and whether to extend these organizations eastward led the regional organizations instead to abandon interest and to leave regional security and boundary drawing to the United Nations.

But the UN Security Council is an extension of the European balance of power, not a neutralizing agent to regional quarrels. It was less able to speak with one voice of global security than it might have done against a non-European or a nonaligned state. Its resolutions provided the global authority and military force necessary to impose norms chosen by the EC but which the EC did not have the power or authority to impose on its own. The UN became an extension of the regional organization, in a servicing, compensatory, and subcontracting relationship. Once it became involved, it was inevitable that the Security Council would become the arena for conflicts between the major powers over their national interests and their views on intervention, for these had preceded UN involvement. Thus the ineffectual performance of Europe was brought to the UN.

The instruments of intervention also implied membership or established sovereignty. In European organizations (such as the CSCE) of which Yugoslavia was a member, it could veto intervention. The CSCE response to this obstacle was to introduce new emergency rules of consensus minus one and to suspend Yugoslav membership. Although it was an economic organization without military force, the EC then carried the banner of CSCE norms on the use of force (in part to get around this veto). But the EC demanded that parties it accused of aggression respect the obligations of signatories to the Helsinki Final Act not to change borders by force when the signatory state for one party (the Yugoslav federal army) had evaporated because of international intervention and the other party (Serbia and Montenegro) had been denied membership in the two norm-obliging organizations (the CSCE and the UN) until it agreed to "obey."

The issue of incorporation makes it doubly significant that an economic organization was given the lead in mediating the Yugoslav threat to international security. The domestic structures of Yugoslavia and the international norms on human rights and legitimate claims to territory applied in its case recall the systems of governance devised by Britain as a colonial power and postimperial security guard and described so well in Milton Esman's overview (Chapter 1), which have elsewhere also led to ethnic conflict and to devices of power sharing and partition which only worsen that conflict in time. Just as Britain's financial power undergirded those systems and then threatened their demise under global economic crisis, no analysis of the Yugoslav conflict can ignore the role the IMF and international organizations of major banks played in the 1980s, the changes in international economic governance its role reflected, and the primary responsibility of G-7 aid and the IMF to guide the transition and incorporation of former socialist states into the West.

The primary concern of Western powers through May 1991 was to restore the capacity of the Yugoslavian federal government to service its foreign debt and that of its republics. The austerities of the IMF conditionality programs, the shifts in economic power (particularly between republican and federal governments over the money supply, foreign exchange allocations, and the federal budget) through obligatory economic reforms and, eventually, radical political and then antisocialist reforms go a long way toward explaining the immediate causes of the Yugoslav conflicts at both mass and elite levels. The EC and Bretton-Woods institutions, until the secessions and wars after June 25, 1991, took the approach that economic rationality would prevent Yugoslav disintegration. Yet international financial organizations (and for that matter religious organizations such as the Vatican) are rarely

considered relevant to ethnic conflict. It is difficult to imagine how
there can be preventive diplomacy toward possible ethnic conflict if
the reasons that economic and political conflict becomes national and
then ethnicized are not recognized until they take on this character
and become intractable. The lack of coordination in the external demands placed on Yugoslavia, such as U.S. demands to respect human
rights, IMF demands for political reform, EC conditions for membership and demands to respect CSCE norms, further divided the already
competing interests within the country and jumbled the mixed signals
given by competing national interests of foreign powers.

The actions of international organizations had far less to do with the
Yugoslav conflict than with its mirror image among the member states
of those organizations—their own assertion of identity and power in
the course of redefining Europe and the relation between economic
and military power in the transition to a new international system.

The European (EC, NATO) refusal to use counteractive force, either
to make Europe's diplomacy credible or to acknowledge that its recognition policy required military means on the ground, was not only a
failure of instruments but an assertion of identity. Despite the use of
force by Slovenia to change borders and by Croatia to cleanse ethnically
and to create a Bosnian Croat state, Herzeg-Bosnia, it was essential
to view these actions as self-defense and to identify aggression with
barbarians on the other side of the line. Thus, Foreign Minister
Genscher's moral revulsion at Serbian actions in Croatia became the
dominant explanation of his policy. Humanitarian aid could be sent to
Bosnia-Herzegovina, but in order to avoid taking a political position
and placing soldiers at risk in an area that was judged culturally outside the line. The risk of creating Muslim extremists out of secular,
Europeanized Bosnians came with the perceptual territory, and when
the Bosnian government rejected the peace agreement for the partition
of Bosnia-Herzegovina into three ethnic states and reports of atrocities
and ethnic cleansing by Muslim militia diluted their image as victims,
the reasons for not intervening militarily seemed reaffirmed.

At the same time, European identity possessed a territorial aspect
that complicated the drawing of this new line, for the Third World
option of neglect was not completely available, for two reasons. Neither
the refugee flow nor television pictures could be distanced, and the
idea of European leadership was one of civilization. As Europeans
began to say when the atrocities in Bosnia seemed invulnerable to their
actions, it was the very "soul" of Europe that was on the line: the "line
in the sand" was a moral line, between what was Western and what
was not.

Yet this choice for economic power and moral identities and rejection of the military bases of security created a dilemma that has not been resolved. The EC decision to act in Yugoslavia was an attempt to address the foreign policy and security implications of greater economic and political integration under Maastricht. The United States initially pushed for CSCE mechanisms of conflict regulation to avoid conflict over NATO's role and the French preference for WEU (and discussion of a French-German corps) which EC involvement would raise, and in the belief that the question at hand for European integration was largely how to incorporate Eastern Europe. This being an economic and regional problem, it was looking to German leadership in Central Europe. By April 1993 U.S. pressure to act in the Yugoslav conflict led NATO to undertake its first military mission out of area, to enforce the air exclusion zone over Bosnia-Herzegovina, and a German constitutional ruling permitted German pilots of those planes in the first German participation in a combat operation since World War II. Marginal adjustments had also been made in the organization of NATO in response to Central European demands for membership, by creating a forum for consultation called the North Atlantic Cooperation Council for former members of the Warsaw Pact (including countries of the former Soviet Union) and a year later, the Partnerships for Peace. But intervention in the Yugoslav conflict remained limited by the unwillingness of major powers to finance such actions and the unresolved quarrels over command and control of military action in the absence of new multilateral (regional or global) security regimes.

If the international community had recognized sovereignty on grounds other than national self-determination, would politicians and intellectuals in the former Yugoslavia have been able to exploit ethnic differences for political gain? If it had had the instruments and political will to ensure peaceful resolution of border conflicts and satisfactory guarantees for multiethnic communities and people placed in a minority position in the new national states, once the path of political disintegration led in this direction, would there have been the ethnic conflict that the wars for national territory seemed to reveal? The unprovable counterfactual of the Yugoslav outcome must be taken seriously if the construction of an international order after the cold war is to reduce, rather than increase, the likelihood of ethnonational conflict, with its threat to individual lives as well as to global stability and peace. Precisely because Western incorporation will remain problematic for both rule setters and applicants, because the issues were far broader and more contemporary than Balkan history, the failure of Western powers to formulate a policy or make more than marginal adjustments in their international organizations and norms in response to Yugoslavia left the world more insecure.

9

The International Community and the Yugoslav Crisis

Steven L. Burg

The wars in former Yugoslavia have made it clear that principles and practices that provided a stable framework for international security in the era of the cold war are no longer sufficient to preserve international peace. Internal contradictions among principles embedded in the documents of the Conference on Security and Cooperation in Europe (CSCE) and the United Nations Charter have been exploited by new international actors to justify acts of repression and aggression within the Euro-Atlantic community. The mounting human tragedy in Bosnia-Herzegovina has revealed the inadequacies of decision-making principles, operational guidelines, and conflict-management capabilities of Euro-Atlantic institutions such as the CSCE, NATO, and the European Community (now the European Union) and the limitations of relying exclusively on the United Nations Security Council to enforce peace. Their failure to respond quickly and decisively to the mounting crisis in Yugoslavia and the inadequacy of international responses to the outbreak of war demonstrate the need to improve the regional and global conflict-management capacities of the international system. Most of all, the wars in former Yugoslavia have reaffirmed the central importance of political leadership by the advanced democratic states

This work is part of a larger project on nationalism, democracy, and American foreign policy in post-Communist Europe supported by the Twentieth Century Fund. It is published with the permission of the Fund.

of the Euro-Atlantic community. Renewed agreement on basic principles and approaches among the major democratic powers, together with renewed willingness to commit resources to preventing their transgression and enforcing them against transgressors, is essential to the construction of a new framework for international peace in the post-cold-war era.

The International Context of the Yugoslav Crisis

Interregional conflict with clear interethnic dimensions steadily escalated in Yugoslavia from the early 1980s (Burg 1986). The veto power exercised by each of the republics paralyzed the federal government, and conflict reached unmistakable crisis proportions by late 1989. The breakup of the Communist party (formally known as the League of Communists of Yugoslavia) at its January 1990 extraordinary congress resulted from the ongoing clash between the Slovenian leadership, intent on pursuing the further confederalization of Yugoslavia, and Slobodan Milošević, the nationalist authoritarian leader of Serbia, intent on recentralizing power and authority in the federation at the expense of the regions. Slovene and other regional leaders refused to acquiesce in the diminution of their power or in the political domination of Serbia and the Serbs which appeared likely in a recentralized system. The breakup of the party left the Yugoslav People's Army (Jugoslovenska Narodna Armija, or JNA) as the only supraregional organization still committed to, in fact, dependent on, the continued survival of the federation.

The electoral victories of independence-oriented, noncommunist coalitions in postwar Yugoslavia's first free, competitive elections in Slovenia and Croatia in the spring of 1990 and the formation of autonomist movements in other regions accelerated the disintegration of the federation. In August, Serbs of the central Dalmatian region of Croatia began an open insurrection against the authority of the new Zagreb government. Fearful that the nationalist campaign of the governing Croatian Democratic Union and its move to disarm local police and replace them by special militia was a portent of further repression, the Serbs of Dalmatia declared their intention to remain part of Yugoslavia or become an independent Serbian republic, to be called Krajina. Their uprising should have been a clear warning to all concerned. The existing internal borders, established by the communist regime in the postwar period, were vulnerable to challenges from minority communities that did not share the ethnic identity of the postcommunist governments emerging in the republics.

Minority communities were alienated and felt threatened when these new governments took on nationalist definitions. If existing borders were to be preserved, substantial political guarantees had to be provided for the several ethnic minority enclaves in the republics, thereby constraining the nationalist definition of the new states and their governments. If new states were to be defined in nationalist terms, then borders would have to be redrawn to avoid conflict between dominant majorities and their minority populations. But a threat by the Yugoslav minister of defense in December to use force to prevent the newly elected governments of Slovenia and Croatia from seceding signaled that any effort to act unilaterally would likely lead to violence. The simultaneous electoral victory in Serbia of Milošević, at the head of the renamed communist party, assured a continuing clash of irreconcilable political views. A narrow window of opportunity to negotiate a peaceful solution of the growing dispute among the republics and to address the demands raised by ethnic communities remained open from December 1990 to March 1991, but international actors failed to respond.

Western unresponsiveness can be attributed to three primary factors. First, American leaders were preoccupied with preparations for military action against Iraq. Second, the continuing political crisis in the Soviet Union appeared to preclude any attempt to facilitate the peaceful dissolution of Yugoslavia, which Western, and particularly American, policy makers feared would create an undesirable precedent for the USSR. Third, new international arrangements for responding to the emerging threats of violence within the post-cold-war Euro-Atlantic community, rather than between East and West, were not yet fully agreed.

The wars in Yugoslavia erupted at a moment when military-political arrangements for responding to the threat of conflict in the Euro-Atlantic arena had not yet been adapted to the changed circumstances of the post-cold-war era. At the same time, neither the economic-political mechanisms of the EC nor the international diplomatic and political capacities of the CSCE were sufficiently developed to take over this task. This shortfall of capabilities left the United States, the only remaining superpower, with expanded responsibilities for leadership, but American attention was diverted from Yugoslavia by greater concern for the fate of the USSR, by the mistaken assumption that Yugoslavia was no longer of strategic importance, and by the demands of building and leading a coalition of forces to roll back Iraqi aggression in the Middle East.

Onset of Crisis and the Search for a Principled Solution

The Serbian leadership seems to have decided upon the use of force to hold the Yugoslav federation together by March 1991. The Serbian president of the collective federal presidency, Borisav Jović, deployed JNA troops to Pakrac, Croatia, in March, following the outbreak of violence between Serbs and local Croatian police units. Although this action was justified as an effort to suppress interethnic violence, it also extended to other republics the precedent set in Kosovo of using the JNA as an internal police force in instances of interethnic tensions. But the collective Yugoslav state presidency refused to endorse a request to establish de facto martial law in the country. This situation led Milošević to declare that Yugoslavia was "dead," and to shift his strategy from seeking to establish a more centralized federation to seeking to redraw borders as a condition for dissolution.

Negotiations among regional leaders intensified in April and May 1991, against the background of increasing antagonism and open interethnic conflict. Slovenia, which had been attempting to negotiate its way out of the federation since December, had offered to assume a share of Yugoslavia's international debts and to provide financial support for a three-year phased withdrawal of JNA troops from the republic, in much the same manner as West Germany had negotiated the withdrawal of Soviet troops from the former East Germany. But the Serbs refused to agree, afraid of setting a precedent for the secession of Croatia and the other republics, as well. Western concern over events in Yugoslavia was expressed in a series of diplomatic warnings and the application of mild economic and political pressures. Western statements failed, however, to address the growing probability that the Serbian leadership in Belgrade and its ethnic Serb allies in the military would use the JNA either to prevent the secession of Slovenia and Croatia or to detach Serb-populated territories of Croatia and Bosnia-Herzegovina and annex them to Serbia. Nor did they address the special interests and concerns of the Serbian communities outside Serbia or other territorially compact ethnic communities such as the Albanians of Kosovo, the Muslims of the Sandzak, or the Hungarians of Vojvodina. Statements issued by the European Community and the United States instead stressed support for the continued unity of Yugoslavia.

EC leaders visiting Belgrade in May reminded Yugoslav leaders of "the Community's attachment to certain principles such as adherence to the existing institutional framework and respect for territorial integrity, [and] the need for dialogue to seek a peaceful settlement to the issue of the country's new structures *within current internal and external borders*" (*Bulletin of the Commission of the European Communities* [Henceforth *Bull. EC*] 5 (1991): 63, emphasis added). At the same time, the United States Department of State expressed support for "democracy, dialogue, human rights, market reform, and unity" in Yugoslavia, defining unity as *"the territorial integrity of Yugoslavia within its present borders."* The U.S. statement went on to suggest dismemberment would worsen ethnic tensions and that unity must be democratic and mutually agreed. It affirmed that "the United States will not encourage or reward secession" and that borders must be changed by "peaceful consensual means" (U.S. Department of State, Bureau of Public Affairs, *Dispatch,* June 3, 1991, 394–96, emphasis added). Such positions seemed to deny the possibility that border changes might have to take place if the growing conflict in Yugoslavia was to be resolved peacefully.

In an apparent effort to stimulate a peaceful resolution of the conflict, the U.S. secretary of state, James Baker, visited Belgrade in June. He devoted little time to hearing the grievances of regional leaders, however, and offered no new initiatives to resolve their disputes peacefully. In remarks following his meeting with Yugoslav leaders, he stressed the "importance of . . . continuing a dialogue to create a new basis for unity" and "the need to avoid unilateral acts that could preempt the negotiating process." He remarked a few days later in Washington, following declarations of independence by Slovenia and Croatia and the onset of fighting in Slovenia, that he "found an air of unreality [in Belgrade], an inability on the part of several republic leaders to understand the dangerous consequences of their actions." He reiterated, "We will not reward unilateral actions that preempt dialogue or the possibility of negotiated solutions, and we will strongly oppose intimidation or the use of force." But he reflected the continuing confusion in American and Western policy toward the conflict when he asserted that "the United States continues to recognize and support *the territorial integrity of Yugoslavia, including the borders of its member republics.* At the same time, we can support greater autonomy and sovereignty for the republics—in other words a new basis for unity in Yugoslavia—but only through peaceful means" (*Dispatch,* July 1, 1991, 468, 463, emphasis added). European governments and the EC similarly disapproved of the Slovenian and Croatian actions. Western governments seemed to be saying that formerly internal borders now enjoyed the status of inviolability heretofore reserved for internationally recognized state borders, and that the previously internationally recognized state could no longer protect its territorial integrity or the inviolability of its borders.

The outbreak of fighting in Slovenia prompted Western states, especially those sharing borders with Slovenia, to activate CSCE conflict-management mechanisms. The Conflict Prevention Center (CPC) consultative committee was convened in early July when Austria and Italy invoked the "unusual military procedure" mechanism. The CPC meeting, used by Yugoslav representatives to argue for their government's right to use force against an illegal declaration of independence (*Times* (London), July 2, 1991, 10), appealed for an immediate cease-fire but had no effect on the conflict. The first emergency meeting of the Committee of Senior Officials of the CSCE was convened shortly thereafter and issued an urgent appeal for a cease-fire, offered a good-offices mission to facilitate dialogue, and supported an EC initiative to send a mediation team of senior officials to Yugoslavia. The chair-in-office (Germany) was empowered to hold additional meetings as necessary to deal with the crisis, and four additional meetings were held on this basis during 1991 (U.S. Commission on Security and Cooperation in Europe 1992, 22, 28). The CSCE remained severely constrained in its ability to respond to Yugoslav events, however, because Yugoslavia was itself a member state and exploited the principle of consensual decision making to exercise an effective veto over the organization.

Even in the face of escalating violence, including large-scale movements of troops and heavy weapons from Belgrade toward Slovenia and Croatia, joint Western action was constrained by genuine disagreement over the probable consequences of particular actions and by the divergent interests and concerns of individual states. American and European policy makers differed, for example, in their estimates of the probable effects of diplomatic recognition of Slovenia and Croatia. The United States and France opposed recognition. The French foreign minister Roland Dumas warned, for example, that recognition would "throw oil on the flames." German, Austrian, and Danish officials, in contrast, urged the EC to recognize the breakaway republics as a way to pressure the Serbs to abandon the use of force.

The responses of individual states were also affected by concerns about the precedent they might be setting for potential parallel situations elsewhere, especially in their own countries. The existence of Corsican terrorists in France, British experience with nationalist movements in Scotland and Wales and with continuing conflict in Northern Ireland, and Italian and Spanish concerns about regional autonomy movements made these countries reluctant to extend immediate recognition to Slovenia and Croatia. Dumas, for example, warned that "tomorrow what we have done for Yugoslavia would be applied to other cases" (*New York Times*, July 6, 1991, 4, and July 7, 1991, 6; *Times* (London), July 6, 1991, 1, 10, 13). Germany, in contrast, because of its own recent experience of national unification, its perceived cultural affinities with the Slovenes and Croats, and its ideological hostility toward the authoritarian regime in Serbia, was more eager to assert the right of Croats and Slovenes to "national self-determination." Germans were unwilling, however, to acknowledge that arguments in favor of such a "right" might logically be applied to the Serbs of Croatia (Tietze 1993).

Individual European states were unable or unwilling to act alone, and the CSCE was rendered incapable of action because of the veto power of both Yugoslavia and the Soviet Union. The latter had a vested interest in denying the CSCE any precedent for intervention in support of the Baltic or other Soviet republics that might declare independence. Three factors persuaded the European Community to take the initiative in seeking a negotiated solution to the conflict. First, the EC perceived an opportunity for Europe to demonstrate a capacity for collective international leadership and thereby validate deeper political integration of the community. Second, the prospect of unilateral action by Germany compelled joint action by the EC to prevent the possibility that deeper integration might be thrown off track. Third, EC members shared a common interest in opposing the use of force to settle disputes in Europe.

The EC approach combined assistance in negotiating and monitoring a cease-fire, the facilitation of peace talks, the imposition of sanctions and, when fighting spread to Croatia, the threat of force. With the political support of the CSCE, the EC initially dispatched a mission to Yugoslavia to promote negotiations, while adopting an embargo on arms shipments and suspending financial assistance to Yugoslavia (*Bull. EC* 7/8 (1991): 107–8). Strenuous and tense negotiations involving Yugoslav leaders and the EC mediation team (*New York Times*, July 7, 1991, 6, and July 8, 1991, A1) produced an agreement among representatives of all six republics, concluded on the island of Brioni on July 7. This agreement called for a cease-fire in Slovenia, the withdrawal of JNA troops from Slovenia and their return to barracks in Croatia, a three-month delay in implementation of the Slovenian declaration of independence, and the initiation of new talks on the future structure of the federation. The Slovenian parliament ratified this agreement but emphasized that Slovenia was not giving up its sovereignty by doing so.

This agreement reflected the convergence of interests between Slovenia and Serbia. Circumstantial evidence suggests that the Slovenian president Milan Kučan and the Serbian president Slobodan Milošević worked out a secret pact permitting secession of the ethnically homogeneous Slovenian republic in exchange for tacit Slovene acquiescence to Serb efforts to redraw other borders. Such an agreement may also have been produced as the result of intensive negotiations between Janez Drnovšek, the popularly elected Slovenian representative in the Yugoslav state presidency, and Serbian leaders. Whatever the case, the Slovene objective of Serbian acquiescence to secession was achieved. Serbian interests in the withdrawal of military assets from Slovenia and the neutralization of Slovenia in the dispute between Serbia and the other former Yugoslav republics also were achieved. During the Brioni negotiations Milošević declared that those who wished to leave Yugoslavia should be permitted to do so but that the JNA should continue to defend those who wished to stay. And he asserted the equal right of Serbs to self-determination (Foreign Broadcast Information Service 1991, 56–57). His statement clearly signaled willingness to allow Slovenian independence, coupled with determination to hold on to ethnic Serb territories of other republics that had declared their intention to leave the Yugoslav federation, which amounted to de facto territorial claims against both Croatia and Bosnia-Herzegovina. EC mediators, like the Slovene and Serbian political leaders engaged in direct negotiations, thus did not have to deal with the most vexing issue in the breakup of the country: the status of Serb communities outside Serbia.

The EC faced far greater difficulties in attempting to end the growing violence in Croatia, where Serb communities had already mobilized against the Zagreb government, and irregular Serb forces were already waging war against ethnic Croatians. The G-7 leaders, meeting in mid-July, concluded that war could not be prevented in Croatia and called for the establishment of a United Nations peace-keeping mission to that republic. But such action was clearly premature, inasmuch as no agreement of any kind had yet been reached among the conflicting parties. UN action was, in any event, blocked by the opposition of the Soviet Union (*Washington Post*, July 20, 1991, A1).

Until the August 1991 coup attempt in Moscow and the ensuing collapse of the USSR, the reactions of the Western states were heavily constrained by concern about the implications of any action in Yugoslavia for developments in the Soviet Union. The West remained committed to supporting Gorbachev and upholding his attempt to keep the Soviet Union together. Western powers were therefore unwilling to move decisively to prevent the use of force against the breakaway republics in Yugoslavia. President George Bush, for example, visited Kiev on August 1 and delivered a speech to the leaders of Ukraine, then already staking out its claim to independence, opposing Ukrainian independence and urging support for the USSR. Both the Western and Soviet leaderships viewed the Yugoslav and Soviet cases as parallel situations.

Negotiation of a peaceful resolution of the conflicts in Croatia and, later, Bosnia-Herzegovina was made more difficult by the collapse of common interests among the Yugoslav leadership. The collective state presidency of Yugoslavia, regional leaders, and national military-security leaders convened for intensive discussions in an effort to defuse the growing conflict in Croatia, but they were unable to reach agreement on a peaceful solution within the confines of the status quo. Indeed, fighting in Croatia intensified during August 1991, as Croatian and Serbian leaders appeared committed to changing existing borders, in the hope of maximizing their gains. Although no Croatian leader could agree to any plan that relinquished territory of the Croatian republic to Serbia, secret talks had already taken place between Croatian president Franjo Tudjman and Serbian president Milošević to plan the partition of Bosnia-Herzegovina. Ethnically Serb and Croat areas would be annexed by Serbia and Croatia, respectively, leaving a smaller, predominately Muslim state in central Bosnia (*Times* [London], July 12, 1991, 10, and July 13, 1991, 11). The prospect of such a realignment of borders made it futile for either outside powers or internal leaders to attempt to play the role of honest broker in an effort to establish agreement on the basis of the territorial status quo.

Serbian refusal to agree to a cease-fire in Croatia in late July marked the failure of the EC mediation effort, and led the EC foreign ministers to call for UN intervention. The EC considered mounting an intervention effort of its own, but was unable to reach agreement. Germany, France, and Luxembourg favored such an effort, but they were deterred by an analysis prepared by British military specialists, which made clear the substantial effort that would be required for such an action to succeed. European states instead threatened economic sanctions and diplomatic recognition of the breakaway republics in an effort to compel the Serbian leadership to abandon its use of force against Croatia. European efforts had no effect, however, until the August coup attempt in Moscow had radically altered the international parameters of the conflict.

The EC call on August 28 for convocation of a peace conference on Yugoslavia was accepted within days. The EC approach involved negotiations among federal and regional representatives and the leaders of the EC, based on the principles of "no unilateral change of borders by force, protection for the rights of all in Yugoslavia and full account to be taken of all legitimate concerns and legitimate aspirations." It also called for the establishment of an arbitration procedure to decide issues submitted by the parties to the conference (*Bull. EC* 7/8 (1991):115–16 and 9 (1991):63).

The EC peace conference was initially linked to the establishment of a cease-fire, but heavy fighting continued even as EC military observers arrived in Croatia. As a result, this linkage was quickly abandoned. The Yugoslav parties' lack of readiness to negotiate was evident from the first session of the conference to the last. Only Serbia and Montenegro favored continuing the federation. Slovenia, Croatia, and Macedonia favored independence. Bosnia-Herzegovina favored federation only if both Croatia and Serbia participated. The Serbian delegation, in particular, frustrated the negotiations by refusing even to discuss most community proposals, on the grounds that the drafts assumed that Yugoslavia did not exist anymore, a proposition it was unwilling to accept.

The first in a long series of EC-mediated cease-fires was concluded on September 17. As would be the case in more than a dozen subsequent "cease-fires" over the next several months, neither the JNA nor the Croats took this agreement seriously. Each side continued to pursue its military options. As a result, the EC again considered sending in its own military force to put an end to the fighting. The Netherlands proposed sending thirty thousand European troops to Croatia. Since the EC has no military capacity of its own, the proposal was directed to the West European Union. Although the French and Italians supported it, the British opposed it. All agreed, however, that any action would require the consent of all warring parties as well as all EC/WEU members and that the force would have to be of sufficient size and strength to defend itself if necessary. These conditions ensured that the proposal would never be approved.

As this proposal was being considered, Lord Peter Carrington reported that the session of the EC peace conference convened earlier in the day had been dominated by the continuation of mutual recriminations between Serbia and Croatia. The Croatian foreign minister called for military intervention to establish peace, while his Serbian counterpart warned that intervention without consent would be considered an "invasion." Not surprisingly, therefore, European leaders rejected military intervention. The British were reported to have warned against "an open-ended long-term commitment," citing lessons learned from Northern Ireland to the effect that it is easier to put troops in than to get them out and that the inevitable result would be increasing levels of military involvement (*New York Times,* September 17, 1991, A3, September 18, 1991, A7, and September 20, 1991, A6).

The scope and intensity of conflict in Yugoslavia accelerated while the Europeans debated their next steps. Croatian forces seized several military garrisons, gaining control of large numbers of heavy weapons, including tanks and advanced antitank weapons. These were deployed immediately to reinforce a counteroffensive against advancing JNA troops. In an effort to limit the conflict, the Committee of Senior Officials of the CSCE agreed to impose an arms embargo on Yugoslavia. The United Nations Security Council unanimously adopted the embargo on September 25, 1991. This and later efforts would have little effect on the ability of the Serbian/JNA forces to wage war, however. They controlled considerable stockpiles of material established by the old regime. Some of these arms caches would come under the control of Croatian forces, improving their fighting capacity. In addition, both the Croats and the Serbs continued to receive considerable supplies from international arms merchants. Only Bosnian government forces, surrounded on all sides by either Croatian or Serbian opponents, felt the effects of the embargo. Eventually, however, Bosnian government forces, too, would secure access to the international arms market. Thus, in Yugoslavia as elsewhere, embargoes and, later, sanctions proved to have little effect.

The United States used the occasion of the Security Council debate to criticize all parties to the conflict. Secretary of State Baker accused Serbia and the JNA of "outright military intervention against Croatia." He warned that "the United States cannot and will not accept repression and the use of force" (*Dispatch*, September 30, 1991, 723, *New York Times*, September 27, 1991, A6). There was, however, little reason to believe that the conflicting parties would heed Baker's call for a peaceful settlement or be much persuaded by a vague threat of further action. The collective presidency of the old regime, which had served as an arena for negotiations among the regional leaders, soon split apart and ceased to play a significant role. The collapse of internal interregional negotiation may have been accelerated by the onset of EC-sponsored negotiations. Each regional leadership directed its attention to winning EC support for its own position, instead of negotiating a mutually acceptable agreement. The Serbs continued to use negotiations as a means to pursue a settlement that would preserve a federated arrangement placing all ethnic Serbs under the ultimate authority of Belgrade. The Croats sought European support to force the withdrawal of the JNA and regain territories under Serbian occupation, as well as European ratification of Croatian independence.

Despite a European Community statement of October 6 recognizing that "the right to self-determination of all the peoples of Yugoslavia cannot be exercised in isolation from the interests and rights of ethnic minorities within the individual republics" (*Bull. EC* 10 [1991]:86), the

EC conference remained unable to address Serbian concerns. In fact, as the bases for political settlement proposed by the EC mediators evolved in October and November, they not only threatened Serbs with the permanent separation from Serbia of those territories in Croatia for which they were fighting but also raised the possibility that Serbia itself might forfeit substantial control over Kosovo (*New York Times,* October 11, 1991, A6, and October 26, 1991, 5; *Bull. EC* 10 [1991]: 89). The draft convention proposed by the EC established "a special status of autonomy" for areas in which a national or ethnic group made up the majority of the population, and implementation of such autonomy arrangements were to be subject to international monitoring, but no reordering of borders was contemplated (EC Conference on Yugoslavia 1991, art. 2 c). Serbia was unwilling to accept parallel treatment of the Serbs in Croatia and the Albanians in Kosovo. The EC proposals also alienated the Slovenes, who were unwilling to compromise Slovenian independence by entertaining any suggestion of association among the former republics. The EC remained unable or unwilling to provide the military force that would be necessary to achieve Croatian objectives.

The inability of the conference to achieve agreement led the EC to turn to sanctions against Serbia and Montenegro. The EC also "forcefully remind[ed] the leadership of the Yugoslav People's Army and all those exercising control over it of their personal responsibility under international law for their actions, including those in contravention of relevant norms of international humanitarian law." This echoed an earlier statement by the CSO of the CSCE which had also threatened to hold Serbian military and political leaders to account for the war crimes of which they were being accused. In addition, the EC foreign ministers ordered the preparation of broad economic sanctions against "those not cooperating with the Conference"—code words for Serbia, whose representatives continued to reject the fundamental presumption of the conference: that Yugoslavia had disintegrated and formerly internal borders of the federal units had acquired international status. The EC called for stronger UN action and agreed to ask the UN secretary-general to use the coercive powers granted by chapter 7 of the UN Charter to bring peace to the region (*Bull. EC* 10 [1991]: 89 and 11 [1991]: 70–72, 91).

The secretary-general's special envoy, former U.S. secretary of state Cyrus Vance, traveled to Yugoslavia three times following adoption of the September arms embargo. He secured agreement to a cease-fire in Croatia on November 23 in Geneva and later negotiated agreement on the deployment of a UN peace-keeping mission to Yugoslavia (United Nations Security Council Documents [henceforth UNSC] S/23280, December 11, 1991, and S/23592, February 15, 1992). Serbia's willingness to accept a UN peace-keeping role, in contrast to its resistance to EC involvement, can be explained by the different conditions under which such intervention would occur. Under existing principles of UN involvement, UN peace-keeping troops could only "freeze" the situation in Croatia and thereby allow local Serbian forces to consolidate their control over UN-protected areas. By this time, these amounted to about one-third of the Croatian republic. This was precisely the outcome opposed by Germany (*Times* [London], November 16, 1991, 11). A UN-sponsored cease-fire might prevent Germany and other European supporters of Croatia from gathering support for an attempt to force Serbia to relinquish the territory it had seized. For Croatia, however, a UN cease-fire halted further Serbian advances, prevented Serbia from annexing Croatian territory outright, and at least held out the possibility that that territory might be regained.

Diplomacy without Force

By this time, Yugoslavia was in evident dissolution. The arbitration commission established as part of the EC conference rendered its decision to this effect in December 1991. The resignation of federal prime minister Ante Marković later in the same month, marking the end of the old federation, passed with hardly any notice. The United States and its European allies remained divided, however, over the timing and consequences of diplomatic recognition of the breakaway republics. Despite direct warnings of the explosive consequences of extending diplomatic recognition from the UN secretary-general, the chair of the EC Conference on Yugoslavia, and the president of Bosnia, German insistence on early recognition won out in mid-December. Britain and other member states opposed to recognition acquiesced in exchange for German concessions on the European monetary union under negotiation in the same period as part of the Maastricht agreement (Newhouse 1992).

The December 1991 EC decision stipulated that, to receive recognition, the former Yugoslav republics would have to meet a broad range of political criteria, including internal democracy; a good-faith commitment to peaceful negotiation of their conflicts; respect for the UN Charter, the Helsinki Final Act, the rule of law, human rights, and the rights of ethnic and national minorities; respect for the inviolability of borders and the principle that they may be changed only by peaceful means and common agreement; and commitment to peaceful settlement of disputes. No mention was made of any right to national self-determination, but the former internal borders had already achieved presumptive recognition. The EC further stipulated that states applying for recognition would have to accept the peace process embedded in its Conference on Yugoslavia (*Bull. EC* 12 [1991]: 119–20).

Bosnia-Herzegovina, Croatia, Slovenia, and Macedonia all submitted applications. The Serbs of Krajina and the Albanians of Kosovo also submitted applications, but the EC refused to accept them. This refusal reflected the continuing support of the community for the preexisting borders of the former federal republics. It also denied ethnic communities not granted republic status under the old regime the same right to self-determination accorded to former federal republics. Serbia and Montenegro did not apply for recognition. Instead, claiming they were the successor state of Yugoslavia, they began to prepare to declare a reduced state. It even appeared at the time that they might lay claim to the self-declared Serbian autonomous regions of Croatia and Bosnia-Herzegovina.

Acceptance of the Vance-mediated UN peace plan for Croatia did not represent a commitment by either Serbia or Croatia to peaceful resolution of their conflict. Contrary to an explanation of Serbian and Croatian actions offered at the time (*New York Times,* January 8, 1992, A3), neither side had agreed to the UN peace-keeping mission because it was war weary. Each continued its military actions following the Geneva agreement, seeking to exploit the opportunities for gain inherent in UN occupation. Illegal arms shipments to Croatia continued, and Serbia showed no sign of abandoning territorial ambitions regarding Serb-populated areas in other republics. Shortly thereafter, Serbia threatened to recognize the independence of the so-called Krajina Republic in Croatia and to incorporate it in a reduced Yugoslavia.

The United Nations peace-keeping plan for Croatia did not address the most obvious concern of both Serbian and Croatian nationalists: the redrawing of borders. Croatian and Serbian leaders continued to negotiate the partition of Bosnia-Herzegovina between them (*Financial Times* [London], January 16, 1992). The failure to deploy UN troops or other personnel to forestall war in Bosnia constituted an obvious strategic weakness of the plan. The EC attempted to mediate the peaceful "cantonization" of Bosnia-Herzegovina into distinct ethnic territories enjoying considerable autonomy. A tentative agreement appeared to have been reached in March, as the Croats abandoned their Muslim allies and aligned themselves with the Serbs in favor of an ethnically based division of the republic (*International Herald Tribune,* August 15–16, 1992). The Bosnian Muslims also appear to have agreed but were less enthusiastic about the plan, concerned about their ability to preserve an independent republic in the event Serbia and Croatia went their separate ways. Any hope that "cantonization" might produce at least some diplomatic breathing space in which to negotiate the peaceful settlement of outstanding issues was destroyed, however, when the American ambassador encouraged the Muslims to reject the plan outright (*New York Times,* August 29, 1993, 10).

Any international effort to settle the conflict by establishing new entities within Bosnia-Herzegovina would also have had to take into account areas outside the republic. Otherwise, the recognition of secession as the appropriate means by which to exercise the right to self-determination of the Serbs and Croats in Bosnia would only fuel conflicts elsewhere. Serbs in Croatia, Muslims in the Sandzak, and Albanians in Kosovo and Macedonia would correctly view such a settlement as a precedent legitimating their own demands for autonomy and, ultimately, secession from their respective republics. By taking a more comprehensive approach, the international community might have been able to mediate among the several contradictory values and goals of local actors. Extreme demands by Serbs to fulfill their right to self-determination by secession from an ethnically alien state and union with an ethnic homeland might have been counterbalanced, for example, by the prospect that adoption of such a principle might lead to the loss of Kosovo. Croatian ambitions with respect to Herzegovina might similarly have been moderated by the desire to hold on to Krajina. Under such circumstances, it might have been possible to achieve an overall settlement based on trade-offs among the parties involved. But such an approach would have required the international community to place the peaceful settlement of conflicting demands for self-determination above the principle of territorial integrity of states or, at least, of constituent units of a disintegrating federation. Alternatively, if republic borders were to remain the basis of state succession, and the dissolution of Yugoslavia was to remain peaceful, the United States and its European allies would have had to have taken more forceful action to guarantee the rights of ethnic minorities and to negotiate internal differences over the future political order in Bosnia than they were willing to undertake at the time. In any event, such approaches stood a reasonable chance of success only before the cycle of interethnic violence had set in. After that, they were futile.

With the cease-fire in Croatia, violent conflict in Bosnia-Herzegovina appeared inevitable. In October 1991 an alliance of the Muslim and Croatian government parties, together with other smaller parties in the parliament of Bosnia-Herzegovina, had declared the sovereignty of the republic and its neutrality in the conflict between Croatia and Serbia. They did so over the objections of the Serbian Democratic party, the third member of the tri-ethnic ruling coalition. The Serbs contended that this action violated an earlier agreement to rule by consensus among the three parties. The Serbs of Bosnia then conducted a referendum in November that recorded the preference of Bosnia's Serbs for union with Serbia in a common Yugoslav state.

Despite the lessons of events in Croatia and Slovenia, and the clear signs of impending conflict provided by developments in Bosnia-Herzegovina, the international community failed to act to prevent war. Instead, when the EC granted formal diplomatic recognition to Slovenia and Croatia in January 1992, its Arbitration Commission ruled that Bosnia-Herzegovina met most of the conditions for recognition. It still needed to demonstrate popular support for a sovereign and independent state. The commission therefore suggested a referendum under international supervision, in which all citizens would participate, as a means of demonstrating such support. The parliament of Bosnia-Herzegovina, again over the objections of the Serbs, scheduled a referendum for February 29–March 1. The republic's Serbs boycotted the referendum. The remaining Muslim and Croat populations voted overwhelmingly in favor of independence.

Recognition provided the spark that ignited war in Bosnia-Herzegovina and brought the UN peace-keeping mission in Croatia to the verge of collapse. The Croats, emboldened by diplomatic recognition and the false hope of military as well as political support, not only renewed their efforts to regain territory but also demanded fundamental changes in the agreed plan for deployment of the UN Protection Force (UNPROFOR) in Croatia. Understandably, the Croats now sought to avert a Cyprus-like de facto partition that would give the local Serbs control over one-third of the republic. And neither Serbia nor Croatia gave up its pursuit of territories in Bosnia-Herzegovina. Diplomatic recognition by the West thus did not have the intended effect of pressuring Serbia and the Serbs into negotiating peaceful resolutions of the conflicts in Croatia and Bosnia-Herzegovina.

The UN peace-keeping operation in Croatia finally approved by the Security Council in February 1992 was authorized for one year but was to remain in effect until a negotiated settlement was achieved. Croatian resistance to the plan raised fears that Croatia would demand the withdrawal of UN troops once the JNA and Serbian irregular forces were withdrawn or disarmed, as called for by the plan, and the protected areas were successfully pacified. Such a withdrawal might then become, as was the case for Israel after the withdrawal of UN forces from Egypt in 1967, a *causus belli*. Invocation of the coercive authority of chapter 7 was opposed by Third World countries, however, concerned not to set the precedent of acting without the consent of the country involved and thereby greatly expanding the power of the Security

Council (*New York Times*, February 14, 1992, A1, February 18, 1992, A3, and February 22, 1992, 3). The United Nations Protection Force in Croatia and its small headquarters operation in Bosnia would thus continue to have to negotiate with hostile local authorities in order to carry out even its limited mission.

Meanwhile, Serb irregular forces, supported by the JNA and the leadership of Serbia, escalated the conflict in Bosnia-Herzegovina. The Serbian and Montenegrin leaderships proclaimed a new Yugoslav state in April and formally disavowed both territorial claims on neighboring states and the use of force to settle disputes. Shortly thereafter, the new Yugoslav regime renounced control over JNA forces in Bosnia-Herzegovina. It formally released soldiers of local origin from service and pledged to return Serbian troops to Serbia. These measures had the effect of converting large numbers of ethnically Serb JNA troops (and substantial heavy weapons supplies) into the military arm of the Bosnian Serb political leadership. Moreover, JNA heavy weapons continued to cross from Serbia into Bosnia in support of actions by irregular forces. In early May, the self-declared Interior Ministry of the Serbian Republic of Bosnia-Herzegovina published a map depicting the division of the republic into separate Croatian, Muslim, and Serbian regions whose lines of demarcation corresponded closely to the pattern of Serb military occupation of the republic. Thus, early in the conflict, the Bosnian Serb goal of dismembering Bosnia-Herzegovina was articulated clearly and publicly.

Even as UN troops began their deployment in Croatia, heavy fighting continued in Bosnia-Herzegovina. Serb forces undertook the "ethnic cleansing" of territories that fell under their control, engaging in widespread terror against non-Serb civilian populations and subjecting cities to fierce artillery and heavy weapons attack. In the Herzegovina region, local Croats, with the support of military forces of the Croatian republic and paramilitary forces of extreme nationalist organizations from Croatia, established control over largely ethnically Croat territories bordering Croatia. In Sarajevo, fighting forced the EC observer team and the UN peace-keeping headquarters unit to withdraw from the city in May. Throughout the republic, large numbers of civilians were killed, many were taken prisoner and subjected to cruel tortures, and hundreds of thousands fled the fighting to become refugees in neighboring republics and other European countries. War crimes were attributed to all factions but most extensively and as an apparently purposeful policy to the Serbs. By the end of July 1992 the Office of the UNHCR estimated that some 2.25 million refugees had fled the fighting.

The EC efforts to mediate a cease-fire and to encourage a negotiated agreement among the warring groups failed repeatedly. This failure of the EC to find any basis for a negotiated solution, the mounting civilian casualties in Bosnia-Herzegovina, the growing refugee flow to Europe, and the scope of Western media attention to the attack on Sarajevo led some European and other states to seek direct UN intervention. But the UN undersecretary-general for peace-keeping operations recommended against such an undertaking, and the secretary-general concluded that a United Nations peace-keeping operation of the scale that would be required in Bosnia-Herzegovina was "not at present feasible." The secretary-general suggested that perhaps a European effort might be more appropriate (New York Times, May 14, 1992, A1).

Secretary of State Baker had earlier been reported to be "disappointed with the lack of success of earlier United States efforts to influence events in Yugoslavia" and to have "decided to disengage from the issue" because "there is no solution" (New York Times, May 5, 1992, A10). Now, however, he declared the situation in Bosnia-Herzegovina "unconscionable" and a "humanitarian nightmare" and called for delivery of humanitarian aid (New York Times, May 23, 1992, A1). A European military intervention, he said, should be viewed as a last resort, to be contemplated only after diplomatic, political, and economic measures had failed. With the support of the EC, which had already adopted an embargo of its own, the United States called for the UN to impose an immediate, complete embargo on Serbia.

On May 30, 1992, the Security Council adopted a trade embargo against the Serbian-Montenegrin federation. It affirmed that borders cannot be changed by force and renewed demands for an immediate cease-fire, an end to outside interference, the withdrawal or disarming of JNA and Croatian military units in Bosnia-Herzegovina, and the disarming and disbanding of all irregular units. The council called for an end to forced expulsions of local populations. It also called for the establishment of a security zone around Sarajevo airport to facilitate a humanitarian airlift.

These sanctions were imposed almost one year after the onset of violence, after increasing numbers of refugees had entered Western states—the first actual "spillover" of the Yugoslav crisis into Western Europe. There were few meaningful differences between conditions in Vukovar in October and November 1991, on the one hand, and those in Sarajevo in May and June 1992, on the other. Because Sarajevo was larger and more recognizable for having hosted the 1984 Winter Olympics, however, it commanded greater international attention. This ensured that American domestic political considerations, a crucial policy determinant with a presidential election less than six months away, played as great a role in motivating American support for stronger actions as conditions in Sarajevo itself.

The reopening of Sarajevo airport under UN control in June to permit the airlift of humanitarian supplies did not, however, advance the solution of the conflict. Ironically, UN occupation of the airport facility and the denial of this land to either warring party completed the encirclement of the city. Moreover, as Bosnian government officials complained at the time, the UN-negotiated agreement to reopen the airport did not require a cease-fire. It required only that local forces not fire upon the airport. Thus, even those Serbian forces under direct UN supervision were able to continue to shell the city. The Bosnian government appealed for air strikes against Serbian gun positions to alleviate the shelling of Sarajevo, but without effect. In fact, as efforts to secure the airport and deliver relief supplies were underway, both Serbian and Croatian forces continued to engage in large-scale military actions, even in the immediate vicinity of the airport. Both Muslim and Serbian forces soon began shooting and shelling UN personnel involved in the airlift. The arrival of UN peace-keepers in Sarajevo and their adherence to the strict principles of neutrality and evenhandedness associated with peace-keeping operations served simply to highlight the futility of such a deployment in the absence of an underlying political agreement between the warring parties.

Western states were deterred from more extensive military intervention by the estimated scale of the commitment that would be necessary either to secure the relief effort against further attacks, to put an end to the fighting or especially, to impose an overall settlement on the warring parties. One Western military affairs expert estimated, for example, that simply to secure the airport and UN relief personnel against further attack might require the commitment of as many as fifty thousand heavily equipped ground troops to establish the twenty-mile-deep security zone around the airport necessary to eliminate the threat of artillery or mortar fire. To establish a ground corridor from the coast to Sarajevo through which greater quantities of supplies might be transported would require an even greater commitment for it would involve 125-mile journeys through "God-given terrain for guerilla operations" (New York Times, June 29, 1992, A1).

Every individual state, group of states, and regional organization involved in the crisis made further action contingent on authorization by the United Nations. Although Secretary of State Baker, for example, was reported to have suggested that "the only way to solve [the situation in Bosnia-Herzegovina] is selective bombing of Serbian targets, including Belgrade" (New York Times, June 19, 1992, A6), the president made it clear that the United States would act only as part of a UNsanctioned multinational effort aimed at humanitarian relief. It would not attempt to solve the political conflict by force (*New York Times,* July 10, 1992, A6). In the absence of member support for the use of coercive force under the provisions of chapter 7, however, a more extensive UN commitment remained contingent on a local political agreement.

A political settlement remained out of reach in July. Representatives of the Serbs, the Croats, and the Bosnian government had met in London in mid-July for indirect talks under the sponsorship of Lord Carrington. Communicating with each other through an EC mediator because each refused to meet directly with the others, the parties appeared to agree to a truce, and to place heavy weapons under UN supervision. They further agreed to begin indirect talks on future constitutional arrangements for the republic and to allow refugees to return to their homes. But as was the case with so many previous ceasefire agreements, no cease-fire was actually established. Serbian shelling of Sarajevo did not let up even during the visit a few days thereafter of the British foreign minister Douglas Hurd, who remarked, "Where there is no will for peace we cannot supply it" (*New York Times,* July 16, 1992, A8).

Bosnian government officials revealed just how little of the good will necessary to negotiate a solution was left when they admitted that "the only reason the Government signed the accord in London was that failure to do so would have allowed the Serbian leaders to present the Government as the party obstructing peace, and because Western nations, including the United States, had placed 'intense pressure' on Bosnian officials to go along" (*New York Times,* July 18, 1992, 4). Similarly, Serbian leaders of the Krajina region agreed to drop their demand that participation in EC-sponsored talks with Croatia be based on the independence of their region and to accept "special status" within Croatia instead only after Lord Carrington "made it abundantly plain that in no circumstances would they be recognized as independent, and that they have to come to the negotiations on that basis" (*New York Times,* July 16, 1992, A8). International actors could coerce local leaders into participating in peace talks, but they could not coerce them into acting in good faith or prevent them from manipulating negotiations to score public relations victories and gain political advantage over their opponents.

A negotiated solution to the conflict required the commitment of local leaders as well as the cooperation of the Milošević government in Serbia and the Tudjman government in Croatia. More moderate, less nationalistic, more democratically inclined regimes did not appear likely to emerge anytime soon in either Serbia or Croatia. Elections to the parliament of the newly declared Yugoslav federation in June 1992 were boycotted by opposition parties and thus produced an even more nationalist parliament. Although repeated popular demonstrations against the Milošević regime followed, there appeared little prospect of its replacement. Indeed, in December 1992 new elections to the Serbian parliament produced a more nationalist institution. In Croatia, Tudjman was also under pressure from more extreme nationalist forces. In December a senior adviser to Tudjman reported that the government was eager to make political concessions to end the fighting, including complete local autonomy for Serbian areas within the Croatian state. But according to this official, "no one in Croatia would survive politically" the surrender of territory (*New York Times*, December 23, 1992, A1). By July it seemed less clear that the Tudjman government was willing to make even political concessions. Elections in August 1993 consolidated Tudjman's hold on the Croatian presidency and produced an overwhelming parliamentary majority for his Croatian Democratic Union.

As long as the governments of Croatia and Serbia base their claims to popular support on nationalist appeals, it will be very difficult for either of them to abandon their expansionist ambitions, to make extensive concessions to local autonomy, or to relinquish territories already taken by force. Western states might be able to help local governments retain popular support in the face of such concessions by providing direct economic assistance to their populations. But it is extremely unlikely that any Western government could provide assistance to a Croatian or Serbian government tainted by support for the kind of violence that has taken place in Bosnia-Herzegovina. Thus, local political circumstances are ill suited to an internationally brokered agreement.

Until August 1992 direct international efforts to achieve a peaceful settlement had been divided between UN officials responsible for peace-keeping and enforcement operations and EC authorities engaged in mediation. In August a conference of concerned parties was convened in London under joint UN-EC sponsorship. The International Conference on the Former Yugoslavia (ICFY) in London was aimed at bringing all parties to the conflicts in former Yugoslavia under the umbrella of a single, coordinated negotiating process. It was intended to intensify pressure on belligerents to cease hostilities and reach a settlement. And it was designed to encourage settlement of those disputes in the former Yugoslavia which had not yet led to open warfare.

The mediation effort that began at the London conference was also motivated by the need on the part of Western governments to demonstrate to their publics that they were responding to the crisis. Increasing media coverage of the atrocities being perpetrated on the civilian population in Bosnia-Herzegovina had given rise to increased pressure for Western military action to stop the fighting and, in the United States, to accusations by the Democratic candidate for president that the Bush administration had failed to act forcefully enough in Bosnia. President Bush and American foreign policy makers, therefore, briefly assumed more active roles in attempting to strengthen Western responses to the mounting tragedy in Bosnia-Herzegovina. President Bush was reported, for example, to be seeking allied support for the use of force to protect the delivery of humanitarian supplies to Sarajevo, the deployment of WEU ground troops in a more aggressive role than UN peace-keepers, and the use of NATO airpower to protect them. But Secretary-General Boutros-Ghali cautioned that the threat of force might make UN troops already in Sarajevo the direct targets of attack. And the British reminded the Americans publicly that "the only objective that would justify the massive use of force would be the achievement of a peace settlement" (New York Times, August 9, 1992, 1).

The Security Council adopted a resolution in August carefully limiting authorization to use "all measures necessary" to the delivery of humanitarian assistance, rather than the imposition of an overall settlement. American enthusiasm for the use of force was quickly dampened, however, by estimates of the scale of the commitment that would be required. Western military analyses leaked to the media suggested that 60,000–120,000 troops would be necessary to secure a land route from the coastal city of Split to Sarajevo, and to establish a twenty-mile security zone around the Sarajevo airport for the protection of relief flights. As many as 400,000 troops would be needed to impose a cease-fire in the republic. (New York Times, August 12, 1992, A8, and August 14, 1992, A6). In the absence of a political settlement among the warring parties, however, even intervention on this scale held out little promise of settling the conflict. Moreover, under such conditions it would be difficult to define the specific mission of an intervention force and impossible to determine when its mission had been completed and it could be withdrawn. The recent experience of UNPROFOR in Croatia suggested that a traditional peace-keeping mission would lead only to an unstable de facto partition of the republic and the continuation of interethnic violence both within and across partition lines. The prospect that intervention would become an open-ended commitment ensured that it would not take place.

The absence of any threat to use force clearly reduced the incentive for the Bosnian Serbs, who enjoyed military dominance, to compromise in the interest of achieving an agreed settlement with the Muslims and the Croats. On the other hand, the prospect that Western military intervention might yet be achieved reduced the willingness of the Bosnian government to negotiate a political agreement with the Serbs. The Muslim-dominated government was confident that any internationally sanctioned intervention would have to support its claims against its opponents. Faced with these difficulties, the Americans and Europeans launched a renewed effort to encourage a negotiated agreement among the warring parties.

The London Conference and the ICFY

The London Conference brought all interested parties together to discuss the conflicts in former Yugoslavia. Conference discussions reflected the great differences in positions among the participants (International Conference on the Former Socialist Federal Republic of Yugoslavia, August 1992). Although some advocated direct military intervention by an international force, none wanted to circumvent the recognized authority of the United Nations Security Council to legitimate such action. It was clear that none of the permanent members of the Security Council were as yet ready to support it. Indeed, no new positions were revealed at the conference. The Bosnian government delegation requested that it be exempted from the arms embargo established by the United Nations, arguing that in the absence of outside intervention Bosnia should be permitted to exercise the right of self-defense. But the conference took no action on this request.

The conference adopted a statement of general principles for the negotiation of a settlement, which included calls for the cessation of fighting and the use of force, nonrecognition of gains won by force, recognition of the sovereignty and territorial integrity of states, and the inviolability of recognized borders. Significantly, the principle of national self-determination was not reiterated. Instead, the conference stressed respect for individual rights as embodied in existing international conventions, implementation of constitutional guarantees of the rights of minorities, and the promotion of tolerance. Thus, the international community appeared to be moving toward the substitution of human rights and civil liberties protections for ethnic-based claims to national self-determination, although it retained the potentially problematic concept of "minority rights." The conference explicitly condemned forced expulsions and called for the closing of detention camps, safe return of refugees, adherence to the Geneva Conventions, and settlement of questions of state succession by consensus or arbitration.

The conference determined that an International Conference on the Former Yugoslavia (ICFY) would remain in being until a settlement had been reached. A steering committee co-chaired by representatives of the UN secretary-general and the EC presidency was established. It included representatives of concerned international organizations— the EC, the CSCE, the permanent members of the Security Council, the Organization of the Islamic Conference, neighboring states of the former Yugoslavia, and Lord Carrington. Working groups were formed for six major aspects of the conflict: a Bosnia-Herzegovina group to promote a cessation of hostilities and constitutional settlement, a humanitarian issues group to promote humanitarian relief, an ethnic and national communities and minorities group that included a special group on Kosovo to recommend initiatives for resolving ethnic questions, and working groups for succession issues, economic issues, and confidence- and security-building and verification measures. The ICFY, which was based at the United Nations headquarters in Geneva and co-chaired by Cyrus Vance and Lord David Owen, became the focus of coordinated international efforts to resolve the conflict.

The London conference briefly appeared to have made a positive beginning with an agreement on humanitarian actions signed by the leaders of the three warring parties: Radovan Karadžić, Alija Izetbegović, and Mate Boban. That agreement committed the signatories to collaborate in efforts to deliver relief throughout Bosnia by road, to secure humane conditions for those in detention, to end unlawful detention of civilians, to provide for the safety of refugees, to comply with international humanitarian law including the Geneva Conventions, and to bring undisciplined elements in their respective areas under control. Furthermore, all parties formally undertook to establish an effective and durable cessation of hostilities in all of former Yugoslavia and Bosnia in particular, including lifting the sieges of cities and towns, placing heavy weapons under international supervision, and withholding transborder military assistance. They agreed to cooperate in confidence-building measures, including a ban on military flights and the deployment of observers to monitor heavy weapons and borders; to dismantle detention camps and to consider the establishment of safe areas for refugees; and to strengthen international support for the rigorous application of sanctions, for monitoring, and for the enforcement of international humanitarian law.

Ensuing events on the ground in Bosnia, and the difficulty of negotiations in Geneva revealed that these were empty commitments. The ICFY mediators produced draft proposals for the cessation of hostilities in Bosnia-Herzegovina and for the future constitutional and political organization of the postwar state. The proposals, quickly labeled the Vance-Owen Plan, called for the establishment of a decentralized state, consisting of ten provinces, whose boundaries were drawn on the basis of ethnic, geographic, economic, and politicomilitary considerations.

Three of these provinces, which recorded ethnic Serb majorities in the 1991 census, were designated Serbian; three were Muslim; and three were Croat. The tenth province, surrounding Sarajevo, was designated nonethnic or multiethnic. The plan provided for transitional governments for each province and for the central government, and for further negotiations over the final constitutional arrangements for the republic and its provinces. But the final arrangements had to comply with international human and civil rights standards established in a long list of international conventions and agreements specifically enumerated in the plan.

The provisions of the Vance-Owen Plan reflected an attempt to forge a compromise among contradictory international principles and values, as well as the conflicting interests of the warring parties. As a result, they were highly controversial. The warring parties were able to agree in Geneva only on the provisions dealing with the cessation of hostilities and on the general constitutional principles for construction of the postwar state. They could not reach agreement on the number or boundaries of the provinces, the definition of their character, or the division of authority between them and the central government. The Serb delegation continued to press for the simple partition of the republic into three ethnically defined units that enjoyed international recognition and would enter into a loose confederative relationship with one another.

As the provisions of the plan became public, it was attacked for having given away too much to the Serbs. One critic argued that it "amounted to appeasement," and another warned, "Beware of Munich" (*New York Times*, January 7, 1993, A23, and January 8, 1993, A25). The specific provisions of the Vance-Owen Plan suffered from some serious deficiencies. As I have argued in detail elsewhere, however, these could have been corrected through further good-faith negotiation (Burg and Shoup 1993). Of far greater importance was the continuing absence of any provision for enforcement of the territorial, institutional, and legal provisions of the plan against those who might not comply with them. The absence of such provisions reflected the judgment of the international mediators that those international actors capable of providing such support remained unwilling to commit themselves to intervention. Most of all, the negotiations remained hampered by the unwillingness of the United States to support any form of intervention, or even the Vance-Owen negotiation process itself.

The obvious unwillingness of the United States to support a military effort to enforce an eventual settlement undermined the ability of ICFY negotiators to persuade the warring parties to reach agreement. The task of the negotiators was made even more difficult by the uncertain position of the new Clinton administration. Candidate Clinton had urged more forceful action during the presidential campaign. President Clinton therefore ordered a full policy review by his principal foreign policy advisers immediately upon taking office. The review was animated by doubt that the ICFY negotiations could, in the words of Secretary of State Warren Christopher, "find an agreement, find a solution that's peaceful that the parties would, in fact, agree to" (*New York Times*, January 22, 1993, A1). A long list of options was considered, including the lifting of the UN arms embargo to allow the United States and other states to arm the Bosnian government, enforcement of the UN flight ban over Bosnia, more aggressive delivery of humanitarian aid within Bosnia, establishment of safe havens for refugees within Bosnia, tightening economic sanctions on Serbia, punitive air strikes against Serbian forces, establishment of a military cordon around Serbia to enforce sanctions, and alternative levels of direct military intervention (*New York Times*, January 28, 1993, A7). In the end, the positions announced by Secretary Christopher in mid-February did not substantially change American policy. It remained clear that the United States was opposed to military involvement on the ground in Bosnia and unhappy with the Vance-Owen Plan but could offer no viable alternative of its own.

The administration found that it had no choice but to support the Vance-Owen negotiations, but on the essential issue its position remained carefully hedged. Secretary Christopher reported that "the United States is prepared to do its share to help implement and enforce an agreement that is acceptable to all parties. If there is a viable agreement containing enforcement provisions, the United States would be prepared to join with the United Nations, NATO, and others in implementing and enforcing it, including possible U.S. military participation" (U.S. Department of State, Office of the Assistant Secretary/ Spokeman 1993, 4). Thus, the administration continued to cede the initiative to the warring parties and deny critical leverage to the ICFY negotiators. Despite reports that the United States was urging NATO to prepare for a large-scale intervention (*New York Times*, March 11, 1993, A1), no specific actions were taken as the Bosnian Serbs mounted a new military offensive in March and April and overran besieged Muslim towns in eastern Bosnia. Despite pressure from Milošević and other supporters to accept the Vance-Owen Plan, the Bosnian Serb "parliament" voted to reject it in April 1993.

Neither War nor Peace

Rejection of the plan led the United States to abandon efforts to negotiate a settlement to the conflict. The Clinton administration proposed lifting the arms embargo against the Bosnian government and using air power to protect the Bosnians while they received the weapons and training necessary for them to defend themselves. This proposal led to sharp differences among the allies. The British and French, with peace-keepers on the ground vulnerable to potential attack, wanted limit the use of force to the protection of "safe areas." Their approach was consistent with the European attempt to address humanitarian concerns without offering partisan support to any of the opposing forces. But the basic stumbling block to the kind of involvement proposed by the Americans remained unchanged. Without an underlying political agreement, peace would have to be imposed by force—either by large numbers of combat-ready Western troops on the ground or by lifting the arms embargo and supplying the government of Bosnia-Herzegovina with the arms necessary for self-defense. The risk of substantial losses over an indeterminate period made the former option politically unacceptable to Western leaders. Despite the assertions of prominent political figures and media commentators to the contrary, there was considerable disagreement even among military experts over whether the latter option would end the fighting. If it failed to deter the Serbs or if it encouraged the Muslims to launch new offensives, it would prolong the war, contribute to its escalation, and threaten to spill over to neighboring countries, with the result that outside powers, including NATO member states, might be drawn into the fighting. Key European states thus opposed the American proposal, while the U.S. administration remained opposed to deploying American troops on the ground until a political settlement had been reached.

The apparent willingness of the European Community to accept the status quo rather than become more deeply involved militarily produced intense opposition from the Bosnian government, from Islamic countries, and from nonpermanent members of the United Nations Security Council, as well as internal dissension among NATO member states. In the United States, the Clinton administration abandoned its attempt to win allied support for arming the Bosnian government. Instead, the administration shifted toward a strategy of containment accepting the European proposal to establish safe havens in territories still held by forces loyal to the Bosnian government. Consciously or not, the Clinton administration signaled its willingness to accept the territorial gains achieved by the Serbs, rather than impose a reduction in those territories, as called for by the Vance-Owen Plan (*Washington Post*, May 23, 1993, A1). Although the administration deployed a contingent of U.S. troops in Macedonia to serve as monitors under UN authority, it also appears to have decided, in the words used by Secretary Christopher in a confidential letter to U.S. ambassadors, that the conflict in Bosnia was "not central to our vital interests" (*New York Times*, June 16, 1993, A13).

Under these circumstances, the Security Council adopted resolution 836 in early June 1993, with the United States voting in favor, but Britain, France, and Russia abstaining. The resolution commended the now-dead Vance-Owen Plan but, at the same time, reaffirmed the UN commitment to establishing the full sovereignty, territorial integrity, and political independence of Bosnia-Herzegovina. Later that month, the United States voted with the minority in favor of a resolution calling for the lifting of the arms embargo. International mediators, however, had already shifted their efforts toward negotiating a partition of the republic intended to bring the fighting to an end. Despite diplomatic and political pressure from European states and the international mediators, and concessions from the Croats and Serbs, no agreement could be reached. Deep divisions within the Muslim-dominated Bosnian government between those willing to compromise and those intent on reestablishing control over the whole of Bosnia-Herzegovina by force made it impossible for the Bosnian Muslim leadership to agree to any settlement short of a complete victory on the battlefield. The hope for such a victory drew sustenance not only from such formal statements of support as resolution 836 but from the repeated resurfacing of the American proposal to lift the arms embargo and provide air support for the government, and from the continued success of all three warring parties at securing weapons on the illegal international arms market (*Boston Globe*, December 5, 1993, 1).

Working through NATO institutions as a means of ensuring close political and military control over operations, the United States continued to press for the use of air power to end the Serbian siege of Sarajevo and impose a cease-fire that might permit negotiations to proceed. The prospect of increased Western military involvement in a form that would constitute de facto support for the Bosnian government produced a hardening of Muslim negotiating positions, however, dimming the prospect that any settlement could be negotiated. The Muslim and the Serbian sides continued their well-established strategies of manipulating international negotiations and deflecting NATO threats to use force in ways designed to advance their own political and military agendas. Moreover, the American resort to NATO as a venue for consideration of the use of force effectively minimized the role of Russia in policy deliberations and increased the resistance of the Russian government to extending Security Council authorization to any NATO action.

By early 1994 a number of factors converged to bring about an expansion of direct international involvement in the fighting in Bosnia-Herzegovina. Western governments were growing increasingly impatient with the lack of progress toward a settlement as public pressure to "do something" had been mounting over the previous six months. A NATO "warning" in August 1993 that it was preparing to take effective action against those violating UN resolutions had raised public expectations of action. Governments with peace-keeping troops on the ground were growing increasingly concerned about their vulnerability and about the interminability of their commitment and the lack of any prospect for success. The U.S. administration was growing concerned that continued inaction would jeopardize the credibility and coherence of the NATO alliance and destabilize fragile new democracies elsewhere in Eastern Europe (*New York Times*, February 14, 1994, A6). Fighting in Bosnia had appeared to be escalating rather than winding down over the previous several months, and evidence that all three sides were preparing for a new spring offensives was mounting. The prospect that Croatia and Serbia would be drawn into direct involvement in the war, with untold consequences for events in Kosovo, Macedonia, and beyond, also was increasing (*New York Times*, January 31, 1994, A9, and February 1, 1994, A8; *Boston Globe*, February 1, 1994, 8). And the latest round of negotiations had ended in deadlock when the Bosnian government rejected compromises intended to facilitate partition (UNSC S/1994/64, January 21, 1994, and S/1994/173, February 14, 1994; cf. *New York Times*, February 1, 1994, A8).

The NATO summit in January 1994 adopted a cautious and well-hedged approach to the use of force in Bosnia which reflected the continuing differences among the member states. The French government broke ranks with its allies, however, and began pressing for direct international military intervention, with American participation, to bring the fighting to an end (*New York Times*, January 6, 1994, A8). Against the background of a renewed contentious debate fought out in the public press among Western policy makers over what should be done to end the fighting, another in a long series of dramatic incidents sparked a public outcry in the West for immediate action. When a mortar shell exploded in the central marketplace in Sarajevo early in February, instantaneous worldwide news coverage and background reporting on the war and the failure of international efforts up to then to bring it to a conclusion intensified the pressure on Western policy makers to "do something." It brought President Clinton, who had heretofore for the most part declined to participate, into direct involvement in policy deliberations in the White House and pushed him to lobby other NATO leaders to support action (*New York Times*, February 14, 1994, A6).

NATO issued an ultimatum to the Serbs to cease their attacks on Sarajevo and withdraw their heavy weapons from an exclusion zone established around the city or face NATO air attacks against them. Bosnian government forces were at the same time admonished not to launch assaults of their own from within the city. In an effort to control the initiative, NATO based its actions on existing Security Council resolutions. Despite the objections of the Russians, no effort was made to seek renewed explicit Security Council authorization for the use of airpower. Simultaneously, however, the UN commander in Bosnia, Lieutenant General Sir Michael Rose, negotiated a cease-fire agreement between the Serbs and Muslims, and the interpositioning of peace-keeping troops to oversee it. At the same time, the Serbs negotiated a separate agreement with the Russians calling for Russian troops to participate in this deployment. The Western powers, the UN, and the Bosnian government were compelled to accept these arrangements, which made the use of airpower more difficult to carry out. The introduction of Russian troops on the ground, especially in the absence of a similar commitment on the part of the Americans, restored the political balance of forces in the conflict and helped to take ultimate authority for the use of force out of NATO and place it back in the Security Council.

The creation of a NATO-enforced weapons exclusion zone around Sarajevo and later a similar one around Goražde and the four other other "safe areas" created by earlier Security Council actions highlighted the differences in philosophy and practice between United Nations peace-keeping operations and the kind of coercive diplomacy adopted by NATO. The inclinations of peace-keepers to maintain strict neutrality and to afford warring parties ample opportunities to "save face" in the interest of establishing voluntary compliance clashed with the inclinations of NATO countries, particularly the United States, to counteract the use of force with counterforce. United Nations officials on the ground in Bosnia repeatedly clashed with NATO and Western leaders in their assessment of events and of the need for force. The secretary-general's personal envoy Yasushi Akashi was drawn into a particularly bitter dispute with the Americans, arising out of his inclination to negotiate a settlement rather than resort to force and his criticism of the Clinton administration's unwillingness to contribute troops to the peace-keeping effort (*New York Times*, April 26, 1994, A6, and April 30, 1994 3). Neither UN officials nor the NATO Leadership, however, appeared to be guided by a coherent strategic concept for the settlement of the conflict. Rather than embark on a coordinated effort to bring the fighting to an end and encourage the warring parties to make concessions in the interest of a durable settlement, individual

NATO countries, the United Nations, and Russia all seemed to be working at cross-purposes.

Russian involvement appeared to be motivated by a desire to thwart any Western effort to impose a settlement on the Serbs by force. United Nations officials appeared intent on preventing NATO from using force, out of concern both for the safety of UN personnel in Bosnia and for the prospects of negotiating a settlement. The United States appeared to be motivated primarily by the desire to reaffirm the effectiveness of American leadership in NATO and the broader international community and by a desire to bring the war to a conclusion. The American administration appeared unwilling, however, to use the measures required for any strategy of coercive diplomacy to succeed. The president repeatedly ruled out the use of U.S. ground troops to impose a settlement. Despite assertions to the contrary by anonymous diplomatic sources, it remained clear that the United States was at the same time not willing to compel the Muslim-led Bosnian government to accept its defeat and agree to a partition that reflected that defeat.

The escalation of NATO, Russian, and American involvement highlighted the degree to which the warring parties in Bosnia were able to manipulate outside powers, international organizations, and the negotiations they sponsored, to advance their own political and military agendas rather than to move toward peace. American officials, for example, repeatedly defined their involvement as an effort "to reinvigorate the negotiations and produce the kinds of results the Bosnians have been looking for" (*New York Times*, February 12, 1994, 5). This and other statements like it handed veto power over American negotiating positions to the Muslims (e.g., *New York Times*, March 13, 1994, 10) and encouraged Bosnian claims that were designed not to achieve a negotiated peace but to ensure the failure of negotiations and to draw the West into more direct military involvement. At the same time, the Clinton administration was unwilling to acknowledge publicly that no settlement could be reached without the agreement of the Serbs and that Serb agreement would come only at the cost of recognizing a substantial proportion of their territorial and political goals. The American-brokered plan to create a federation of Bosnian Muslim and Bosnian Croat territories which would then enter into confederal relations with Croatia, for example, announced with much official fanfare at a formal signing ceremony in Washington in March, could not be meaningfully implemented without Serb agreement.

Halfhearted coercive diplomacy on the part of the United States and the NATO allies offered little hope of achieving a political settlement. At the same time, UN-brokered talks between the warring parties appeared headed toward institutionalizing the status quo. On the same

day that Washington unveiled the Croat-Muslim agreement, the
United Nations announced that Bosnian Serbs and the Bosnian government had agreed to reestablish limited movement of the civilian population and relief supplies across the Sarajevo siege lines, under UN
supervision (*New York Times*, March 18, 1994, A1). This agreement
brought the Bosnian war a large step closer to a Cyprus-like conclusion: a de facto partition accepted by neither party and a condition of
"neither war nor peace." Indeed, President Alija Izetbegović of Bosnia
indicated that this was the strategy of his government and that such
an outcome would simply mark the start of a prolonged period of
terrorism and guerrilla war conducted across UN-monitored cease-fire
lines. Izetbegović was reportedly influenced by discussions with PLO
leader Yasir Arafat, who counseled him to accept any deal that legitimated Muslim control of territory and then use it as a base for a guerrilla war (*New York Times*, October 11, 1993, A1).

Lessons of the Yugoslav Crisis

The Yugoslav experience revealed the organizational and procedural
weaknesses in the capacity of regional and international institutions,
as well as individual states, to manage such a complex crisis. The most
obvious of these is the reactive, rather than proactive, nature of the
international effort. Despite clear evidence that Yugoslavia was disintegrating and the high probability that disintegration would lead to
violence, few efforts were undertaken to address the underlying conditions of conflict and thereby avert the crisis. In order to become more
proactive, Western states will have to overcome their long-standing
reluctance to become involved in the internal affairs of other states.

A proactive approach is especially important in disputes involving
competing ethnic territorial claims. Violence in such cases escalates
rapidly and engulfs the civilian population. Mechanisms established
through the CSCE for the peaceful resolution of disputes must be more
fully developed and made mandatory for member states if they are to
function successfully. In particular, the Yugoslav experienced suggests
the need to develop nonmilitary means by which to assist member
governments in the impartial investigation and ajudication of "incidents" of interethnic violence so as to avert the militarization and rapid
escalation of conflict. The hostility generated by civilian casualties and
large-scale population displacement arising out of the militarization of
conflict makes it very difficult to negotiate a peaceful settlement.

The cease-fire in Slovenia and the later agreement to establish a
UN peace-keeping operation in Croatia make it clear that it is local

interests, not the interests of outside mediators, which determine the success or failure of mediation. The war in Bosnia-Herzegovina demonstrates, however, the extent to which the authority and control of local leaders become dissipated under conditions of ethnic war and the great difficulty leaders have in recapturing it. It is therefore in the interest of outside actors to engage local leaders in negotiations before the stakes involved, and especially the costs of making concessions to achieve agreement, are raised by the human toll of war. The spread of violence erodes the authority and control of local leaders, making it more difficult for them to enforce any agreement that might be reached. The United States and other Western states, however, did little to encourage and support a negotiated solution prior to the outbreak of violence.

Western states were unwilling to support the peaceful redrawing of borders early in the Yugoslav conflict, as part of the redefinition of interrepublic relationships. Negotiations among regional leaders over the redrawing of the Yugoslav map might have allowed local leaders to achieve their goals through mutual concessions. Those who refused the opportunity to do so could then have been held accountable for their actions from the outset. The key to such negotiations, however, lay in the recognition that international principles, and the rights derived from them, were equally applicable to all parties. And successful application of those principles would have required the international community to withhold recognition from those who refused to negotiate in good faith.

International institutions and organizations were paralyzed early in the conflict by the inherent contradiction between the right of national self-determination claimed by ethnic minorities and national groups to legitimate their claims to statehood, and another principle of greater importance to the dominant states of the international system: the principle of territorial integrity. Instead of pressuring all parties to reach peaceful agreement, the United States and other Western states chose to support the territorial status quo. By doing so they increased the opportunity for local supporters of the status quo to use force against their opponents. Strong principles must be found, other than support for a discredited status quo, by which to settle such questions before they turn violent.

This is not to argue, as others have (Zametica 1992, 78), in favor of subordinating principles of territorial integrity and the inviolability of borders to the right of ethnic groups to national self-determination. Rather, if the United States and other international actors are to prevent the outbreak of such violence elsewhere, they must affirm the moral and political superiority of principles of human rights and democratic government over those of territorial integrity and national self-determination (Burg 1992). The establishment and protection of individual human rights makes possible the free expression of linguistic and cultural identities. The enforcement of principles of national self-determination, however, does not guarantee individual freedom. On the contrary, nationalist bases of political legitimation often subordinate the individual to the collective and lead to ethnic exclusivity and political privilege.

Human rights should therefore take priority over ethnic self-determination in the resolution of conflict. Authoritarian movements that seek to legitimate their claims to power through appeals to nationalism do not deserve the support of the international community. Nor do nationalist-separatist movements that offer no greater democracy than has already been established under an existing regime. Democracy, defined as that political order which results from the institutionalization of individual human rights, must be treated as superior to ethnic affinity as a basis for sustaining the claims of political regimes to sovereignty.

Similarly, the principle of territorial integrity must be subordinated to the principle of preserving or advancing democracy. The existence of an internationally recognized human rights regime—not the existence of coercive power prepared to enforce existing borders—represents the limiting criterion for denying secessionist claims. In this way, the creation of an increasing number of microstates that contribute little to the advance of human rights may be avoided, while changes that improve the human condition may be recognized and supported.

The Yugoslav case demonstrates that insistence on territorial integrity and the preservation of existing borders may in some situations discourage democratic change and encourage the use of force. Early insistence by outside powers on the democratic legitimation of existing borders might have encouraged the establishment of human rights regimes and avoided the escalation of ethnic tensions in Croatia and Bosnia. The disintegration of Yugoslavia allowed many opportunities for international actors to influence events. The importance of articulating the preceding principles clearly, publicly, and early in such a situation cannot be overemphasized. By doing so, international actors may affect popular perceptions and politics. In Yugoslavia, for example, the regional elections held in 1990 might have produced more moderate governments. By insisting on these principles, international actors may even affect the calculations of local leaders. Serb, Croat, and Muslim leaders in Bosnia, as well as leaders of Serbia and Croatia might have chosen to continue with negotiations underway in 1990 if they had held out the prospect of change.

The most difficult conflicts to resolve are those involving competing ethnically legitimated claims to the same territory, as is the case in Croatia and Bosnia. Where such claims do not exist, as for example in Slovenia, simple partition may eliminate the basis of interethnic conflict. In some instances, partition may also advance the cause of democracy. But the existence of competing claims to territory does not by itself account for the magnitude of human destruction that has occurred in Yugoslavia. The extreme violence in Yugoslavia must also be attributed to the establishment of ethnically defined governments that failed to provide democratic safeguards for the human rights of minority communities. For these reasons, the repression of Kosovo and its ethnic Albanian population by Serbia represents another, equally violent conflict waiting to happen. If the international community is to facilitate the peaceful settlement of even this category of ethnic conflict, therefore, it must devise instrumentalities by which to safeguard human rights in such territories.

One such instrumentality may be the establishment of international transitional authorities for newly emerging multiethnic states that have not yet institutionalized democratic safeguards. Transitional arrangements may allow each ethnic group to avoid accepting subordination to rule by the other, thereby deescalating the conflict. In the short run, such deescalation is by itself an important achievement. But the primary longer-term function of transitional arrangements should be to foster the emergence of a democratic system. To be successful, therefore, transitional arrangements must avoid substituting rule by outside actors for the consolidation of democratic self-rule. While outsiders will necessarily be centrally involved in the resolution of extremely sensitive issues, they must encourage and rely on self-administration by the local population across a broad range of governmental functions, especially those that transcend the local ethnic communities and integrate them with neighboring states and the broader international community. This strategy will permit many identities and interests to compete for the loyalties of these populations, and the same integrative forces that transformed the West European states into the European Union may begin to displace the disintegrative forces of nationalism. In this way, transitional arrangements offer the means by which the international community may engage in genuine and lasting peace making, and ethnic communities may avoid the human tragedy and destruction of war.

Such action requires democratic states, working in concert and through legitimate international agencies, to overcome their reluctance to intervene in the affairs of other states. As a result of the end of the cold war, the commitment to democratic politics by the successor states, and the evolution of the Helsinki-CSCE process, there is considerable justification for constructive concern and a legitimate international framework for involvement in human-rights-related issues throughout the Euro-Atlantic community. Membership in this international community and the benefits to be derived from economic, political, and security arrangements developing within it must be made contingent on acceptance of the principle that such issues are the legitimate object of international concern.

The Yugoslav experience provides further evidence of another well-known reality: even under conditions of crisis and in the context of a "collective" security approach, leaders of individual states in the Euro-Atlantic community advocate widely differing and even contradictory responses. Such differences reflect their pursuit of differing national interests arising out of historical factors, traditional "spheres of influence," economic and political ambitions, or such simple geographic facts as a common border with the country in crisis. Successful international management of Yugoslav-like crises therefore requires counterbalancing individual national interests by strengthening concern for the core values and principles of political behavior common to the members of Euro-Atlantic community. The common institutions of the CSCE must be rededicated to advancing the principles of human rights and democracy. More effective decision-making procedures must be developed which prevent conflicting parties from obstructing international action and increase the pressure on states to support these broad principles of international community.

The CSCE took the first tentative steps in this direction at its Prague meeting in January 1992 by adopting a "consensus-minus-one" principle of decision making which would prevent any single member from preventing action "in cases of clear, gross and uncorrected violations of relevant CSCE commitments." In such cases, appropriate peaceful action to protect human rights, democracy, and the rule of law may be taken "in the absence of the consent of the State concerned." This provision was prompted by the Yugoslav crisis and by concerns that the accession to membership of the post-Soviet republics made it likely that, similar situations would arise in the future. Such actions, however, were to be limited to "political declarations or other political steps to apply outside the territory of the State concerned" (CSCE, 1992, paras. 16, 22, 23). This principle must now be adopted for all CSCE actions.

The Yugoslav crisis also demonstrated the clear need to develop a regional capacity for peace keeping. Both NATO and the WEU countries acknowledged as much in June 1992 when NATO agreed in principle on the possibility of undertaking peace-keeping operations in

Eastern Europe if asked to do so by the CSCE, and the WEU countries agreed on the possibility of assigning troops to the WEU for such missions. Under present CSCE rules, however, any request that NATO play such a role would still require a unanimous vote, and the decision to assign forces to the WEU remains under the authority of each individual member state. Peace keeping alone, moreover, may not be sufficient to ensure political stability among the Euro-Atlantic states still in transition to democracy. The continued threat of interethnic violence calls for the establishment of a credible capacity for military intervention to enforce the principles of democratic government already established in the Euro-Atlantic community. The absence of such a capacity makes peaceful efforts to resolve Yugoslav-like conflicts more difficult. Only a credible threat that force might be used to impose a less favorable settlement than might be reached through negotiation may persuade the parties to severe ethnic conflicts to participate in more peaceful efforts to resolve their differences. The Yugoslav crisis demonstrates, however, that while such a threat represents a necessary condition for the successful collective management of ethnic conflicts, force alone is not sufficient to achieve the kind of political settlement required to secure international peace.

PART IV

Conclusion

10

An Outline of a Comparison Between Yugoslavia and Lebanon

Barry Preisler

Comparisons between the tragic experiences of Lebanon and Yugoslavia have been quite common over the years. Walid Khalidi, in his discussion of the initiating events of the Lebanese Civil War of 1975–1976, spoke of the Ain Rumanneh bus massacre of April 1975 as the "Sarajevo" of the civil war (Khalidi 1983). Branka Magaš, for her part, characterized the collapse of the Yugoslav state by the end of 1991 as the "Lebanization" of Yugoslavia (Magaš 1993). Such comparisons implicitly recognize a great deal that is common to the historical experiences of these two societies. Both are significantly divided on ethnic, subnational, or sectarian lines, and these divisions have been part of the basis of significant strife in the historical past as well as in the present.

When we come to the question of outside involvement, especially by international organizations, in the internal strife of Lebanon and Yugoslavia, the comparisons are both more obvious and more difficult to make. Besides nearly continuous international diplomatic and mediational efforts in Lebanon over the years, direct intervention in the form of international peace-keeping troops has occurred on many occasions. The entry of Arab League troops in late 1976, United Nations troops in 1978, and the Multinational Forces in 1982 constituted major efforts to intervene in the internal affairs of Lebanon by outside powers acting not alone but in some international or at least multinational coordinated effort.

The international efforts in regard to the former Yugoslavia, though more compacted in time, also passed through many phases. A number of major international organizations have been involved in the Yugoslav crisis, sometimes in sequence, sometimes in concert. The European Community (now the European Union), the United Nations, NATO, and the CSCE have all tried to influence the escalating conflict since at least the spring of 1990.

What seems to be common to essentially all direct (that is, military) interventions in both cases is the overall aim: to minimize death and destruction among people caught in the battles, by acting as buffers and cease-fire monitors ("separating the warring sides") and by providing humanitarian assistance. What seems to be common to most indirect (that is, good-offices, diplomatic) intervention is the overall aim of resolving the basic causes of conflict. These aims seem to coincide most clearly with the norms of international intervention (both old and new). The issues involved when these are the aims tend to be timing, clarity of backing from the international organizations they represent, and concern for the safety and welfare of the units that will be sent to intervene.

Allowing these most elemental points of similarity, however, there are other broad and important dimensions in which to compare and contrast the Lebanese and Yugoslav cases. In this chapter, I focus on two major areas that show the greatest promise for fruitful comparison: structural characteristics and risks for interveners. With regard to structural characteristics, I explore how the involvement of international organizations is prompted by the unilateral involvement of outside states, and I examine the nature and implications of the "collapse" of the state in the two instances. I then present an outline for a more precise structural comparison. "Lessons" from other conflicts are continually being invoked in regard to the risks of intervention in Yugoslavia. In the second part of the essay, I consider the general risks of involvement for international organizations in any such dispute, paying special attention to the risks for member states that participate, and I discuss the particular risks entailed in humanitarian intervention in ethnic strife.

Structural Comparisons

International Intervention after Unilateral Intervention

In all three cases of major direct involvement by international organizations in Lebanon, the international intervention followed in the wake of a unilateral intervention or invasion by a single outside state: Syria in 1976 and Israel in both 1978 and 1982. In each case, the outside power was militarily overpowering in relation to the Lebanese (or Lebanese/Palestinian) forces they faced. Each of these Syrian and Israeli offensives into Lebanon proceeded until the military or political costs of further advance grew too great. In other words, these military advances came to a halt more for reasons outside Lebanon (such as diplomatic pressure by other countries) and much less because of the military opposition facing them on the ground in Lebanon. When that point was reached in each case, the path was open for international intervention, mainly in the form of troops to provide a buffer between the sides and to monitor any breaches of the cease-fires. Consent of both (or all) sides, one of the conditions of successful intervention discussed by Milton Esman and Shibley Telhami in this volume, was thus obtained more or less by default in that the side capable of military advance had achieved most if not all of its objectives. The factions and forces trying so unsuccessfully to oppose such military advances would, of course, "agree" to almost any international intervention that promised to halt the offensive against them. Indeed, militarily weak factions are typically the ones that call most stridently for outside intervention.

The point here is more than the simple one of demonstrating that a crucial factor for initiating international intervention with the hope that it will be relatively successful is the willingness of both sides to accept international participation at these junctures. These cases illustrate a more profound point, especially in the context of Lebanon. It was not until the *internal* crisis of Lebanese politics became an *interstate* crisis involving direct military involvement by other states that international organizations acted. That is, international intervention took place pretty much within the bounds of traditional norms of intervention: to contain a threat to international peace. The "trip wire" legitimating IO involvement was the involvement of (at least) two recognized states in the conflict. The 1976 Arab League intervention, the 1978 UNIFIL action, and (to a lesser degree) the 1982 MNF intervention were all clearly within the bounds of traditional justifications. The conflicts were no longer simply the internal affairs of a single state.

In each of these cases, as well, the unilateral actions of Syria and Israel had serious repercussions for the regional cold wars (both Arab-Israeli and inter-Arab) as well as the global cold war between the superpowers. That is, these unilateral interventions raised serious risk of drawing in other regional or global actors (comparable to the major superpower involvement in the Arab-Israeli wars of 1967 and 1973).

This quite genuine risk acted as an extra spur for international involvement.

By contrast (at least until early 1994), it seems that the Yugoslav case could never be defined *in any simple way* as an internal or domestic conflict that had "drawn in" outside state involvement. Certainly many states were highly concerned about events in Yugoslavia, especially in regard to the treatment of minorities with which they shared an ethnic or religious association. But even the most concerned, such as Austria, Hungary, Albania, Greece, Germany, and Bulgaria (to name just a few), did *not* intervene directly in the events in Yugoslavia, certainly not unilaterally, in the way Syria and Israel did in Lebanon. Thus, there was no relatively simple trip wire to legitimate (by traditional standards) direct intervention by international organizations such as the EC, NATO, and the UN in the Yugoslav crisis.

Just such a legitimating trip wire was supplied in principle, however, by diplomatic recognition of the distinct sovereignty of Slovenia, Croatia, and Bosnia-Herzegovina, promoted most strenuously by the Germans in December 1991 and January 1992. Clearly, it can be debated whether international recognition ameliorated or exacerbated the difficulties on the ground in Yugoslavia (Glenny 1992), but it certainly served to legitimate IO involvement. With independent Croatia, Bosnia-Herzegovina, etc., facing the military might of Belgrade-directed JNA, the conflict theoretically switched from an internal Yugoslav affair to a conflict among "states." Thus, the conflict became the legitimate concern of international bodies such as the UN and the EC.

Although diplomatic recognition laid the groundwork, it did not automatically bring direct IO involvement in Yugoslavia. The repeated estimates that an outside military peace-making mission would demand hundreds of thousands of troops and probably sustain high casualties restrained IO involvement for very practical reasons.

Yet if the European and international diplomatic sleight of hand left the basic struggle within Yugoslavia unchanged in some ways and failed to generate direct involvement of outside actors, it is nevertheless the most appropriate point of comparison with the Lebanese cases. As emphasized before, direct IO involvement followed direct military intervention in Lebanon by Syria and Israel. International pressures of various sorts ultimately persuaded Syria and Israel to accept international peace-keepers to separate the contending parties, but only after both these states had achieved almost all of their military and political objectives. By contrast, Yugoslavia had *not* reached such a point in late 1991 and early 1992, even though very similar international pressures were being applied. That is, neither the Belgrade-backed Croatian Serbs nor, for that matter, the Croatian government, had achieved all the objectives it was pursuing by force of arms. Short of (highly un-likely) direct outside military intervention to stop them, the Croatian Serb forces and their backers had very little incentive to honor any cease-fire or adhere to any peace agreements that promised them less than they knew they were capable of achieving by military means (Church 1992b).

Once these goals were reached—as they were, slowly but eventually, after sufficient ethnic cleansing and civilian casualties—then relatively "successful" international intervention in such forms as peace-keeping units policing cease-fires was achieved. Again, the precondition of "consent of the warring sides" seems to have been achieved only when the losing side was willing to accept anything and the (militarily) win-ning side had achieved most of its aims.

The Bosnian tragedy seems to have followed exactly the same format, with military "solutions" pursued until very little more could be gained, followed by international supervision of whatever final results had been achieved by force. The only fundamental difference is how particularly vulnerable the Bosnian government and the Bosnian Mus-lim population has been, once it became clear that military means or, more accurately, unrestrained violence would decide the final outcomes.

These basically "realist" conclusions about the ultimate victory of vio-lence need to be qualified for these two case studies in only one, also "realist," dimension. Specifically, the Syrian intervention in Lebanon in June 1976 was indeed constrained in one major way, aside from the diplomatic efforts of other Arab states and extraregional actors. The movement of Syrian military forces to the southern parts of Lebanon was denied to the Syrians, not by the Lebanese National Movement/ Palestinian forces arrayed against them but by the (apparently quite explicit) threat of Israeli military engagement if the Syrian troops moved beyond the so-called red line (Haley and Snider 1979; Wein-berger 1986). Although Israeli warnings might be characterized as "in-ternational action" or pressure which had a measurable effect on events, it is much more accurate to see it in more conventional terms as "state action"—that is, as Israel's threat to act in its own state interests.

Collapse of State versus Collapse of Federation

The second major dimension in which to compare the possible roles of international actors in the Lebanese and Yugoslav cases is the notion of the "collapse of the state," which has been applied quite often to both cases. Some notion of the breakdown of internal order lies at the heart of both tragedies and helped to spur international involvement in these affairs. Although the same notion, collapse of the state, has been applied to the internal disruptions of Lebanon in 1975–1976 and Yugoslavia in 1991–1992, however, the structural characteristics of the two cases are profoundly different and have quite different implications for the nature and appropriateness of international intervention. Briefly, the Lebanese experience indeed seems to be the collapse of the state, whereas the Yugoslav experience might better be termed the collapse of the federation.

The fundamental political characteristic of the Lebanese civil war of 1975–1976 was the complete breakdown of all state institutions that might be expected to maintain or restore order. Independent militias and irregular political/military forces, as well as more clearly criminal or mercenary bands, dominated most of the streets of Beirut and the countryside of Lebanon during much of the period of civil strife. The Lebanese police, even the more impressive Deuxième Bureau and "Squad 16" (the Sittᶜash) were clearly unable to deal with all the heavily armed forces that had taken control of Lebanon and unwilling even to try. The Lebanese army stayed out of the fighting as well, even though in theory it was both large enough and well enough equipped to deal with the militias.

In this respect, the army held to its traditional function in Lebanese politics: to do nothing under any circumstances and most especially not to become involved in any internal ethnic or sectarian dispute. Even though it did nothing, however, its mere existence acted as something of a line of last resort before the final and complete breakdown of the state. Indeed, in March 1976 when the army finally did break apart, it either disbanded entirely or else took sides in the political-sectarian conflict, according to each soldier's sectarian or political sympathies.

From the international perspective, this true and final "collapse of the state" in Lebanon, the dissolution of the army, made the choice of international involvement quite clear if by no means easy. By spring 1976 there was no *internal* force capable of stopping the destruction (unless, of course, one of the sides—most likely the LNM-Palestinian alliance—were to achieve a full military victory). If the fighting was to stop (or, more specifically, if a leftist Lebanese-Palestinian victory was to be avoided), then some outside force would have to do it. In the event, the "outside force" was not an international body, at least not initially, but rather the Syrians acting unilaterally and quite forcefully.

The Yugoslav case, especially at the stage when Slovenia and Croatia and then other constituent republics of Yugoslavia began unambiguously to pursue the course of independence from Belgrade, was quite a different phenomenon. The state at that point was not so much breaking down as breaking apart, along formal lines of partition already in existence: the constituent republics of the old Yugoslav federation. At least in the more ethnically homogeneous sections of Slovenia and Croatia, there was no breakdown of public order. The existing police structures continued to operate more or less as they had before the breakup, since their immediate superiors had always been their respective republican governments. Most Croats and Slovenes accepted the "legitimacy" of these now national institutions of government. Eventually, this was matched by the recognition of their international legitimacy by most EC countries and the United States.

The violent strife that attended this breakup came specifically from the rejection of precisely that legitimacy by, in particular, the Serb-dominated regions of the new state of Croatia and later both the Serb and Croat regions of Bosnia-Herzegovina. The conflict that evolved was perhaps much more "territorial" than the Lebanese case ever became. In the former Yugoslavia the refrain has been claims to sovereignty and nationhood, first, for the former republics of the Yugoslav federation (such as Croatia and Slovenia) and then for the smaller Bosnian Serb, Bosnian Croat, and Croatian Serb populations within the new republics.

This pursuit of sovereignty has not been a major constituent of the Lebanese crisis. The Lebanese state did not splinter along the lines of formally recognized preexisting units. There was a de facto partition of the country during the civil war into rightist/Christian-held and leftist/Palestinian-held territories, but this was not the basis of any claim to sovereignty of a smaller state. Although a "Marounistan" solution (that is, a separate Christian state) was sometimes mooted in rightist circles, it was in practical terms a nonviable option. As for the Lebanese Leftist Alliance (as well as for the Syrians), any "solution by partition" was emphatically rejected (Al-Azmeh 1976).

Thus, the Lebanese and Yugoslav cases are structurally distinct as regards the "breakdown of the state." The Lebanese case compares more closely to the Somalia situation of 1990–1992 (which led to UN intervention in 1992–1993), in which central government institutions, especially those in charge of maintaining public order, broke down completely. The Yugoslav case more closely resembles the breakup of the Soviet Union into its constituent republics.

An Outline for a More Precise Structural
Comparison

It should be clear that precise comparisons between the Yugoslav and Lebanese situations are quite difficult to make. Nevertheless, there do seem to be periods and situations when close similarities can be identified which seem to indicate that the international community involved in events in Yugoslavia was actually following the precedent set by Lebanese events, however implicitly and unintentionally.

Consider, in particular, spring 1976 in Lebanon, and fall and winter 1991–1992 in Croatia, and spring 1992 in Bosnia-Herzegovina. During these periods the fighting was between groups *within* each (new) state: Serbs against Croatians in Croatia; Serbs against Croatians against Muslims in Bosnia; Lebanese against Lebanese against Palestinians in Lebanon. At these times the killing and destruction seemed to be completely out of hand and there was no internal political or military force ready, willing, or able to stop it from happening. (In the Yugoslav cases, essentially all internal forces, in particular the JNA, were already heavily involved in the conflict from an early stage. From the international perspective, no local forces existed in theory or in practice who might have helped to halt the fighting or to check aggression. Predictably, negotiated cease-fires did not last.

Granting as always that international organizations are hesitant to involve themselves in the internal affairs of sovereign states, it is nevertheless at times like these that outside "unilateral" intervention becomes most probable. That is, some particularly interested state may and often does act either out of humanitarian concern or, more likely, out of fears for its own security should the internal disruption of the (usually neighboring) state spill over its borders. In addition or alternatively, a state may act to preempt the intervention of some other interested state. Once unilateral intervention takes place or becomes clearly imminent, regional or international involvement is more likely because *international* peace is usually threatened.

The Lebanese case in the spring of 1976 follows exactly this pattern. "International intervention" did not take place. But *unilateral* Syrian intervention did. With the collapse of the Lebanese army in March and the LNM/Palestinian offensive that followed, both Syria and Israel seriously considered unilateral intervention (Schiff and Yaari 1984; Weinberger 1986). President Asad of Syria gave many reasons for intervening, but clearly the most compelling strategic reason was the fear that if Syria did not stop the Lebanese leftist offensive (whose forces he had until then backed), then Israel would do so. An Israeli military presence in Lebanon would have created an enormous strategic disadvantage for Syria vis-à-vis Israel. In the event, Syria moved first, even at the cost of fighting the leftist Lebanese and Palestinian forces that Syria had previously supported. Whatever its wisdom and however compelling the reasons for it, Syria's unilateral act spurred the eventual participation of the Arab League, once the Syrians had checked and reversed the leftist Lebanese and Palestinian forces.

The Croatian (1991–1992) and Bosnian (1992–1993) situations would seem to be different in that no "unilateral outside intervention" ever took place. Clearly, neither Greece nor Albania nor Hungary nor any other single state intervened. Nevertheless, with the diplomatic recognition of the breakaway republics of Slovenia and Croatia in January 1992, at least theoretically the situation changed dramatically. In particular, the active involvement of the Belgrade-directed JNA in Croatia (and later in Bosnia), basically on the side of the Serb populations in those states, was transformed from the actions of a national army within its national territory to the actions of an outside army involving itself in the affairs of another sovereign state.

In principle, this transformation of an internal conflict into a case of "outside" intervention, albeit a diplomatic sleight of hand, had the potential to legitimate greater international or regional (EC) involvement. In fact, there was more IO involvement in Yugoslavia after January 1992. Thus, in a sense, it parallels the case in Lebanon in 1976 after the full-scale intervention of the Syrians. This was not, of course, a peace-making intervention, which was clearly what some Europeans (especially the Germans) and other diplomats seemed to want.

With the actual deployment of international troops in Croatia and Bosnia, as it turns out, attention shifted to the issue of risk. The international troops and observers in the former Yugoslavia were committed for both peace keeping and humanitarian assistance. Because the fighting continued to rage, both roles entailed great risks. In the next section, I consider the many parallels Lebanon offers to the question of the risks of intervention in the former Yugoslavia.

The Risks of International Intervention

Risks of International Organizations and Their Member States

Aside from structural characteristics, the other major dimension in which to search for meaningful comparisons between the Lebanese and Yugoslav experiences has to do with the variety of risks which may attend any international involvement in a state's internal and especially its ethnic conflicts. Not all risks, of course, are physical. There is a risk, for example, that any action taken in regard to the former Yugoslavia may create precedents for action in the breakup of other states—say, the former Soviet Union—which some (such as the present Confederation of Independent States [CIS]) may well not want to see established (Gamba 1993; Burg, this volume). There is a risk, moreover, especially in the most violent and intractable situations, of falling down the "slippery slope" of greater and greater involvement with less and less hope of resolving issues or even improving the situation (Haas 1993). On the other hand, *lack* of intervention also has risks; in some situations failure to act in time may allow the internal conflict of a particular state to spread to another state or states, or it may draw in the direct military involvement of states in the region, escalating the conflict and threatening international peace.

All these are important risks to consider in Lebanon and Yugoslavia. Here, however, I want to discuss two areas of risk which offer perhaps the most important parallels and comparisons between the two cases. The first has to do with the basic physical risk to any international (or multinational or regional) force that becomes involved in the internal or ethnic conflicts of disrupted states. The second concerns the particular problems and risks of humanitarian relief efforts in ethnic conflict.

It is worth recalling that a basic precondition for any "successful" intervention in such conflicts is the consent of the warring sides. This principle stems from the simple but sometimes forgotten notion that not all actors in a state's internal conflicts will benefit from an end to hostilities, that parties to the conflict may have perfectly rational (from their perspective) incentives to oppose peace-keeping efforts. Unless the mandate of international intervention is enforcement and military confrontation with recalcitrant forces is anticipated, then lack of consent by the warring sides can prove politically devastating and physically dangerous to the interveners.

It is important to recognize that the combatants may not believe claims of neutrality or may not perceive outside intervention as neutral to their interests. The outside force may well be made up of soldiers of constituent states that have by no means been neutral previously (or at least have not been regarded as neutral by the local protagonists). If the foreign policies of those states (particularly but not exclusively those of a superpower such as the United States) continue to be seen as prejudicial to local interests, then the physical risks for those "neutral" troops can be expected to increase greatly. This was clearly the case in Lebanon, and it can be argued that it is a relevant lesson for intervention in Yugoslavia. A brief comparison of two interventions in Lebanon may help to illustrate these points and give some basis for evaluating the risks of intervention in the former Yugoslavia.

The specific cases worth considering in some detail here are the commitment of UNIFIL (United Nations Interim Force in Lebanon) troops in 1978 after Israel's first major invasion and the Multinational Force intervention (especially phase II) after Israel's second major invasion in 1982. In the case of UNIFIL, both its mandate and its composition seemed designed as much to minimize risks to their own physical security as to carry out any positive policy in the volatile area of southern Lebanon where its troops were stationed. The major troop contributors initially were Canada, Sweden, Norway, Nigeria, Nepal, Senegal, and even Fiji—that is, nonregional and non-great-power countries whose involvement had the best chance of being considered truly neutral by local Lebanese, Palestinian, and Israeli actors with whom the UNIFIL troops would need to interact (Gilmour 1984; also Hudson, this volume). In addition, their mandate was a classic "separate the (potentially) warring sides" (that is, peace-keeping) mission. Despite many complaints that the UNIFIL forces were not effective enough in keeping one side or another from shooting or infiltrating across cease-fire lines, the forces never actively took sides in the conflict and thus never invited retaliation against themselves. As long as the UN refrained from taking sides (and was not perceived to be taking sides by the local actors, mainly Palestinian and Lebanese) and as long as its constituent governments (e.g., Fiji, Norway) did not take sides, UNIFIL had a reasonable chance to be considered as truly neutral by local actors and thus to minimize its physical risks.

The example of "international" intervention provided by the MNF provides a stark contrast to the UNIFIL example. Most obviously, the MNF did not act in the name of the UN or any other international organization. It was basically an action of the United States government with the requested assistance of France, Italy, and eventually Britain as well. It entailed the direct involvement of the soldiers of a major superpower, precisely contrary to common wisdom. In fact, it was very nearly a unilateral action, with the superpower actively pursuing its own policy in both Lebanon and the broader Middle East. Yet although the intervention was partisan by almost any standard, the MNF tried to present its troops as neutral peace-keepers in their role in Lebanon.

These points need some elaboration. U.S. (and French) regional policies had their reverberations in Lebanon. By 1982 both the United States and France found themselves tilting toward increasing support of Iraq in its war with Iran, less, in the U.S. case at least, from any love of Iraq or Saddam Hussein than from fear of the implications of an Iraqi collapse and an Iranian victory for U.S. interests. Since major factions (especially among the Shiʿa Muslim population) in Lebanon were connected to or supported by Iran, American and French policy could well be expected to increase the risks for the American and French soldiers in the MNF.

In Lebanon the MNF, particularly the Americans and the French, gave increasing and increasingly direct support to the central government. Given the sectarian partiality of that government, this support constituted an extraordinary gamble with the safety of the U.S. and French troops in Lebanon. It was a gamble that was lost in the most dramatic fashion when the U.S. Marine compound in Beirut and, almost simultaneously, the French military compound were decimated by suicide bomb attacks on October 23, 1983. The fact that the Italians, who were *not* pursuing similar policies in Lebanon and in the region (Fisk 1990), were *not* the targets of similar attacks seems a clear confirmation of the importance of neutrality.

All these factors seem inherently relevant to events in the former Yugoslavia. Indeed, an argument can be made that policy makers, either consciously or unconsciously, have been acting with exactly the Lebanese precedent in mind. Any international involvement has been and will continue to be viewed with suspicion by the various factions and militias in Croatia and Bosnia. Not only is involvement almost inevitably partisan in its implications—for example, in consolidating and sanctifying the gains made by violence and ethnic cleansing— but the troops most likely to be involved tend to be the ones most distrusted locally.

That is, the most likely "international" volunteers for duty in Yugoslavia are the countries most concerned with events there, in particular, European nations. There is clearly a trade-off here. Those most willing to become involved in Yugoslavia as part of some EU or UN force are also the ones running the most risks in such involvement. Their greater concern has typically been expressed in a history of support for one or another of the nationalities in the former Yugoslavia which unfortunately makes them "partisan" in the eyes of other groups and thus, in principle, poor candidates to play the role of a neutral force. Germany provides perhaps the most obvious example. The Germans are as concerned over events in Yugoslavia as any outside power, but any action they take or have taken seems to be interpreted by many Serbs as evidence of a new Nazism, a "fourth Reich" (Glenny 1992).

The way out of this dilemma would seem to be to employ "Fijians"— that is, troops from distant nations truly neutral in their prior commitments and sympathies. The other side of the trade-off, however, is that there are not that many "Fijians" (in the generic sense) to go around, and it will always be difficult to persuade any truly disinterested outside power to commit its soldiers into a dangerous situation for a cause that does not really concern it. The residual alternative—using many troops representing nations that will probably not be considered neutral in the conflict—would seem to be at least partly a repeat of the situation of the MNF in Beirut: soldiers running extremely great risks because of their nation's questionable neutrality in the context of the ethnic or sectarian conflict they face.

There is perhaps an interesting twist on this analysis for the situation in Yugoslavia. European and other international diplomats seem completely aware of the dangers involved, so aware, in fact, as to cripple the ability of the European and world community to develop a more forceful policy in Bosnia and elsewhere. Although many UN and EU troops are already present (and quite vulnerable) in Croatia and Bosnia, attempting to perform peace-keeping duties, the French, German, and other diplomats deciding policy back in their national capitals have been significantly handicapped in any efforts to stop the genocidal policies of the many factions. The most often heard refrain from these leaders is that any more forceful intervention on their part would threaten the safety of their soldiers already in place there (Church 1992a). In essence, these troops became a type of hostage to the factions in Yugoslavia. This logic can be said to take its most extreme form, moreover, when the international intervention is for humanitarian purposes.

Humanitarian Intervention in Ethnic Conflicts

The logic of risk becomes even more twisted when intervention is primarily for humanitarian purposes. Perhaps in no other case do the assumptions and motives of outside actors fail as profoundly as in the attempt to intervene in ethnic conflicts for humanitarian purposes. The faulty assumption is that in such conflicts humanitarian concerns can be divorced and treated separately from the reasons for the conflict itself. Unfortunately, perhaps the classic indicator of ethnic and sectarian conflict is that civilian populations are not simply the unfortunate and unintended victims of the conflict but its *targets*. In such a situation, what does it mean to supply food and medicine to civilians?

Various international agencies, from the International Red Cross to the UN, have tried to bring in food and medical supplies for the relief of civilian populations "caught in the middle of the conflict" in both Lebanon and Yugoslavia. The most dramatic such efforts, but by no means the only ones, were the International Red Cross efforts in the siege of the Palestinian refugee camp of Tel al-Zaatar in east Beirut in the summer of 1976 and the UN's efforts in the siege of Sarajevo from 1992 to the breaking of the siege in early 1994.

There is clearly an air of unreality in such IO actions and professed goals. These civilian populations are not simply "caught in the middle of conflict"; they are very much the target of aggression. The international press can and does report the reality that "civilians are the primary target" (in the Serbian siege of Sarajevo and elsewhere in Bosnia), that the attack is meant to kill those civilians or drive them out of their homes by the "rational use of terror" ("Atrocity and Outrage" 1992). The implications for any outside effort to help such civilians should be starkly clear, even though they are seldom explicitly stated. That is, since the civilians themselves are the target, the "enemy," any international agency seeking to help them cannot help but be perceived as partisan by those targeting the civilians. It is clearly an understatement to point out, then, that the risks to the lives and safety of those participating in such efforts are quite extraordinary.

Indeed, looking at the casualty lists of the Tel al-Zaatar and Sarajevo relief efforts and listening to the testimony of those who were shot in their attempts to aid these besieged populations corroborate our expectations. What is interesting, however, is that the casualties are perhaps less than one might have imagined from this logic. That *anyone* is allowed to bring in relief of any sort needs to be explained.

Clearly, the besiegers will be opposed to any relief effort that helps the besieged to survive and thus to hold out, but they cannot afford to target relief personnel, at least not obviously. They must at least partially restrain themselves for larger political and strategic reasons. Any all-out attack on relief agencies might provide a "last straw" precipitating full-scale military involvement by outside parties (as for instance in Somalia, where food distribution efforts came under attack and precipitated forceful involvement by U.S.-UN forces). In lieu of open attack, therefore, the besiegers may be expected to subject relief workers to "random" sniper fire and "indiscriminate" bombing that may well be neither random nor indiscriminate but can be disclaimed as such to avoid drawing forceful retribution from the outside.

The logic of ethnic conflicts can become even more perverse, for humanitarian relief can be recognized as actually aiding the aggressors as much as it helps the victims of the aggression. In a slightly different context, it has often been stated, especially for the events in Yugoslavia, that international mediation, including cease-fire negotiations and monitoring, in effect helps one side more than another. In particular, cease-fires in Croatia and Bosnia have often had the effect of legitimating and solidifying the fruits of aggression (Smolowe 1992). In the case of humanitarian efforts, the presence of relief workers helps the besieged to last another day, but it also in effect implies international legitimation of the attack on these civilians in the first place. If the relief workers are allowed in and they are themselves not shot at too much, then the basic offensive against civilians can continue. Concern over the welfare of the international personnel carrying out their duties becomes a major factor in the calculations of outside national leaders in relation to the situation on the ground in places such as Sarajevo. In effect, the presence of international humanitarian relief efforts makes at least one policy alternative extremely unlikely: forceful intervention to stop the aggression. Any such action would jeopardize the safety of the relief personnel.

My primary interest in this chapter has been to provide the basis for more informed, less facile comparisons of the Lebanese and Yugoslavian cases of ethnic/sectarian conflict. There are major differences as well as significant similarities. With regard to the structural characteristics of the two cases, the crisis situations in Lebanon and Yugoslavia evolved differently. In particular, "international" intervention in Lebanon (including regional efforts by the Arab League) almost always took place in the aftermath of some state's unilateral intervention or invasion of Lebanon, usually in response to internal disruption there. This "trip wire"—unilateral intervention leading to international intervention— was technically reached in Yugoslavia only when Slovenia and Croatia were recognized as separate states, whereupon the actions of the Belgrade-directed Yugoslav National Army in Croatia and Bosnia were no longer simply the domestic concern of a sovereign Yugoslavia but the legitimate focus for an "international" action.

Similarly, the "collapse of a state" (most appropriate for Lebanon after 1975) differs from the "breakup of a federation" into its constituent units (appropriate for Yugoslavia after January 1992). The role of the national armies in the two cases highlights the differences in the superficially similar situations. Simply put, in Lebanon it was the collapse of the Lebanese National Army (in spring 1976) which indicated the final collapse of all central state authority, the irremediable descent into total chaos. In Yugoslavia, by contrast, the problem was the *survival* of the Yugoslav National Army (the JNA) or, more explicitly, its active use against the former republics.

In their structural characteristics, therefore, Lebanon and Yugoslavia differed. But comparison helps to provide a better understanding of the role of international agencies dealing with ethnic conflict. In particular, the implications for intervention of the international moves toward recognition of the constituent republics of the former Yugoslavia becomes clearer.

I also discussed the element of risk in the calculations of states and international bodies in regard to Lebanon and Yugoslavia. The fundamental risks for any "neutral" international force that involves itself in ethnic conflict are well evidenced by consideration of the Lebanese experiences. The risks are even more profound when IOs and others attempt to provide humanitarian aid in the context of ethnic strife.

One conclusion reached in this analysis is the large extent to which these principles seem to be recognized and to form the basis for action, especially in the continuing crisis in Yugoslavia. That is, outside actors working through international organizations such as the UN and the EU seem to have the lessons of Lebanon, as discussed, very much in mind. Indeed, if anything, the lessons of Lebanon seem to have been learned too well.

Response to the "humanitarian nightmare" in Bosnia and elsewhere (to use former secretary of state James Baker's words) has been incremental and ad hoc. Troops were sent in with the ostensible purpose of helping Yugoslavs. Instead, they seem to have become hostages to the armed factions ("Land of the Slaughter" 1992).

Of all the metaphors for Yugoslavia, especially Bosnia—"another Viet Nam," "another Northern Ireland," "another Munich" (Talbott 1992; Church 1992a and c)—the image uppermost in the minds of the outside leaders most concerned with events there seems to have been "another Beirut massacre." All seem to bear in mind the slaughter of international troops who considered themselves neutral peace-keepers but who appeared otherwise to local factions when those troops or the nations they came from became actively engaged in the Lebanese fighting.

Clearly, intervention in ethnic conflicts is no simple matter. For those who feel compelled to do something to stop "humanitarian nightmares," the dilemma is great. Essentially, all the alternatives have been and continue to be fraught with peril, both for outsiders and for the people in the former Yugoslavia. No easy solution can be offered here, only an appreciation of what the various alternatives imply.

11

Changing Roles

Shibley Telhami

This book addresses two related themes: first, how the role of international organizations in ethnic conflict and civil strife has generally evolved and, second, the actual response to two specific cases of ethnic conflict, Lebanon and Yugoslavia. In the preceding chapter, Barry Preisler draws some conclusions from similarities and differences between the cases of Lebanon and Yugoslavia. In this final chapter, I address the broader issue of the changing role of international organizations in ethnic conflict and then suggest some questions for future research.

The driving force behind this book was obvious: the end of the Soviet-U.S. rivalry was followed by an increase in ethnic and civil strife in several areas and by a more active role in these conflicts for the United Nations. A set of questions were posed about the potential effectiveness of IO interventions and about the likely evolution of these interventions in the post-cold-war world.

One of the preliminary questions pertained to the logic of our focus on "ethnic" conflict, as opposed to other forms of civil strife (Somalia, Haiti). It is evident from Jack Donnelly's chapter that the "ethnic factor" has rarely been the reason for UN intervention, and when intervention has occurred in ethnic conflict, it took place either because of humanitarian concerns or because of perceived threats to international peace and security. Yet, despite the absence of theoretical differentiation between cases of ethnic conflict and other instances of domestic strife, our study reveals good empirical reasons to focus on ethnic strife.

First, as Raymond F. Hopkins points out, although the end of the cold war did not create ethnic rivalries, it did "open new space for them to be played out." Ethnic groups that were coercively restrained from expressing separatist demands during the cold war found new opportunities following its demise. Donnelly and Hopkins agree that the end of the cold war removed external props for fragile multiethnic states, thus leading to a devolution of power similar in scope to the period of decolonization following World War II. Second, the survey of IO interventions in ethnic conflict by Milton Esman and the two detailed cases of intervention in Lebanon and Yugoslavia reveal that IO intervention in domestic strife is more likely to occur after outside actors are drawn in, thus constituting an "international" crisis. To the extent that ethnic identity is transnational, ethnic conflict is more likely than other types of civil strife to draw outside actors—with the Cyprus conflict representing a good case in point.

Given our focus in this book, three central questions were addressed: To what extent is the role of IOs in ethnic conflict changing? How effective are IOs in dealing with ethnic conflict? And how are the means and venues of intervention changing? I will now review our findings in each area:

The Nature of Change in the Role of IOs

There was full agreement among our contributors that the scope of IO intervention, especially UN intervention, has grown substantially since the end of the cold war. As Jack Donnelly points out, in just a few years, the UN has intervened nearly as many times as in the entire cold-war period, which spanned decades. Moreover, the costs of one case of UN peace-keeping in Cambodia in 1992–1993 ($1.3 billion) surpassed the combined costs of all UN peace-keeping operations in the previous forty-six years. Yet, despite these impressive numbers, the nature of change in the role of IOs was hotly debated. Jack Donnelly concluded that "the post-cold-war era seems to be one of (quantitatively) greater activity for international organizations, not (qualitatively) enhanced powers and authority."

At the heart of this debate are two perceived obstacles to enhanced authority for IOs. The first and more fundamental is the prevalence of the "sovereignty norm" in international relations, which simultaneously limits the ability of external agencies to intervene in the internal affairs of states and limits the possibility for multilateral cooperation.

The second obstacle is the insufficient capabilities of IOs to meet the demand for intervention.

IOs and the Sovereignty Norm

All our contributors ruled out the idea that the end of the cold war has fundamentally transformed international politics by transcending the dominant norm of sovereignty. The debate focused on the extent to which the norm of sovereignty has been weakened and on the extent to which such change is reversible. On this issue, Hopkins was mildly more optimistic than Donnelly, who concluded that both the progressive nature of change and its limits need to be emphasized.

One reason Hopkins remains pessimistic about fundamental change is that, despite the collapse of the cold-war norms that helped regulate state behavior, the world remains "anarchic," reflecting the absence of a hierarchical order and the relative independence of nation-state units. In addition, there is ample evidence in recent cases of UN intervention to suggest that the historical tension between "humanitarian" norms and "sovereignty norms," although changing, is still generally resolved in favor of sovereignty. Despite the increase in the scale and frequency of UN interventions, international authorization for these interventions, even in the most purely humanitarian cases, such as Somalia, has been based on findings of a "threat to international peace and security," suggesting that state sovereignty remains the dominant norm in international relations. Moreover, as Donnelly points out, the selectivity of IO intervention (northern Iraq, but not Sudan, for example), suggests that the magnitude of humanitarian need has not been the primary criterion for intervention. Even worse, Donnelly conceives the substantial increase in UN activity and authority since the end of the cold war to be merely another episode in a period of devolution of power in certain areas of world politics. Consequently, these increased UN activities are likely to remain "encapsulated," rather than spill over into similar kinds of activities in more settled circumstances: "Nothing in these cases provides evidence of a mandate to deal with ethnic conflict." Susan Woodward, too, finds little evidence for change in international norms. She wonders if the very norm recognizing sovereignty on grounds of national self-determination enabled "politicians and intellectuals in former Yugoslavia . . . to exploit ethnic differences for political gain."

The basis for some optimism about a degree of progressive change is twofold. First, despite the selectivity of IO interventions and despite their justification in the "threat to international peace," it is clear that there is practical change. The scope of UN-mandated intrusion into

Iraq's sovereignty following the Iraqi invasion of Kuwait was unprecedented; and despite the legal justification provided for intervention in Somalia and for UN support for possible intervention in Haiti in 1994, one would be hard pressed to make the case for a serious threat to "international peace and security" in these cases. At a minimum, the interpretation of such threat is being stretched to new limits. As Lori Fisler Damrosch puts it, recent UN resolutions "evidence a newly emerging consensus that the Security Council's enforcement powers may be invoked in a more purely domestic situation than had been the case with respect to either Iraq or Yugoslavia" (Damrosch 1993, 105).

Yet, despite such observable trends, one can take an extreme realist position on these matters. The selection bias in these cases of intervention is easily explained by the expedient interests of the permanent members of the UN Security Council, most notably the United States. Indeed, much of the rise in expectations about the role of the UN in international affairs has resulted from the international intervention to reverse Iraq's invasion of Kuwait—an intervention that cannot be explained without reference to U.S. economic and strategic interests. And in instances where the UN failed to follow through on UNSC resolutions, it was the role of the United States, acting for its own political reasons, that best explains the restraint. The Israeli refusal in early 1993 to implement a UNSC resolution calling for the immediate return of Palestinian deportees from South Lebanon, for example, created a crisis in the UN which was ultimately averted by extraordinary U.S. diplomatic intervention resulting in a solution that was closer to the Israeli position than to the UNSC resolution. In short, a realist could make a good case that the UN has in effect become an instrument of policy for the United States and other major powers. But this account ignores some important, even if unintended, side effects.

Whatever the motives of the members of the UN or the interests of the United States in mobilizing UN actions, the fact remains that new precedents were set, producing expectations that in turn affect future decisions on intervention. The legal and political justifications employed in mobilizing the required international effort in the Persian Gulf in 1991 helped establish new norms of intervention. Thus, the subsequent humanitarian intervention in Somalia became more likely partly because of rising international and U.S. domestic expectations resulting from the intervention in the Persian Gulf; the Bush administration felt the need to show that the intervention in Kuwait was not an exception. If U.S. considerations for intervention in Somalia were themselves partly political—that is, partly an attempt to respond to accusations, especially by Arab and Muslim allies, that the United States pursued a double standard—the action in Somalia nevertheless set another precedent, adding to a pattern that might eventually result in a new international norm. In short, no matter what the motives for intervention, the consequence may be the emergence of a new and unintended norm.

One can take a different view of the U.S. intervention to avoid UN measures against Israel in 1993. Although the United States succeeded in preventing action against Israel without forcing Israel fully to implement UNSC resolutions, there were some costs for both Israel and the United States. First, Israel agreed to a compromise formula calling for the immediate return of some, but not all, Palestinians; and the United States used a great deal of political leverage to secure the support of other members of the Security Council. In previous years, during the cold war, the United States would not have hesitated to veto a UNSC resolution; in fact, the majority of such vetoes during the cold war pertained to Israel. In short, even if one posits the UN as an expedient instrument of U.S. policy in the new era, it is obvious that the United States still has to compromise in order to maintain credibility and to prevent a veto by other permanent members of the Security Council. It is true of course that the increasing consensus among members of the council is reversible, that the United States or any other permanent member may decide to exercise its veto. But the costs of such veto in any given case will be to reduce the value of the UN as an instrument of policy in instances where unilateral policy options are considerably more costly. The net result is that, despite the disproportionate power the United States wields, UN norms have an increasing, if still small, power of their own.

Thus the progressive shifts in the norms of international intervention about which there was general agreement among our contributors are at best small and incremental. Moreover, they are consistent with "the regime literature" in international relations, which found instances of normative importance even during the cold war. The question is whether there is stronger evidence for optimism about the prospects of a progressive shift away from the sovereignty norms in world politics. On this issue, Raymond Hopkins was somewhat more optimistic than the rest.

The basis for Hopkins's guarded optimism is his belief that world politics have entered a transitional period during which new norms have not emerged to replace those previously imposed by the U.S.-Soviet rivalry. Instead, a condition of "anomie" prevails, making major change more likely. Now, while violations of human rights are less tolerated, norms for action are in disarray, and strategy calculations have become less certain as the interests of states have become difficult to identify in the absence of the cold-war rivalry. With declining domestic support and unclear interests, states are less able to deal with these threats on their own. Yet, increasing ethnic conflict and decreasing state control create collective problems, such as weakened control over nuclear weapons, which threaten international peace and stability. The consequence is that a growing number of states look to international organizations to solve issues involving the international public good. This situation creates unprecedented possibilities for the UN.

Yet, as Hopkins notes, possibilities and expectations are one thing, the limitations of reality are another. A substantial disparity exists between needs and expectations, on the one hand, and UN capabilities, on the other. Even besides the resource constraints facing the UN (discussed in the next section), the subtle weakening of sovereignty norms that Hopkins detects in some areas has to be measured against the continued dominance of sovereignty norms in most other areas. One can easily envision a reversal of this weakening trend.

The fundamental problem remains. The United Nations is still an organization representing individual states whose interests are often not harmonious and whose power, even within the UN, is unequal. Structurally, the value of membership in the Security Council has increased substantially with the end of the cold war. Ultimately, it is the Security Council that interprets the UN Charter, establishes new norms through resolutions, and selects the cases for its action. Within the UNSC, the relative power of the five permanent members has also increased. Although the United States theoretically wields no more power than the other permanent members, in practice it exercises substantially more influence through issue linkages that exploit its trade advantages (with China), foreign aid (Russia), and its role in European politics.

So far, this arrangement has worked to maintain reasonable consensus within the United Nations. Even when China had great reservations about a 1994 UNSC resolution authorizing the use of force in Haiti, for example, the Chinese chose to abstain rather than veto the resolution. But for China, Haiti is a marginal issue, and although it is concerned about setting a precedent for intervention in the domestic affairs of other states, it can ultimately veto any such resolution that applies to itself or its allies. What was said of China applies as well to other permanent members of the UNSC. In short, the consensus is being maintained by avoiding issues of high importance to the permanent members of the Security Council over which there may be conflict of interest. That this state of affairs can be maintained for long is rather doubtful, and if it is maintained, it may generate resentment among other states. As it is, a number of UN members believe that the Security Council, whose structure was created half a century ago, no longer reflects the new configuration of states. Two of the wealthiest and most influential, Germany and Japan, lack permanent seats, and a large number of new and old UN members feel that they lack adequate representation in the council.

On the prescriptive side, one can imagine how this structure could be improved in a way that would increase representation without undermining consensus. For example, the number of "permanent" members could be increased from five to ten, including Japan, Germany, and three "rotating" members from the developing states. To increase the chance of consensus, a veto of any resolution would require the negative votes of two permanent members. But this idea, like many others around, can be implemented only if the Security Council, as presently constituted, votes to implement it, and there are selfish sovereign interests for all permanent members that count against such an idea. If Russia and China have been willing to cooperate with the United States on some issues on which they disagree, they have done so partly out of confidence that, on issues of vital interest to them, they can unilaterally prevent UN action through their veto power. Why should they give it up? In short, it is unlikely that any permanent member of the council will be willing to yield on this issue.

A more likely change is some increase in the "permanent" membership of the Security Council without bestowing veto power on the new members. Germany and Japan have enough direct and indirect influence to secure permanent seats without veto power. Like the United States, they can use economic power for issue linkage, and they can promise substantial increases in badly needed contributions to the UN. In revising the council structure to include Germany and Japan, the inclusion of representatives from the developing world would become unavoidable. Ultimately, however, such restructuring will not fundamentally alter the dominance of sovereign interests in shaping UN actions.

The Costs of Intervention and IO Capabilities

As the costs of intervention are escalating, existing UN mechanisms and resources are unable to meet the demand. Both Milton Esman and Raymond Hopkins point out several areas of weakness in the existing capabilities of the UN: the lack of autonomous military forces capable of peace enforcement, autonomous sources of income to replace ad hoc contributions that are difficult to collect, and intelligence and other information-gathering capabilities; the weakness of existing logistical capabilities; and a bureaucracy Hopkins called "feudal."

Proposals abound for correcting the UN's shortcomings. Realistically, however, one has to consider only options that do not so threaten the sovereignty norm that their implementation becomes impossible. Besides bureaucratic reform and incremental improvement of existing logistical and military capabilities, two proposals are noteworthy. The first is Milton Esman's idea about autonomous revenue sources. UN peace-keeping and humanitarian operations could be partially funded by such sources as royalties on minerals extracted from deep seabeds and small charges on international communications and commerce. One can imagine, of course, that sovereignty could interfere with the implementation of this proposal. It is likely that governments will be more responsive to domestic interest groups lobbying against such fees than to international agencies that have no say in electing these governments. Moreover, mechanisms to enforce collection could prove to be a serious obstacle to implementation.

The second proposal is to designate a portion of the national military forces of each state, appropriately trained, for use by the UN in humanitarian and peace-keeping operations authorized by the Security Council. Already in 1994 the U.S. military began training more than six thousand troops for peace-keeping tasks. As recent cases of UN action indicate, the current ad hoc basis for mobilizing multinational forces is highly problematic in that critical time is lost and the troops ultimately deployed are usually ill trained for the mission. Although this proposal too will likely encounter objections, the fact that individual states will have the ultimate say on the deployment of their own troops in any given case improves the chance of its attainment.

Effectiveness of Intervention

The increase in the frequency and scope of intervention by the UN and other IOs will undoubtedly result in greater scrutiny of their effectiveness. In this regard, three criteria are relevant: the nature of intervention; the spatial effectiveness of intervention, that is, the extent to which it succeeds not only in the specific case but also in deterring other potential conflicts; and the longitudinal effectiveness of intervention, that is, whether the success is temporary and short-term or provides a long-term solution to the problem faced.

In discussing intervention in ethnic conflict, it is easy to forget the many different types of intervention available to IOs, and to focus instead on the most difficult and costliest, those that involve some military power capable of enforcing peace if not fighting a war. Indeed, where there has been pessimism about the projected role of IOs, it has been with military intervention in mind. Yet, as pointed out in the

Introduction, the UN and other IOs have been relatively successful at peace keeping, economic sanctions, humanitarian relief, and good offices but less successful at peace enforcement and peace making.

Spacial Effectiveness of Intervention

It is useful to contrast IO interventions to interventions by the super-powers during the cold war. It is generally assumed that one major reason for the UNs ineffectiveness is limited military, economic, and logistical capabilities, in comparison, for example, to the United States. But besides the limits imposed by the sovereignty norm, there is a fundamental structural problem that should make it difficult for the UN to intervene effectively even if all the resources of the United States were at its disposal: its inability to project deterrence.

Even a dominant power such as the United States lacks the ability to intervene in all the trouble spots around the globe. During the cold war, the United States intervened selectively in cases (Korea, Vietnam) where the local interests of the United States did not warrant the costs of intervention. Leaders in the United States believed that effective actions in these cases would deter aggression against vital American interests elsewhere, thus justifying the costs of intervention. When deterrence worked (and there are many who argue that it was not effective in any case), it was for two primary reasons: areas of "vital" American interests were clearly defined and limited, and the targets of deterrence were also few and well defined, mostly the Soviet Union and its allies. Even here, however, the United States lacked the re-sources to intervene in all areas of vital interest; the logic of deterrence was to intervene effectively when necessary, thus making it too risky for the targets of your deterrence to challenge your interests elsewhere. From intervention that was perceived to have failed, such as the U.S. intervention in Lebanon in 1982–1983, the Reagan administration drew the lesson that forces should be committed to military action overseas only when "vital" interests were at stake and that such commitment should be made only with the clear intent and support needed to win (Reagan 1990, 466).

UN intervention in ethnic conflicts has much less potential to deter. First, if deterrence depends on the potential aggressor's fear of punish-ment, it is hard to know, in most cases of ethnic conflict, whom to punish. The source of conflict is either a collapse of central authority or a number of small internal aggressors. Second, since in principle the measure of relevance in any given case of conflict is not the vital interest of any single member state but UN norms, all violations of these norms present potential cases for intervention. From this perspective, one cannot differentiate between civil strife in Sudan and civil strife in northern Iraq. At any given time there is a large set of potential targets for UN intervention, many of which require simultaneous responses, thus presenting the UN, even with substantially enhanced resources, with an impossible task. At the same time, failure to intervene in only a few of these cases undermines the very norm that the UN strives to establish.

When one adds the sovereignty issue to this deterrence problem, additional complications emerge. The UNSC resolution authorizing intervention in Somalia, for example, included a finding of "threat to international peace and security" at the insistence of China and some Third World countries, which were worried that this might set a precedent for intervention in their own domestic politics. Similarly, during the U.S. effort to mobilize UNSC authorization for military intervention in Haiti in 1994, Latin American states and China expressed concerns that this case too might establish a threatening precedent, prompting the U.S. ambassador to the UN to stress that this case is "unique," that Haiti is a case of nothing but Haiti. By contrast, most Third World countries had little trouble supporting UN action after Iraq invaded Kuwait, even if most saw it as action precipitated by U.S. national interest. Just as the cold war was ending, weaker states had no desire to establish a precedent of a strong state, Iraq, invading its weak neighbor, Kuwait—and to do so against the wishes of the United States, the most powerful state of all. In short, sovereignty and calculations of state interest play a complicating role, limiting the degree to which the UN can hope to be effective through reputation and precedent setting.

Since enhanced resources alone cannot overcome the structural barriers to effectiveness of certain types of UN intervention, there will be a growing need to set realistic priorities, in the same way that effective states do. For example, serious violations of human rights such as genocide, which fortunately have been limited in number, should be accorded substantial resources, in the same way that states accord resources to the defence of "vital" interests. Only by setting such priorities, even if limited in scope, can the UN become incrementally more effective; otherwise, the increasing disparity between international expectations and the ability to meet them will soon diminish UN influence.

Longitudinal Effectiveness of Intervention

IO interventions are considerably more likely to be effective in the short term than to provide a long-term solution to any given conflict. International efforts have provided humanitarian relief to Kurds in northern Iraq, but not a solution to their plight. They addressed the famine in Somalia, but did not resolve the civil conflict that produced it. UN peace-keeping forces in Cyprus have minimized the violence between the conflicting groups but only through a long-term commitment of resources without evidence that the conflict is coming any closer to resolution, perhaps even reducing the local parties' incentives to reach a lasting settlement.

Part of the difficulty is that ethnic conflicts remain substantially a national problem whose resolution rests largely with subnational actors. The Kurds of Iraq will have to face the consequences of their conflict with the Iraqi state long after the international determination to provide them with help has diminished. Long-term success of IO interventions could be enhanced only by developing a fuller understanding of the internal dynamics of conflict. With the internal contexts of the Yugoslav and Lebanese conflicts in mind, several contributors made specific recommendations for enhancing the effectiveness of IO interventions.

Both Michael Hudson and Steven Burg, for example, echo Secretary-General Boutros Boutros-Ghali's call for preventive diplomacy before the outbreak of violence. Given the substantial resource constraints facing the UN and the far greater costs of intervention after ethnic hostilities become violent, the UN and other IOs should invest relatively more resources in establishing effective mechanisms for early diplomatic intervention. As Milton Esman pointed out, early warning systems could be set up, and small observer units could be dispatched to potential trouble spots, to enable the UN to act in preventive capacity, to initiate good offices and mediation procedures while there is still time to preempt the outbreak of violence.

Both Burg and Hudson also see timing as critical. In the case of Yugoslavia, for example, Burg believes that the international community should have supported the "peaceful redrawing of borders as part of the redefinition of interrepublic relationships, before the outbreak of violence." In his view, negotiations among regional leaders over the redrawing of the Yugoslav map could have permitted local leaders to achieve their goals through mutual concessions. From the Lebanon case, Michael Hudson suggests that interventions stand the best chance of success if they occur either at the very beginning of the crisis or after a long period of conflict when the local actors are becoming exhausted. In addition, Hudson suggests that IO interventions should be as short as possible because, as time goes on, IOs risk becoming just another party to the conflict, thus jeopardizing the requirement of relative neutrality—a requirement that Naomi Weinberger found to be essential in her own study of the Lebanon case.

Changing Means and Venues

Because the UN's reliance on national resources in major instances of intervention is likely to continue for the foreseeable future, any assessment of the prospects of UN intervention must take into account national calculations of interest. It has been evident that states are not likely to commit substantial resources, especially in the military arena, if important national interests are not at stake. In contrast, the issues are always vital to local parties to any ethnic conflict, and they are generally willing to commit most of their resources. Thus, if an international intervention has any chance of success at all, it usually requires substantial external resources. That only external actors with important interests are willing to pay the costs of intervention presents a serious dilemma for the UN.

The difficulty, as Hopkins, Hudson, Weinberger, and Preisler indicate, is that IOs must appear "neutral" when they intervene in ethnic conflict. The chance of failure increases with every sign of partiality detected by local actors. As Hopkins points out, the potential effectiveness of the UN stems from its universality. "Regional organizations, such as the OAU or the Arab League, suffer from less ability for their members to be neutral."

Yet, it is those states whose interests are at stake in the conflict which have the will and incentive to commit the resources required for intervention. It is no surprise that Syria and the Arab League intervened in Lebanon or that the United States mobilized large resources to defend oil-rich Kuwait. When intervention occurs in areas of no vital interest to the national interveners, as happened to the United States in Somalia, the will cannot be sustained. Those expressing faith in the power of television pictures of human suffering found that television is a double-edged sword: the blood of a single compatriot is far more powerful than the rest. Moreover, suffering is all too common, and the public can be saturated. Far more people followed the O. J. Simpson case in 1994 than paid attention to the horrifying tragedy in Rwanda.

One result of the end of the cold war has been that the incentives for the superpowers to intervene in ethnic conflict have substantially declined at the same time that the opportunities for intervention have increased. If the end of the cold war contributed to the outbreak of hostilities in Yugoslavia, it did so partly because powerful states were less likely to intervene. During the cold war, the United States, European states, and the USSR would have cared much more about the consequences of the conflict, so close to the heart of Europe. In short, despite increased public awareness of ethnic conflict globally, fewer states have reason to rank the resolution of these conflicts very high in their national priorities.

In most instances, it is neighboring states that are most affected by ethnic conflict. Members of the Organization of American States are more alarmed than others by events in Haiti; Europeans are more alarmed by events in Yugoslavia; OAU states are more concerned about the bloodbath in Rwanda. These priorities have fostered a recent trend in which the UN empowers regional organizations (OAU in the case of Rwanda) and other multilateral groups (NATO in Bosnia; "a multilateral force under unified command and control" in Haiti) to intervene in problem areas. This trend is likely to continue.

Although such a development means that interveners will inevitably be less "neutral" than some hope, it is nonetheless unavoidable given the resource constraints that the UN will continue to face. Moreover, even though regional actors may not be the ideal interveners, our studies show that, under some circumstances, they can be successful. Michael Hudson, for example, found that the Arab League intervention leading to the Ta'if Accords was successful, despite substantial obstacles. There are also ways to reduce the appearance of partiality. First, it is important to avoid unilateral interventions; the broader the regional organization, the better. Second, the UN should consolidate formal working relationships with regional organizations, as suggested by the secretary-general. Third, as Esman points out, regionals must be encouraged to upgrade their own structures to deal with the new tasks. Fourth, even when regional organizations intervene, such interventions should take place preferably under an authorizing resolution of the Security Council spelling out a specific mandate.

Still, the powerful states, especially the United States, will remain indispensable for their ability to carry out some operations in a timely fashion. Even in purely humanitarian cases, such as providing relief to Rwandan refugees, the logistical support for efficient and timely implementation required the type of capability that few states other than the United States could project.

Reflections for Future Research

This volume points out the need for additional work in several areas related to the role of IOs in ethnic conflict. In the broad context, issues of nationalism, sovereignty, and ethnicity open up a larger question about the formation of collective identity in world politics—a subject that is appropriately popular these days among Western social scientists. Knowledge of how such identity is formed could shed light on the proposition that shifts away from sovereignty norms are taking place. It could also place ethnic identity in a broader framework and enhance our understanding of the causes of ethnic conflict. Social scientists could inform us about the proposition, advanced by Jack Donnelly, that the proliferation of ethnic conflict following the end of the cold war is an episode unlikely to become a global trend. As it stands, most separatist ethnic groups aspire to a state of their own, not to some new form of collective identity.

More immediate from the point of view of this work is the need to examine several issues with the assumption that sovereignty norms will remain paramount in the foreseeable future and states will remain the key actors in world politics. A more focused investigation should appraise the effectiveness of IO interventions from the perspective, supported by studies in this volume, that ethnic conflicts have both internal and external sources; IOs should aim, not to impose solutions from the outside, but to aid local actors in the best way possible in ameliorating conflict. IOs must avoid expending resources without benefit, or worse, acting only to postpone future settlement of ethnic conflict. To understand how they may do so, we must expand the empirical base of cases for IO intervention in ethnic conflict, with special focus on long-term effectiveness.

Given our conclusion that effective UN intervention conducive to normative change requires the establishment of realistic priorities, there is a need for interdisciplinary investigations of areas of important international norms that lend themselves to enforcement. How would it be possible, for example, to establish effective measures to punish extreme violators of human rights, as in cases of genocide, even if those found responsible are subnational actors.

The conclusion that regional organizations are likely to play an increasing role in ethnic conflicts highlights the need to examine their capabilities. As Raymond Hopkins points out, regional organizations are even less prepared for intervention than the UN. As their mission inevitably changes, we must examine ways to enhance the structure and capabilities of regionals and to consolidate their relationship with the UN. Moreover, there is a need to explore the possibilities of turning old but effective alliances, such as NATO, whose primary mission is clearly changing, into international organizations with defined relationships to the UN.

Other areas of relevance for future study include issues that have not caught the imagination of most students of international relations: the roles of diaspora communities and nongovernmental organizations in ethnic conflict. As argued earlier, the transnational nature of ethnic identity makes ethnic conflicts more likely to be internationalized and in turn increases the chance of intervention by IOs. Diaspora communities are an important variable in this regard. Moreover, recent examples in settlement of disputes reveal an important role for nongovernmental organizations, including human rights groups and religious and academic organizations. It has been argued, for example, that such groups played an important role in the process leading to the Israel-PLO agreement in 1993 (Telhami 1995, 94). Thus, though we have, I hope, helped to answer some important questions about the role of international organizations in ethnic conflict, much work remains to be done.

References

Abou Diab, Khattar. 1985. *Le role de la force multinationale au Liban de 1982 à 1984.* Paris: Presses Universitaires de France.

Achebe, Chinua. 1959. *Things Fall Apart.* Greenwich, Conn.: Fawcett.

Adelman, Howard. 1992. "The Ethics of Humanitarian Intervention: The Case of the Kurdish Refugees." *Public Affairs Quarterly* 6 (1): 61–87.

Africa Recovery Briefing Paper No. 7. 1993. United Nations Publications, January 15.

Agwani, M. S. 1965. *The Lebanese Crisis, 1958: A Documentary Study.* New York: Asia.

Anderson, James. 1992. "New World Order and State Sovereignty: Implications for UN-Sponsored Intervention." *Fletcher Forum of World Affairs* 16 (2): 127–37.

Armstrong, John. 1982. *Nations before Nationalism.* Chapel Hill: University of North Carolina Press.

"Atrocity and Outrage." 1992. *Time,* August 17, 20 and passim.

Azar, Edward E. 1990. *The Management of Protracted Social Conflict: Theory and Cases.* Dartmouth: Gower.

al-Azmeh, Aziz. 1976. "The Progressive Forces." In *Essays on the Crisis in Lebanon,* ed. Roger Owen. London: Ithaca Press.

Baer, Gabriel. 1982. *Fellah and Townsmen in the Middle East.* London: F. Cass.

Bakić, Biljana. 1994. "The Role of the Media in the Yugoslav Crisis." M.A. thesis, University of Pittsburgh, draft.

Banac, Ivo. 1992a. "Post-Communism as Post-Yugoslavism: The Yugoslav Non-Revolutions of 1989–1990." In *Eastern Europe in Revolution,* ed. Banac. Ithaca: Cornell University Press.

——. 1992b. "The Fearful Asymmetry of War: The Causes and Consequences of Yugoslavia's Demise." *Daedalus* (Spring): 141–74.

——. 1984. *The National Question in Yugoslavia: Origins, History, Politics.* Ithaca: Cornell University Press.

Barakat, Halim, ed. 1988. *Toward a Viable Lebanon.* London: Croom Helm; Washington, D.C.: Georgetown University Center for Contemporary Arab Studies.

Barua, Prodeep P. 1992. "Ethnic Conflict in the Military of Developing Nations: A Comparative Analysis of India and Nigeria." *Armed Forces and Society: An Interdisciplinary Journal* 19 (3): 123–37.

Bebler, Anton. 1992. "The Yugoslav Crisis and the 'Yugoslav People's Army.'" *Zürcher Beiträge zur Sicherheitspolitik und Konfliktforschung.* Vol. 23.

Beker, Avi. 1988. *The United Nations and Israel.* Lexington, Mass.: Lexington Books.

Beyerlin, Ulrich. 1981. "Humanitarian Intervention." In *Encyclopedia of International Law,* ed. Rudolf Bernhardt. Amsterdam: Elsevier North Holland.

Bialer, Seweryn. 1980. *Stalin's Successors.* New York: Cambridge University Press.

Bilandžić, Dušan. 1979. *Historija Socijalističke Federativne Republike Jugoslavije.* Zagreb: Skolska knjiga.

Bloed, Arie, ed. 1990. *From Helsinki to Vienna: Basic Documents of the Helsinki Process.* Boston: Martinus Nijhoff.

Boban, Ljubo. 1973. *Svetozar Pribićević u opoziciji (1928–1936).* Zagreb: Institut za hrvatsku povijest.

Boulding, Elise. 1992. Introduction to *Internal Conflict and Governance,* ed. Kumar Rupesingher. New York: St. Martin's Press.

Boutrous-Ghali, Boutrous. 1992a. *An Agenda for Peace: Report to the UN Security Council.* New York: United Nations, January 31.

——. 1992b. *An Agenda for Peace: Preventive Diplomacy, Peacemaking, and Peacekeeping.* New York: United Nations.

——. 1992c. "Empowering the United Nations." *Foreign Affairs* 71 (5): 89–102.

Bowring, John. 1840. *Report on the Commercial Statistics of Syria.* London: Clowes.

Branigin, William. 1992a. "United Frustrations: The U.N. Is Tripping over Its Own Bloat and Corruption." *Washington Post National Weekly Edition,* November 30–December 6, 5

——. 1992b. "A Costly Way to Keep the Peace," *Washington Post National Weekly Edition,* December 7–13, 9–10.

Brass, Paul R. 1985. *Ethnic Groups and the State.* Totowa, N.J.: Barnes and Noble.

——. 1976. *Ethnicity in an International Context.* New Brunswick: Transaction.

Bread for the World. 1992. *Hunger, 1993: Displaced People.* Washington: Bread for the World.

Brucan, Silviu. 1987. *World Socialism at the Crossroads.* New York: Praeger.

Bull, Hedley. 1977. *The Anarchical Society.* London: Macmillan.

Burg, Stephen L. 1992. "Avoiding Ethnic War: Lessons of the Yugoslav Crisis." *Twentieth Century Fund Newsletter* 2 (3).

——. 1986. "Elite Conflict in Post-Tito Yugoslavia." *Soviet Studies* 38 (2): 170–93.

——. 1983. *Conflict and Cohesion in Socialist Yugoslavia: Political Decision Making since 1966.* Princeton: Princeton University Press.

Burg, Stephen L., and Paul S. Shoup. 1993. *A Workshop on Peace in Bosnia-Hercegovina: Co-Chairs' Report.* Washington, D.C.: International Research and Exchanges Board and Woodrow Wilson International Center for Scholars, March.

Cerović, Stojan. 1993. "Letter from Serbia: 'Greater Serbia' and Its Discontents." In *Why Bosnia?* ed. Rabia Ali and Lawrence Lifschultz. Stony Creek, Conn.: Pamphleteer's Press.

Chamoun, Camille. 1963. *Crise au Moyen-Orient.* Paris: Gallimard.

Chazan, Naomi, et al. 1992. *Politics and Society in Contemporary Africa* 2d ed. Boulder: Lynne Rienner.

Chevallier, Dominique. 1971. *La société du Mont Liban a l'époque de la révolution industrielle en Europe.* Paris: Librairie Orientaliste.

Chisholm, Michael, and David N. Smieds. 1990. *Shared Space, Divided Space: Essays on Conflict and Territorial Organization.* Boston: Unwin Hyman.

Chopra, Jarat, and Thomas G. Weiss. 1992. "Sovereignty Is no Longer Sacrosanct: Codifying Humanitarian Intervention." *Ethics and International Affairs* 6: 95–117.

Church, George. 1992a. "Saving Bosnia—at What Price?" *Time,* July 13, 60.

——. 1992b. "Aggression 1, International Law 0." *Time,* July 27, 47.

——. 1992c. "Munich All Over Again?" *Time,* August 31, 48.

Churchill, Charles H. 1862. *The Druzes and Maronites under the Turkish Rule.* London: Spottiswood.

——. 1853. *Mount Lebanon: A Ten Year Residence from 1842–52.* Vol. 3. London: Saunders and Otley.

Claude, Inis. 1955. *National Minorities, an International Problem.* Cambridge: Harvard University Press.

Coate, Roger, and Donald Puchala. 1990. "Global Policies and the United Nations System." *Journal of Peace Research* 27 (May): 127–40.

Cohen, Lenard J. 1992. "The Disintegration of Yugoslavia." *Current History: A World Affairs Journal* 91 (11): 369–75.

Cohen, Lenard, and Paul Warwick. 1983. *Political Cohesion in a Fragile Mosaic: The Yugoslav Experience.* Boulder: Westview Press.

Collings, Deirdre, ed. 1993. *Peace for Lebanon? From War to Reconstruction.* Boulder: Lynne Rienner, 1993.

Comay, Michael. 1983. "UN Peacekeeping: The Israeli Experience." In *Peacekeeping: Appraisals and Proposals,* ed. Henry Wiseman. New York: Pergamon Press.

Conference on Security and Cooperation in Europe. 1992. *Prague Document on Further Development of CSCE Institutions and Structures.* Prague: CSCE.

——. 1991a. *Report of the CSCE Meeting of Experts on National Minorities.* Geneva: CSCE.

——. 1991b. *Report of the CSCE Meeting of Experts on Peaceful Settlement of Disputes.* Valletta: CSCE.

——. 1991c. *CSCE Missions: A Summary Prepared by the Staff of CSCE.* September 1, 17 pp. Available from US Helsinki Commission, 237 Ford Office Building, Washington, D.C.

Connaughton, Richard M. 1992. *Military Intervention in the 1990s: Multilateral Military Intervention as a Collective Security Measure for the 1990s.* New York: Routledge.

Cooper, Robert, and Mats Berdal. (1993). "Outside Intervention in Ethnic Conflicts." *Survival* 35 (1): 118–42.

Copeland, Miles. 1969. *The Game of Nations.* London: Weidenfeld and Nicolson.

Corm, Georges. 1988. "Myths and Realities of the Lebanese Conflict." In *Lebanon: A History of Conflict and Consensus,* ed. Shehadi and Haffar-Mills. London: I. B. Tauris.

Corr, Edwin G., and Stephen Sloan. 1992. *Low-Intensity Conflict: Old Threats in a New World.* Boulder: Westview Press.

Coufoundakis, Van. 1991. "Greece in the Cold War: Domestic Politics and External Intervention." *Journal of Political and Military Sociology* 19 (1): 157–67.

Cox, Robert W. 1984. "Social Forces, States, and World Order." In *Culture, Ideology, and World Order,* ed. R. B. J. Walker. Boulder: Westview Press.

Damrosch, Lori Fisler. 1993. "Changing Conceptions of Intervention in International Law." In *Emerging Norms of Justified Intervention,* ed. Laura W. Reed and Carl Kaysen. Cambridge, Mass.: American Academy of Arts and Sciences.

——. 1989. "Politics across Borders: Nonintervention and Nonforcible Influence over Domestic Affairs." *American Journal of International Law* 83 (January): 1–50.

Damrosch, Lori Fisler, and David J. Scheffer. 1991. *Law and Force in the New International Order.* Boulder: Westview Press.

Davison, Roderic. 1963. *Reform in the Ottoman Empire, 1876–1896.* Princeton: Princeton University Press.

Dawisha, Adeed I. 1980. *Syria and the Lebanese Crisis.* London: Macmillan.

Dean, Robert. 1976. "Civil-Military Relations in Yugoslavia, 1971–1975." *Armed Forces and Society* 3 (1): 17–58.

Dempsey, Judy. 1991. "Yugoslavia Seeks $4.5bn to Help Its Economic Reforms," *Financial Times,* May 23, 2.

Deng, Francis M. 1990. "The Identity Factor in the Sudanese Conflict." In *Conflict and Peacemaking in Multiethnic Societies,* ed. Joseph V. Montville. Lexington, Mass.: Lexington Books.

Deutsch, Karl W. 1953. *Nationalism and Social Communication.* Cambridge: MIT Press.

——. 1954. *Political Community at the International Level.* Garden City, N.Y.: Doubleday.

Diehl, Paul F., 1988. "Peacekeeping Operations and the Quest for Peace." *Political Science Quarterly* 103 (Fall): 485–507.

Diehl, Paul F., and Chetan Kumar. 1991. "Mutual Benefits from International Intervention: New Roles for United Nations Peace Keeping Forces." *Bulletin of Peace Proposals: To Motivate Research; to Inspire Future-Oriented Thinking; to Promote Activities for Peace* 22 (12): 369–75.

Donnelly, Jack. 1993. *International Human Rights.* Boulder: Westview Press.

——. 1989. *Universal Human Rights in Theory and Practice.* Ithaca: Cornell University Press.

——. 1988a. "Human Rights: The Impact of International Action." *International Journal* 43 (Spring): 241–63.

——. 1988b. "Human Rights at the UN, 1955–85: The Question of Bias." *International Studies Quarterly* 32 (3): 275–303.

Doyle, Michael. 1986. "Liberalism and World Politics." *American Political Science Review* 80 (4): 1151–69.

Durkheim, Emile. 1964. *The Division of Labor in Society.* New York: Free Press.

EC Conference on Yugoslavia. 1991. *Treaty Provisions for the Convention.* Corrected Version.

Elaraby, Nabil A. 1983. "UN Peacekeeping: The Egyptian Experience." in *Peacekeeping: Appraisals and Proposals,* ed. Henry Wiseman, New York: Pergamon Press.

Emerson, Rupert. 1960. *From Empire to Nation: The Rise to Self-Assertion of Asian and African Peoples.* Boston: Beacon Press.

Esman, M. J. 1990. "Ethnic Pluralism and International Relations." *Canadian Review of Studies in Nationalism* 17 (1–2): 83–93.

Fabian, L. L. 1971. *Soldiers without Enemies: Preparing the United Nations for Peacekeeping.* Washington, D.C.: Brookings Institution.

Fairley, H. Scott. 1980. "State Actors, Humanitarian Intervention, and International Law: Reopening Pandora's Box." *Georgia Journal of International and Comparative Law* 10: 1.

Feste, Karen A., ed. 1990. *American and Soviet Intervention: Effects on World Stability.* New York: Taylor and Francis.

——. 1992. *Expanding the Frontiers: Superpower Intervention in the Cold War.* New York: Praeger.

Fisk, Robert. 1990. *Pity the Nation: The Abduction of Lebanon.* New York: Atheneum.

Ford Foundation. 1990. "A World of Leadership: Tomorrow's United Nations." *Ford Foundation Letter* 21 (3): 8–11.

Foreign Broadcast Information Service. 1991. *Daily Report—Eastern Europe* (Washington, D.C.), July 8, 91–130.

Forsythe, David P. 1969. "United Nations Intervention in Conflict Situations Revisited: A Framework for Analysis." *International Organization* 23 (1): 131–39.

Franck, Thomas M. 1985. *Nation against Nation: What Happened to the U.N. Dream and What the U.S. Can Do about It.* New York: Oxford University Press.

Freysinger, Robert C. 1991. "US Military and Economic Intervention in an International Context of Low-Intensity Conflict." *Political Studies* 39 (6): 321–34.

Fukuyama, Francis. 1989. "The End of History." *National Interest* no. 16 (Summer).

Gagnon, V. P., Jr. 1994. "Serbia's Road to War." *Journal of Democracy* (Spring): 117–31.

———. 1992. "Ideology and Soviet-Yugoslav Relations, 1964–1969: Irrational Foreign Policy as a Rational Choice." Ph.D. diss., Columbia University.

Gamba, Virginia. 1993. "Justified Intervention? A View from the South." In *Emerging Norms of Justified Intervention,* ed. Laura W. Reed and Carl Kaysen. Cambridge, Mass.: American Academy of Arts and Sciences.

Garofano, John. 1991. "Feasibility, Intervention, and the Definition of Interests: U.S. Military Intervention in Asia, 1945–70." Ph.D. diss., Cornell University.

Geddes, Charles, ed. 1991. *A Documentary History of the Arab-Israel Conflict.* New York: Praeger.

Geertz, Clifford, ed. 1963. *Old Societies and New States.* New York: Free Press.

Gehrke, William. 1991. "The Mozambique Crisis: A Case for United Nations Military Intervention." *Cornell International Law Journal* 24 (4): 135–64.

Gellner, Ernest. 1988. *Culture, Identity, and Politics.* Cambridge: Cambridge University Press.

George, Alexander L. 1983. *Managing U.S.-Soviet Rivalry: Problems of Crisis Prevention.* Boulder: Westview Press.

Gerges, Fawaz A. 1993. "The Lebanese Crisis of 1958: Risks of Inflated Self-Importance." *Beirut Review* 11 (5): 83–113.

Gilmour, David. 1984. *Lebanon: The Fractured Country.* New York: St. Martin's Press.

Gilpin, Robert. 1981. *War and Change in World Politics.* New York: Cambridge University Press.

Girard, René. 1977. *Violence and the Sacred.* Baltimore: Johns Hopkins University Press.

Glenny, Misha. 1992. *The Fall of Yugoslavia: The Third Balkan War.* Harmondsworth: Penguin.

Goodby, James. 1992. "Peacekeeping in the New Europe." *Washington Quarterly* 15 (2): 153–71.

Gordenker, Leon. 1991. "International Organizations in the New World Order." *Fletcher Forum of Human Affairs* 15 (Summer): 71–86.

Gordon, D. C. 1980. *Lebanon, the Fragmented Nation.* Stanford: Hoover Institution Press.

Gow, James. 1993. "The Role of the Military in the Yugoslav War of Dissolution." *Armed Conflicts in the Balkans and European Security,* an international conference of the Center for Strategic Studies, Slovene Ministry of Defence, Ljubljana, April 20–22, 1993 (Ljubljana, June 1993), 69–92.

———. 1991. "Deconstructing Yugoslavia," *Survival* 33 (4): 308.

Greenwood, Christopher. 1991. "Iraq's Invasion of Kuwait: Some Legal Issues." *World Today* 47 (3): 39–43.

Gregory, Barbara F. 1984. *The Multinational Force—Aid or Obstacle to Conflict Resolution.* Conflict Studies 170. Institute for the Study of Conflict.

Group for the Advancement of Psychiatry, Committee on International Relations. 1987. *Us and Them: The Psychology of Ethnonationalism.* Brunner/Mazel.

Grundy, Kenneth. 1991. *South Africa.* Boulder: Westview Press.

Gurr, Ted Robert. 1993. *Minorities at Risk.* Washington, D.C.: United States Institute of Peace.

Guys, Henri. 1850. *Beyrouth et le Liban.* Vol. 2. Paris: Ramquet.

Haas, Ernst B. 1993. "Beware the Slippery Slope: Notes toward the Definition of Justifiable Intervention." *Emerging Norms of International Intervention,* ed. Laura W. Reed and Carl Kaysen. Cambridge, Mass.: American Academy of Arts and Sciences.

——. 1990. *When Knowledge Is Power: Three Models of Change in International Organizations.* Studies in International Political Economy. Vol. 22. Berkeley: University of California Press.

——. 1987. "The Collective Management of International Conflict, 1945–1984." In United Nations Institute for Training and Research (UNITAR), *The United Nations and the Maintenance of International Peace and Security.* Dordrecht, Netherlands: Martinus Nijhoff.

——. 1986. *Why We Still Need the United Nations: The Collective Management of International Conflict, 1945–1984,* Berkeley: Institute of International Studies, University of California.

——. 1983. "Regime Decay: Conflict Management and International Organizations, 1945–1981." *International Organizations* 37 (2): 189–256.

Hadawi, Sami. 1989. *Bitter Harvest: A Modern History of Palestine.* New York: Olive Branch Press.

Haddad, Wadi D. 1985. *Lebanon: The Politics of Revolving Doors.* Center for Strategic and International Studies, the Washington Papers 114. New York: Praeger.

Haggard, Stephan. 1991. "Structuralism and Its Critics: Recent Progress in International Relations Theory." In *Progress in Postwar International Relations,* ed. Emanuel Adler and Beverly Crawford. New York: Columbia University Press.

Hagglund, G. 1990. "Peace Keeping in a Modern War Zone." *Survival* 33 (3): 233–40.

al-Halabi, Antun. 1927. *Hurub Ibrahim Basha al-Misri fi Suriya Wal Anadul* [The wars of Ibrahim Pasha in Syria and Anatolia]. 2 vols. Ed. Asad Rustum and Bulus Qua'ali. Heliopolis: Syrian Press.

Haley, Edward, and Lewis Snider, eds. 1979. *Lebanon in Crisis.* Syracuse: Syracuse University Press.

Hallenbeck, Ralph A. 1991. *Military Force as an Instrument of U.S. Foreign Policy: Intervention in Lebanon, August 1982–February 1984.* New York: Praeger.

Halpern, Manfred. 1963. *The Morality and Politics of Intervention.* New York: Council on Religion and International Affairs.

Hamashita, Takeshi. 1991. "Emigration and the Formation of an Extended Economic Zone." Unpublished paper.

Hannum, Hurst, ed. 1992. *Guide to International Human Rights Practice.* 2d ed. Philadelphia: University of Pennsylvania Press.

——. 1990. *Autonomy, Sovereignty, and Self-Determination: The Accommodation of Conflicting Rights.* Philadelphia: University of Pennsylvania Press.

Harik, Iliya. 1987. "Communalist and National Cooperation in Lebanon." In *The Islamic Impulse,* ed. Barbara Freyer-Stowasser. London: Croom Helm.

———. 1968. *Politics and Change in a Traditional Society: Lebanon, 1711–1845.* Princeton: Princeton University Press.

Hassouna, Hussein A. 1975. *The League of Arab States and Regional Disputes: A Study of Middle East Conflicts.* Dobbs Ferry, N.Y.: Oceana.

Heiburg, Marianne. 1991. *Ethnic Conflict, Peacekeeping, and Peacemaking towards 2000.* Nupi Paper 442. Norwegian Institute of International Affairs, April.

Heiburg, Marianne, and Johan Jorgen Holst. 1986. "Peacekeeping in Lebanon: Comparing UNIFIL and the MNF." *Survival* 28 (September–October): 411–23.

Helman, Gerald, and Steven Ratner. 1992. "Saving Failed States." *Foreign Policy* 89 (Winter): 3–20.

Henkin, Louis, et al. 1991. *Right vs. Might: International Law and the Use of Force.* New York: Council on Foreign Relations.

Henrikson, Alan K. 1991. *Defining a New World Order: Toward a Practical Vision of Collective Action for International Peace and Security: Discussion Paper.* Medford: Fletcher School of Law and Diplomacy.

Heraclides, A. 1991. *The Self-Determination of Minorities in International Politics.* Portland, Ore.: F. Cass.

Hirschman, Albert O. 1971. *Exit, Voice and Loyalty.* Cambridge: Harvard University Press.

Hitti, Philip. 1957. *Lebanon in History.* London: Macmillan.

Hobsbawm, E. J. 1985. *Bandits.* Harmondsworth: Penguin.

Hoffmann, Stanley. 1984. "The Problem of Intervention." In *Intervention in World Politics,* ed. Hedley Bull. Oxford: Clarendon Press.

———. 1962. "In Search of a Thread: The UN in the Congo Labyrinth." *International Organization* 16 (Spring): 331–61.

Hondius, Frits W. 1968. *The Yugoslav Community of Nations.* The Hague: Mouton.

Hopkins, Raymond F. 1992. "International Food Organizations and the United States: Drifting Leadership and Diverging Interests." In *The United States and Multilateral Institutions: Patterns of Changing Instrumentality and Influence,* ed. Margaret P. Karns and Karen A. Mingst. New York: Routledge.

Horowitz, D. L. 1985. *Ethnic Groups in Conflict.* Berkeley: University of California Press.

Houghton, Robert B., and Frank G. Trinka. 1984. *Multinational Peacekeeping in the Middle East.* Washington, D.C.: Foreign Service Institute, U.S. Department of State.

Hourani, Albert. 1976. "Ideologies of the Mountain and the City." In *Essays on the Crisis in Lebanon,* ed. Roger Owen. London: Ithaca Press.

Hudson, Michael C. 1985. *The Precarious Republic: Political Modernization in Lebanon.* Boulder: Westview Press.

Huntington, Samuel. 1993. "Clash of Civilizations." *Foreign Affairs.* 72 (3): 22–49.

———. 1973. "Transnational Organizations in World Politics." *World Politics* 25: 333–68.

Hurewitz, J. C. 1979. *The Middle East and North Africa in World Politics: A Documentary Record.* vol. 2. New Haven: Yale University Press.

———. 1956. *Diplomacy in the Near and Middle East: A Documentary Record.* Princeton: Van Nostrand.

Hybel, Alex Roberto. 1990. *How Leaders Reason: US Intervention in the Caribbean Basin and Latin America.* London: Blackwell.

Inegbedion, John. 1992. "The ECOWAS Intervention in Liberia: Toward Regional

Conflict Management in Post–Cold War Africa?" Paper for the Academic Committee on the UN System and the American Society of International Law Summer Workshop on International Organizations. Hanover, N.H.

International Court of Justice. 1991. *Case Concerning Border and Transborder Armed Actions (Nicaragua vs. Costa Rica)*. International Court of Justice.

Irvine, Jill. 1993. *The Croat Question: Partisan Politics in the Formation of the Yugoslav Socialist State*. Boulder: Westview Press.

Issawi, Charles. 1967. "British Consular Views on Syria's Economy in the 1850's–1860's." *American University of Beirut Festival Book* (Festschrift). Beirut: Centennial.

Jackson, Robert M. 1990. *Quasi-States: Sovereignty, International Relations, and the Third World*. Cambridge: Cambridge University Press.

Jackson, Robert H., and Carl G. Rosberg. 1982. "Why Africa's Weak States Persist." *World Politics* 35 (1): 1–24.

James, Alan. 1990. *Peacekeeping in International Politics*. London: Macmillan.

——. 1989. "The UN Force in Cyprus." *International Affairs*, 65 (Summer): 481–500.

——. 1984. "Options for Peace-Keeping." In *Armed Peace: The Search for World Security*, ed. Josephine O'Connor Howe. London: Macmillan.

"Japan, the U.S., Regional Crisis Management, and the U.N." 1993. Tokyo, March 29–31. Co-sponsored by the Asia Pacific Association of Japan and the United Nations Association of the USA.

Jelavich, Charles, and Barbara Jelavich. 1977. *The Establishment of the Balkan National States, 1804–1920*. Seattle: University of Washington Press.

Jelić-Butić, Fikreta. 1978. *Ustaše i Nezavisna Država Hrvatska*. Zagreb: Sveučilišna Naklada Liber.

Jervis, Robert, 1976. *Perception and Misperception in International Politics*. Princeton: Princeton University Press.

Johanssen, Robert C. 1990. "UN Peacekeeping: the Changing Utility of Military Force." *Third World Quarterly* (12): 53.

Johnson, A. Ross. 1978. *Role of the Military in Communist Yugoslavia: An Historical Sketch*. Rand Paper Series P-6070. Santa Monica: Rand Corporation, January.

Jumblatt, Kamal. 1982. *I Speak for Lebanon*. London: Zed Press.

Kabbara, Nawaf. 1988. "Shehabism in Lebanon, 1958–1970: The Failure of a Hegemonic Project." Ph.D. diss., University of Essex.

Kaloudis, George Stergiou. 1991. *The Role of the UN in Cyprus from 1964 to 1989*. New York: Peter Lang.

Kaplan, Morton A. 1957. *System and Process in International Politics*. New York: Wiley.

Karns, Margaret P. 1987. "The U.S., the Contact Group, and Namibia." *International Organization* 41 (1): 93–123.

——. 1986. "Multilateral Statecraft: The Theory and Practice of International Organizations in American Foreign Policy." Paper presented at the Annual Meeting of the American Political Science Association, Washington, D.C., August 27–31.

Kasfir, Nelson. 1990. "Peacemaking and Social Cleavage in Sudan." In *Conflict and Peacemaking in Multiethnic Societies*, ed. Joseph V. Montville. Lexington, Mass.: Lexington Books.

Kellas, James. 1991. *The Politics of Nationalism and Ethnicity*. London: Macmillan Education.

Kennedy, Paul. 1987. *The Rise and Fall of Great Powers*. New York: Random House.

Keohane, Robert. 1989. *International Institutions and State Power*. Boulder: Westview Press.

———. 1988. "International Institutions: Two Approaches." *International Studies Quarterly* 32 (4): 379–96.

———. 1984. *After Hegemony: Cooperation and Discord in the World Political Economy.* Princeton: Princeton University Press.

Keohane, Robert O., and Joseph S. Nye. 1977. *Power and Interdependence: World Politics in Transition.* Boston: Little Brown.

———. 1974. "Transnational Relations and International Organizations." *World Politics* 27: 39–62.

Kerr, Malcolm. 1957. *Lebanon in the Last Years of Feudalism, 1840–1866.* Beirut: Catholic Press.

Khalaf, Samir. 1993. *Beirut Reclaimed.* Beirut: Dar al-Nahar.

———. 1987. *Lebanon's Predicament.* New York: Columbia University Press.

———. 1979. *Persistence and Change in 19th Century Lebanon.* Beirut: American University of Beirut and Syracuse University Press.

Khalaf, Samir, and Philip S. Khoury, eds. 1993. *Recovering Beirut.* Leiden: E. J. Brill.

Khalidi, Walid, 1983. *Conflict and Violence in Lebanon.* Cambridge: Harvard Center for International Affairs.

Khalil, Muhammad, ed. 1962. *The Arab States and the Arab League.* 2 vols. Beirut: Khayat's.

el-Khazen, Farid. 1992. "Lebanon's Communal Elite-Mass Politics." *Beirut Review* 1 (3): 53–82.

Khoury, Philip S., and Joseph Kostiner, eds. 1990. *Tribes and State Formation in the Middle East.* Berkeley: University of California Press.

Khuwayri, Antwan. 1977. *al-Harb fi Lubnan, 1976* [The war in Lebanon, 1976]. 3 vols. Junyih, Lebanon: Al-Matba'ah al Bulsiyyah.

Kimche, David. 1991. *The Last Option.* New York: Charles Scribner's Sons.

Kohn, Hans. 1965. "Minorities," *Encyclopedia Brittanica* 15: 542–53.

Krasner, Steven D. 1988. "Sovereignty: An Institutional Perspective." *Comparative Political Studies* 21 (1): 66–94.

———. 1985. *Structural Conflict: The Third World against Global Liberalism.* Berkeley: University of California Press.

———, ed. 1983. *International Regimes.* Ithaca: Cornell University Press.

Kratochwil, Friedrich. 1989. *Rules, Norms, and Decisions.* Cambridge: Cambridge University Press.

———. 1982. "On the Notion of 'Interest' in International Relations." *International Organization* 36 (1): 1–30.

"Land of the Slaughter." 1992. *Time,* June 8, 32.

Lasswell, Harold. 1935. *World Politics and Personal Insecurity.* New York: McGraw-Hill.

The Lebanese Constitution: A Reference Edition in English. 1960. Beirut: American University of Beirut, Department of Political Studies and Public Administration.

Lefever, Ernest. 1967. *Uncertain Mandate: Politics of the UN Congo Operation.* New York: Johns Hopkins University Press.

Lehne, Stefan. 1991. *The Vienna Meeting of the Conference on Security and Cooperation in Europe, 1986–1989.* Boulder: Westview Press.

Leites, Nathan, and Charles Wolf Jr. 1970. *Rebellion and Authority: An Analytic Essay on Insurgent Conflicts.* Chicago: Markham.

Levite, Ariel, Bruce W. Jentleson, and Larry Berman, eds. 1992. *Foreign Military*

Intervention: The Dynamics of Protracted Conflict. New York: Columbia University Press.

Lewis, William H. 1991. "The Security Role of the UN." Washington: National Defense University's Institute for National Strategic Studies, October.

Lijphart, Arend. 1981. "Karl Deutsch and the New Paradigm in International Relations." In *From National Development to Global Community,* ed. Richard L. Merritt and Bruce M. Russett. London: G. Allen and Unwin.

Little, Richard. 1975. *Intervention: External Involvement in Civil Wars.* Totowa, N.J.: Rowman and Littlefield.

Lobel, Jules. 1990. "The Legality of U.S. Funding of the Nicaraguan Opposition under International Law." *Guild Practitioner: Current Problems, Law and Practice* 47 (4): 7–12.

Lone, Salim. 1992. "Enlarging the UN's Humanitarian Mandate." *United Nations Spotlight on Humanitarian Issues.* United Nations Publications, December.

Longrigg, Stephen Hemsley. 1958. *Syria and Lebanon under French Mandate.* London: Royal Institute of International Affairs and Oxford University Press.

Luard, Evan. 1984. "Collective Intervention." In *Intervention* and Guatemalan Refugees." *Public Affairs Quarterly: Philosophical Studies of Public Policy Issues* 6 (1): 45–60.

Mackinlay, John. 1989. *The Peacekeepers.* Boston: Unwin Hyman.

Mackinlay, John, and Jarat Chopra. 1992. "Second-Generation Multinational Operations." *Washington Quarterly* (Summer): 113–31.

Magaš, Branka. 1993. *The Destruction of Yugoslavia.* New York: Verso.

Malanczuk, Peter. 1993. *Humanitarian Intervention and the Legitimacy of the Use of Force,* Amsterdam: Het Spuihuis.

Mansbach, Richard, et al. 1976. *The Web of World Politics: Non-State Actors in the Global System.* Englewood Cliffs, N.J.: Prentice-Hall.

Ma'oz, Moshe. 1968. *Ottoman Reform in Syria and Palestine, 1840–1861.* New York: Oxford University Press.

Mapel, David R. 1991. "Military Intervention and Rights." *Millennium: Journal of International Studies* 20 (1): 41–55.

Maynes, Charles W. 1993. "Containing Ethnic Conflict." *Foreign Policy* 90: 3–21.

McDermott, Anthony, and Kjell Skjelsbaek, eds. 1991. *The Multinational Force in Beirut, 1982–1984.* Miami: Florida International University Press.

McNeely, Connie L. 1993. "The Determination of Statehood in the United Nations, 1945–1985." *Research in Political Sociology* 6.

Mearsheimer, John J. 1990. "Back to the Future: Instability in Europe after the Cold War." *International Security* 15 (1): 5–56.

Melko, Matthew. 1990. *Peace in Our Time.* New York: Paragon House.

Meyer, John. 1980. "The World Polity and the Authority of the Nation State." In *Studies of the Modern World System,* ed. Albert Bergesen. New York: Academic Press.

Midlarsky, Manus, ed. 1992. *The Internationalization of Communal Strife.* London: Unwin Hyman.

Miedlig, Hans Michael. 1992. "Greunde und Hintergreunde der Aktuellen Nationaliteatenkonflikte in den Jugoslowischen Leandern." *Seudosteropa: Zeitschrift feur Gegenwartsforschung* 41 (2): 116–30.

Miller, Linda B. 1967. *World Order and Local Disorder: The United Nations and Internal Conflicts.* Princeton: Princeton University Press.

Minear, Larry, and Thomas Weiss. 1991. *Humanitarianism under Seige: Operation Lifeline Sudan*. Lawrenceville, N.J.: Red Sea Press.

Modelski, George. 1990. "Is World Politics Evolutionary Learning?" *International Organization* 44 (1): 1–24.

Montville, Joseph V., ed. 1990. *Conflict and Peacemaking in Multiethnic Societies*. Lexington, Mass.: Lexington Books.

Moynihan, Daniel P. 1993. *Pandaemonium: Ethnicity in International Politics*. New York: Oxford University Press.

Mueller, John. 1989. *Retreat from Doomsday: The Obsolescence of Major War*. New York: Basic Books.

Murphy, Robert. 1965. *Diplomat among Warriors*. New York: Pyramid.

Nachmani, Amikam. 1990. *International Intervention in the Greek Civil War: The United Nations Special Committee on the Balkans, 1947–1952*. New York: Praeger.

Nagel, Joane, and Brad Whorton. 1992. "Ethnic Conflict and the World System: International Competition in Iraq (1961–1991) and Angola (1964–1991)." *Journal of Political and Military Sociology* 20: 1–35.

Nakarada, Radmila. 1991. "The Mystery of Nationalism: The Paramount Case of Yugoslavia." *Millenium: Journal of International Studies* 20(4): 369–82.

Nasr, Salim, et al. 1991. *Conference on Lebanon Working Paper*. Washington: American Task Force on Lebanon.

Neale, F. A. 1852. *Eight Years in Syria, Palestine, and Asia Minor*. London: Colburn.

Nelson, Richard W. 1984. "Multinational Peacekeeping in the Middle East and the United Nations Model." *International Affairs* (London) 61 (Winter): 67–89.

Newhouse, John. 1992. "The Diplomatic Round: Dodging the Problem." *New Yorker*, August 24.

Nye, Joseph S., Jr. 1990. *Bound to Lead: The Changing Nature of American Power*. New York: Basic Books.

O'Brien, Connor Cruise. 1962. *To Katanga and Back*. New York: Simon and Schuster.

Ogata, Shijuro, and Paul Volcker. 1993. *Financing an Effective United Nations*. New York: Ford Foundation.

Owen, Roger, ed. 1976. *Essays on the Crisis in Lebanon*. London: Ithaca Press.

Oye, Kenneth A., ed. 1986. *Cooperation under Anarchy*. Princeton: Princeton University Press.

Ozgur, Ozdemir. 1982. *Apartheid: The United Nations and Peaceful Change in South Africa*. Dobbs Ferry, N.Y.: Transnational.

Pakradouni, Karim, 1984. *La paix manquée: Le mandat d'Elias Sarkis (1976–1982)*. 2d ed. Beirut: Editions FIMA [Fiches du Monde Arabe].

Parkerson, John Embry, Jr. 1991. "United States Compliance with Humanitarian Law Respecting Civilians during Operation Just Cause." *Military Law Review* 133 (2): 31–140.

Peck, Steven. 1994. *US Peacekeeping Policy: An Update*. Briefing paper prepared by the Center for Strategic and International Studies, Political Military Studies Program, Washington, D.C., February 10.

Penna, David R. 1991. "The Right to Self-Defense in the Post–Cold War Era: The Role of the United Nations." *Denver Journal of International Law and Policy* 20 (3): 41–54.

Perovič, Latinka. 1991. *Zatvaranje kruga: Ishod političkog rascepa u SKJ 1971/72*. Sarajevo: Svjetlost.

Pogany, Istvan. 1987. *The Arab League and Peacekeeping in Lebanon.* Aldershot, U.K.: Avebury.

Polk. William. 1963. *The Opening of South Lebanon, 1788–1840.* Cambridge: Harvard University Press.

Posen, Barry R. 1993. "The Security Dilemma and Ethnic Conflict" *Survival* 35 (1): 27–47.

Priesler, Barry. 1988. "Lebanon: The Rationality of National Suicide." Ph.D. Diss., University of California at Berkeley.

Puchala, Donald J. 1994. "The History of the Future of International Relations." *Ethics and International Affairs* 8: 177–202.

Puchala, Donald J., and Raymond F. Hopkins. 1983. "International Regimes: Lessons from Inductive Analysis." In *International Regimes,* ed. Stephen D. Krasner. Ithaca: Cornell University Press.

Qubain, Fahim I. 1961. *Crisis in Lebanon.* Washington, D.C.: Middle East Institute.

Quigley, John. 1992. *The Ruses for War: American Interventionism since World War II.* Buffalo, N.Y.: Prometheus Books.

Ra'anan, Uri, ed. 1991. *State and Nation in Multi-Ethnic Societies: The Break-up of Multinational States.* New York: St. Martin's Press.

Rabinovich, Itamar. 1984. *The War for Lebanon, 1970–1983.* Ithaca: Cornell University Press.

Rabinow, Paul. 1989. *France Modern.* Cambridge: MIT Press.

Ramet, Pedro. 1987. "The Limits to Political Change in a Communist Country: The Yugoslav Debate, 1980–1986." *Crossroads* no. 23: 67–79.

——. 1984. *Nationalism and Federalism in Yugoslavia, 1963–1983.* Bloomington: Indiana University Press.

Ramet, Sabrina P. 1992. *Nationalism and Federalism in Yugoslavia, 1962–1991.* Bloomington: Indiana University Press.

Reagan, Ronald. 1990. *An American Life.* New York: Simon and Schuster.

Reddy, E. S. 1986. *Apartheid: The United Nations and Peaceful Change in South Africa.* Dobbs Ferry, N.Y.: Transnational.

Reed, Laura W., and Carl Kaysen, eds. 1993. *Emerging Norms of Justified Intervention.* Cambridge, Mass.: American Academy of Arts and Sciences.

Reisman, W. Michael. 1990. "International Law after the Cold War." *American Journal of International Law* 84 (4): 859–66.

Remington, Robin Allison. 1974. "Armed Forces and Society in Yugoslavia," In *Political-Military Systems: Comparative Perspectives,* ed. Catherine McArdle Kelleher. Beverly Hills: Sage.

al-Rfouh, Faisal. 1984. *United Nations, League of Arab States, and Palestinians.* New Delhi: Bhalla Books.

Rikhye, Indar Jit. 1984. *The Theory and Practice of Peacekeeping.* London: C. Hurst.

Rikhye, Indar Jit, and Kjell Skjelsbaek, eds. 1991. *The United Nations and Peacekeeping: Results, Limitations, and Prospects, the Lessons of Forty Years of Experience.* New York: St. Martin's Press.

Riley, Eileen. 1991. *Major Political Events in South Africa, 1948–1990.* New York: Facts on File.

Robinson, Linda. 1991. *Intervention or Neglect: The United States and Central America beyond the 1980s.* Council for International Relations.

Robinson, William I. 1992. *A Faustian Bargain: U.S. Intervention in the Nicaraguan Elections and American Foreign Policy in the Post–Cold War Era.* Boulder: Westview Press.

Rodley, Nigel S., ed. 1992. *To Loose the Bands of Wickedness: International Intervention in Defence of Human Rights.* New York: Macmillan.

Roksandić, Drago. 1991. *Srbi u Hrvatskoj od 15. stoljeća do naših dana.* Zagreb: Vjesnik.

Rosenau, James. 1973. "Theorizing across Systems: Linkage Politics Revisited." In *Conflict Behavior and Linkage Politics,* ed. Jonathan Wilkenfeld. New York: David McKay.

Rothchild, Donald. "Regime Management of Conflict in West Africa." Manuscript of forthcoming volume.

Rothchild, Donald, and Victor A. Olorunsola. 1983. *State versus Ethnic Claims: African Policy Dilemmas.* Boulder: Westview Press.

Rothschild, Joseph. 1981. *Ethnopolitics: A Conceptual Framework.* New York: Columbia University Press.

———. 1974. *East Central Europe between the Two World Wars.* Seattle: University of Washington Press.

Ruggie, John Gerard. 1993. "Territoriality and Beyond." *International Organization* 47 (1): 139–74.

———. 1992. "Multilateralism: The Anatomy of an Institution." *International Organization* 46 (3): 521–98.

Rule, James. 1988. *Theories of Civil Violence.* Berkeley: University of California Press.

Rupesinghe, Kumar. 1992. "The Disappearing Boundaries between Internal and External Conflicts." In *Internal Conflict and Governance,* ed. Rupesinger. New York: St. Martin's Press.

Rustow, Dankwart A. 1967. *A World of Nations.* Washington, D.C.: Brookings Institution.

Ryan, Stephen. 1990a. *Ethnic Conflict and International Relations.* Aldershot, U.K.: Dartmouth.

———. 1990b. "Ethnic Conflict and the United Nations." *Ethnic and Racial Studies* 13 (1): 25–49.

Sabec, Christopher John. 1991. "The Security Council Comes of Age: An Analysis of the International Legal Response to the Iraqi Invasion of Kuwait." *Georgia Journal of International and Comparative Law* 21 (1): 63–122.

Salem, Paul. 1991. "Two Years of Living Dangerously: General Awn and Lebanon's 'Second Republic.'" *Beirut Review* 1 (1): 62–87.

Salibi, Kamal. 1988. "The Tribal Origins of the Religious Sects in the Arab East." In *Toward a Viable Lebanon,* ed. Halim Barakat. London: Croom Helm; Washington, D.C.: Georgetown University Center for Contemporary Arab Studies.

———. 1965. *The Modern History of Lebanon.* London: Weidenfeld and Nicolson.

Samatar, Abdi Ismail. 1992. "Destruction of State and Society in Somalia: Beyond the Tribal Convention." *Journal of Modern African Studies* 30 (4): 625–43.

Schachter, Oscar. 1991. "United Nations Law in the Gulf Conflict." *American Journal of International Law* 85 (3): 452–73.

Schecterman, Bernard, and Martin Slann, eds. 1993. *The Ethnic Dimension in International Relations.* New York: Praeger.

Schermerhorn, R. A. 1978. *Comparative Ethnic Relations: A Framework for Theory and Research.* Chicago: University of Chicago Press.

Schiff, Zeev, and Ehud Ya'ari. 1984. *Israel's Lebanon War*. New York: Simon and Schuster.

Schraeder, Peter J. ed. 1992. *Intervention into the 1990s: U.S. Foreign Policy in the Third World*. Boston: South End Press.

Scott, James. 1990. *Domination and the Arts of Resistance*. New Haven: Yale University Press.

————. 1985. *Weapons of the Weak*. New Haven: Yale University Press.

Shalom, Stephen Rosskamm. 1993. *Imperial Alibis: Rationalizing U.S. Intervention after the Cold War*. Boston: South End Press.

Siilasvuo, Ensio. 1992. *In the Service of Peace in the Middle East, 1967–1979*. New York: St. Martin's Press.

Silva, K. M. de, and R. J. May. 1991. *Internationalization of Ethnic Conflict*. London: Pinter.

Silva, K. M. de, and S. W. R. de A. Samarasinghe, eds. 1993. *Peace Accords and Ethnic Conflict*. New York: St. Martin's Press.

Singham, A. W., and Shirley Hune. 1986. *Namibian Independence: A Global Responsibility*. Westport, Conn.: Lawrence Hill.

Skjelsbaek, Kjell. 1989. "United Nations Peacekeeping and the Facilitation of Withdrawals." *Bulletin of Peace Proposals* 20 (3): 253–64.

Skogmo, Bjorn. 1989. *UNIFIL: International Peacekeeping in Lebanon, 1978–1988*. Boulder: Lynne Reinner.

Smolowe, Jill. 1992. "Why Do They Keep on Killing?" *Time* May 11, 48.

Somerville, Keith. 1990. *Foreign Military Intervention in Africa*. New York: St. Martin's Press.

Southall, Aidan. 1980. "Social Disorganization in Uganda." *Journal of Modern African Studies* 18 (4): 627–56.

Sparks, Donald, and December Green. 1992. *Namibia: The Nation after Independence*. Boulder: Westview Press.

Spencer, Herbert. 1874. *The Study of Sociology*. New York: D. Appleton.

Stavenhagen, Rodolfo. 1991. "Ethnic Conflicts and Their Impact on International Society." *International Social Science Journal* 43 (1): 117–31.

————. 1990. *The Ethnic Question: Conflicts, Development, and Human Rights*. Tokyo: United Nations UP.

Stavenhagen, Rodolfo, and Martha Pou. 1990. "Ethnic Conflicts and Their Internationalization." *Estudios Sociologicos* 8 (24): 623–45.

Talbott, Strobe. 1992. "Why Bosnia Is Not Viet Nam," *Time*, August 24, 49.

Telhami, Shibley. 1995. "Israeli Foreign Policy: A Realist Ideal Type or a Breed of Its Own?" In Michael Barnett, ed., *The Politics of Uniqueness: The Status of the Israeli Case*. Albany: SUNY Press. Forthcoming.

————. 1990. *Power and Leadership in International Bargaining: The Path to the Camp David Accords*. New York: Columbia University Press.

Tessitore, John, and Susan Wolfson, ed. 1990. *Issues 44: Issues before the 44th General Assembly of the United Nations*. Lexington, Mass.: Lexington Books.

Thakur, Ramesh. 1987. *International Peacekeeping in Lebanon: United Nations Authority and Multinational Force*. Boulder: Westview Press.

Thornton, T. P. 1991. "Regional Organization in Conflict Management." *Annals* no. 518: 132–41.

Tibawi, A. L. 1969. *A Modern History of Syria*. Edinburgh: Macmillan.

Tibi, Bassam. 1990. "The Simultaneity of the Unsimultaneous: Old Tribes and Impost Nation-States in the Modern Middle-East." In *Tribes and State Formation in the Middle East*, ed. Philip S. Khoury and Joseph Kostiner. Berkeley: University of California Press.

Tietze, Nikola. 1993. "Reactions of German Government, German Parties, and Journalists during the Crisis in Yugoslavia." Unpublished manuscript, Department of Politics, Brandeis University.

Tillema, Herbert K. 1991. *International Armed Conflict since 1945: A Bibliographic Handbook of Wars and Military Interventions.* Boulder: Westview Press.

Tilly, Charles, ed. 1975. *The Formation of Nation States in Western Europe.* Princeton: Princeton University Press.

Touraine, Alain. 1981. *The Voice of the Eye.* Cambridge: Cambridge University Press.

Towell, Pat. 1992. "Senators Broach Using Military to Quiet Bosnia-Herzegovina: Push to Put Teeth in UN Sanctions May Test Bush's Post–Cold War Foreign Policy." *Congressional Quarterly Weekly Report* 50 (13): 1714–15.

Trachtenberg, Marc. 1992. "The Past and Future of Arms Control." In *The International Practice of Arms Control*, ed. Emanuel Adler. Baltimore: Johns Hopkins University Press.

Tuéni, Ghassan. 1979. *Peace-Keeping in Lebanon: The Facts, The Documents. . . .* New York: William Belcher Group.

UNA/USA. 1992. *A Global Agenda: Issues before the 47th General Assembly of the United Nations.* Ed. John Tessitore and Susan Wolfson. Lanham, Md.: University Press of America.

"The United Nations: Mr. Human Rights" 1991. *The Economist* 325: 57–60.

United Nations. 1992a. *An Agenda for Peace: Preventive Diplomacy, Peacemaking, and Peacekeeping.* United Nations, General Assembly A/47/277, June 17.

———. 1992b. *United Nations Handbook.* New Zealand, Ministry of External Relations and Trade.

United Nations, Department of Public Information. 1992. *United Nations Peace-Keeping Operations: Information Notes.* New York.

———. 1990. *The Blue Helmets: A Review of United Nations Peacekeeping.* New York.

United Nations Institute for Training and Research (UNITAR). 1987. *The United Nations and the Maintenance of International Peace and Security.* Dordrecht, Netherlands: Martinus Nijhoff.

United States Senate Committee on Foreign Relations. 1992. *The Ethnic Cleansing of Bosnia-Hercegovina: A Staff Report.* Washington, D.C.: The Committee.

United States Commission on Security and Cooperation in Europe. 1992. *The Conference on Security and Cooperation in Europe: An Overview of the CSCE Process, Recent Meetings, and Institutional Development.* Washington, D.C.: The Commission February.

———. 1989. *Concluding Document of the Vienna Follow-Up Meeting.* Washington, D.C.: The Commission, January.

United States Department of State, Office of the Assistant Secretary/Spokesman. 1993. *Statement by U.S. Secretary of State Warren Christopher*, February 10.

United States House Committee on Ways and Means. 1992. *Foreign Contributions to the Costs of the Persian Gulf War: Hearing, July 31, 1991.* Washington, D.C.: The Committee.

Urquhart, B. 1990. "Beyond the 'Sheriff's Posse.'" *Survival* 33 (3): 196–205.

Van Dyke, Vernon. 1977. "The Individual, the State, and Ethnic Communities in Political Theory." *World Politics* 29: 343–69.

———. 1975. "Justice as Fairness: For Groups?" *American Political Science Review* 69: 607–14.

Voll, John. 1990. "Northern Muslim Perspectives." In *Conflict and Peacemaking in Multiethnic Societies*, ed. Joseph V. Montville. Lexington, Mass.: Lexington Books.

Walker, Jenonne. "European Regional Organizations and Ethnic Conflict." Unpublished paper.

———. 1993. "International Mediation of Ethnic Conflicts." *Survival* 35 (1): 102–17.

Waltz, Kenneth Neal. 1979. *Theory of International Politics*. Reading, Pa.: Addison-Wesley.

Weinberger, Naomi, 1986. *Syrian Intervention in Lebanon*. Oxford: Oxford University Press.

———. 1983. "Peacekeeping Options in Lebanon." *Middle East Journal* 37 (3): 341–69.

Weiner, Myron. 1992. "Security, Stability, and International Migration." *International Security* 17 (3): 91–126.

Weiner, Myron, and Samuel Huntington, eds. 1987. *Understanding Political Development: An Analytical Study* Boston: Little Brown, 1987.

Weiss, Thomas G. 1993. "New Challenges for UN Military Operations: Implementing an Agenda for Peace." *Washington Quarterly* (Winter): 51–66.

———. 1992. *Natural Disaster and Military Relief*. New York: St. Martin's Press.

———. ed. 1990. *Humanitarian Emergencies and Military Help in Africa*. New York: St. Martin's Press.

Weiss, Thomas G., and S. Neil MacFarlane. 1992. "Regional Organizations and Regional Security." *Security Studies* 2 (1): 6–37.

Weller, Marc. 1992. "The International Response to the Dissolution of the Socialist Federal Republic of Yugoslavia." *American Journal of International Law* 86 (3): 569–607.

Wendt, Alexander. 1992. "Anarchy Is What States Make of It: The Social Construction of Power Politics." *International Organization* 46 (2): 391–425.

Wettig, Gerhard. 1992. *Nation und Konflikt in Osteuropa nach dem Ausammenbruch des Kommunismus*. Germany: Bundesinst Ostewiss und Internat Studien.

White, N. D., and H. McCoubrey. 1991. "International Law and the Use of Force in the Gulf." *International Relations* 10 (11): 347–73.

Williams, Robin. 1977. *Mutual Accommodation: Ethnic Conflict and Cooperation*. Minneapolis: University of Minnesota Press.

Willoughby, John. 1991. "Nationalism and Globalism: Beyond the Neo-Leninist Tradition." *Rethinking Marxism* 4 (2): 134–42.

Wiseman, Henry. 1987. "The United Nations and International Peacekeeping." In UNITAR, *The United Nations and the Maintenance of International Peace and Security*. Dordrecht, Netherlands: Martinus Nijhoff.

Woodward, Susan L. 1995. *Balkan Tragedy: Chaos and Dissolution after the Cold War*. Washington, D.C.: Brookings Institution.

World Bank. 1989. *Sub-Saharan Africa: From Crisis to Sustainable Growth*. Washington, D.C.: World Bank.

Yaniv, Avner. 1987. *Dilemmas of Security: Politics, Strategy, and the Israeli Experience in Lebanon*. New York: Oxford University Press.

Yared, Marc. 1992. "Somalie, pourquoi?" *Jeune Afrique* 32 (3): 30–32.

Young, M. Crawford, ed. 1993. *The Rising Tide of Cultural Pluralism*. Madison: University of Wisconsin Press.

Young, Oran. 1989a. *International Cooperation*. Ithaca: Cornell University Press.

———. 1989b. "Politics of International Regime Formation." *International Organization* 43(3): 349–76.

Zacher, Mark W. 1979. *International Conflicts and Collective Security, 1946–1977.* New York: Praeger.

Zametica, John. 1992. *The Yugoslav Conflict.* Adelphi Papers 270. London: Brassey's for the International Institute for Strategic Studies.

Zamir, Meir. 1985. *The Formation of Modern Lebanon.* Ithaca: Cornell University Press.

Zartman, William. 1991. "Conflict and Resolution: Context, Cost, and Change." *Annals of the American Academy* no. 518: 11–22

Zenner, Walter F. 1991. *Minorities in the Middle: A Cross-Cultural Analysis.* Albany: State University of New York Press.

Zinnes, Dina. 1983. *Conflict Processes and the Breakdown of International Systems.* Denver: Graduate School of International Studies, University of Denver.

Žižek, Slavoj. 1993. "Caught in Another's Dream in Bosnia." In *Why Bosnia?* ed. Rabia Ali and Lawrence Lifschultz. Stony Creek, Conn.: Pamphleteer's Press.

Contributors

STEVEN L. BURG is Associate Professor of Politics at Brandeis University. His most recent book is *War or Peace? Nationalism, Democracy and American Foreign Policy in Eastern Europe,* prepared for the Twentieth Century Fund.

JACK DONNELLY is Associate Professor of Political Science at the University of Denver. He is author of *The Concept of Human Rights,* (St. Martins Press, 1984) and *Universal Human Rights in Theory and Practice* (Cornell University Press, 1989).

MILTON J. ESMAN is Professor of Government and the John S. Knight Professor of International Studies, Emeritus, at Cornell. His most recent book, *Ethnic Politics,* was published in 1994 by Cornell University Press.

V. P. GAGNON JR., a political scientist, is a Visiting MacArthur Foundation Post-doctoral Fellow at the Peace Studies Program, Cornell University. He is spending the academic year 1994–1995 at the Department of Sociology, University of Zagreb, and the Institute for Philosophy and Social Theory at the University of Belgrade.

RAYMOND F. HOPKINS is Director of the Program in Public Policy and Professor in the Department of Political Science, Swarthmore College. During 1995 he is serving as Distinguished Professor of International Economics at the University of Tuscia (Viterbo), Italy.

MICHAEL C. HUDSON is Professor of International Relations and the Seif Ghobash Professor of Arab Studies in the School of Foreign Service at Georgetown University. He has written on Lebanon, the Palestinians, and the problem of legitimacy in Arab politics.

SAMIR KHALAF is Professor of Sociology at the American University in Beirut and author of *Lebanon's Predicamant* (Columbia University Press, 1987) and *Recovering Beirut: Urban Design and Post-war Reconstruction* (Brill, 1993).

BARRY PREISLER teaches political science at California State University at Hayward. He has taught at the University of California at Berkeley, California State University at Sacramento, and at San Francisco State University.

SHIBLEY TELHAMI is Associate Professor of Government at Cornell and currently a visiting fellow at the Brookings Institution. He served on the United States delegation to the United Nations during the Persian Gulf crisis of 1990–1991. He is author of *Power and Leadership in International Bargaining: The Path to the Camp David Accords* (Columbia University Press, 1990).

NAOMI WEINBERGER is Assistant Professor of Political Science at Barnard College. Her publications include *Syrian Intervention in Lebanon* (Oxford University Press, 1986) and *Achieving Security in the West Bank and Gaza* (forthcoming).

SUSAN L. WOODWARD is a Senior Fellow in the Foreign Policy Studies program at the Brookings Institution. Her most recent publication is *Balkan Tragedy: Chaos and Dissolution after the Cold War,* published in 1995 by Brookings.

Index

Addis Ababa Agreement of 1972, 33
ADF. *See* Arab Deterrent Force
Afghanistan, 5, 62, 85
  and the cold war, 66
  ethnic conflict in, 72
  quasi decolonization of, 64
  Soviet invasion of, 39, 41
Africa, 27, 36, 48, 75, 85. *See also specific*
  countries
African Commission on Human and
  Peoples' Rights, 56, 68
African National Congress (ANC), 11, 39
Agenda for Peace, An (Boutros-Ghali), 171,
  227
Aidid, General Mohammed Farah, 174, 175
Akashi, Yasushi, 264–65
Albania, 45, 217, 275, 280
Albanians, 189, 191, 202, 213
  ethnic discrimination against, 192, 205–6,
  269
  in Kosovo, 204, 208, 217, 220–21, 224, 238,
  246, 249
  and recognition by EC, 247–48
Algeria, 144
Allied powers, 127, 181, 182
Amal movement, 135, 136, 138–42, 145,
  146
Amin, Idi, 70, 90
Anarchy, 74, 77
ANC. *See* African National Congress
Angioni, General Franco, 170
Anglo-Egyptian condominium, 32
Angola, 5, 89, 90
  and cold war, 66
  integrated UN operations in, 43, 69
  quasi decolonization of, 64
  Soviet-backed Cuban troops in, 39–40
Anomie, 73, 74, 77, 79, 83, 96, 292
Aoun, General Michel, 135, 144–46
Apartheid, 35–38, 80

Arab Deterrent Force (ADF), 137–39, 147,
  150, 158
Arab-Israeli wars, 27, 85, 139, 151, 274
Arab League, 2, 3, 73, 123
  and ADF, 137–39
  and members' interests, 146–47
  and neutrality, 84, 299
  and 1958 Lebanon crisis, 131–35
  and 1976 intervention in Lebanon, 272,
  274, 280, 286
  and Syrian intervention in Lebanon, 7–8,
  9, 150
  and Ta'if Accord, 144–46, 300
Arab nationalism, 130, 131, 133, 134
Arab states, 26–29, 90, 133. *See also specific*
  states
Arab Summit Conference (Riyadh), 137
Arafat, Yasir, 140, 150, 266
Arms embargo, 13, 36, 43, 212, 224, 228,
  241, 245
  and illegal weapons sales, 207, 224
  and London Conference, 257, 260
  U.S. proposal on, 214, 260–62
Asad, Hafiz al-, 112, 138, 139, 279
Asian minorities, in South Africa, 35
Assimilationist policies, 22–23, 25, 102
Association of Southeast Asian Nations, 73
Atrocities, 223, 229, 233, 255–56. *See also*
  Ethnic cleansing
Austria, 24, 109, 114, 119, 196, 201
  and fighting in Slovenia, 240
  illegal provision of weapons by, 207
  and intervention in Yugoslavia, 208, 220,
  221, 227, 275
  and the Règlement Shakib Effendi of
  1843, 117
Austro-Hungarian Empire, 181–83
Authoritarian rule, 87, 88, 182

Badinter Commission, 213
Baker, James, 239, 245, 252, 253, 287

Somalia (*cont.*)
  and IO capabilities, 85–86, 88–93
  and Lebanon compared, 278
  and principles of intervention, 72–74, 78, 82, 290–92
  and quasi decolonization, 64–67
  and theories regarding IO roles, 3–5
  and UNOSOM and MNF experiences compared, 172–75
Somaliland, 91
South Africa, 45, 53, 75, 76
  and apartheid, 35–38, 80
  and decolonization, 58
  and General Assembly coalition against, 27
  and Namibia, 38–40
  resistance to IO intervention by, 11
Southern Peoples' Liberation Army (SPLA), 34
South Korea, 78
South Lebanon Army, 140, 141
South Slavs, 180–83
Southwest Africa Peoples' Organization (SWAPO), 39, 40
South Yemen, 137
Sovereignty. *See* State Sovereignty
Soviet bloc, 27, 74, 88, 184
Soviet Union, 48, 86–89, 234, 296
  and Angola, 39–40
  and criteria for intervention, 8
  and CSCE, 40–43
  and Cyprus, 30
  and decolonization, 63–64
  and intervention in Yugoslavia, 212, 214, 218, 228, 237, 241, 280
  and Lebanese civil war, 144–46
  and post-cold-war political transition, 4, 5, 75–76, 94, 171, 300
  and reform in Yugoslavia, 184, 185, 201
  and Sinai MFO, 152
  and Yugoslavia compared, 278
  See also Russia
Soweto, 36
Spain, 215, 217
Special UN Committee on Apartheid, 36
SPLA. *See* Southern Peoples' Liberation Army
"Squad 16" (Sitt'ash), 277
Sri Lanka, 72, 85, 86, 89
Stalinist economic system, 184, 185
State socialism, 130, 188–89
State sovereignty, 11–12, 21–22, 34, 43–44, 48, 289
  advantages of, 79
  during cold war, 88
  and CSCE, 41, 42
  and decolonization, 51, 57, 58, 64
  and deterrence, 297
  and human rights, 55, 72, 79–83, 96

and IO intervention in Yugoslavia, 199, 223, 225, 226, 228–29, 230, 232
and Iraqi invasion of Kuwait, 1–2, 8, 63
and JNA, 280
and League of Nations Minorities treaties, 24, 25
and need for external norms, 83–84
new states' perception of, 89–90
and norm of nonintervention, 73
and post-cold-war normative changes, 47, 74, 76, 290–94, 301
and quasi decolonization, 64–65
and regional IOs, 46
and role of UN, 68, 77–79, 89–90, 94, 96, 97
and South African apartheid, 35–37
theoretical arguments about, 5–7, 60–62
and types of intervention, 49–50
and UN costs and capabilities, 294–95
Western support for, in Yugoslavia, 239–40
and Yugoslav and Lebanese crises compared, 278
and Yugoslav conflict over control of economy, 200, 201, 203–8
and Yugoslav republican bid for independence, 208–18
State system values, 1, 6
Stigmatization of regimes, 21. *See also* Economic sanctions
Stoltenberg, Thorvald, 216
Structural argument, 61
Sudan, 32–35, 93, 133, 290
  and ADF, 137
  civil war in, 63
  ethnic conflict in, 72
  and limited capabilities of IOs, 43
  state failure in, 75
  UN humanitarian intervention in, 68
Suez Crisis (1956), 123
SWAPO. *See* Southwest Africa Peoples' Organization
Sweden, and UNIFIL, 282
Syria, 9, 85, 109, 119, 299
  and ADF, 137–39
  and Arab nationalism, 130, 131, 133
  and effectiveness of peace-keeping operations in Lebanon, 159, 161, 163, 165
  and Iraqi invasion of Kuwait, 63
  and Lebanese and Yugoslav cases compared, 274–77, 279
  and Lebanese civil war (1975–1990), 135, 136, 144
  motives for intervention in Lebanon, 7–8, 150–51, 153
  and Ta'if Accord, 145, 146
  and UNIFIL, 141–42
Syrian Social National party, 136